T0271266

Behavioral Rationality and Heterogeneous Expectations in Complex Economic Systems

Recognizing that the economy is a complex system with boundedly rational interacting agents, the book presents a theory of behavioral rationality and heterogeneous expectations in complex economic systems and confronts the nonlinear dynamic models with empirical stylized facts and laboratory experiments. The complexity modeling paradigm has been strongly advocated since the late 1980s by some economists and by multidisciplinary scientists from various fields, such as physics, computer science and biology. More recently the complexity view has also drawn the attention of policy makers, who are faced with complex phenomena, irregular fluctuations and sudden, unpredictable market transitions. The complexity tools – bifurcations, chaos, multiple equilibria – discussed in this book will help students, researchers and policy makers to build more realistic behavioral models with heterogeneous expectations to describe financial market movements and macroeconomic fluctuations, in order to better manage crises in a complex global economy.

CARS HOMMES is Professor of Economic Dynamics at the University of Amsterdam (UvA). After his PhD in Mathematical Economics at the University of Groningen, he founded the Center for Nonlinear Dynamics in Economics and Finance (CeNDEF), an interdisciplinary research group at UvA, pursuing theoretical, experimental and empirical research on complex systems, bounded rationality and behavioral agent-based models in economics and finance.

"Professor Hommes' work is a major contribution to the understanding of intertemporal economic fluctuations. In a world in which production and investment behavior is motivated by expectations of the future, the way those expectations are formed becomes of the utmost importance. These expectations lead to dynamic systems, and the author draws on the rich literature developed for the study of mechanical and gravitational phenomena. These lead to the emergence of very complex behavior in markets driven by expectations, especially when different economic agents have different modes of forming expectations from data. The study of this book will have a profound impact on the theoretical and empirical analysis of securities markets and other forms of investment."

Kenneth J. Arrow, Joan Kenney Professor of Economics and Professor of Operations Research, Emeritus, Stanford University. Winner of the Nobel Prize in Economics 1972

"Cars Hommes has written an excellent book that is a combination of theory, economic modeling and economic experiments. The book is an outgrowth of a course on Nonlinear Economic Dynamics that he has given mostly at the University of Amsterdam for the last 20 years."

Professor Carl Chiarella, Head of Finance Discipline Group, University of Technology, Sydney

"Henri Poincaré, the great French mathematician and father of non linear dynamic analysis, at the turn of the 20th century chided Walras for his unrealistic assumptions about how individuals make their decisions. He also declared that Bachelier's random walk hypothesis for financial markets overlooked the tendency of people to act like sheep. Yet Walras and Bachelier are, with reason, regarded as the founders of modern economic and financial theory.

Cars Hommes' excellent book puts us firmly back on the path that we should have followed had we heeded Poincaré's warnings and built our economic theory on the foundations that he laid. The book's careful formal analysis, empirical and experimental evidence provides a solid basis for understanding the volatile evolution of economies. It provides the framework for a better understanding of how economies do actually behave rather than how current economic theory says they should behave. This book could not have come at a more opportune moment."

Alan Kirman, Professor Emeritus of Economics at Université d' Aix-Marseille III, France and Director of Studies at Ecole des Hautes Etudes en Sciences Sociales

"Assumptions about the homogeneity of individuals' expectations have limited economic modeling for some time. In this very complete book, Cars Hommes shows the reader how the world of heterogeneous expectations works in several different contexts. It distinguishes itself by covering theory along with empirical and experimental validation. Researchers interested in getting up to speed in this relatively new area of economics will find this book an excellent overview and tutorial."

Professor Blake LeBaron, International Business School, Brandeis University

"Without doubt, rational expectations has been a powerful and useful assumption in pushing applied work forward in the last 40 years. But positing that agents have heterogeneous beliefs that deviate from the measure implied by a model opens up new possibilities that promise to allow us to resolve some of our many remaining puzzles about asset prices and quantities. Cars Hommes' book is a leading example of how productive this approach can be."

Thomas J. Sargent, W. R. Berkley Professor of Economics and Business, New York University and Senior Fellow, Hoover Institution, Stanford University. Winner of the Nobel Prize in Economics 2011

Behavioral Rationality and Heterogeneous Expectations in Complex Economic Systems

Cars Hommes

University of Amsterdam
Center for Nonlinear Dynamics in Economics and Finance (CeNDEF)
Amsterdam School of Economics and Tinbergen Institute

CAMBRIDGE
UNIVERSITY PRESS

University Printing House, Cambridge CB2 8BS, United Kingdom

One Liberty Plaza, 20th Floor, New York, NY 10006, USA

477 Williamstown Road, Port Melbourne, VIC 3207, Australia

314-321, 3rd Floor, Plot 3, Splendor Forum, Jasola District Centre, New Delhi - 110025, India

79 Anson Road, #06-04/06, Singapore 079906

Cambridge University Press is part of the University of Cambridge.

It furthers the University's mission by disseminating knowledge in the pursuit of
education, learning and research at the highest international levels of excellence.

www.cambridge.org
Information on this title: www.cambridge.org/9781107019294

First published 2013
3rd printing 2014

A catalogue record for this publication is available from the British Library

Library of Congress Cataloging in Publication data
Hommes, Carsien Harm, author.
Behavioral rationality and heterogeneous expectations in complex economic systems / Cars Hommes.
    pages   cm
Includes bibliographical references and index.
ISBN 978-1-107-01929-4
1. Rational expectations (Economic theory).   2. Economics–Psychological aspects.   I. Title.
HB3731.H66   2012
330.01 ′9–dc23   2012033806

ISBN 978-1-107-01929-4 Hardback
ISBN 978-1-107-56497-8 Paperback

Voor Annelies, Thomas & Saar

Contents

Figures

Preface

This book has a long history. It grew out of courses on Nonlinear Economic Dynamics (NED), which I have been teaching in the past 20 years at the University of Amsterdam (UvA) and various other places. The NED course has been part of the MSc Econometrics program of the Amsterdam School of Economics, University of Amsterdam since I started at UvA in 1992. I have also taught a condensed version of NED bi-annually between 1996 and 2004 in the Network Algemene en Kwantitatieve Economie (NAKE), a quantitative network of economics PhD courses in the Netherlands. Since 2004 the NED course has been part of the Graduate Program of the Tinbergen Institute, the Graduate school in Economics, Econometrics and Finance in Amsterdam and Rotterdam. More recently, much of the material in this book has been taught at various summerschools and lecture series, in particular the Advanced School on Nonlinear Dynamical Systems in Economics, Udine, Italy, June 2004, the Lecture Series on Heterogeneous Agent Models, Pisa, Italy, June 2006, the Trento Summerschool on Agent-based Finance, Trento, Italy, July 2007 and the International School on Multidisciplinary approaches to Economic and Social Complex Systems, Siena, Italy, June 2010.

I am grateful to many colleagues and friends for inspiration and help over more than two decades. My main PhD thesis advisor at the University of Groningen, Helena Nusse, raised my enthusiasm for chaos and complexity. In Groningen, Floris Takens further deepened my knowledge of nonlinear dynamics and strange attractors, and Ad Pikkemaat taught me the first lessons in mathematical economics. At the University of Amsterdam, this role was taken over by Claus Weddepohl, who was one of the first mathematical economists in the Netherlands and Europe recognizing the importance of nonlinear dynamics and complexity for economics.

I am most grateful to William "Buz" Brock for his inspiration and support over so many years. My visits to the University of Wisconsin, Madison, in the summers of 1994, 1995 and 1997 and our regular discussions thereafter over a coffee or a "spotted cow" either in Amsterdam or Madison, have been extremely stimulating and productive. Our joint work on bounded rationality and heterogeneous expectations in complex economic systems forms the theoretical basis of this book. Buz's contributions go far beyond science and his warm friendship has been another reason to keep coming back to Madison.

Since 1998 the Center for Nonlinear Dynamics in Economics and Finance (CeNDEF) provided a most stimulating research environment within the Amsterdam School of Economics at UvA. The CeNDEF group has not only further explored the theory and applications of nonlinear dynamics and complexity in economics, but has also brought these models to the data by testing them with empirical time series data and laboratory experiments with human subjects. At the start of CeNDEF, experimental and empirical work for me were a "jump in the dark" and this book has benefitted enormously from my almost daily discussions and joint work in the past 15 years with CeNDEF researchers, coauthors and friends, particularly with Mikhail Anufriev, Peter Boswijk, Cees Diks, Maurice Koster, Roald Ramer, Joep Sonnemans, Jan Tuinstra and Florian Wagener. I have been fortunate with continuous intellectual challenges from excellent PhD students and postdocs at CeNDEF and would like to thank Tiziana Assenza, Te Bao, Adriana Cornea, Pietro Dindo, Gerwin Griffioen, Peter Heemeijer, Sander van der Hoog, Tatiana Kiseleva, David Kopanyi, Marco van der Leij, Michiel van der Leur, Tomasz Makarewicz, Sebastiano Manzan, Domenico Massaro, Saeed Mohammadian Moghayer, Marius Ochea, Valentyn Panchenko, Raoul Philipse, Daan in't Veld, Henk van de Velden, Robin de Vilder, Juanxi Wang, Roy van der Weide, Marcin Wolski, Paolo Zeppini, Mei Zhu and Ilija Zovko.

Complexity, bounded rationality and heterogeneity are new and still somewhat controversial topics in economics and my work benefitted greatly from many stimulating discussions, encouragement and joint work with many colleagues and friends: Jasmina Arifovic, Volker Böhm, Giulio Bottazzi, Jean Philip Bouchaud, Bill Branch, Jim Bullard, Serena Brianzoni, Carl Chiarella, Silvano Cincotti, David Colander, Herbert Dawid, Dee Dechert, Paul DeGrauwe, Domenico Delli-Gatti, Roberto Dieci, Giovanni Dosi, Edward Droste, John Duffy, George Evans, Doyne Farmer, Gustav Feichtinger, Mauro Gallegati, Laura Gardini, Andrea Gaunersdorfer, Jacob Goeree, David Goldbaum, Jean-Michel Grandmont, Roger Guesnerie, Tony He, Dirk Helbing, Thorsten Hens, Seppo Honkapohja, Hai Huang, Ken Judd, Alan Kirman, Mordecai Kurz, Yuri Kuznetsov, Laurence Laselle, Blake LeBaron, Axel Leijonhufvud, Marji Lines, Thomas Lux, Rosario Mantegna, Bruce McGough, Alfredo Medio, Paul Ormerod, Damjan Pfajfar, J. Barkley Rosser, Klaus-Reiner Schenk-Hoppé, Andras Simonovits, Gerhard Sorger, Didier Sornette, Shyam Sunder, Leigh Tesfatsion, Fabio Tramontana, Miroslav Verbic, Duo Wang, Frank Westerhoff, Remco Zwinkels and many others.

I hope this book will provide the readers with some of the excitement about nonlinear dynamics and complex systems in economics and finance that I have experienced over the years. The book should not be seen as an in-depth mathematical treatment of nonlinear dynamics, but rather as a collection of the most important and relevant tools to be applied by researchers and policy makers in economics and finance. In the courses I have been teaching about the subject, computer simulations have always played an important role for students as an illustration of the concepts and richness of nonlinear dynamics. Most of the figures in this book have been generated by the *E&F Chaos* software package, jointly developed at CeNDEF with Cees Diks, Valentyn Panchenko and Roy van der Weide, and freely downloadable at http://www1.fee.uva.nl/cendef/.

A special word of thanks goes to Dávid Kopányi, for his assistance in the last year with carefully editing the text and especially producing many illuminating figures and illustrations in the book. Without his help the book would still be unfinished. In addition, I would like to thank Chris Harrison and Phil Good at CUP for their technical support and patience. I gratefully acknowledge financial support for many years of complexity research by the Netherlands Organization for Scientific Research (NWO) and the EU through several FP6 and FP7 EU grants.

Finally and most of all, I thank Annelies, Thomas and Saar for their love and patience over so many years. They are my stable attractors in a complex world.

1 Introduction

The economy is a complex system with nonlinear interactions and feedback loops. Early traces of this view date back, for example, to Schumpeter and Hayek, and to Simon. The complexity modeling paradigm has been strongly advocated since the 1980s by economists and multidisciplinary scientists from various fields, such as physics, computer science and biology, linked to the Santa Fe Institute.[1] More recently the complexity view has also drawn the attention of policy makers, who are faced with complex phenomena, irregular fluctuations and sudden, unpredictable market transitions. For example, the chairman of the FED, Ben Bernanke, noted that the 1000-point collapse of the Dow Jones Industrial Average on the afternoon of May 6, 2010, reflected the complexity of financial-market systems:

> The brief market plunge was just a small indicator of how complex and chaotic, in the formal sense, these systems have become. Our financial system is so complicated and so interactive – so many different markets in different countries and so many sets of rules. What happened in the stock market is just a little example of how things can cascade or how technology can interact with market panic.
>
> (interview Ben Bernanke, IHT, May 17, 2010).

The recent financial-economic crisis is a dramatic example of large movements, similar to critical transitions that are so characteristic for complex evolving systems. These large changes of global financial markets can hardly be viewed as a rational response to news about economic fundamentals and cannot be explained by traditional representative rational agent macro-finance models. A more compelling and intuitive explanation is that these extreme large movements have been triggered by bad economic news, and subsequently strongly amplified by an "irrational" overreaction of a heterogeneous population of boundedly rational, interacting agents. In a well-known speech the former president of the ECB, Jean-Claude Trichet, called for a new approach for policy makers to managing crises:

> First, we have to think about how to characterise the homo economicus at the heart of any model. The atomistic, optimising agents underlying existing models do not capture behaviour during a

---

[1] See, e.g., the early collections of papers in the Santa Fe conference proceedings Anderson et al. (1988) and Arthur et al. (1997a).

1

crisis period. We need to deal better with heterogeneity across agents and the interaction among those heterogeneous agents. We need to entertain alternative motivations for economic choices. Behavioural economics draws on psychology to explain decisions made in crisis circumstances. Agent-based modelling dispenses with the optimisation assumption and allows for more complex interactions between agents. Such approaches are worthy of our attention.

Second, we may need to consider a richer characterisation of expectation formation. Rational expectations theory has brought macroeconomic analysis a long way over the past four decades. But there is a clear need to re-examine this assumption. Very encouraging work is under way on new concepts, such as learning and rational inattention.

(Speech by Jean-Claude Trichet, ECB Central Banking Conference, Frankfurt, November 18, 2010)

This book presents some simple, stylized complexity models in economics. Our main focus will be an underlying *behavioral theory of heterogeneous expectations* of boundedly rational individual agents in a complex, adaptive economic environment. We will also discuss empirical validation, both at the micro and at the macro level, of a behavioral theory of heterogeneous expectations through financial time series data and laboratory experiments with human subjects. The need for an empirically grounded behavioral theory of expectations for economic dynamics has already been stressed by Herb Simon (1984, p. 54):

A very natural next step for economics is to maintain expectations in the strategic position they have come to occupy, but to build an empirically validated theory of how attention is in fact directed within a social system, and how expectations are, in fact, formed. Taking that next step requires that empirical work in economics take a new direction, the direction of micro-level investigation proposed by Behavioralism.

1.1   Economic dynamics, nonlinearity and complexity

Economic dynamics is concerned with modeling fluctuations in economic and financial variables, such as commodity prices, output growth, unemployment, interest rates, exchange rates and stock prices. Broadly speaking, there are two contrasting views concerning the main sources of economic fluctuations. According to the first, business cycles are mainly driven by "news" about economic fundamentals, that is, by random *exogenous* shocks to preferences, endowments, technology, firms' future earnings or dividends, etc. These random shocks typically act on an inherently stable (linearized) economic system. This view dates back to the 1930s, to Frisch, Slutsky and Tinbergen, who showed that a stable linear system subject to an irregular sequence of external, random shocks may produce fluctuations very similar to those observed in real business cycles.

The *linear, stable view* was criticized in the 1940s and 1950s, mainly because it did not offer an *economic* explanation of observed fluctuations, but rather attributed those fluctuations to external, non-economic forces. As an alternative, Goodwin, Hicks and Kaldor developed nonlinear, *endogenous* business cycle models, with the savings-investment mechanism as the main economic force generating business fluctuations. According to this *nonlinear view*, the economy may be intrinsically unstable and, even in the absence of external shocks, fluctuations in economic variables can arise. These early Keynesian nonlinear business cycle models, however, were criticized for at least three reasons. Firstly, the limit cycles generated by these models were much too regular to explain the sometimes highly irregular movements in economic and financial time series data. Secondly, the "laws of motion" were considered to be "ad hoc," since they had not been derived from micro foundations, i.e., from utility and profit maximization principles. A third important critique was that agents' behavior was considered as *irrational*, since their *expectations were systematically wrong* along the regular business cycles. Smart, rational traders would learn from experience to anticipate these cyclic movements and revise their expectations accordingly, and, so the story goes, this would cause the cycles to disappear.

These shortcomings triggered the rational expectations revolution in the 1960s and 1970s, inspired by the seminal papers of Muth (1961) and Lucas (1972a and b). New classical economists developed an alternative within the exogenous approach, the stochastic real business cycle (RBC) models, pioneered by Kydland and Prescott (1982). RBC models fit into the general equilibrium framework, characterized by utility-maximizing consumers, profit-maximizing firms, market clearing for all goods at all dates and all traders having rational expectations. More recently, New Keynesian Dynamic Stochastic General Equilibrium (DSGE) models have moved to the forefront of macroeconomic modeling and policy analysis (Clarida et al., 1999; Woodford 2003). Typically these DSGE models are log linearized and assume a representative rational agent framework. A representative, perfectly rational agent nicely fits into a linear view of a globally stable, and hence predictable, economy. By the late 1970s and early 1980s, the debate concerning the main source of business cycles seemed to have been settled in favor of the exogenous shock hypothesis, culminating in the currently dominating DSGE macro models for policy analysis.

1.1.1 The discovery of chaos

In mathematics and physics the view on modeling dynamic phenomena changed dramatically in the 1960s and 1970s due to the discovery of *deterministic chaos*. One of its pioneers, the MIT meteorologist Edward Lorenz (1963), discovered by computer simulations that a simple nonlinear system of three differential equations can generate highly irregular and seemingly unpredictable time series patterns.[2] Moreover, his stylized model of weather prediction was characterized by *sensitive dependence on initial conditions* (the "butterfly effect"): a small perturbation of the initial state leads to a completely different time path prediction in the medium or long run. In the 1970s, Ruelle and Takens (1971) presented a mathematical proof that a simple nonlinear system of three or four differential equations, without any external random disturbances, can indeed exhibit complicated, irregular long run dynamical behavior. They introduced

---

[2] See, e.g., Gleick (1987) for a stimulating historical overview of "chaos theory." It is interesting to note that one of the traditional Keynesian business cycle models from the 1950s, Hicks' classical nonlinear trade cycle model with ceilings and floors, can in fact generate irregular, chaotic time series. In particular, figures 9 and 10 in Hicks (1950, pp. 76–79), computed by hand at the time, are similar to the computer simulated chaotic series in Hommes (1995), so that in some sense Hicks was close to discovering chaos in his trade cycle model.

the notion of a *strange attractor* to describe irregular long run behavior in a nonlinear deterministic dynamical system. The discovery of deterministic chaos and strange attractors shattered the Laplacian deterministic view of perfect predictability and made scientists realize that, because initial states can only be measured with finite precision, long run prediction may be fundamentally impossible, even when the laws of motion are perfectly known.

In the 1970s, there was yet another important mathematical article with the illuminating title "Period three implies chaos" (Li and Yorke, 1975), which played a stimulating role and was particularly important for applications. Li and Yorke showed that for a large class of simple nonlinear difference equations in one single state variable, a simple sufficient "period three" condition already implies complicated, chaotic dynamical behavior. The best-known example concerns logistic population growth in biology, as described by May (1976). These and other simple mathematical examples together with the rapidly increasing availability of computers for numerical simulations led to an explosion of interest in nonlinear dynamics in mathematics, physics and other applied sciences.

The "chaos revolution" in the 1970s had its roots, however, much earlier, at the end of the nineteenth century in the famous French mathematician Henri Poincaré. In 1887 king Oskar II of Sweden promised a prize to the best essay concerning the question "Is our solar system stable?" In his prize-winning essay, Poincaré (1890) showed that the motion in a simple three-body system, a system of sun, earth and moon, need not be periodic, but may become highly irregular and unpredictable. In modern terminology he showed that chaotic motion is possible in a three-body system. Poincaré introduced the notion of a so-called *homoclinic point*, an intersection point between the stable and the unstable manifolds of an equilibrium steady state. His notion of homoclinic orbits turned out to be a key feature of complicated motion and strange attractors and may be seen as an early signature of chaos.

1.1.2   *Economic applications of chaos*
In the 1980s, inspired by "chaos theory" and within the tradition of endogenous business cycle modeling, economic theorists started looking for nonlinear, deterministic models generating erratic time series similar to the patterns observed in real business cycles. This search led to new, simple nonlinear business cycle models, within the Arrow–Debreu general equilibrium paradigm of optimizing behavior, perfectly competitive markets and rational expectations, generating chaotic business fluctuations (e.g., Benhabib and Day, 1982 and Grandmont, 1985; see, e.g., Lorenz, 1993 for an overview of nonlinear business cycle models and chaos). These model examples show that irregular, chaotic fluctuations can arise under the New Classical Economics paradigm in a perfectly rational representative agent framework. It turned out to be more difficult, however, to calibrate or estimate such chaotic business cycle models to real economic data.

Simultaneously, the search for nonlinearity and chaos in economics was undertaken from an empirical perspective. In physics and mathematics nonlinear methods to distinguish between truly random and deterministic chaotic time series had been developed. For example, correlation dimension tests and Lyapunov exponent tests had been developed by Takens (1981) and Grassberger and Procaccia (1983). When the correlation dimension of a time series is low, this suggests evidence for low-dimensional chaos. In economics, for example, Brock and Sayers (1988) found a correlation dimension of about 3 for macroeconomic data (postwar quarterly US unemployment rates), and Scheinkman and LeBaron (1989) a correlation dimension of about 6 for stock market data (weekly stock returns). A problem for applying these empirical methods, particularly relevant for economic data, is that they require very long time series and that they are extremely sensitive to noise. Furthermore, it turned out that time series generated by fitted stochastic alternative models, such as linear, near unit root autoregressive models for macro data or GARCH-models for stock returns, also generate low correlation dimensions of comparable size. Hence, from these empirical findings, one *cannot* conclude that there is evidence for low-dimensional, purely deterministic chaos in economic and financial data. Brock, Dechert, Scheinkman and LeBaron (1996) have developed a general test (the BDS test), based upon the notion of correlation dimension, to test for *nonlinearity* in a given time series; see Brock et al., (1991) for the basic theory, references and applications. The BDS test has become widely used, in economics but also in physics, and has high power against many nonlinear alternatives. From an empirical viewpoint, evidence for low-dimensional, purely deterministic chaos in economic and financial data is weak, but there is strong evidence for nonlinear dependence. At the same time, it seems fair to add that, because of the sensitivity to noise of these methods, the hypothesis of chaos buffeted with (small) dynamic noise has *not* been rejected either.[3] Nor has higher-dimensional chaos been rejected by these time series methods.

Empirical difficulties, both in calibrating new classical nonlinear endogenous business cycle models to economic data and in finding evidence for low-dimensional chaos in economic and financial time series, thus prevented a full embracement and appreciation of nonlinear dynamics in economics in the 1980s and early 1990s.

1.1.3 Expectations
The most important difference between economics and the natural sciences is perhaps the fact that decisions of economic agents today depend upon their *expectations* or *beliefs* about the future. To illustrate this difference, weather forecasts for tomorrow will not affect today's weather, but investors' predictions about future stock prices may affect financial market movements today. A classic example is the Dutch "tulip mania" in the seventeenth century, as described in Kindleberger (1996). The dreams and hopes of Dutch investors for excessive high returns on their investments in tulip bulbs may have exaggerated the explosion of the price of tulip bulbs by a factor of more than 20 at the beginning of 1636, and its crash back to its original level by the end of that year. Another more recent example is the "dot-com bubble," the rapid run up of stock

---

[3] See Hommes and Manzan (2006) for a brief recent discussion.

prices in financial markets worldwide in the late 1990s, and the subsequent crash. This rise in stock prices was triggered by good news about economic fundamentals, a new communication technology, the internet. An overoptimistic estimate of future growth of ICT industries seems to have contributed to and strongly reinforced the excessively rapid growth of stock prices in 1995–2000, leading to extreme overvaluation of stock markets worldwide, and their subsequent fall in 2000–2003. A more recent example is the 2008–2012 financial-economic crisis. It is hard to believe that the decline of worldwide financial markets in 2008 of more than 50% was completely driven by changes in economic fundamentals. Rather it seems that the large decline was strongly amplified by pessimistic expectations and market psychology. A similar observation applies to the 2011–2012 EU debt crisis. While the budget deficits of EU countries are partly caused by economic fundamentals, the sharp rise in the spread of, e.g., Italian and German bonds in 2011 seems to have been exaggerated by investors' pessimistic expectations. The predictions, expectations or beliefs of consumers, firms and investors about the future state of the economy are part of the "law of motion." The economy is a highly nonlinear *expectations feedback* system, and therefore a *theory of expectations* is a crucial part of any dynamic economic model or theory.

Since the introduction of rational expectations by Muth (1961) and its popularization in macroeconomics by Lucas (1972a and b) and others, the *rational expectations hypothesis* (REH) became the dominating expectations formation paradigm in economics. According to the REH all agents are rational and take as their subjective expectation of future variables the objective prediction by economic theory. In economic modeling practice, expectations are given as the mathematical conditional expectation given all available information. Rational agents do not make "systematic mistakes" and their expectations are, on average, correct. The REH provides an elegant "fixed-point" solution to an economic expectations feedback system by imposing that, on average, expectations and realizations coincide. In the absence of exogenous shocks, rational expectations implies that agents have perfect foresight and make no mistakes at all. This shortcut solution excludes all irrationality and market psychology from economic analysis, and instead postulates that expectations are in equilibrium and perfectly self-fulfilling.

The rational expectations revolution in economics took place *before* the discovery of chaos, at least before the time that the irregular behavior and complexity of nonlinear dynamics were widely known among economists. The fact that chaos can arise in simple nonlinear systems and its implications for limited predictability, however, shed important new light on the expectations hypothesis. In a simple (linear) stable economy with a unique steady state, predictability prevails and it seems natural that agents may have rational expectations, at least in the long run. A representative, perfectly rational agent model nicely fits into a linear view of a globally stable and predictable economy. But how can agents have rational expectations or perfect foresight in a *complex, nonlinear world*, when the true law of motion is unknown and prices and quantities move irregularly on a strange attractor exhibiting sensitivity to initial conditions? A boundedly rational world view with agents using simple forecasting strategies, which may not be perfect but are at least approximately right, seems more appropriate for a complex nonlinear environment. Indeed, already around 1900 Poincaré, one of the founding fathers of nonlinear dynamics, expressed his concerns about the implications of limited predictability in nonlinear systems for economics in a letter to Walras, one of the founders of mathematical economics:[4]

> You regard men as infinitely selfish and infinitely farsighted. The first hypothesis may perhaps be admitted in a first approximation, the second may call for some reservations.

1.1.4 Bounded rationality and adaptive learning

In economics in the 1950s, Herbert Simon emphasized that rationality requires extreme assumptions concerning agents' information gathering and computing abilities. Firstly, rational agents are typically assumed to have perfect information about economic fundamentals and perfect knowledge about underlying market equilibrium equations. This assumption seems unrealistically strong, especially since the "law of motion" of the economy depends on the expectations of *all other* agents. Secondly, even if such information and knowledge were available, typically in a nonlinear market equilibrium model it would be very hard, or even impossible, to derive the rational expectations forecast analytically, and it would require quite an effort to do it computationally. As an alternative, Simon strongly argued for *bounded rationality*, with limited computing capabilities and agents using simple rules of thumb instead of perfectly optimal decision rules, as a more accurate and more realistic description of human behavior. Simon's reasoning lost against the rational expectations revolution in the 1970s, but in the last two decades similar reasoning has caused an explosion of interest in bounded rationality. Modeling a world with boundedly rational agents, who adapt their behavior and learn from past experiences over time, leads to a complex and highly nonlinear dynamic system.

A common assumption underlying models of bounded rationality is that agents do *not* know the actual "law of motion" of the economy, but instead base their forecasts upon time series *observations*. They behave like economic statisticians, forming expectations based upon time series observations, using a simple statistical model for their perceived law of motion. *Adaptive learning*, sometimes also referred to as *statistical learning*, means that agents adapt their beliefs over time by updating the parameters of their perceived law of motion according to some learning scheme (e.g., recursive ordinary least squares), as additional observations become available. The adaptive learning approach has been used extensively in macroeconomics. Sargent (1993) gives an early overview of learning in macroeconomics, while Evans and Honkapohja (2001) contains a more recent extensive and detailed treatment; see also Conlisk (1996) for a stimulating discussion of bounded rationality. An important issue that has received much attention in the literature is the *stability* of rational expectations equilibria under adaptive learning. If adaptive learning enforces convergence to a rational

---

[4] Front quotation in Grandmont (1998) and Ingrao and Israel (1990), from letter of October 1, 1901 of Henri Poincaré to Léon Walras.

expectations equilibrium, the REH would be more plausible as a (long run) description of the economy, since the underlying informational assumptions could be considerably relaxed. However, many examples have been found where adaptive learning does *not* converge to rational expectations, but rather settles down to some kind of "learning equilibrium" displaying endogenous, sometimes even chaotic, fluctuations and excess volatility (e.g., Bullard, 1994, Grandmont, 1998, Hommes and Sorger, 1998 and Schönhofer, 1999).

1.1.5 Heterogeneity in complex adaptive systems

The representative agent model has played a dominant role in modern economics for quite some time. Most rational expectations models assume a single, *representative agent*, representing average consumer, average firm or average investment behavior. An important motivation for the rational agent model dates back to the 1950s, to Milton Friedman (1953) who argued that non-rational agents will be driven out of the market by rational agents, who will trade against them and earn higher profits. In recent years however, this view has been challenged and heterogeneous agent models are becoming increasingly popular in finance and in macroeconomics. Kirman (1992, 2010), for example, provides an illuminating critique on representative rational agent modeling.

Bounded rationality and learning in a complex environment naturally fit with *heterogeneous expectations*, with the economy viewed as a complex evolving system composed of many different, boundedly rational, interacting agents, using different decision strategies, heuristics and forecasting rules. Heterogeneous strategies compete against each other and an evolutionary selection mechanism, e.g., through genetic algorithm learning, disciplines the class of strategies being used by individual agents. In such a complex system, expectations and realizations coevolve over time. The work at the Santa Fe Institute has played a stimulating role and the collections of papers in Anderson et al. (1988) and Arthur et al. (1997a) of Santa Fe conferences provide early examples of the complexity modeling approach in economics.

The complexity view in economics is naturally linked to *agent-based computational economics (ACE)*, characterized by agent-based computer simulation models with many heterogeneous agents; see, e.g., the recent *Handbook* of Tesfatsion and Judd (2006) for surveys of the state of the art of ACE. An advantage of agent-based models is that one can use a "bottom up" approach and build "realistic" models from micro interactions to simulate and mimic macro phenomena. However, in agent-based models with many interacting agents, the "wilderness of bounded rationality" is enormous, there are infinitely many possibilities for individual decision rules and, for a given model, it is often hard to pin down what exactly causes certain stylized facts at the macro level in agent-based micro simulations.

1.1.6 Behavioral rationality and heterogeneous expectations

A good feature of the rational expectations hypothesis (REH) is that it imposes strong discipline on agents' forecasting rules and minimizes the number of free parameters in dynamic economic models. In contrast, the "wilderness of bounded rationality" in agent-based models leaves many degrees of freedom in economic modeling, and it seems far from clear which rules are the most reasonable out of an infinite class of potential behavioral rules. Stated differently in a popular phrase: *"There is only one way (or perhaps a few ways) you can be right, but there are many ways you can be wrong."* To avoid "ad hoccery," a successful bounded rationality research program needs to discipline the class of expectations and decision rules. The REH assumes *perfect consistency* between beliefs and realizations. For a successful bounded rationality research program a *reasonable* and *plausible* form of consistency between beliefs and realizations is necessary.

This book focusses on "simple" complexity models, where only a few different types of heterogeneous agents interact. Our main focus is on the role of *behavioral rationality* and *heterogeneous expectations* within stylized complexity models. Our consistency story of bounded rationality contains three important elements: (i) agents use simple decision rules, with an intuitive behavioral interpretation; (ii) agents switch between different decision rules based on evolutionary selection and learning; and (iii) the models of bounded rationality are empirically validated, at both the micro and the macro levels.

Behavioral rationality emphasizes the use of simple, intuitive decision rules – *heuristics* – with a plausible behavioral interpretation. These heuristics are not perfect and need not be optimal, but within an environment that is too complex to fully understand individual agents look for simple decision rules that perform reasonably well to a first-order approximation; for a similar approach and extensive discussions, see, e.g., the collection of papers on smart heuristics and the adaptive toolbox in Gigerenzer et al. (1999) and Gigerenzer and Selten (2001).

Two forms of learning further discipline the class of decision heuristics. First, we use the heterogeneous strategy switching framework of Brock and Hommes (1997a, 1998) of *endogenous evolutionary selection* or *reinforcement learning* among heterogeneous decision or forecasting rules. The main idea here is that agents tend to switch to rules that have performed better, according to some suitable economic performance measure such as realized profits or forecasting accuracy, in the recent past. The forecasting rules may be divided into different classes, with different degrees of rationality, ranging from simple behavioral rules such as naive or adaptive expectations, trend extrapolating rules or contrarian rules, to more sophisticated rules, such as statistical learning rules, fundamental market analysis or even rational expectations. These more sophisticated rules may be more costly – due to information-gathering costs – than alternative forecasting heuristics. The second form of learning takes place within each class of forecasting heuristics, with some parameters changing over time following some adaptive learning process. For example, within the class of trend-following heuristics, the trend coefficient or the anchor from which the trend is extrapolated may change over time and depend upon market realizations. This type of learning also has a behavioral interpretation and can be linked to the *anchor and adjustment* heuristics used in psychology (e.g., Tversky and Kahneman, 1974, Kahneman, 2003).

To discipline behavioral models and boundedly rational decision heuristics, *empirical validation both at the micro and at the macro level* is important. Laboratory experiments with human subjects, in particular experimental macroeconomics, plays a key role here, with the experimenter having full control over the type of micro interactions and the macroeconomic fundamentals. Duffy (2006, 2008a and b) provides a stimulating overview of experimental macroeconomics; the learning-to-forecast experiments surveyed in Hommes (2011) can be used to study the interactions of individual heterogeneous expectations and their aggregate effect in the laboratory.

Behavioral rationality and heterogeneous expectations naturally lead to highly *nonlinear* dynamical systems, because the fractions attached to the different rules are changing over time. Evolutionary selection of heterogeneous expectations sometimes enforces convergence to a rational expectations equilibrium. More often, however, the evolutionary system may be unstable and exhibit complicated, perpetual fluctuations, with several simple forecasting heuristics surviving evolutionary selection. In particular, we will see that when some rules act as "far from the steady state stabilizing forces" and other rules act as "close to the steady state destabilizing forces," evolutionary selection of expectations rules may lead to Poincaré's classical notion of a homoclinic orbit and may be seen as a signature of potential instability and chaos in a complex adaptive system with behaviorally rational agents.

An economy with heterogeneous, behaviorally rational agents is a highly nonlinear complex evolving system. The tools of nonlinear dynamics and complex systems are crucial to understand the behavior of markets with heterogeneous boundedly rational agents and to provide the insights to managing complex adaptive systems. This book introduces the most important analytical and computational tools in simple nonlinear complexity models and applies them to study economic dynamics with heterogeneous boundedly rational agents and learning. The remainder of this introduction gives the reader a quick overview of the contents of the book, discussing important concepts such as behavioral rationality and heterogeneous expectations in some simple examples of complex economic systems and briefly discussing their empirical validation with time series data and laboratory experiments with human subjects.

1.2   Adaptive expectations in a nonlinear economy

The simplest economic example nicely illustrating the role of expectations feedback is the "hog cycle" or *cobweb model*. Traditionally it has played a prominent role as a didactic benchmark model and has been used, for example, in the seminal article of Muth (1961) introducing rational expectations. Here we focus on the role of simple expectation rules, in particular adaptive expectations, in a *nonlinear* cobweb model.

The model is partial equilibrium and describes an independent competitive market for a non-storable consumption good, such as corn or hogs. Production takes a fixed unit of time, and suppliers therefore have to base their production decision upon their anticipation or expectation p_t^e of the market equilibrium price p_t that will prevail.

Demand, supply and market clearing are described by

$$D(p_t) = a - dp_t + \epsilon_t, \qquad\qquad a,d > 0, \qquad\qquad (1.1)$$

$$S_\lambda(p_t^e) = c + \arctan(\lambda(p_t^e - \bar{p})), \qquad c,\lambda > 0, \qquad\qquad (1.2)$$

$$D(p_t) = S_\lambda(p_t^e). \qquad\qquad\qquad (1.3)$$

Demand D in (1.1) is a linearly decreasing function in the market price p_t, with slope $-d$, and ϵ_t is a random term representing (small) exogenous demand shocks. The supply curve S_λ in (1.2) is *nonlinear*, increasing and S-shaped, with the parameter λ tuning the nonlinearity of the supply curve and $\bar{p}$ denoting the inflection point of the nonlinear supply curve, where marginal supply assumes its maximum. It should be noted that such a nonlinear, increasing supply curve can be derived from producer's profit maximization with a convex cost function. Finally, (1.3) dictates that the price adjusts such that the market clears in each period.

To close the model we have to specify how producers form price expectations. The simplest case, studied in the 1930s, e.g., by Ezekiel (1938), assumes that producers have *naive expectations*, that is, their prediction equals the last observed price, $p_t^e = p_{t-1}$. Under naive expectations, when demand is decreasing and supply is increasing and bounded, there are only two possibilities concerning the price dynamics, depending on the ratio of marginal supply over marginal demand at the steady state price p^* (i.e., the price where demand and supply intersect):

- if $|S'(p^*)/D'(p^*)| < 1$, then the steady state is (locally) *stable* and prices converge to p^*;
- if $|S'(p^*)/D'(p^*)| > 1$, then the steady state is *unstable* and prices diverge from p^* and converge to a (stable) 2-cycle.

The unstable case is illustrated in Figure 1.1 (top panel). Due to the nonlinearity of the supply curve, in the unstable case prices converge to a stable 2-cycle, with up and down "hog cycle" price fluctuations.

In the 1960s, simple mechanical expectation rules such as naive expectations became heavily criticized as being "irrational," since these forecasts are *"systematically wrong"*. Rational farmers would discover the regular, cyclic pattern in prices, learn from their systematic mistakes, change expectations accordingly and the hog cycle would disappear, so the argument goes. Similar considerations lead Muth (1961) to the introduction of *rational expectations*, where the expected price coincides with the price predicted by economic theory. In a rational expectations equilibrium, agents use economic theory, and compute their expectations as the conditional mathematical expectation derived from the market equilibrium equations. In the cobweb model, taking conditional mathematical expectations on the left- and right-hand sides of the market equilibrium equation (1.3), one derives that the rational expectations forecast is exactly given by the steady state price p^*. In a rational expectations equilibrium, expectations are self-fulfilling and agents make no systematic forecasting errors. In a cobweb world without uncertainty (i.e., $\epsilon_t \equiv 0$), the forecast $p_t^e = p^*$ will always

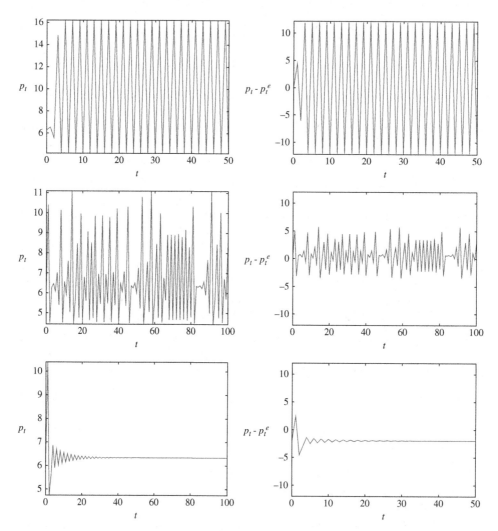

Figure 1.1. Time series of prices (left panel) and forecasting errors (right panel) in the nonlinear cobweb model with adaptive expectations for different values of expectations weight factor w: stable 2-cycle for $w = 1$ (top panel), chaotic price series for $w = 0.5$ (middle panel), and stable steady state for $w = 0.3$. Other parameter values are $\lambda = 4.8$, $c = 1.5$, $a = 4.1$, $d = 0.25$, $\bar{p} = 6$ and initial state $p_0 = 6$.

be exactly right and rational expectations coincides with perfect foresight. In a noisy cobweb world with uncertainty, the rational expectations forecast $p^e_t = p^*$ will be correct on average and agents make no systematic mistakes, since forecasting errors are proportional to the exogenous random demand shocks ϵ_t.

Now consider the case of adaptive expectations, discussed by Nerlove (1958) (but only in the case of linear demand and supply). *Adaptive expectations* are given by

$$p^e_t = (1 - w)p^e_{t-1} + w p_{t-1}, \qquad 0 \leq w \leq 1, \qquad (1.4)$$

where w is the expectations weight factor. The expected price is a weighted average of yesterday's expected and realized prices, or equivalently, the expected price is adapted by a factor w in the direction of the most recent realization. The weight factor w determines the magnitude of the "error-correction" in each period. In fact, adaptive expectations means that today's expected price is a weighted average, with geometrically declining weights, of all past prices. In the cobweb model with *linear* demand and supply curves, naive and adaptive expectations lead to the familiar "hog" cycle," characterized by up and down oscillations between a high and a low price level. In the case of *nonlinear* (but monotonic) demand and/or supply curves, things become more complicated, however. A simple computation, using (1.1–1.3) and (1.4), shows that the dynamics of expected prices becomes

$$p_t^e = f_{w,a,d,\lambda}(p_{t-1}^e) = (1-w)p_{t-1}^e + w\frac{a+\epsilon_t - c - \arctan(\lambda(p_{t-1}^e - \bar{p}))}{d}. \quad (1.5)$$

Dynamics of (expected) prices in the cobweb model with adaptive expectations is thus given by a one-dimensional (1-D) system $x_t = f_{w,a,b,\lambda}(x_{t-1})$ with four model parameters. *What can be said about the price–quantity dynamics in this nonlinear dynamic model, and how does it depend on the model parameters?*

Figure 1.1 illustrates time series of prices and corresponding forecasting errors, for different values of the expectations weight factor w. Under naive expectations ($w = 1$; top panel) prices converge to a stable 2-cycle and expectational errors are large and systematic. When agents are cautious in adapting their expectations, i.e., when the expectations weight factor is small ($w = 0.3$, bottom panel), prices converge to the RE stable steady state and forecasting errors vanish in the long run. For intermediate values of the expectations weight factor ($w = 0.5$; middle panel) prices as well as forecasting errors are chaotic. These forecasting errors are considerably smaller than under naive expectations and, because they are *chaotic*, they are much more irregular and it is more difficult for producers to learn from their errors. The degree of consistency between realizations and adaptive expectations in the chaotic case is much higher than in the 2-cycle case of naive expectations, and it may therefore be a more reasonable, boundedly rational description of market behavior.

A powerful tool to investigate how the dynamical behavior of a nonlinear model depends on a single parameter is a *bifurcation diagram*. A bifurcation is a qualitative change in the dynamics as a model parameter changes. Critical transitions in complex systems arise because of some bifurcation, some qualitative change in the dynamics of the system. A bifurcation diagram shows the long run dynamical behavior as a function of a model parameter. Figure 1.2 shows a bifurcation diagram of the cobweb model with adaptive expectations with respect to the expectations weight factor w, illustrating the long run dynamics (100 iterations) after omitting a transient phase of 100 iterations.[5] For small values of w, $0 \leq w \leq 0.31$, prices converge to a stable steady

---

[5] Most figures in this book have been made using the E&F Chaos software for simulation of nonlinear systems, as described in Diks et al. (2008). The software is flexible and the user can, for example, easily include her own favorite nonlinear dynamic system. The software is freely downloadable at www.fee.uva.nl/cendef.

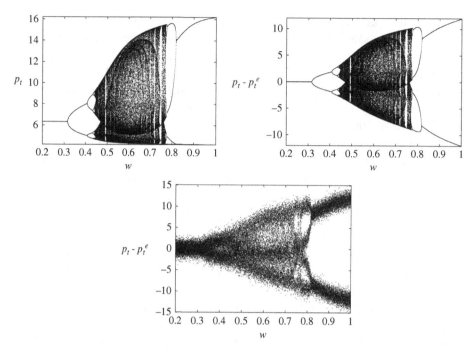

Figure 1.2. Bifurcation diagram for the expectations weight factor w, $0.2 \leq w \leq 1$, showing long run behavior of prices (top left panel) and forecasting errors (top right panel). The bottom panel shows a bifurcation diagram in the presence of small noise. Other parameter values are $\lambda = 4.8$, $c = 1.5$, $a = 4.1$, $d = 0.25$, $\bar{p} = 6$ and initial state $p_0 = 6$.

state, while for high values of w, $0.82 < w \leq 1$ (close to naive expectations) prices converge to a stable 2-cycle with large amplitude. Along the 2-cycle agents make systematic forecasting errors. For intermediate w-values however, say for $0.45 < w < 0.77$, chaotic price oscillations of moderate amplitude arise. In particular, the chaotic price fluctuations for $w = 0.5$ have been illustrated already in Figure 1.1. Figure 1.2 (bottom panel) also shows a simulation in the presence of small noise. The fine structure of the bifurcation diagram disappears, but the initial period-doubling bifurcations remain visible.

This example illustrates that a simple adaptive expectations rule in a noisy, nonlinear environment may be a reasonable forecasting strategy, which may be correct on average and which may not be easy to improve upon in a boundedly rational world.

1.3 Rational versus naive expectations

Heterogeneity of expectations among traders introduces an important *nonlinearity* into the market dynamics and is a potential source of market instability and erratic, chaotic price fluctuations. To illustrate this point by an example, we briefly discuss the cobweb model with heterogeneous expectations, rational versus naive producers, as introduced in Brock and Hommes (1997a); see Chapter 5 for a more detailed treatment. Agents can either buy a rational expectations forecast at positive information-gathering costs or freely obtain a simple, naive forecasting rule. This relates to Herbert Simon's idea to take deliberation and information-gathering costs into account in behavioral modeling. Information costs for rational expectations represent the idea that sophisticated prediction of prices, for example based upon detailed market analysis of economic fundamentals, is more costly than a simple prediction scheme, such as naive expectations or extrapolation of a price trend. The fractions of the two types change over time depending on how well both strategies performed in the recent past. Agents are boundedly rational in the sense that they tend to switch to the strategy that has performed better in the recent past.

To be more concrete, suppose that in the cobweb economy there are two types of producers, with different price expectations. At the moment of their production decision, producers can either buy the rational expectations price forecast at positive information costs C, or freely obtain the naive forecast. The two forecasting rules are

$$p^e_{1,t} = p_t, \tag{1.6}$$

$$p^e_{2,t} = p_{t-1}. \tag{1.7}$$

Rational agents have perfect foresight, while naive agents use the last observation as their forecast. In a cobweb world with rational versus naive expectations, the market equilibrium price is determined by demand and aggregate supply of both groups, i.e.,

$$D(p_t) = n_{1,t} S(p_t) + n_{2,t} S(p_{t-1}), \tag{1.8}$$

where $n_{1,t}$ and $n_{2,t}$ represent the fractions of producers holding rational respectively naive expectations. Notice that rational agents have perfect knowledge about the market equilibrium equation (1.8). Hence, rational traders not only have exact knowledge about prices and their own beliefs, but in a heterogeneous world they must also have perfect knowledge about expectations or beliefs of *all other* traders. We take a linear demand curve as before and, to keep the model as simple as possible, also a linear supply curve $S(p^e) = sp^e$. Market clearing in this two-type cobweb economy then yields

$$a - dp_t = n_{1,t} sp_t + n_{2,t} sp_{t-1}. \tag{1.9}$$

The second part of the model describes how the fractions of rational and naive producers are updated over time. The basic idea is that fractions are updated according to evolutionary fitness. Producers are boundedly rational in the sense that most of them will choose the forecasting rule which has highest fitness as measured by an economic performance measure, such as realized profits. To simplify the discussion, we focus here on the case where predictor selection is based upon last period's squared forecasting error plus the costs for obtaining that forecasting rule.[6] After the market equilibrium price

---

[6] As we will see in Chapter 5, Section 5.2 for linear demand and supply curves the fitness measure minus squared prediction error is, up to a constant factor, identical to realized profits.

has been revealed by (1.9), the new updated fractions of rational and naive producers will be given by a discrete choice or logit model:

$$n_{1,t+1} = \frac{e^{-\beta C}}{e^{-\beta C} + e^{-\beta(p_t - p_{t-1})^2}}, \tag{1.10}$$

$$n_{2,t+1} = \frac{e^{-\beta(p_t - p_{t-1})^2}}{e^{-\beta C} + e^{-\beta(p_t - p_{t-1})^2}}. \tag{1.11}$$

Note that these fractions add up to one. The key feature of the evolutionary selection or reinforcement learning scheme (1.10–1.11) is that the rule that performs better will attract more followers. More precisely, as long as the squared forecasting error $(p_t - p_{t-1})^2$ from naive expectations is smaller than the per period costs C for rational expectations, the majority of producers will "free ride" and not bother to buy the rational expectations forecast. But as soon as squared prediction errors for naive expectations become larger than the per period information-gathering costs for rational expectations, most producers will switch prediction strategy and buy the rational expectations forecast. The parameter β is called the *intensity of choice*, and it measures how fast the mass of traders will switch to the optimal prediction strategy. In the special case $\beta = 0$, both fractions will be constant and equal, and producers never switch strategy. In the other extreme case, $\beta = +\infty$, in each period *all* producers will use the same, optimal strategy. We call this latter case the *neoclassical limit*, since it represents the highest degree of rationality with respect to strategy selection based upon past performance in a heterogeneous world.

Now suppose that the market is *unstable* under naive expectations, that is, as long as all producers are naive, prices will diverge from the steady state price p^*. This situation is quite common and arises when the sensitivity of production decisions to expected price changes is larger than the sensitivity of consumers to price changes. The evolutionary dynamics exhibits a *rational route to randomness*, that is, a bifurcation route to strange attractors occurs, when the intensity of choice to switch to optimal forecasting strategies becomes larger. Figure 1.3 illustrates chaotic time series of prices and fractions as well as a strange attractor in the phase space.

The economic intuition behind the complicated evolutionary dynamics is simple. Suppose that we start from a situation where prices are close to the steady state p^* and almost all producers are naive. With prices close to the steady state, forecasting errors of naive expectations will be small, and therefore most producers will remain naive. Prices start fluctuating and will diverge from the steady state, so that the forecasting errors from naive expectations will increase over time. At some point, these forecasting errors will become larger than the costs for rational expectations. If the intensity of choice to switch strategies is high, then most producers will switch to rational expectations, causing prices to return close to the steady state. But with prices close to the steady state, it makes no sense to buy a rational expectations forecast, and most producers will become naive again. Hence, boundedly rational switching between forecasting

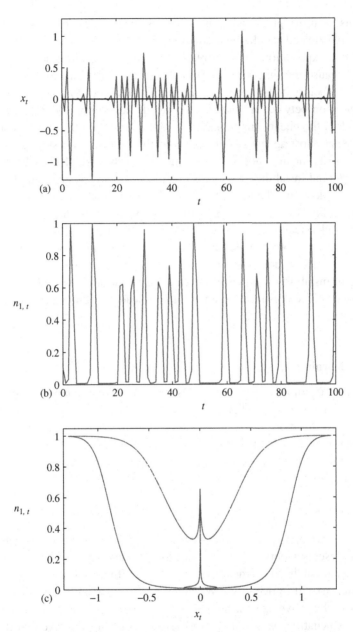

Figure 1.3. Chaotic time series of price deviations $x_t = p_t - p^*$ from steady state (top) and fractions $n_{1,t}$ of rational agents (middle) and corresponding strange attractor in the (x, n_1)-phase space (bottom). The market switches irregularly between an unstable phase of "free riding" with naive expectations dominating and a stable phase of costly rational expectations. Parameters are $\beta = 5$, $a = 0$, $d = 0.5$, $s = 1.35$ and $C = 1$.

strategies leads to an irregular switching between "cheap, destabilizing free riding" and "costly, sophisticated stabilizing prediction."

Heterogeneous expectations in a simple linear cobweb economy lead to a natural *nonlinearity*, because the time-varying fractions of the different trader types appear as multiplicative factors in the market equilibrium equation (1.8). The economic evolutionary interaction between a "close to the steady state destabilizing force" when most agents adopt the cheap, simple strategy, and a "far from the steady state stabilizing force" when most agents switch to the costly, sophisticated strategy, is in fact closely related to Poincaré's notion of a homoclinic orbit, which may be seen as a signature of potential instability and chaos in an evolutionary system with boundedly rational agents. Indeed, in Chapter 5, Section 5.2 we will see that for a high intensity of choice, the nonlinear evolutionary adaptive system is close to having a *homoclinic orbit*, Poincaré's classical notion nowadays known to be a key feature of chaotic systems. The nonlinear adaptive evolutionary system describing strategy selection of a population of boundedly rational agents thus incorporates a simple economic mechanism leading to instability and chaos. In particular, a rational choice between cheap free riding and costly sophisticated prediction may lead to highly erratic equilibrium price fluctuations.

1.4 Adaptive learning

For commonly used simple expectations rules, such as naive or adaptive expectations, the parameters of the rule are fixed. *Adaptive learning*, sometimes also called *statistical learning*, refers to the more flexible situation with time-varying parameters, where agents try to learn the parameters of their forecasting rule as new observations become available over time. As a simple example, suppose agents use a linear AR(1) forecasting rule, of the form

$$p_t^e = \alpha + \rho(p_{t-1} - \alpha), \tag{1.12}$$

with two parameters α and ρ. This linear rule has a simple *behavioral* interpretation. The parameter α represents agents' belief about the long run average of prices, while ρ represents the belief about the first-order autocorrelation coefficient, that is, the persistence (or anti-persistence) of the price series. When ρ is positive, agents believe that if the last observed price is above average, the next price will also be above average. On the other hand, when ρ is negative, agents are *contrarians*, that is, they believe that if the last observed price is above (below) average, the next price will be below (above) average. But what are the "true" or "optimal" parameters α and ρ of the linear rule in a complex market? In general, agents do *not* know the "true" parameters of their perceived law of motion, but they may try to learn the optimal parameters as additional observations become available. A more flexible forecasting rule with time-varying parameters is

$$p_t^e = \alpha_{t-1} + \rho_{t-1}(p_{t-1} - \alpha_{t-1}). \tag{1.13}$$

A simple example of an adaptive learning rule is given by

$$\alpha_t = \frac{1}{t+1} \sum_{i=0}^{t} p_i, \qquad\qquad t \geq 1 \qquad\qquad (1.14)$$

$$p_t = \frac{\sum_{i=0}^{t-1}(p_i - \alpha_t)(p_{i+1} - \alpha_t)}{\sum_{i=0}^{t}(p_i - \alpha_t)^2}, \qquad t \geq 1, \qquad\qquad (1.15)$$

where α_t is the *sample average* and p_t is the first-order *sample autocorrelation coefficient*. We refer to this adaptive learning schema as *sample autocorrelation learning* (SAC learning)[7]; see Chapter 4, Subsection 4.7.2 for a more detailed discussion. Here, we emphasize the behavioral interpretation of SAC learning. Agents try to learn the long run average α_t and the first-order autocorrelation or the "degree of persistence" of their linear forecasting rule. Hence, in a complex, nonlinear environment, agents try to match the first two moments, the long run average and the first-order autocovariance, to observed time series data.

The price dynamics in the cobweb model with linear demand and supply and SAC learning is given by

$$p_t = \frac{a - s p_t^e}{d}, \qquad\qquad (1.16)$$

with the expected price p_t^e given by SAC learning (1.13), (1.14) and (1.15). The model with learning is a *nonlinear* system. When demand and supply are monotonic, however, that is, demand is decreasing and supply is increasing, the system has nice properties and always converges to the RE steady state, as illustrated in Figure 1.4.

But are all individual agents sophisticated enough to use such a statistical adaptive learning rule? Stated differently, in an unknown complex environment will individual agents coordinate on a simple adaptive learning procedure to enforce convergence of aggregate price behavior to the rational expectations benchmark?

1.4.1 Cobweb learning-to-forecast experiments

Hommes et al. (2007) ran *learning-to-forecast* laboratory experiments with human subjects to address this question; see Chapter 8 for a much more detailed discussion of learning-to-forecast experiments. Participants in the experiments were asked to predict next periods' market price of an unspecified good. The realized price p_t in the experiment was determined by the (unknown) cobweb market equilibrium equation

$$D(p_t) = \frac{1}{K} \sum_{i=1}^{K} S(p_{i,t}^e), \qquad\qquad (1.17)$$

---

[7] SAC learning has been introduced in Hommes and Sorger (1998) and is closely related to recursive ordinary least squares (OLS)learning, which is used extensively in the literature on adaptive learning, see Evans and Honkapohja (2001).

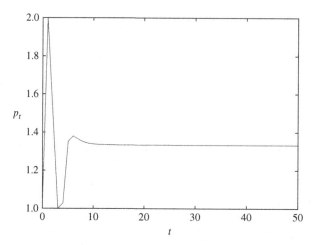

Figure 1.4. Price series under sample autocorrelation (SAC) learning converging to the unique rational expectations equilibrium. Parameters are $a = 2$, $d = 0.5$, $s = 2$ and $p_0 = 1$.

where $D(p_t)$ is the demand for the good at price p_t, K is the size of the group, $p_{i,t}^e$ is the price forecast by participant i and $S(p_{i,t}^e)$ is the supply of producer i, derived from profit maximization given the forecast by participant i. Demand and supply curves D and S were fixed during the experiments (except for small random shocks to the demand curve) and unknown to the participants. We focus on the group experiments with $K = 6$, as in Hommes et al. (2007).

The main question in these experiments was whether agents can learn and coordinate on the unique REE, in a world where consumers and producers act as if they were maximizing utility and profits, but where they do *not* know underlying market equilibrium equations and only observe time series of realized market prices and their own forecasts. Our choice for a nonlinear, S-shaped supply curve enables us to investigate whether agents can avoid systematic forecasting errors, as would, for example, occur along a 2-cycle under naive expectations, or can even learn a REE steady state in a nonlinear cobweb environment.

In their experiment, Hommes et al. (2007) considered a stable and an unstable treatment, which only differ in the parameter λ tuning the nonlinearity of the supply curve as in (1.2). In the stable treatment, if all subjects use naive expectations, prices converge to the RE steady state. In contrast, in the unstable treatment, if all subjects use naive expectations, prices diverge from the RE steady state and converge to the stable 2-cycle, with large and systematic forecasting errors.

Figure 1.5 shows time series of the realized prices in two typical group experiments, one stable and one unstable treatment, that only differ in the magnitude of the parameter λ tuning the nonlinearity of the supply curve. For both treatments, the sample mean of realized prices is very close to the (unknown) RE price. Moreover, in the stable treatment, the sample variance is close to the variance (0.25) of the RE

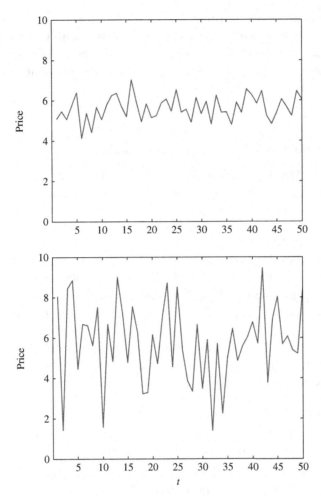

Figure 1.5. Realized market prices in two different cobweb group experiments. In the stable treatment (upper panel) the price quickly converges to the RE price with small random fluctuations, whereas in the unstable treatment (lower panel)) prices do not converge and exhibit excess volatility, with strongly fluctuating prices around the RE price.

benchmark. In contrast, in the unstable treatment the sample variance is significantly higher than the variance (0.25) of the RE benchmark, so that the unstable treatment exhibits excess volatility. Hommes et al. (2007) also look at autocorrelations in realized market prices, and find that there is no statistically significant autocorrelations in realized market prices, for both the stable and the unstable treatments. Apparently, the heterogeneous interactions of individual forecasting rules have washed out all linear predictable structure in realized aggregate market prices.

Hence, in a stable cobweb environment with unknown demand and supply curves, rational expectations may be a reasonable description of long run aggregate price

behavior. In an unstable cobweb environment, however, full coordination on rational expectations does not arise and the market exhibits excess volatility. Homogeneous
expectation models are – to our best knowledge – unable to explain all laboratory experiments simultaneously, and therefore heterogeneity is a key feature in explaining
experiments across different treatments.

1.5 Behavioral rationality and heterogeneous expectations

A theory of bounded rationality and learning must be based on some reasonable consistency between expectations and realizations. Broadly speaking, we have discussed
two stories of learning. One story of adaptive learning, where all agents use the same
simple rule, the perceived law of motion, and try to learn the optimal parameters of
the forecasting heuristic. According to this view, a representative agent optimizes the
parameters of his forecasting rule within a given (simple) class of rules. The second
story assumes that there are different classes of rules and that evolutionary selection or
reinforcement learning determines which classes are more popular. According to this
view, agents are heterogeneous and tend to switch to heuristics that have been more
successful in the recent past. More sophisticated classes of rules may require higher
information-gathering costs. We now combine these two bounded rationality stories of
adaptive learning and evolutionary selection into a theory of behavioral rationality and
heterogeneous expectations.

As an example, assume that agents can choose between a simple rule, naive expectations, and a more sophisticated SAC learning rule. The SAC rule requires more effort,
therefore it is more costly and can only be obtained at per period information costs
$C \geq 0$. Hence, agents can choose between two forecasting rules:

$$p_{1,t}^e = \alpha_{t-1} + \rho_{t-1}(p_{t-1} - \alpha_{t-1}), \tag{1.18}$$

$$p_{2,t}^e = p_{t-1}. \tag{1.19}$$

In a cobweb world with SAC learning versus naive expectations, the market equilibrium
price is determined by

$$p_t = \frac{a - n_{1,t} s p_{1,t}^e - n_{2,t} s p_{t-1}}{d}, \tag{1.20}$$

where $n_{1,t}$ and $n_{2,t}$ represent the fractions of producers using SAC learning respectively
naive expectations.

Evolutionary selection or reinforcement learning determines how many agents will
adopt each strategy. The fractions of SAC learners and naive producers depend upon
an evolutionary performance measure given by (minus) squared prediction errors, and
the fractions of the two types are again represented by a logit model

$$n_{1,t+1} = \frac{e^{-\beta[(p_t - p_{1,t}^e)^2 + C]}}{e^{-\beta[(p_t - p_{1,t}^e)^2 + C]} + e^{-\beta(p_t - p_{t-1})^2}}, \tag{1.21}$$

$$n_{2,t+1} = \frac{e^{-\beta(p_t - p_{t-1})^2}}{e^{-\beta[(p_t - p_{1,t}^e)^2 + C]} + e^{-\beta(p_t - p_{t-1})^2}}. \tag{1.22}$$

This model is very similar to the model with costly rational versus free naive expectations in the previous section, with rational agents replaced by SAC learning. Recall that rational expectations requires perfect information, including knowledge about market equilibrium equations and beliefs of all other agents. SAC learning assumes *no* knowledge about beliefs of other agents, but instead SAC learning tries to extract information (including how prices may be affected by expectations of other agents) from *observable* quantities using a simple, linear model with time-varying parameters in an unknown nonlinear environment.

According to (1.21–1.22), as long as the squared forecasting error $(p_t - p_{t-1})^2$ from naive expectations is smaller than the squared forecasting error $(p_t - p_{1,t}^e)^2$ from SAC learning plus the per period costs C, most producers will "free ride" and not bother about statistical learning. When the squared prediction errors for naive expectations become larger, however, most producers will switch prediction strategy and buy the SAC learning forecast.

Figure 1.6 illustrates the dynamics in the cobweb model with SAC learning versus naive expectations. The price dynamics becomes chaotic, with a complicated underlying strange attractor. Prices fluctuate irregularly, but at the same time adaptive learning enforces convergence of the learning parameters, the sample average α_t and the sample autocorrelation ρ_t. The sample average α_t converges to the (unknown) steady state price p^*, where demand and supply intersect, while the sample autocorrelation coefficient converges to a constant of about -0.4. Agents thus *learn to be contrarians*, as $\rho_t \to -0.4$, consistent with the SAC in realized prices. The presence of the SAC learning rule in the ecology of forecasting strategies ensures that much of the strongly negative autocorrelation in realized market prices is "arbitraged away," similar to the learning-to-forecast laboratory experiments.

In the cobweb market with heterogeneous agents, adaptive learning picks up the correct sample average and first-order sample autocorrelation. Interactions and evolutionary switching between these strategies cause complicated dynamical behavior. The bifurcation diagram in Figure 1.6 (bottom panel) illustrates a *rational route to randomness*, that is, complicated dynamics arises when agents become more sensitive to past performance of the strategies. The irregular price fluctuations are caused by the interaction of a simple, destabilizing strategy and a more sophisticated, costly, stabilizing strategy. This example illustrates that, agents are able to learn the optimal linear AR(1) rule in an unknown, complex heterogeneous environment.

When we apply the same 2-type model with SAC learning versus naive expectations to a stable cobweb model, evolutionary selection and adaptive learning enforce convergence to the rational expectations price. Hence, this simple 2-type heterogeneous

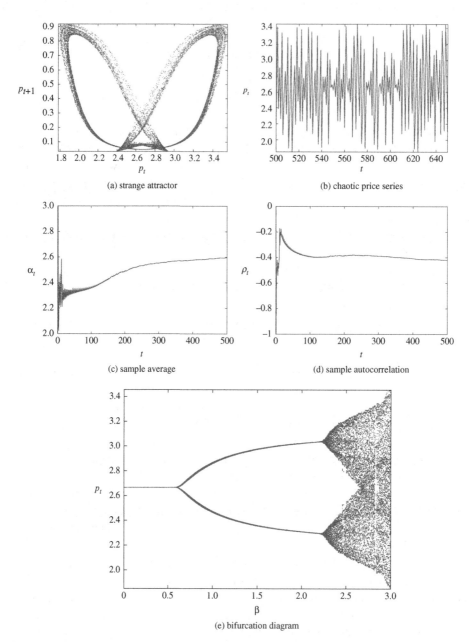

(a) strange attractor

(b) chaotic price series

(c) sample average

(d) sample autocorrelation

(e) bifurcation diagram

Figure 1.6. SAC learning versus naive expectations. Agents learn to be contrarians, as the first-order autocorrelation coefficient ρ_t approaches -0.4. The bifurcation diagram shows a rational route to randomness, as the intensity of choice β increases. Parameters are $\beta = 3$, $a = 4$, $d = 0.5$, $s = 1$, $C_1 = 1$, $p_0 = 2$, $\alpha_0 = 2$, $\rho_0 = 0$.

expectations model is able to explain both the coordination onto rational expectations in the stable treatment and the excess volatility with erratic price fluctuations in the unstable treatment of the cobweb laboratory experiments.

1.6   Financial markets as complex adaptive systems

The cobweb commodity market model discussed in the previous two sections is the simplest nonlinear framework in which the role of heterogeneous expectations has been studied extensively. In the last two decades, several structural heterogeneous agent models have been introduced in the finance literature; see LeBaron (2006) and Hommes (2006) for extensive surveys. In most of these heterogeneous agent models different groups of traders, having different beliefs or expectations about future asset prices, coexist. Two broad classes of traders can be distinguished. The first are *fundamentalists*, believing that the price of an asset is determined by underlying economic fundamentals, as measured, for example, by the expected future dividend stream. Fundamentalists predict that the asset price will move in the direction of its fundamental value and buy (sell) the asset when the price is below (above) its fundamental value. The second typical trader type are *chartists* or *technical analysts*, believing that asset prices are not determined by fundamentals only, but that they can be predicted by simple technical trading rules based upon observed patterns in past prices, such as trends or cycles.

An important critique from "rational expectations finance" upon behavioral finance with boundedly rational agents is that "irrational" traders will *not* survive in the market, because they will on average lose money and therefore they will be driven out of the market by rational investors, who will trade against them and drive prices back to fundamentals. According to this view it can be assumed, at least in the long run, that all agents behave "as if" they are all rational (Friedman, 1953). This "Friedman hypothesis" is essentially an evolutionary argument, suggesting that wealth- or profit-based reinforcement learning will drive out irrational investors.

At the Santa Fe Institute (SFI), Arthur et al. (1997b) and LeBaron et al. (1999) have built an early artificial stock market, where traders select their forecasting rules and trading strategies from a large population of trading rules, based upon an evolutionary "fitness measure," such as past realized profits or squared prediction errors. Strategies with higher fitness have a bigger chance of being adopted by individual traders. Computer simulations with genetic algorithms of this artificial stock market are characterized by two different regimes: close to the fundamental fluctuations, where the efficient market hypothesis (EMH) holds, and periods of persistent deviations from fundamentals and excess volatility, where the market is dominated by technical trading. Asset prices switch irregularly between these different regimes, creating stylized facts, such as time-varying, clustered volatility (GARCH effects) and fat tails, similar to those observed in real financial data. Here we briefly discuss the asset pricing model with heterogeneous beliefs of Brock and Hommes (1998), which may be viewed as a stylized, more tractable version of the SFI artificial stock market. We only illustrate the main features of the model by a simple 4-type example; an extensive treatment of the model is given in Chapter 6.

Agents can either buy an infinitely lived risky asset that pays an uncertain dividend y_t, or invest in a risk free asset that pays a fixed rate of return r. Dividends follow an exogenous stochastic process, known to all agents. In a perfectly rational world, all traders expect the future price of the risky asset to follow the fundamental price p_t^*, given by the discounted sum of expected future dividends. Boundedly rational traders, however, believe that in a heterogeneous world prices can in general *deviate* from their fundamental value. Let

$$x_t = p_t - p_t^* \tag{1.23}$$

denote the price deviation from the fundamental value. In the asset pricing model with heterogeneous beliefs, with different trader types h, $1 \le h \le H$, the market clearing price deviation from the fundamental benchmark is determined by

$$(1+r)x_t = \sum_{h=1}^{H} n_{ht} f_{ht}, \tag{1.24}$$

where n_{ht} is the time-varying fraction of trader type h in period t and f_{ht} is the forecast of type h at time t. Each forecasting rule f_h may be viewed as a "model of the market" of type h according to which prices will deviate from the fundamental price. For example, a forecasting strategy f_h may correspond to a technical trading rule, based upon short run or long run moving averages, or a trading range break strategy of the type used in real markets.

A convenient feature of our model formulation in terms of deviations from a benchmark fundamental is that it can be used for empirical and experimental testing of the theory. In this general setup, the benchmark rational expectations asset pricing model will be *nested* as a special case, with all forecasting strategies $f_h \equiv 0$.

An evolutionary selection mechanism describes how the fractions of different trader types will be updated over time. Fractions are updated according to an evolutionary fitness measure U_{ht}, given, e.g., by past realized profits or forecasting performance. Without discussing it in detail here, we give the expression for *realized profits* in deviations from the fundamental[8]:

$$U_{ht} = \left(x_t - (1+r)x_{t-1}\right)\left(\frac{f_{h,t-1} - Rx_{t-1}}{a\sigma^2}\right). \tag{1.25}$$

We assume here that there are no information-gathering costs, so that all forecasting strategies are freely available to all agents. Fractions of each type are given by a discrete

---

[8] Realized profits for type h in (1.25) are obtained by multiplying the realized excess return of the risky asset over the risk free asset times the demand for the risky asset by traders of type h. The demand is derived from mean-variance maximization of expected next period's wealth. The parameter a represents risk aversion while σ^2 represents constant conditional belief about the variance; see Chapter 6, Section 6.3 for details.

choice or multinomial logit model

$$n_{ht} = \frac{e^{\beta U_{h,t-1}}}{Z_{t-1}}, \qquad Z_{t-1} = \sum_{h=1}^{H} e^{\beta U_{h,t-1}}, \qquad (1.26)$$

where Z_{t-1} is a normalization factor, so that all fractions n_{ht} add up to one. The crucial feature of (1.26) is that the higher the fitness of trading strategy h, the more traders will select strategy h. As before, the parameter β is the intensity of choice, measuring how sensitive the mass of traders is to selecting the optimal prediction strategy. The financial market with heterogeneous traders is represented by the market equilibrium equation (1.24) coupled with an evolutionary selection of strategies (1.25–1.26). Prices and beliefs thus coevolve over time.

What do price fluctuations in this stylized asset pricing model with heterogeneous beliefs look like? Brock and Hommes (1998) present an analysis of the evolutionary dynamics in the case of simple, *linear* forecasting rules

$$f_{ht} = g_h x_{t-1} + b_h, \qquad (1.27)$$

where the parameter g_h represents a *trend* and the parameter b_h represents an upward or downward *bias* in prices. These very simple linear predictors were chosen as the simplest class of rules and to keep the analysis of the dynamical behavior tractable. It turns out that a rational route to randomness, that is, a bifurcation route to strange attractors arises as the intensity of choice to switch prediction or trading strategies becomes high, even when there are no information-gathering costs and all fundamental and technical trading strategies are freely available to all agents. Figure 1.7 shows chaotic price fluctuations on a strange attractor in a typical example, with four different types, fundamentalists versus three different classes of chartists. The chaotic price fluctuations are characterized by an irregular switching between phases of close-to-the-EMH-fundamental-price fluctuations, phases of "optimism" with prices following an upward trend, and phases of "pessimism," with (small) sudden market crashes. In fact, one could say that prices exhibit evolutionary switching between the fundamental value and temporary speculative bubbles.

Under homogeneous, rational expectations and a constant mean dividend process, the asset price dynamics is extremely simple: one constant price equal to the fundamental at all dates. Under the hypothesis of *heterogeneous expectations* among traders, the situation changes dramatically, and an extremely rich dynamics of asset prices and returns emerges, with bifurcation routes to strange attractors. In contrast to Friedman's hypothesis, in the evolutionary competition driven by (short run) realized profits, fundamentalists *cannot* drive out chartists trading strategies. The market is characterized by an irregular switching between periods where fundamental analysis dominates and other periods where technical trading is more profitable. Short run profit opportunities lead boundedly rational agents to adopt trend-following strategies, causing persistent price deviations from fundamentals. In empirical work, e.g., Brock et al. (1992), it has

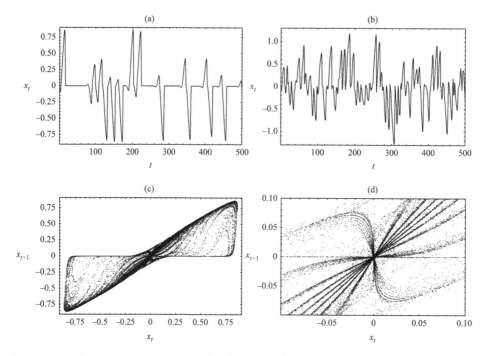

Figure 1.7. Chaotic (top left) and noisy chaotic (top right) price time series of asset pricing model with heterogeneous beliefs with four trader types. Strange attractor (bottom left) and enlargement of strange attractor (bottom right). Belief parameters are $g_1 = 0$, $b_1 = 0$; $g_2 = 0.9$, $b_2 = 0.2$; $g_3 = 0.9$, $b_3 = -0.2$ and $g_4 = 1 + r = 1.01$, $b_4 = 0$; other parameters are $r = 0.01$ and $\beta = 90.5$.

been shown that simple technical trading rules applied to real data such as the Dow Jones Index can indeed yield positive returns.

1.6.1 Estimation of a model with fundamentalists versus chartists

From a *qualitative* viewpoint, the chaotic price fluctuations in the asset pricing model with heterogeneous beliefs bear a close resemblance to observed fluctuations in real markets. But do the endogenous irregular fluctuations explain a statistically significant part of stock price movements? Here, we briefly discuss an estimation of a heterogeneous agent model, with fundamentalists versus trend followers, using yearly S&P 500 stock market data; see Chapter 7 for a more detailed discussion.

Figure 1.8 shows time series of yearly log prices of the S&P 500 stock market index, 1880–2003, around a benchmark fundamental (top left panel) and the corresponding price-to-earnings (PE-)ratio (top right panel). The fundamental price is a nonstationary stochastic process, following an exogenous stochastic earnings process with constant mean growth rate. The S&P 500 shows large swings around this RE benchmark fundamental. These large swings become even more pronounced from the PE-ratio plots. If the asset price would perfectly track its fundamental value, the PE-ratio would be constant at 17.5, as indicated by the horizontal line (right panel). For the S&P 500,

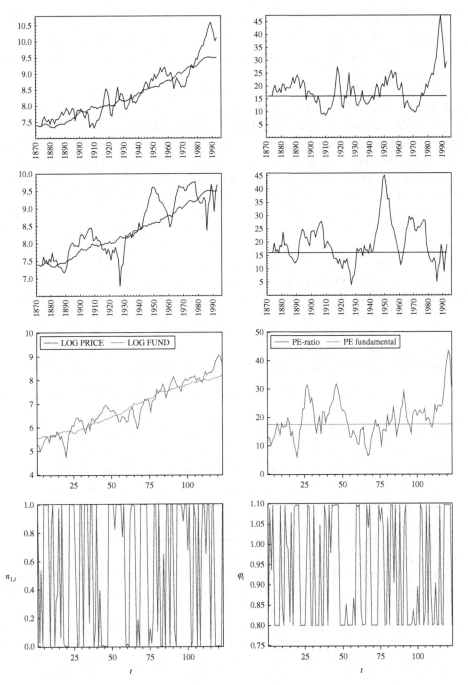

Figure 1.8. Simulated log price series (left panel) and PE-ratios (right panel) for estimated 2-type model with fundamentalists versus trend followers. Parameters: $g_1 = 0.80$, $g_2 = 1.097$ and $\beta = 7.54$. Top-panel: logarithm S&P 500 and fundamental (left) and PE ratio (right). Second panel: fitted model with reshuffled residuals. Third panel: simulated model with normally distributed shocks with mean 0 and $\sigma = 2.975$. Bottom panel: estimated fraction of fundamentalists (left) and average extrapolation coefficient (right).

however, the PE-ratio is characterized by long swings and persistent deviations from the benchmark fundamental ratio. The PE-ratio fluctuates between 8 and 28 for about 100 years, but in the late 1990s, the PE-ratio "explodes" to unanticipated high values of more than 45.

Boswijk et al. (2007) estimated a 2-type model with evolutionary strategy switching for the S&P 500 PE-ratio. The two forecasting functions were $f_{1t} = g_1 x_{t-1}$ and $f_{2t} = g_2 x_{t-1}$, with estimated parameter values $g_1 = 0.80$ and $g_2 = 1.097$, implying that type 1 behaves as a fundamentalist expecting mean-reversion of the PE-ratio toward the fundamental benchmark, while type 2 are trend followers expecting the trend to continue and the price to deviate further from fundamental value. Figure 1.8 shows plots of the fitted model time series and simulations of the estimated model, with shuffled estimated residuals (second panel) as well as normally distributed shocks with mean zero and the same variance (third panel). The simulation with reshuffled residuals shows temporary bubbles similar to the original data series, except that the timing of the large bubble is different (due to the reshuffling). A typical model simulation with normally distributed shocks of the same variance will show occasionally large deviations, up to 45 or even higher, of the PE-ratio from its fundamental benchmark. The time series of the fraction of fundamentalists (bottom left panel) is characterized by irregular switching between periods where almost all agents are fundamentalists or trend followers respectively. Finally, a simulated time series of the average market sentiment, that is, the extrapolation coefficient averaged over the population of traders,

$$\varphi_t = n_{1t} g_1 + n_{2t} g_2, \tag{1.28}$$

is shown (right bottom panel). The average extrapolation coefficient switches irregularly, and occasionally exceeds 1, causing phases of strong trend extrapolation.

These simulations show that endogenous speculative dynamic of a simple asset pricing model with two different belief types, fundamentalists versus chartists, around a benchmark fundamental may explain a significant part of observed stock price fluctuations in real markets. According to our model temporary price bubbles are *triggered by news* about fundamentals, but may become strongly amplified by trend-following strategies. For example, positive news about the economy during a number of consecutive periods may trigger a rise in stock prices, which then may become strongly reinforced by trend-following trading behavior. This may explain the strong rise in stock prices worldwide in the late 1990s, when a new internet technology provided "good news" for the growth of the economy, triggering a rise in stock prices. Our estimated model suggests that, driven by short run profit opportunities, trend-following strategies strongly amplified the rise in stock prices in the late 1990s, thus contributing significantly to the subsequent excessive rise in stocks and the "dot-com" bubble.

1.7   Learning-to-forecast experiments

In the nonlinear economic models discussed so far, expectations play an important role. But how do individuals in complex markets actually form expectations, and what is the aggregate outcome at the macro level of the interactions of individual forecasts at the micro level? Laboratory experiments with human subjects, where economic fundamentals are under control of the experimenter, are well suited to study how individuals form expectations and how their interaction shapes aggregate market behavior.

The results from laboratory experiments are somewhat mixed, however. Early experiments, with various market designs such as double auction trading, show convergence to equilibrium (Smith, 1962, Plott and Sunder, 1982), while more recent asset pricing experiments exhibit persistent deviations from equilibrium with temporary bubbles and sudden crashes (Smith et al., 1988). A clear explanation of these different market phenomena is still lacking (e.g., Duffy, 2008a,b) and this is an important challenge for experimental macroeconomics. It is particularly challenging to provide a universal theory of learning which is able to explain both the possibilities of convergence and persistent deviations from equilibrium. It is intuitively plausible that such a theory needs to be based on heterogeneous expectations and learning.

Here we briefly discuss some recent results from Anufriev and Hommes (2012a,b) to fit a heuristics switching model to laboratory experiments on expectation formation; see Chapter 8 for more details. In the *learning-to-forecast experiments* of Hommes et al. (2005), three different outcomes have been observed in the same experimental setting. Individuals had to make a two-period-ahead forecast of the price of a risky asset, say a stock. These individual forecasts determine aggregate demand and supply, leading to a market clearing price. The equilibrium price was in fact determined in exactly the same way as the asset pricing model with heterogeneous beliefs, as discussed above. Based upon the realized market price and without knowledge of the forecasts of others, individuals were then asked to make their next forecasts, and so on. The experiment lasted 50 periods. The environment in this experiment is stationary and if all agents would behave rationally or learn to behave rationally, the market price would be equal to (or quickly converge to) a constant fundamental price $p^f = 60$. In the experiment coordination of individual forecasts occurred, but three different aggregate market outcomes have been observed (see Figure 1.9, left panels):

(a) slow, monotonic convergence to the constant fundamental price level;
(b) slowly converging oscillatory movements around the fundamental price; and
(c) persistent oscillatory fluctuations around the fundamental.

A simple model based on *evolutionary selection* of *forecasting heuristics* explains how coordination of individual forecasts arises leading to these different aggregate market outcomes. The nonlinear switching model exhibits *path dependence*, since the only differences between the model simulations in Figure 1.9 are the initial states (i.e., initial prices and initial distribution over the heuristics).

The model works as follows (see Chapter 8 for more details). Agents select rules from a population of simple forecasting rules or heuristics. To keep the model as simple as possible, but rich enough to explain the different observed price patterns in the experiments, only four heuristics have been chosen. These heuristics are intuitively

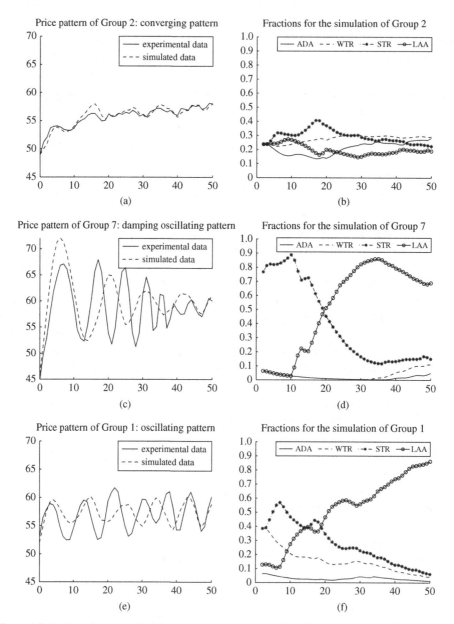

Figure 1.9. Left panels: prices for laboratory experiments (bold) and heuristics switching model (dotted). Right panels: fractions of four forecasting heuristics: adaptive expectations (ADA), weak trend followers (WTR), strong trend followers (STR) and learning anchor and adjustment rule (LAA). Coordination of individual forecasts explains three different aggregate market outcomes: monotonic convergence to equilibrium (top panel), oscillatory convergence (middle panel) and permanent oscillations (bottom panel).

plausible and were among the rules estimated for the individual forecasts in the experiment (these estimations were based on the last 40 observations, to allow for a short learning phase). The following four heuristics have been used in the simulations:

$$p^e_{1,t+1} = 0.65 p_{t-1} + 0.35 p^e_{1,t}, \tag{1.29}$$

$$p^e_{2,t+1} = p_{t-1} + 0.4(p_{t-1} - p_{t-2}), \tag{1.30}$$

$$p^e_{3,t+1} = p_{t-1} + 1.3(p_{t-1} - p_{t-2}), \tag{1.31}$$

$$p^e_{4,t+1} = \frac{1}{2}(p_{t-1} + \bar{p}) + (p_{t-1} - p_{t-2}), \tag{1.32}$$

where $\bar{p}$ in (1.32) is the sample average of realized prices, i.e., $\bar{p} = \sum_{j=0}^{t-1} p_j$.

Adaptive expectations (ADA) in (1.29) means that the price forecast for period $t+1$ is a weighted average of the last observed price p_{t-1} (weight 0.65) and the last own forecast $p^e_{1,t}$ (weight 0.35). Note that the last observed price has two lags (participants had to make a two-period-ahead forecast), while the last own forecast has only one lag. The *weak trend rule* (WTR) takes the last observed price level p_{t-1} as an *anchor* or *reference point* and extrapolates the last observed price change $p_{t-1} - p_{t-2}$ by a (small) factor 0.4. The *strong trend rule* (STR) in (1.31) is the same as the WTR, except that is has a larger extrapolation factor 1.3. Finally, the *learning anchor and adjustment heuristic* (LAA) uses a (time-varying) *anchor* or *reference point*, defined as an (equally weighted) average between the last observed price and the sample average of all past prices, and extrapolates the last price change from there. The LAA rule has been obtained from a related, simpler AR(2) rule $p^e_{t+1} = \frac{1}{2}(p_{t-1} + 60) + (p_{t-1} - p_{t-2})$, after replacing the (unknown) fundamental price 60 by the observable sample average $\bar{p}$. Such an AR(2) rule (or similar ones) has been estimated for a number of individual forecasts in the experiments. The first three rules are first-order heuristics in the sense that they only use the last observed price level, the last forecast and/or the last observed price change. The fourth rule combines adaptive learning of the price level and trend extrapolation, and therefore we refer to it as a learning anchor and adjustment heuristic (LAA).

The simulation model is based upon evolutionary switching or *reinforcement learning* between the four forecasting heuristics, driven by their past relative performance. Heuristics that have been more successful in the past will attract more followers. The performance measure is (minus) squared forecasting errors, similar to the financial rewards in the experiment. The performance of heuristic h is given by

$$U_{ht} = -(p_t - p^e_{h,t})^2 + \eta U_{h,t-1}. \tag{1.33}$$

The parameter η measures the relative weight agents give to past errors and thus represents their *memory strength*. When $\eta = 0$, only the performance of the last period plays a role in the updating of the shares assigned to the different rules. For $0 < \eta \leq 1$, all past prediction errors affect the heuristic's performance.

Given the performance measure, the weight assigned to rules is updated according to a *discrete choice model with asynchronous updating*

$$n_{h,t+1} = \delta n_{ht} + (1-\delta)\frac{e^{\beta U_{ht}}}{\sum_{h=1}^{4} e^{\beta U_{ht}}}.$$
(1.34)

There are two important parameters in (1.34). The parameter $0 \leq \delta \leq 1$ gives some persistence or inertia in the weight assigned to rule h, reflecting the fact that not all the participants are willing to update their rule in every period. Hence, δ may be interpreted as the fraction of individuals who stick to their previous strategy. In the extreme case $\delta = 1$ the initial weights assigned to the rules never change, no matter what their past performance is. If $0 \leq \delta < 1$, in each period a fraction $1 - \delta$ of participants update their rule according to the well known discrete choice model. The parameter β represents the intensity of choice, measuring how sensitive individuals are to differences in strategy performance. The higher the intensity of choice β, the faster individuals will switch to more successful rules. In the extreme case $\beta = 0$, the fractions in (1.34) move to an equal distribution independent of their past performance. At the other extreme $\beta = \infty$, all agents who update their heuristic (i.e., a fraction $1 - \delta$) switch to the most successful predictor.

The left panel of Figure 1.9 shows that the heuristics switching model matches all three different patterns, slow monotonic convergence to the fundamental price, dampened oscillatory price movements and persistent price oscillations, in the laboratory experiments. In all simulations in Figure 1.9, the parameters have been fixed at the same values, and the simulations only differ in the initial states, that is, the initial prices and the initial distribution of agents over the population of heuristics. The nonlinear heuristics switching model therefore exhibits *path dependence*, since the simulations only differ in initial states. In particular, the initial distribution over the population of heuristics is important in determining which pattern is more likely to emerge. The right panels of Figure 1.9 plot the corresponding transition paths of the fractions of each of the four forecasting heuristics. In the case of monotonic convergence (top panel), agents start uniformly distributed over the heuristics and the four fractions (and the individual forecasts) remain relatively close together, causing slow (almost) monotonic convergence of the price to the fundamental equilibrium 60. In the second simulation (middle panel), a large initial fraction of (strong) trend followers leads to a strong rise of market prices in the first 7 periods, followed by large price oscillations. After period 10 the fraction of strong trend followers decreases, while the fraction of the fourth rule, the learning anchor and adjustment heuristic, rises to more than 80% after 30 periods. At turning points, the flexible LAA heuristic predicts better than the static STR rule, which overestimates the price trend. After 35 periods the fraction of the LAA heuristic starts slowly decreasing, and consequently the price oscillations slowly stabilize. In the third simulation (bottom panel) weak and strong trend followers each represent 40% of the initial distribution of heuristics, causing a rise in prices which, due to the presence of weak trend followers, is less sharp than in the previous case. However, already after 5 periods the fraction of the LAA rule starts to increase, because once again at turning points it predicts better than the static STR and LTR rules, which either overestimate or underestimate the price trend at turning points. The fraction of the LAA heuristic gradually increases and dominates the market within 20 periods, rising to more than 80% after 40 periods, explaining coordination of individual forecasts as well as persistent price oscillations around the long run equilibrium level.

These simulations illustrate how the interaction and evolutionary selection of individual forecasting heuristics may lead to coordination of individual behavior upon different price patterns and enforce path-dependent aggregate market outcomes. Individuals are behaviorally rational and use simple heuristics consistent with recent observations. Evolutionary learning leads to switching between simple forecasting heuristics based upon recent performance and different types of aggregate behavior may emerge.

1.8 Simple complex systems

The economy is a complex system, with many interacting consumers, firms, investors, banks, etc. But how complex should a model be to describe economic complexity? One could think of a detailed *agent-based model* (ABM) using a "bottom up" approach to model agents' interactions at the micro level and study its aggregate macro behavior. ABMs are becoming increasingly popular in finance and in macro; see, e.g., the collection of papers in the *Handbook of Computational Economics, Volume 2: Agent-Based Computational Economics* (Tesfatsion and Judd, Eds., 2006) and the *Handbook of Financial Markets. Dynamics and Evolution* (Hens and Schenk-Hoppé, Eds., 2009). For ABMs in macro; see, e.g., the monographs of Aoki (2002) and Delli-Gatti et al. (2008); DeGrauwe (2010a,b) contains a stimulating discussion of a "bottom up" approach of ABMs in behavioral macroeconomics.

While detailed ABMs present an important challenge and promising approach in economic modeling, this book emphasizes *simple complex system models* as complementary tools to gain insights in nonlinear interaction mechanisms. The key features of these models are that they are *nonlinear* and that there is some form of *heterogeneity* and endogenous switching between heterogeneous decision rules. Since the economy is inherently uncertain, the "law of motion" of the economy is stochastic. A simple complex system with heterogeneous agents typically is of the form

$$X_{t+1} = F(X_t; n_{1t}, ..., n_{Ht}; \lambda; \delta_t; \epsilon_t), \tag{1.35}$$

where F is a *nonlinear* mapping, X_t is a vector of state variables, say prices (or lagged prices), n_{jt} is the fraction or weight of agents of strategy type h, $1 \leq h \leq H$, λ is a vector of parameters and δ_t and ϵ_t are (vectors of) noise terms. There are (at least) two types of uncertainty relevant for economic modeling, *intrinsic noise* and *model approximation errors*. Intrinsic noise refers to intrinsic uncertainty about economic fundamentals (preferences, technology, future earnings, future growth, etc.) in the economy. The noise term δ_t then represents unexpected random shocks, "news" about economic fundamentals. The second type of noise, *model approximation errors*, represents the fact that a model can only be an approximation of the real world and that part of the economy remains not modeled. Approximation errors will also be present in a physics model, although the magnitude may be smaller. In a financial market, one may for example have a (small) fraction of "noise traders" who trade randomly and whose behavior therefore is uncertain. The law of motion of the economy is then a nonlinear stochastic system as in (1.35).

In general, the nonlinear stochastic model can be a detailed ABM, a highly nonlinear complex system with many different agent types and of high dimension. For a detailed ABM it will be difficult to use analytical tools and one will mainly have to resort to numerical simulations. In this book, we will emphasize *simple complex systems*, where the dimension of the system is relatively low, the number of different agent types is relatively small, and the system is simple enough to be studied, at least partially, by analytical tools. Since the dynamical behavior of simple complex systems is rich, *a simple nonlinear system model buffeted with noise as in (1.35) may explain a significant part of observed fluctuations and stylized facts in economic and financial markets.* An important goal in simple complex systems modeling is to match the statistical regularities of empirical data both at the macro level and at the micro level. Hence, one would like to match both individual behavioral decision rules, e.g., calibrating them with laboratory experiments, and, at the same time, match aggregate macro behavior and time series properties.

A special case of the nonlinear stochastic system (1.35) arises when all noise terms are set equal to their unconditional mean. We will refer to this system as the *(deterministic) skeleton* denoted by

$$X_{t+1} = F(X_t; n_{1t}, ..., n_{Ht}; \lambda). \tag{1.36}$$

In order to understand the properties of the general stochastic model (1.35) it is important to understand the properties of the nonlinear deterministic skeleton. In particular, one would like to impose as little structure on the noise process as possible, and relate the individual decision rules as well as the aggregate stylized facts of the general stochastic model (1.35) directly to generic properties of the underlying deterministic skeleton. This naturally leads to the study of the dynamics of simple nonlinear dynamical systems.

1.9   Purpose and summary of the book

This book serves three important purposes. First, it presents simple examples of complex systems applications in economics and finance. The simplicity of these examples should help the reader to grasp the essential features of nonlinear complex systems. Second, the methodological part (Chapters 2 and 3) serves as a primer to nonlinear dynamics, introducing the key tools in the analysis of simple nonlinear systems that should be part of the toolbox of any quantitative economist. Third, our main focus is on bounded rationality and heterogeneous expectations in simple complex adaptive economic systems. In particular, we extensively discuss a theory of behavioral rationality, heterogeneous expectations and learning in complex economic systems and confront this theory, both at the macro and the micro level, with empirical time series and laboratory experimental data.

The book is organized in seven chapters following this introduction. Two methodological chapters, Chapters 2 and 3, give an introduction to the mathematical tools of nonlinear, discrete time dynamical systems. Chapter 2 deals with one-dimensional systems, discusses the (in)stability of steady states, introduces elementary bifurcations (tangent, period-doubling, pitchfork, transcritical), defines the notion of chaos and Lyapunov exponents and discusses the period-doubling bifurcation route to chaos. Chapter 3 deals with two- and higher-dimensional systems, discusses the saddle-node and the Hopf (or Neimark–Sacker) bifurcations, introduces the "breaking of an invariant circle" bifurcation route to chaos and strange attractors and introduces the key notions related to chaotic dynamics, such as horseshoes, homoclinic orbits, homoclinic bifurcations, Lyapunov exponents and strange attractors. We have made an attempt to provide an introduction to nonlinear dynamics for non-specialists and a general audience of economists, emphasizing the most important concepts to be used in economic applications and adding references to more advanced mathematical treatments whenever appropriate.

The second part of the book, Chapters 4, 5 and 6, contains simple examples of complex systems modeling in economics and finance. Chapter 4 discusses the *nonlinear cobweb model* with various benchmark *homogeneous expectations*: naive expectations, rational expectations, adaptive expectations and linear backward-looking expectations. In a nonlinear cobweb economy with monotonic demand and supply curves, all of these simple adaptive and backward-looking expectations may lead to chaotic price fluctuations. These benchmark cases provide simple didactic examples of stylized complex dynamics applications to economics, illustrating how expectations feedback may generate complicated dynamics in a *nonlinear* environment. Chapter 4 also discusses the notion of *consistent expectations equilibrium*, where behaviorally rational agents learn the "optimal" linear AR(1) rule in a complex, nonlinear environment. Chapter 5 discusses the cobweb model with *heterogeneous expectations*, focusing on 2-type examples with a sophisticated but costly expectations rule – rational expectations, fundamentalist forecast, a contrarian rule or adaptive learning – competing against a simple, freely available forecasting heuristic such as naive expectations. A common finding is a *rational route to randomness*, i.e., a bifurcation route to chaos, as agents become more sensitive to differences in evolutionary fitness. Moreover, the complexity of the price dynamics increases as the learning detects and exploits more structure in price fluctuations.

Chapter 6 discusses a standard financial market *asset pricing model* with *heterogeneous beliefs*. A number of simple examples, with two, three and four trader types – fundamentalists versus chartists – is discussed. A rational route to randomness arises, even when there are no information-gathering costs for more sophisticated strategies. Hence, simple technical trading rules are not driven out of the market, but survive evolutionary competition driven by (short run) realized profits. Another simple 2-type example, fundamentalists versus conditional trend followers, exhibits coexistence of a stable fundamental steady state and a stable limit cycle. Hence, there is path dependence:

the market may either converge to the stable fundamental price or it may perpetu-
ally oscillate around the fundamental price with the fractions of fundamentalists and
chartists changing over time. In the presence of noise, the system exhibits clustered
volatility, with the market switching irregularly between close to the fundamental price
fluctuations and large swings and excess volatility in asset prices. Finally, the case with
many different expectations types is discussed. The model with many different trader
types is well approximated by the so-called *large type limit* (LTL), a tool that can be
used to study markets with many different trader types.

The final part of the book, Chapters 7 and 8, discusses the *empirical validity* of
heterogeneous expectations models. Chapter 7 discusses the estimation of a simple
2-type asset pricing model with fundamentalists versus trend followers on yearly data
of the S&P 500 stock market index. Behavioral heterogeneity is statistically significant
with large swings in the fractions of both types of traders. In particular, the heuristics
switching model explains the dot-com bubble as being triggered by good news about
economic fundamentals – a new internet technology – strongly amplified by technical
trading.

Finally, Chapter 8 discusses the empirical validity of heterogeneous expectations
models by laboratory experiments with human subjects. *Learning-to-forecast experiments*, where subjects' only task is to forecast prices in an expectations feedback
environment, in the cobweb and the asset pricing frameworks are discussed. Coordination on different types of aggregate market behavior – stable convergence or persistent
price oscillations – arises. A simple heuristics switching model – exhibiting path dependence – can explain coordination on these different aggregate outcomes. Another
striking finding is that negative expectations feedback markets, such as commodity
prices in a cobweb framework where high price expectations yield high production
and thus low realized market prices, are rather stable, while positive feedback markets,
such as speculative asset markets, tend to oscillate around the fundamental price. The
simple heuristics switching model explains both types of aggregate behavior as well
as individual behavior. In the negative feedback market, adaptive expectations dominates evolutionary competition, because the trend-following heuristics perform poorly.
In contrast, in positive feedback markets trend-following rules perform relatively well
and amplify price oscillations, possibly leading to bubbles and crashes.

2 Bifurcations and chaos in 1-D systems

In this chapter we consider the simplest discrete-time nonlinear dynamic models, namely nonlinear difference equations in a single state variable. Consider the *one-dimensional (1-D) nonlinear dynamical system*

$$x_{t+1} = f_\lambda(x_t), \qquad (2.1)$$

where f_λ is a nonlinear map on the real line which depends upon a *parameter* λ. Unless otherwise stated, the map f_λ is continuous and differentiable. Given an *initial state* x_0, the difference equation (2.1) uniquely determines all future states x_t, $t = 1, 2, \ldots$. The *orbit* or *time path* or *solution* with initial state x_0 is the set

$$\{x_0, x_1, x_2, \ldots\} = \{x_0, f_\lambda(x_0), f_\lambda^2(x_0), \ldots\},$$

where f_λ^i is the i-th iterate of the map f_λ, i.e., the map f_λ composed with itself i times.

The central problem in the theory of dynamical systems may be formulated as follows: *what can be said about the orbits of the dynamical system (2.1), for different parameter values λ and for different initial states x_0?* Once we have a complete characterization of all possible orbits for all parameter values, the dynamics of the model is completely understood.

This chapter consists of six sections. In Section 2.1 we concentrate on 1-D monotonic, i.e., either increasing or decreasing, maps f and show that the dynamics of monotonic maps is always simple.[1] In Section 2.2 we consider what is perhaps the simplest example of a non-monotonic map, a quadratic map, and study the occurrence of periodic orbits and chaos. Section 2.3 focuses on bifurcations, that is, qualitative changes in the dynamics as a model parameter changes. In Section 2.4 we present a definition of chaos, while Section 2.5 introduces the Lyapunov exponent, measuring the sensitive dependence on initial conditions in chaotic systems. Finally, Section 2.6 discusses some stochastic aspects of chaotic time series, in particular sample autocorrelations (or the lack thereof) of chaotic series.

---

[1] We will write f instead of f_λ, whenever the dependence upon the parameter is not relevant at that point.

2.1   Monotonic maps

In analyzing the dynamics of a model, usually first the steady states and their stability
are investigated. A *steady state* (or an *equilibrium* or a *fixed point*) of the map f is a
point x^{eq} for which $f(x^{eq}) = x^{eq}$. At a steady state the dynamical system is at rest and
the orbit of a steady state x^{eq} consists of the single point x^{eq}. Graphically, a steady
state x^{eq} is the (x-)coordinate of an intersection point of the graph of the map f with
the diagonal $y = x$.

A steady state x^{eq} is called *(asymptotically) locally stable* if there exists an interval
$I = (x^{eq} - \varepsilon, x^{eq} + \varepsilon)$, $\varepsilon > 0$, such that for all initial states $x_0 \in I$, the orbit of x_0
converges to the steady state x^{eq}, i.e., $\lim_{i \to \infty} f^i(x_0) = x^{eq}$. The steady state x^{eq} is
globally stable if for *all* initial states x_0 (in the domain of f) the time path converges
to x^{eq}. A steady state x^{eq} is called *unstable* if there exists a (small) interval $I = (x^{eq} - \varepsilon, x^{eq} + \varepsilon)$, $\varepsilon > 0$, such that for all initial states $x_0 \in I$, $x_0 \neq x^{eq}$, the orbit of x_0 leaves
I, i.e., there exists $i > 0$ such that $f^i(x_0) \notin I$. The (in)stability of a steady state x^{eq} in
1-D discrete systems is determined by the derivative at the steady state:

1. if $|f'(x^{eq})| < 1$ then x^{eq} is locally stable,
2. if $|f'(x^{eq})| > 1$ then x^{eq} is locally unstable.

This follows essentially from a Taylor series approximation around the steady state x^{eq}:

$$x_{t+1} = f(x_t) \approx x^{eq} + f'(x^{eq})(x_t - x^{eq}) + h.o.t.,$$

where "h.o.t." refers to higher-order terms. To a first-order approximation the dynamics
close to the steady state x^{eq} is determined by the linear term and the stability then
depends on $f'(x^{eq})$ and is not affected by the higher-order terms (except at the hairline
case where $|f'(x^{eq})| = 1$). Figure 2.1 illustrates the four typical cases:

(a) monotonic convergence if $0 < f'(x^{eq}) < 1$;
(b) unstable and monotonic divergence if $f'(x^{eq}) > 1$;
(c) stable and oscillatory convergence if $-1 < f'(x^{eq}) < 0$; and
(d) unstable and oscillatory divergence if $f'(x^{eq}) < -1$.

What happens when an orbit does not converge to a steady state? One possibility is
that fluctuations are (asymptotically) periodic. A point x is called a *periodic point with
period k* if $f^k(x) = x$ and $f^i(x) \neq x$, $0 < i < k$. Hence, a periodic point with period k
is a point that exactly returns onto itself after precisely k periods. Notice that a periodic
point with period k is a fixed point of the k-th iterate f^k of the map f. The corresponding
orbit $\{x, f(x), f^2(x), \dots f^{k-1}(x)\}$ is called a *periodic orbit* or a *k-cycle* and consists of
exactly k points.

The dynamics of *monotonic* (i.e., increasing or decreasing) 1-D maps can be easily
characterized. If the 1-D map f is either increasing or decreasing, then there are only
three possibilities for the (long run) dynamical behavior of (2.1):

1. the time path x_t converges to a steady state, or
2. the time path x_t converges to a period 2-cycle, or

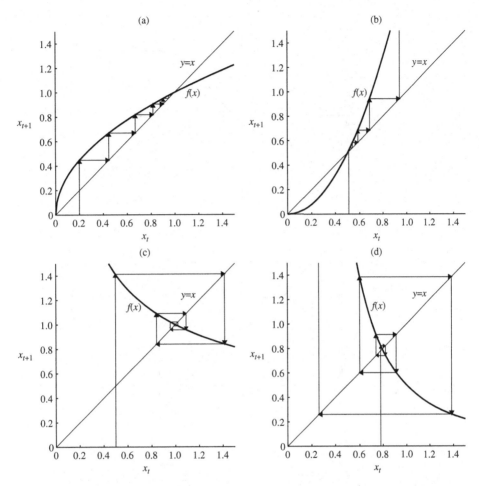

Figure 2.1. Stability of a steady state x^{eq} is determined by its derivative $f'(x^{eq})$, as follows: (a) $0 < f'(x^{eq}) < 1$: stable and monotonic convergence; (b) $f'(x^{eq}) > 1$: unstable and monotonic divergence; (c) $-1 < f'(x^{eq}) < 0$: stable and dampened oscillation; and (d) $f'(x^{eq}) < -1$: unstable and diverging oscillation.

3. the time path is unbounded and x_t increases toward to $+\infty$, decreases toward $-\infty$ or exhibits unbounded, diverging oscillations toward $+\infty$ and $-\infty$.

This result follows from careful graphical analysis. Figure 2.2 illustrates some typical cases. The map f in Figure 2.2a is increasing and has four steady states x_1^*, x_2^*, x_3^* and x_4^*; two steady states x_2^* and x_4^* are (locally) stable, whereas the other two x_1^* and x_3^* are unstable. Depending upon the initial state x_0 there are three possibilities:

1. for $x_0 > x_3^*$ the orbit converges to x_4^*;
2. for $x_1^* < x_0 < x_3^*$ the orbit converges to x_2^*;
3. for $x_0 < x_1^*$ the orbit of x_0 converges to $-\infty$.

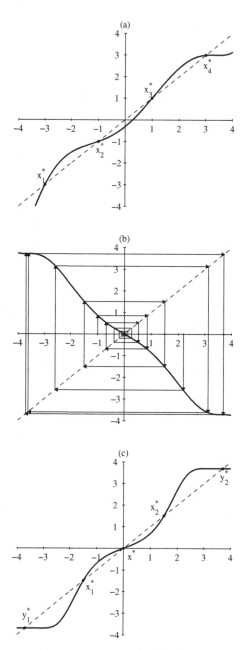

Figure 2.2. Dynamics of $x_{t+1} = f(x_t)$ when f is increasing (a) or decreasing (b–c). (a) Two locally stable steady states x_2^* and x_4^* and two unstable steady states x_1^* and x_3^*; (b–c) Decreasing map f with stable steady state $x^* = 0$ and stable period 2-cycle (y_1^*, y_2^*), separated by unstable period 2-cycle (x_1^*, x_2^*). When f is decreasing (b), its second iterate f^2 is increasing (c). Fixed points of f^2 form 2-cycles (x_1^*, x_2^*) and (y_1^*, y_2^*) of f.

From this example it should be clear, that when f is increasing convergence to a steady state or convergence to $+\infty$ or to $-\infty$ are the only possibilities.

Figures 2.2b–c illustrate an example where f is decreasing. Figure 2.2b shows that f has a stable steady state $x^* = 0$ and a (stable) 2-cycle $\{y_1^*, y_2^*\}$. This can easily be verified by looking at the graph of the second iterate f^2, as illustrated in Figure 2.2c. When f is decreasing, then f^2 will be increasing.[2] In Figure 2.2c, the map f^2 has five fixed points: $x^* = 0, x_1^*, x_2^*, y_1^*$ and y_2^*. The first fixed point, $x^* = 0$, of f^2 is also a fixed point of f. The remaining four fixed points of f^2 form two pairs of period 2-cycles of the map f: a stable 2-cycle $\{y_1^*, y_2^*\}$ and an unstable 2-cycle $\{x_1^*, x_3^*\}$. Depending upon the initial state x_0 we have:

1. for $x_1^* < x_0 < x_2^*$, the orbit converges to the stable fixed point $x^* = 0$;
2. for $x_0 < x_1^*$ or $x_0 > x_2^*$, the orbit converges to the stable 2-cycle $\{y_1^*, y_2^*\}$.

From this example it should be clear that when f is decreasing, convergence to a steady state or convergence to a (possibly unbounded) 2-cycle are the only two possible types of dynamical behavior. In conclusion, as long as the 1-D map f is *monotonic*, the dynamics of the nonlinear difference equation (2.1) is simple and regular.

2.2   The quadratic difference equation

When the 1-D map f_λ in (2.1) is non-monotonic, the dynamical behavior can be very complicated. In order to illustrate the richness of the dynamics of non-monotonic 1-D maps, we start with what is perhaps the simplest example of a nonlinear difference equation, the quadratic difference equation

$$x_{t+1} = f_\lambda(x_t) = \lambda x_t (1 - x_t). \qquad (2.2)$$

We will refer to f_λ as the quadratic map or the quadratic family (depending on the parameter λ). It should be emphasized that this example is by no means special, but captures many of the essential features of the complicated dynamical behavior of *unimodal* maps, i.e., 1-D maps whose graphs have one maximum or minimum. We call the point $x = c$ where a 1-D map f_λ has a maximum or minimum a *critical point* of f_λ. For the quadratic map f_λ in (2.2) the critical point $c = 1/2$, where the quadratic map assumes its maximum.

2.2.1   Steady states and stability

The quadratic difference equation (2.2) has two steady states, $x = 0$ and $x_\lambda^* = 1 - \frac{1}{\lambda}$. The (local) stability of the steady states is determined by the derivative of the quadratic map f_λ

$$f_\lambda'(x) = \lambda - 2\lambda x.$$

---

[2] If f is differentiable and decreasing, this follows immediately from the chain rule, since $(f^2)'(x) = f'(f(x)) \cdot f'(x) \geq 0$, so f^2 is increasing.

The steady states are stable if the derivatives at the steady states, i.e., $f_\lambda'(0)$ and $f_\lambda'(x_\lambda^*)$, are between -1 and $+1$. Straightforward computations combined with a graphical analysis show the following for initial state $x_0 \in [0, 1]$:

1. For $0 \le \lambda \le 1$, $x = 0$ is the unique steady state and it is *globally stable*.
2. For $\lambda > 1$ there are two steady states: $x = 0$ and $x_\lambda^* = 1 - \frac{1}{\lambda}$. The steady state $x = 0$ is unstable. For $1 < \lambda \le 3$ the steady state x_λ^* is stable and attracts all time paths with $x_0 \in (0, 1)$.

Figure 2.3a shows that, for $\lambda = 2.9$, the time series converges to a stable steady state. For $\lambda > 3$, both steady states will be unstable. What can be said about the dynamics when both steady states are unstable?

2.2.2   Periodic and aperiodic time series

Figure 2.3 shows the first 100 points of the time series of the quadratic difference equation (2.2), with initial state $x_0 = 0.1$ for different values of the parameter λ. We observe the following:

1. $\lambda = 2.9$: convergence to a stable steady state.
2. $\lambda = 3.3$: the steady state is unstable, and the time path converges to a stable period 2-orbit.
3. $\lambda = 3.5$: the period 2-orbit is unstable, and the time path converges to a stable period 4-orbit.
4. $\lambda = 3.83$: the initial part of the time path (the first 60 periods) is erratic. Eventually the time path settles down to a stable period 3-cycle. The phenomenon of an erratic initial phase is called *transient chaos*.
5. $\lambda = 4$: two time series are shown in Figures 2.3e–f. Both time series look very erratic and it seems that they do not converge to a stable cycle (at least not with period < 100). Both time series are *chaotic*.

Figures 2.3 e–f show two time series corresponding to the same parameter $\lambda = 4$, with different initial states. The first has initial state $x_0 = 0.1$ and the second has a slightly different initial state $x_0 = 0.1001$. Although the distance between the two initial states is very small (only 0.0001) the two time series are completely different already after a number of periods. For example, after 13 time periods, for the first time series $x_{13} \approx 0.0002$, while for the second $x_{13} \approx 0.9518$. After 13 time periods, the distance between the two time series has therefore increased by a factor of more than 9000! The phenomenon that the time paths of nearby initial states do not stay close to each other, but in fact diverge exponentially fast, is called *sensitive dependence on initial conditions* and it is one of the most important characteristics of a chaotic dynamical system. Because of the sensitive dependence, long term prediction in a chaotic model seems impossible, because in practice initial conditions are only known with finite precision. In fact, this "*butterfly effect*" is the main reason why weather prediction is so

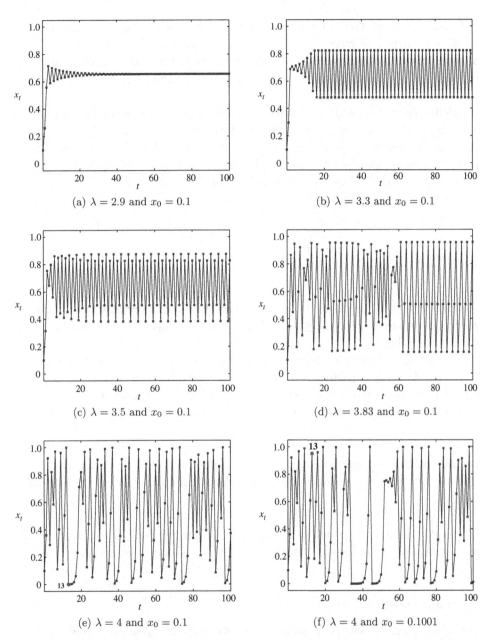

(a) $\lambda = 2.9$ and $x_0 = 0.1$

(b) $\lambda = 3.3$ and $x_0 = 0.1$

(c) $\lambda = 3.5$ and $x_0 = 0.1$

(d) $\lambda = 3.83$ and $x_0 = 0.1$

(e) $\lambda = 4$ and $x_0 = 0.1$

(f) $\lambda = 4$ and $x_0 = 0.1001$

Figure 2.3. Time series for the quadratic map for different values of the parameter λ. (a) $\lambda = 2.9$: convergence to stable steady state; (b) $\lambda = 3.3$: convergence to stable 2-cycle; (c) $\lambda = 3.5$: convergence to stable 4-cycle; (d) $\lambda = 3.83$: transient chaos and convergence to stable 3-cycle; (e–f) $\lambda = 4$: chaotic time series with sensitive dependence on initial conditions; initial states (e) $x_0 = 0.1$ and (f) $x_0 = 0.1001$.

difficult. Nowadays, due to the sensitivity of the atmosphere, meteorologist consider weather prediction of more than 12 days ahead fundamentally impossible. A small disturbance of the current state of the atmosphere, caused, for example, by the flapping of the wings of a butterfly, can lead to a completely different weather forecast over a horizon of more than 12 days.

A definition of chaos and sensitive dependence will be given in Section 2.4. Figure 2.3 shows a number of examples where the time series converges to a stable cycle. Let us define a stable periodic orbit. Let $\{x_1, x_2, ..., x_k\}$ be a periodic orbit of period k. Each point x_i is then a fixed point of the k-th iterate f^k. If x_i is a stable fixed point of f^k, then $\{x_1, x_2, ..., x_k\}$ is called a *stable periodic orbit*. From the chain rule we have

$$(f^k)'(x_i) = (f^k)'(x_1) = f'(f^{k-1}(x_1)) \cdot f'(f^{k-2}(x_1)) ... f'(f(x_1)) \cdot f'(x_1)$$

$$= \prod_{i=0}^{k-1} f'(f^i(x_1)).$$

For each $1 \leq i \leq k$, the slope $(f^k)'(x_i)$ of a periodic point of period k thus equals the product of the slopes $f'(x_i)$, $1 \leq i \leq k$, that is, it is the product of the derivatives along the periodic orbit.

The time series in Figures 2.3b–d show convergence to a stable periodic orbit, with periods 2, 4 and 3 respectively. Apparently, stable cycles of different length occur, for different parameter values λ. On the other hand, the time series in Figures 2.3e–f suggest that for $\lambda = 4$, there are initial states whose orbit does *not* settle down to a stable periodic orbit. We therefore define:

Definition 2.2.1. *A point x is called an* **aperiodic point** *if (1) the orbit of x is bounded, (2) the orbit of x is not periodic and (3) the orbit of x does not converge to a periodic orbit.*

A natural question is: for which parameters does the quadratic difference equation (2.2) have stable cycles and for which parameter values do aperiodic points occur?

2.3   Bifurcations

Figure 2.3 suggests that, as the parameter λ increases, the dynamical behavior of the quadratic difference equation (2.2) changes and becomes more and more complicated. A qualitative change in the dynamics of a nonlinear system, as a model parameter varies, is called a *bifurcation*. For example, a bifurcation occurs when the stability of a steady state changes and/or a periodic orbit is created or destroyed, as a parameter varies. There are different types of bifurcations. In this section we discuss four important bifurcations that can arise in one-dimensional discrete systems, period-doubling, tangent, transcritical and pitchfork bifurcation.

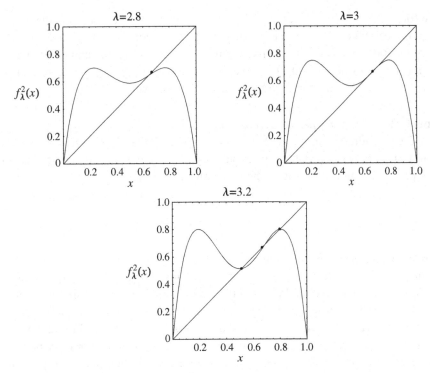

Figure 2.4. Period-doubling bifurcation of the quadratic map (2.2), illustrated by graphs of the second iterate f_λ^2 for three different λ-values around the period-doubling bifurcation at $\lambda = 3$. For $\lambda = 2.8$, f_λ^2 has two intersection points with the diagonal $y = x$, the two steady states 0 and x_λ^*. The same is true for the bifurcation value $\lambda = 3$, and moreover the graph of f_λ^2 is tangent to the diagonal $y = x$. For $\lambda = 3.2$, f_λ^2 has four intersection points with the diagonal $y = x$, the two steady states 0 and x_λ^* and two additional points forming a stable 2-cycle.

2.3.1 Period-doubling bifurcation

For the quadratic map f_λ in (2.2), the slope at the steady state $x_\lambda^* = 1 - \frac{1}{\lambda}$ is given by $f_\lambda'(x_\lambda^*) = 2 - \lambda$. Hence, as λ increases, the steady state becomes unstable at $\lambda = 3$ when the derivative at the steady state crosses the critical value -1. In addition to the loss of stability of the steady state at $\lambda = 3$, there is another important change in the dynamical behavior: a new (stable) 2-cycle is created. Figure 2.4 illustrates the creation of the 2-cycle by the graphs of the second iterate f_λ^2 for different values of λ close to the bifurcation value $\lambda = 3$. Note first that, since $(f_\lambda^2)'(x) = f_\lambda'(f_\lambda(x)) \cdot f_\lambda'(x)$, f_λ^2 has three critical points, namely $x = c = 1/2$ where f_λ^2 has a local minimum and two points d_1 and d_2 for which $f(d_1) = f(d_2) = c$, where f_λ^2 has a global maximum. For $\lambda = 2.9$ the graph of f_λ^2 has two intersection points with the diagonal $y = x$, the points 0 and x^*, which are the two fixed points of f_λ. The same is true at the bifurcation value $\lambda = 3$. For $\lambda = 3$ the slope of the graph of f_λ^2 at the steady state x^* is

$$(f_\lambda^2)'(x^*) = f_\lambda'(f_\lambda(x^*)) \cdot f_\lambda'(x^*) = f_\lambda'(x^*) \cdot f_\lambda'(x^*) = (-1)^2 = +1.$$

Since for $\lambda > 3$, $f_\lambda'(x^*) < -1$, we get $(f_\lambda^2)'(x^*) > 1$. Therefore, for $\lambda > 3$ the graph of f^2 has (at least) four (!) intersection points with the diagonal as shown in Figure 2.4c. Two of the four points are the two fixed points 0 and x_λ^* of f_λ; the remaining two must form a period 2-cycle $\{y_1, y_2\}$ of f_λ. We have $f_\lambda(y_1) = y_2$, $f_\lambda(y_2) = y_1$, $f_\lambda^2(y_1) = y_1$ and $f_\lambda^2(y_2) = y_2$. In summary, we have shown the following:

Property 2.3.1 *(primary period-doubling bifurcation)*:
At $\lambda = 3$ the quadratic map f_λ in (2.2) exhibits a *period-doubling bifurcation* in which, as λ increases, the steady state x_λ^* loses stability and a stable period 2-cycle is created. At the period-doubling bifurcation the first-order condition

$$f_\lambda'(x_\lambda^*) = -1 \tag{2.3}$$

is satisfied.

Bifurcation diagram of the quadratic map
The time series in Figure 2.3 illustrate that the dynamical behavior of the quadratic map becomes more and more complicated as the parameter λ increases. A simple numerical method to investigate how the (long term) dynamical behavior of a model changes as a parameter is varied, is the construction of a *bifurcation diagram*. Figure 2.5 shows a bifurcation diagram for the quadratic family, for $2.9 \leq \lambda \leq 4$. For each parameter value from a grid of say 1000 λ-values between 2.9 and 4, 500 points of the orbit of $x_0 = 0.5$ have been plotted, after leaving out a transient of 100 points. In this way an

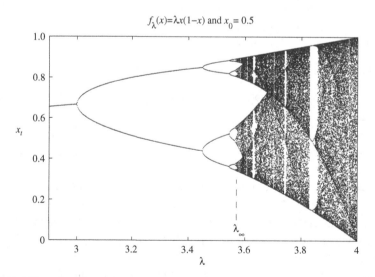

Figure 2.5. Bifurcation diagram of the quadratic map. As the parameter λ increases, a period-doubling bifurcation route to chaos occurs, with limiting value λ_∞. Beyond λ_∞, stable cycles of different periods arise (e.g., cycles of periods 6, 5 and 3 are clearly visible), but often the dynamics is chaotic.

accurate picture of the long term dynamical behavior of the quadratic map, as a function of the parameter λ, is obtained. For example in the bifurcation diagram for $\lambda = 2.9$ all 500 plotted points are close to the stable steady state x_λ^*; for $\lambda = 3.3$ all 500 plotted points are close to the stable 2-cycle; and for $\lambda = 3.5$ all points are close to the stable 4-cycle. The bifurcation diagram shows that for $\lambda \approx 3.45$ a second period-doubling bifurcation has occurred, in which the period 2-cycle becomes unstable and a new stable period 4-cycle is created. In fact the bifurcation diagram suggest the occurrence of an (infinite) cascade of period-doubling bifurcations with the periods of the stable cycles: $1 \rightarrow 2 \rightarrow 4 \rightarrow 8 \rightarrow 16 \rightarrow 32...$, and so on. The bifurcation values λ_n from a stable cycle of period 2^n to a stable cycle of period 2^{n+1} converge to a limiting value λ_∞, with $\lim_{n \rightarrow \infty} \lambda_n = \lambda_\infty \approx 3.5699$.

For $\lambda > \lambda_\infty$ sometimes stable cycles arise, but often the dynamical behavior does not converge to a periodic cycle and is chaotic. For example, a stable 6-cycle occurs for $\lambda \approx 3.63$, a stable 5-cycle for $\lambda \approx 3.75$ and a stable 3-cycle for $\lambda \approx 3.83$. In these cases, however, often transient chaos occurs, since the initial part of the time series (e.g., the first 100 points which are not plotted in the bifurcation diagram) can be very erratic (cf. Figure 2.3d). For many other λ-values, corresponding to the black regions in the bifurcation diagram, the time path does not settle down to a stable cycle with low period, but in fact is chaotic.

2.3.2 Tangent bifurcation

We have seen that, for the quadratic difference equation (2.2), periodic orbits with periods 2^n are created in subsequent period-doubling bifurcations, as the parameter λ increases. However, period-doubling bifurcations *cannot* explain the creation of stable cycles of, e.g., periods 3 or 5, which have been observed in the bifurcation diagram in Figure 2.5. These are created in a so-called *tangent bifurcation*. First we discuss the tangent bifurcation by a simpler example of steady state bifurcations in the one-parameter family $x_{t+1} = x_t^2 + c$.

The steady states of $x_{t+1} = f_c(x_t) = x_t^2 + c$ satisfy $x^2 + c = x$, or

$$x^2 - x + c = 0.$$

The steady state solutions are

$$x_{1,2}^{eq} = \frac{1 \pm \sqrt{1 - 4c}}{2}.$$

For the quadratic difference equation $x_{t+1} = x_t^2 + c$ we have (see Figure 2.6):

1. for $c > 1/4$ there are no steady states;
2. for $c = 1/4$ there is a unique steady state x^{eq}, with $f'(x^{eq}) = 1$;
3. for $c < 1/4$ there are two steady states: one stable and one unstable.

Since the derivative $f_c'(x) = 2x$, at the steady state we get

$$f_c'(x_{1,2}^{eq}) = 1 \pm \sqrt{1 - 4c},$$

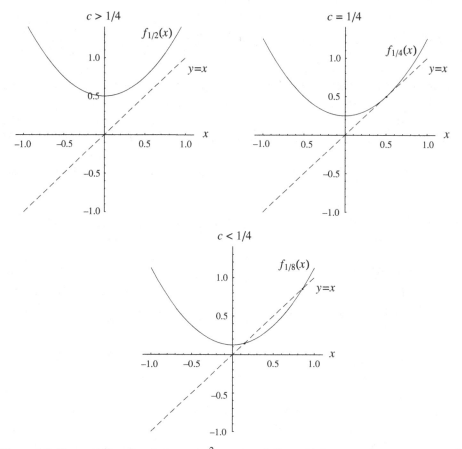

Figure 2.6. Tangent bifurcation for $x_{t+1} = x_t^2 + c$ at $c = 1/4$, at which two steady states are created, one stable and one unstable. (a) $c > 1/4$: no steady states; (b) $c = 1/4$: one steady state, with graph of f_c tangent to diagonal $y = x$; and (c) $c < 1/4$: two steady states, one stable and one unstable.

so that for $0 < c < 1/4$ indeed one steady state is stable and the other one is unstable. We say that f_c exhibits a *tangent bifurcation* at $c = 1/4$. At the bifurcation value $c = 1/4$, the graph of f_c is tangent to the diagonal $y = x$ and two new steady states are created, one stable and one unstable. The tangent bifurcation parameter value is characterized by the first-order condition

$$f_c'(x^{eq}) = +1, \tag{2.4}$$

where x^{eq} is the steady state.

Creation of a period 3-cycle for $x_{t+1} = \lambda x_t(1-x_t)$

The period-3 cycle in the quadratic family (2.2) is created in essentially the same way, through a tangent bifurcation of the third iterate f_λ^3, as illustrated in Figure 2.7. Since

$$(f_\lambda^3)'(x) = f_\lambda'(f_\lambda^2(x)) \cdot f_\lambda'(f_\lambda(x)) \cdot f_\lambda'(x),$$

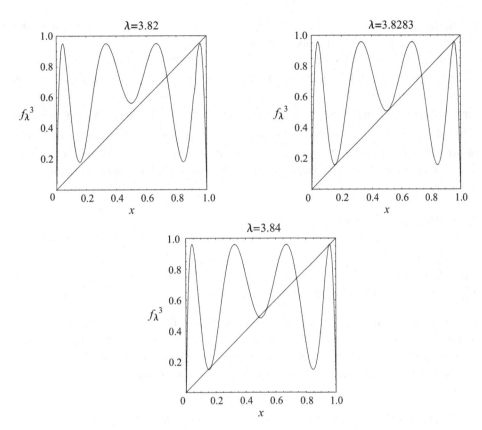

Figure 2.7. Creation of 3-cycle for the quadratic map (2.2) through tangent bifurcation at $\lambda \approx 3.8283$. For $\lambda = 3.82$, there is no 3-cycle. For $\lambda \approx 3.8283$, the graph of f_λ^3 is tangent to diagonal $y = x$, and a 3-cycle is created through a tangent bifurcation. For $\lambda = 3.84$ two 3-cycles, one stable and one unstable have been created.

f_λ^3 has critical points at $x = c = 1/2$, at points d_1 and d_2 for which $f_\lambda(d_1) = f(d_2) = c$, and at four additional points e_j, $1 \leq j \leq 4$, for which $f_\lambda^2(e_j) = c$. For $\lambda \approx 3.8283$, the map f^3 has seven critical points. More precisely, we have (see Figure 2.7):

Property 2.3.2 *(tangent bifurcation of 3-cycle in the quadratic map (2.2))*:
For $\lambda = \lambda^* \approx 3.8283$, f_λ has a tangent bifurcation in which two 3-cycles are created, one stable and one unstable. Equivalently, at $\lambda = \lambda^*$ the third iterate f_λ^3 exhibits a tangent bifurcation in which simultaneously 6 steady states are created, 3 stable and 3 unstable. We have:

1. for $\lambda < \lambda^*$: f_λ has no 3-cycle;
2. for $\lambda = \lambda^*$: f_λ has one 3-cycle $\{x_1, x_2, x_3\}$, and $(f^3)'(x_i) = +1$, for $1 \leq i \leq 3$;
3. for $\lambda > \lambda^*$ (and λ close to λ^*): f_λ has two 3-cycles, one stable and one unstable.

At the bifurcation value $\lambda = \lambda^*$, the graph of the third iterate f^3 is tangent to the diagonal $y = x$ at the three points of the 3-cycle.

We have seen examples of the two most important bifurcations occurring in one-parameter families of 1-D maps, the period-doubling and the tangent bifurcation. A period-doubling bifurcation of a steady state x^* can arise when $f'_\lambda(x^*) = -1$, whereas a tangent bifurcation of a steady state x^* can arise when $f'_\lambda(x^*) = +1$. A period-doubling bifurcation of a period k point y can arise when $(f^k_\lambda)'(y) = -1$, whereas a tangent bifurcation of a period k point y can arise when $(f^k_\lambda)'(y) = +1$. We note that these first-order conditions are necessary, but not sufficient conditions for these bifurcations to occur.[3]

2.3.3 Transcritical bifurcation

A *transcritical bifurcation* occurs when two steady states "collide" and exchange stability. In fact, we have already encountered a transcritical bifurcation in the quadratic map (2.2) for $\lambda = 1$. Recall that the quadratic map has two steady states, $x = 0$ and $x^*_\lambda = 1 - 1/\lambda$, for which the following holds:

1. For $0 < \lambda < 1$, the steady state $x^*_\lambda < 0$ is unstable, while $x = 0$ is stable.
2. For $\lambda = 1$, the steady states coincide, i.e., $x^*_\lambda = 0$. Moreover, at the bifurcation value $f'(x^*_\lambda) = +1$, so that the graph of f_λ is tangent to the diagonal $y = x$.
3. For $1 < \lambda(< 3)$, the steady state $x = 0$ is unstable, while the steady state $x^*_\lambda > 0$ is stable.

The bifurcation diagram of a transcritical bifurcation is shown in Figure 2.8.

2.3.4 Pitchfork bifurcation

Another important bifurcation that may arise in 1-D systems is the *pitchfork bifurcation*. We explain it by an example. Consider the 1-D map

$$x_{t+1} = g_\lambda(x_t) = \tanh(\lambda x_t) = \frac{e^{\lambda x_t} - e^{-\lambda x_t}}{e^{\lambda x_t} + e^{-\lambda x_t}}. \tag{2.5}$$

The map g_λ is increasing, S-shaped and its derivative is $g'_\lambda(x) = \lambda(1 - \tanh^2(\lambda x))$. It is easily verified that $x = 0$ is always a steady state and $g'_\lambda(0) = \lambda$. The map g_λ has the following properties (see Figure 2.9):

1. For $0 \leq \lambda < 1$, $x = 0$ is the unique steady state and it is (globally) stable.
2. For $\lambda = 1$, $x = 0$ is the unique steady state, with $g'_\lambda(0) = +1$, and it is (globally) stable. The graph of g_λ is tangent to the diagonal at the steady state $x = 0$.
3. For $\lambda > 1$, there are 3 steady states: the steady state $x = 0$ has become unstable and two additional steady states x^*_λ and $-x^*_\lambda$ exist, both of which are locally stable.

---

[3] See Kuznetsov (1995) for a detailed mathematical treatment of bifurcation theory, including necessary and sufficient higher-order conditions associated to different types of bifurcations.

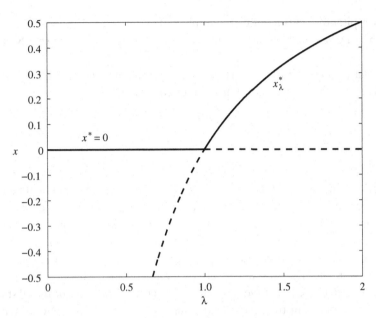

Figure 2.8. Transcritical bifurcation of the quadratic map (2.2). Bold curves correspond to stable steady states, while the dotted curves denote unstable steady states. At $\lambda = 1$ the steady states $x = 0$ and $x_\lambda^* = 1 - 1/\lambda$ "collide" and exchange stability.

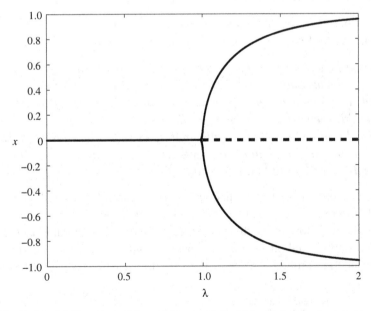

Figure 2.9. Pitchfork bifurcation of the tanh($\cdot$) map (2.5). At $\lambda = 1$ the steady state $x = 0$ becomes unstable and two additional stable steady states x_λ^* and $-x_\lambda^*$ are created.

Hence, at a pitchfork bifurcation the number of steady states changes from 1 to 3; the existing steady state becomes unstable and two additional stable steady states are created.

Notice that a tangent bifurcation, a transcritical bifurcation and a pitchfork bifurcation of a steady state x^{eq} share the same first-order condition[4]:

$$f_\lambda'(x^{eq}) = +1. \qquad (2.6)$$

2.4 Chaos

The numerical simulations in Figures 2.3 and 2.5 show that the dynamical behavior in the quadratic family becomes very complicated, as the parameter λ increases beyond the limiting value λ_∞ of period-doubling bifurcations. The phenomenon that simple nonlinear models exhibit very complicated dynamics is called *deterministic chaos*. The nonlinear models are deterministic (i.e., without noise), so given an initial state with infinite precision, the entire future path is exactly determined. Chaotic solutions exhibit sensitivity to initial states, however, so that a small perturbations of the initial state leads to a completely different time path. Initial state uncertainty in chaotic systems, e.g., due to round-off errors on a computer or the flapping of the wings of a butterfly, leads to unpredictability in the long run.

The intuitive notion of deterministic chaos is easily explained, but an exact mathematical definition is nontrivial. There exist a number of non-equivalent definitions of chaos in the literature. One frequently used definition is the following:

Definition 2.4.1. *The dynamics of a difference equation* $x_{t+1} = f(x_t)$ *is called* **(topologically) chaotic** *if the following three properties are satisfied:*

1. *There exists an infinite set P of (unstable) periodic points with different periods.*
2. *There exists an uncountable set S of aperiodic points (i.e., poinst whose orbits are bounded, not periodic and not converging to a periodic orbit).*
3. *f has sensitive dependence on initial conditions w.r.t.* $\Lambda = P \cup S$, *that is, there exists a positive distance C such that for all initial states* $x_0 \in \Lambda$ *and any ε-neighborhood U of x_0, there exists an initial state* $y_0 \in \Lambda \cap U$ *and a time* $T > 0$ *such that the distance* $d(x_T, y_T) = d(f^T(x_0), f^T(y_0)) > C$.

The first property states that a chaotic system has an infinite number of periodic points with different periods. This property already indicates that in a chaotic system the dynamics can follow many different, periodic patterns. According to the second property for many initial states, the time paths do *not* converge to a periodic orbit, but keep wandering around. The third property, the sensitive dependence on initial

---

[4] A tangent bifurcation is a generic bifurcation, while transcritical and pitchfork bifurcations are non-generic, and require "special features." A transcritical bifurcation, for example, arises in systems such as the quadratic map where $x = 0$ is always a steady state. A pitchfork bifurcations arises in symmetric systems, such as the tanh map, for which $f(-x) = -f(x)$. Once more we refer the reader to Kuznetsov (1995) for an extensive mathematical discussion of bifurcation theory.

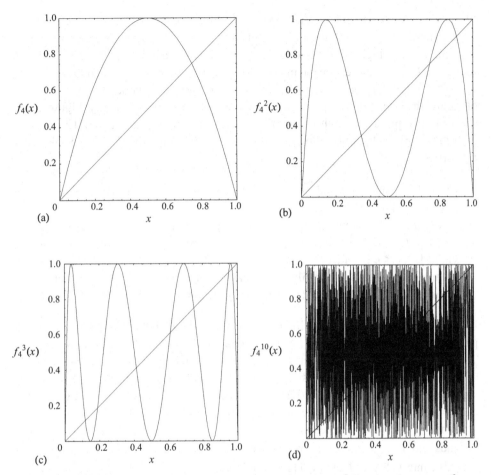

Figure 2.10. Graphs of (a) $f_4(x) = 4x(1-x)$, (b) the second iterate f_4^2, (c) the third iterate f_4^3 and (d) the tenth iterate f_4^{10}. f_4^2 oscillates twice, f_4^3 four times and f_4^{10}, $2^9 = 512$ times. Hence, f_4^{10}, has 1024 intersection points with the diagonal, corresponding to points of periods 1, 2, 5 and 10.

conditions, is the most important characteristic of a chaotic system and implies inherent unpredictability in the long run.

2.4.1 An example

The quadratic difference equation with parameter $\lambda = 4$, i.e., $x_{t+1} = 4x_t(1-x_t)$, satisfies all three properties of the definition of topological chaos. We present an explanation of this fact by the graphical analysis in Figure 2.10. The graph of $f_4(x) = 4x(1-x)$ has its maximum $f_4(\frac{1}{2}) = 1$ at $x = \frac{1}{2}$, so f_4 increases from 0 to 1 on the interval $[0, \frac{1}{2}]$ and decreases from 1 to 0 on the interval $[\frac{1}{2}, 1]$. Figure 2.10b shows the graph of the second iterate f_4^2, which oscillates twice between 0 and 1 on the interval $[0, 1]$, with two different maxima 1 and three different minima 0 (including the minima at 0 and 1).

Moreover, f_4^2 has four intersection points with the diagonal $y = x$, of which two are steady states of f_4 ($x = 0$ and $x_\lambda^* = 1 - 1/\lambda = 3/4$) and the remaining two form an unstable 2-cycle. Figure 2.10c shows the graph of the third iterate f_4^3, which oscillates four times between 0 and 1 on the interval $[0, 1]$, with four maxima at 1 and five minima at 0. The graph of f_4^3 has eight intersection points with the diagonal, two steady states of f_4 and the remaining six points form two (unstable) 3-cycles. Finally, Figure 2.10d shows the graph of the tenth iterate f_4^{10}, which oscillates wildly, $2^9 = 512$ times on the interval $[0, 1]$. It can be shown that for any n, the graph of f_4^n has the following properties:

1. f_4^n has 2^{n-1} maxima equal to 1 and $2^{n-1} + 1$ minima equal to 0 (including minima at the endpoints $x = 0$ and $x = 1$);
2. f_4^n oscillates 2^{n-1} times on the interval $[0, 1]$;
3. the map f_4^n has 2^n fixed points; these correspond to periodic points of period k, where $1 \leq k \leq n$ is a factor of n;
4. for any interval I of arbitrarily small length ε, there exists an $N > 0$ such that I contains points x, y with $f_4^N(x) = 0$ and $f_4^N(y) = 1$.

From these properties it follows immediately that, for each positive integer n, f_4 has a periodic point with period n. The first property in the definition of chaos is thus satisfied. The sensitive dependence on initial states follows immediately from the property (4) of the graph of f_4^N for large N, since the points x and y which are arbitrarily close are separated by a distance 1 after N time periods. Finally, existence of aperiodic time paths can be shown by symbolic dynamics (see Subsection 2.4.3). In fact, for each random sequence of coin tosses, there exists a point x_0 such that $f_4^i(x_0) \in [0, \frac{1}{2}]$ if the i-th toss is heads and $f_4^i(x_0) \in [\frac{1}{2}, 1]$ if the i-th toss is tails. Such a trajectory is aperiodic, if it visits the intervals $[0, \frac{1}{2}]$ and $[\frac{1}{2}, 1]$ in a random order.

2.4.2   Period 3 implies chaos

We have seen that the quadratic map $x_{t+1} = 4x_t(1 - x_t)$ is a simple example of a chaotic system. An important question is: *which 1-D maps exhibit (topological) chaos?* There is a famous theorem by Li and Yorke giving a simple sufficient condition for topological chaos in 1-D systems (see Figure 2.11)[5]:

Theorem 2.4.1. *(Period 3 implies chaos). Let* $x_{t+1} = f(x_t)$ *be a 1-D difference equation, with* f *a continuous map. If there exist a point* x_0 *such that*

$$f^3(x_0) \leq x_0 < f(x_0) < f^2(x_0) \tag{2.7}$$

(or with $>$ instead of $<$) then the dynamics is topologically chaotic.

---

[5] See Li and Yorke (1975) for the original theorem. A detailed textbook mathematical treatment is, for example, Devaney (2003)

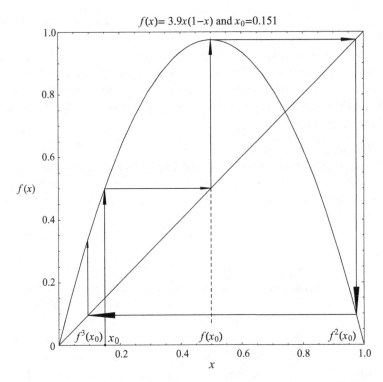

$f(x)= 3.9x(1-x)$ and $x_0=0.151$

Figure 2.11. Period 3 implies chaos. A 1-D continuous map satisfying the Li–Yorke condition $f^3(x_0) \leq x_0 < f(x_0) < f^2(x_0)$ (or with $>$ instead of $<$) is topologically chaotic.

Notice that, if we replace the inequality $\leq$ in the theorem by an equality $=$, then we get

$$f^3(x_0) = x_0 < f(x_0) < f^2(x_0), \tag{2.8}$$

and x_0 is a period-3 point. Hence, as a special case, the theorem says that if a 1-D continuous map has a period-3 point, then the dynamics $x_{t+1} = f(x_t)$ is topologically chaotic.

The Li–Yorke theorem has been important for applications of chaotic dynamics in economics and other fields, because it gives a simple and easy to verify sufficient condition for the occurrence of topological chaos for 1-D maps. Figure 2.11 illustrates how the Li–Yorke condition (2.7) can be verified graphically in a concrete example such as the quadratic map. It suffices to check whether the point x_0 which is mapped onto the critical point, i.e., the point x_0 such that $f(x_0) = c (= 0.5)$, satisfies the Li–Yorke condition.

The Li–Yorke theorem gives a sufficient, but not a necessary condition for topological chaos. For example, for the quadratic map (2.2) it is in fact true that the dynamics is topologically chaotic for all parameter values $\lambda > \lambda_\infty$, i.e., beyond the accumulation point of period-doubling bifurcations. Although for $\lambda > \lambda_\infty$, the Li–Yorke condition need not be satisfied for f_λ, there always exists some $N \geq 1$ such that the N-th iterate f_λ^N satisfies the Li–Yorke condition.

The Li–Yorke theorem is a general result, applying to a large class of maps, but there are two important conditions in the theorem, namely that the map f has to be *one-dimensional* and *continuous*. In general, the theorem "period 3 implies chaos" is not true for discontinuous 1-D maps and also not for continuous 2- or higher-dimensional maps (try to find counterexamples!).

Topological chaos and true chaos

A careful reader may be puzzled by the "period 3 implies chaos" theorem and the apparently contradicting regular behavior in the time series simulation in Figure 2.3d, illustrating convergence to a stable 3-cycle for the quadratic map $x_{t+1} = \lambda x_t (1 - x_t)$ with $\lambda = 3.83$. According to the Li–Yorke theorem the dynamics in this example is topologically chaotic, while a typical time series exhibits regular long run dynamics converging to a stable 3-cycle.

The resolution of this apparent paradox lies in the fact that the chaotic dynamics only occurs for initial states in a Cantor set of Lebesgue measure zero; Subsection 2.4.3 will discuss chaotic invariant Cantor sets in more detail. Therefore, in the example of the quadratic map with $\lambda = 3.83$, chaotic dynamics is in some sense exceptional and only arises with probability zero, for initial states in a zero Lebesgue measure chaotic invariant Cantor set. For almost all (in the sense of Lebesgue measure) other initial states the time series is regular in the long run and converges to the stable period-3 cycle, as in Figure 2.3d. Initial states close to the chaotic Cantor set, however, may mimic the chaotic dynamics for a long period of time. This phenomenon is called *transient chaos*, and explains the erratic initial part of the time series in Figure 2.3d. For applications in economics, transient chaos is important, because in the presence of small noise, the chaotic invariant Cantor set may cause long run irregular fluctuations, as illustrated in Figure 2.12.

To summarize, a topological chaotic system has a set of initial states P with infinitely many periodic points and an uncountable set S with aperiodic points, with sensitive dependence for initial states in the set $\Lambda = P \cup S$. The chaotic dynamics, however, may be restricted to a set of initial states with "probability zero," i.e., the set of initial states $\Lambda = P \cup S$ may have Lebesgue measure zero and therefore may be "unobservable" in the long run in computer simulations. This leads us to a second and stronger definition of chaos[6]:

Definition 2.4.2. *The dynamics of a difference equation $x_{t+1} = f(x_t)$ is called "**truly**" chaotic if there exists a set Λ of positive Lebesgue measure, such that f has sensitive dependence on initial conditions w.r.t. Λ, that is, there exists a positive distance C such that for all initial states $x_0 \in \Lambda$ and any ε-neighborhood U of x_0, there exists an initial state $y_0 \in \Lambda \cap U$ and a time $T > 0$ such that the distance $d(x_T, y_T) = d(f^T(x_0), f^T(y_0)) > C$.*

---

[6] We will refer to this definition as "true chaos." Another term sometimes used in the literature is "thick chaos."

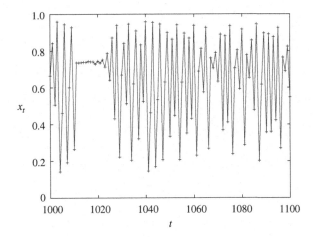

Figure 2.12. Complicated dynamics for the quadratic map buffeted with small noise. The simulation shows a time series for the quadratic map $x_{t+1} = 3.83x_t(1 - x_t) + \epsilon_t$, where ϵ_t is a small noise term, uniformly distributed with mean 0 and SD $\sigma = 0.01$. Small noise prevents the time series from converging to the stable 3-cycle and causes irregular fluctuations mimicking the transient chaotic deterministic skeleton.

An example of a truly chaotic system is the quadratic map with $\lambda = 4$, which does not have a stable periodic cycle. The map f_4 has sensitive dependence on initial conditions w.r.t. the entire interval $[0, 1]$. Almost all orbits are aperiodic and exhibit sensitive dependence on initial conditions. "Truly" chaotic dynamical behavior is not exceptional in the quadratic family $x_{t+1} = \lambda x_t(1 - x_t)$. In fact, the set of parameter values λ for which the quadratic map f_λ is truly chaotic has positive Lebesgue measure.[7]

2.4.3 A chaotic invariant Cantor set

In nonlinear dynamic systems, complicated sets with a fractal structure frequently arise as invariant chaotic sets. At an abstract level, without referring to dynamical systems, fractal sets had already been introduced by the mathematician Cantor, at the end of the nineteenth century (without using the notion "fractal"). An orbit with an initial state in a chaotic Cantor set never leaves the invariant set but jumps irregularly over the fractal set. In this subsection, we discuss a simple example of an invariant chaotic Cantor set.

The middle third Cantor set

The simplest construction of a Cantor set C is as follows (see Figure 2.13). The construction starts with the unit interval $C_0 = [0, 1]$ and removing the middle third interval $(\frac{1}{3}, \frac{2}{3})$ from C_0. This yields the set $C_1 = [0, \frac{1}{3}] \cup [\frac{2}{3}, 1]$. In the second stage of the construction from each of the two intervals of C_1 again the middle third is removed, yielding the set $C_2 = [0, \frac{1}{9}] \cup [\frac{2}{9}, \frac{1}{3}] \cup [\frac{2}{3}, \frac{7}{9}] \cup [\frac{8}{9}, 1]$, the union of four intervals. The

---

[7] This follows from a deep theorem by the Russian mathematician Jacobson (1981); see, e.g., Collet and Eckmann (1980) or de Melo and van Strien (1993) for detailed mathematical treatments.

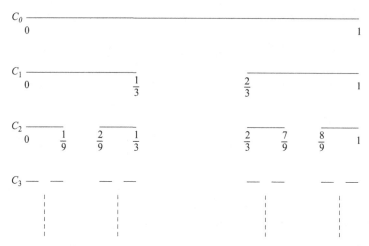

Figure 2.13. The middle third Cantor set. At each stage of the construction, the middle third of the interval is removed. At the n-th stage, the set C_n consists of 2^n intervals; the limiting set $C = C_\infty$ is the Cantor set.

construction of removing the middle third interval is repeated infinitely many times. At the n-th stage of the construction, the set C_n consists of 2^n intervals, each of length $(1/3)^n$. Letting $n \to \infty$, the *Cantor set* is obtained as the limiting set C_∞ .

How "many" points does the Cantor set C_∞ have? Clearly the set is not empty, since the left and right endpoints 0 and 1, as well as all other endpoints of the intervals $1/3$, $2/3$, $1/9$, $2/9, \ldots$, $(1/3)^k$, for all k, belong to C_∞. On the other hand, the Cantor set has infinitely many "holes", due to the removal of intervals. In fact, the Cantor set does *not* contain any arbitrarily small interval, because at the n-th stage of the construction the length of each interval in C_n is $(1/3)^n$. Hence, the Cantor set has infinitely many points, but contains no intervals. Cantor proved the remarkable result that a Cantor set is *uncountable*.

Recall that the set $\mathcal{Z}$ of integers and the set $\mathcal{Q}$ of rational numbers are both infinite, *countable* sets, that is, it is possible to define a list of the numbers in these sets. More precisely, a set A is countable if there exists a one-to-one mapping between the set $\mathcal{N}$ of nonnegative integers and the set A. Cantor showed that any nontrivial interval of real numbers, is an *uncountable* infinite set: there exists no one-to-one mapping between the set of positive integers $\mathcal{N}$ and say the interval $[0, 1]$. Hence, countable and uncountable are different notions of "infinitely many points." To see why a Cantor set is an uncountable set, we have to show that there exists a one-to-one mapping from an interval, say $[0, 1]$, to the Cantor set. The trick is to note that any number $y \in [0, 1]$ has a binary representation $(y_1 y_2 y_3)$, $y_j = 0$ or $y_j = 1$, so that

$$y = y_1 \frac{1}{2} + y_2 \left(\frac{1}{2}\right)^2 + y_3 \left(\frac{1}{2}\right)^3 + \cdots = \sum_{j=1}^{\infty} y_j \left(\frac{1}{2}\right)^j .$$

For each $y \in [0,1]$ the binary representation is unique, with the exception of points of the form $y = (1/2)^k$, $k \geq 1$, which have two binary representations. For example, $1/4 \equiv (0100...) \equiv (00111...)$.

For the Cantor set C_∞ a binary representation also applies. To each point $x \in C_\infty$ there corresponds a unique, infinite symbolic sequence $\sigma = (s_0 s_1 s_2 s_3 ...)$ of symbols $s_i = 0$ or $s_i = 1$, depending upon whether in the n-th stage of the construction of the Cantor set the point x is in the left interval ($s_n = 0$) or in the right interval ($s_n = 1$). For example, the symbolic sequence $\sigma = (0000...)$ corresponds to the left end point 0, while the symbolic sequence $\sigma = (1111...)$ corresponds to the right end point 1. Similarly, $(01111...)$ corresponds to $\frac{1}{3}$ and $(110000...)$ corresponds to $\frac{8}{9}$, etc. The claim that a Cantor set is uncountable then essentially follows from the unique correspondence between a point x in the Cantor set and its symbolic sequence σ and the fact that the same binary sequence corresponds to a point in the unit interval $[0,1]$.

Another important property of the middle third Cantor set is that it has Lebesgue measure 0. In the n-th stage of the construction of the Cantor set, the set C_n consists of 2^n intervals, each of length $(1/3)^n$. Hence, the Lebesgue measure of C_n equals its total length $(\frac{2}{3})^n$. It then follows immediately that the limiting Cantor set C_∞ has Lebesgue measure 0. In conclusion: the Cantor set C_∞ is an uncountable set with Lebesgue measure 0.[8]

An invariant Cantor set for $\lambda > 4$

Figure 2.14a shows the graph of the quadratic map f_λ in (2.2) for $\lambda > 4$ (in what follows we omit the subscript λ). Since $f(\frac{1}{2}) > 1$ there is an interval A_0 of initial states x_0 for which $x_1 = f(x_0) > 1$, so their orbits escape from the unit interval $[0,1]$ and subsequently diverge to $-\infty$. There are two intervals labeled $I_0, I_1 \subset [0,1]$ in Figure 2.14a, consisting of points x_0 such that $f(x_0) \in [0,1]$.

The following question arises: *what is the set of points x_0 whose orbit remains in the unit interval $[0,1]$ for all time?* Clearly this set is nonempty, because it contains the steady states $x = 0$ and $x^* = 1 - 1/\lambda$, as well as the endpoints of the intervals I_0 and I_1. We will see that the invariant set Λ consisting of points that never escape from the unit interval is a *Cantor set* and that the dynamics on this Cantor set is chaotic.

Since $f(I_0) = f(I_1) = [0,1]$ there must be four subintervals $I_{00}, I_{01} \subset I_0$ and $I_{11}, I_{10} \subset I_1$ such that (see Figure 2.14)

$$f(I_{00}) = f(I_{10}) = I_0, \ f(I_{11}) = f(I_{01}) = I_1$$

and

$$f^2(I_{00}) = f^2(I_{01}) = f^2(I_{11}) = f^2(I_{10}) = [0,1].$$

---

[8] One can also construct Cantor sets with positive Lebesgue measure. To do so, instead of removing the same fraction (e.g., 1/3) from each interval in each step of the construction, one can shrink the lengths of the intervals removed at the n-th stage. The remaining Cantor set may then have positive Lebesgue measure. A positive Lebesgue measure Cantor set is called a *thick Cantor set*; cf. Definition 2.4.2 of "true" or thick chaos.

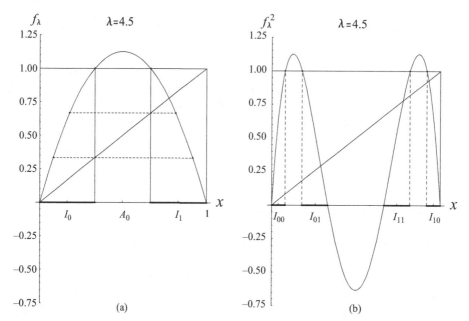

Figure 2.14. Graphs of f_λ (a) and f_λ^2 (b) for $\lambda > 4$. Points in the interval A_0 escape in the first step from the unit interval. Points that do not escape from the unit interval after one period are contained in the intervals I_0 and I_1. These intervals contain four smaller subintervals I_{00}, $I_{01} \subset I_0$ and I_{11}, $I_{10} \subset I_1$, consisting of points that do not escape within the first two time periods. The endpoints of I_{00}, I_{01}, I_{11}, and I_{10} are obtained as the inverse images of the intervals I_0 and I_1 (the dotted lines in the left panel). The invariant set of points that never escape from the unit interval is a Cantor set.

This construction of subintervals can be repeated. Each of the four intervals $I_{s_0 s_1}$ contains two smaller intervals $I_{s_0 s_1 s_2}$ (so a total of eight new subintervals) for which $f(I_{s_0 s_1 s_2}) = I_{s_1 s_2}$ and $f^3(I_{s_0 s_1 s_2}) = [0, 1]$, with $s_i = 0$ or 1, for $0 \le i \le 2$. Let $s_0 s_1 \ldots s_{n-1}$ be a sequence of n symbols 0 or 1. At the n-th stage of the construction one gets 2^n intervals $I_{s_0 s_1 \ldots s_{n-1}}$ with the following properties:

1. f^n is monotonic on $I_{s_0 s_1 \ldots s_{n-1}}$ and $f(I_{s_0 s_1 \ldots s_{n-1}}) = I_{s_1 \ldots s_{n-1}}$ (i.e., applying f means dropping the first symbol s_0 in the symbolic sequence);
2. $f^n(I_{s_0 s_1 \ldots s_{n-1}}) = [0, 1]$ (ensuring that the construction can be repeated);
3. for each $x_0 \in I_{s_0 s_1 \ldots s_{n-1}}$, we have $f^k(x_0) \in I_{s_k}$, for $0 \le k \le n - 1$ (i.e., the symbol s_k encodes whether after k periods the orbit is in I_0 or I_1).

Let Λ_n be the set of points $x \in [0, 1]$ for which $f^k(x) \in [0, 1]$ for all $0 \le k \le n$. From the above construction and properties 1–3, it follows that Λ_n consists of 2^n intervals $I_{s_0 s_1 \ldots s_{n-1}}$. The invariant set Λ, i.e., the set of points whose orbit remains in the interval $[0, 1]$ for all time, is obtained by letting $n \to \infty$ and Λ is a Cantor set. Moreover, it can be shown that the sum of the lengths of the 2^n intervals Λ_n converges to 0 as $n \to \infty$. Hence, the invariant set Λ is a Cantor set with Lebesgue measure 0.

According to property 3 above, the labeling of the intervals $I_{s_0 s_1 \ldots s_{n-1}}$ already contains all information concerning the dynamics of f. The dynamics on the invariant Cantor set Λ can be described by *symbolic dynamics*. Let Σ be the set of all one-sided symbolic sequences of 0's and 1's, so a point $\sigma \in \Sigma$ is an infinite sequence $\sigma = (s_0 s_1 s_2 s_3 \ldots)$, with $s_i = 0$ or 1, $i \geq 0$. Define the *shift map* φ on Σ as

$$\varphi(s_0 s_1 s_2 s_3 \ldots) = (s_1 s_2 s_3 s_4 \ldots), \tag{2.9}$$

so φ shifts a sequence $(s_0 s_1 s_2 s_3 \ldots)$ one entry to the right. The dynamics of the quadratic map f_λ on the invariant Cantor set Λ is equivalent to the dynamics of the shift map φ on Σ. The dynamics of φ on Σ is topologically chaotic, since the following properties hold:

1. φ has a periodic point of period n, for any positive integer n; each periodic sequence σ is a periodic point of φ.
2. Any aperiodic sequence σ is an aperiodic point of φ; hence, φ has uncountably many aperiodic points.
3. φ has sensitive dependence on initial conditions w.r.t. Σ, because for two different sequences after applying φ a number of times the first entry will be different.

We therefore conclude that the dynamics of f_λ, $\lambda > 4$, on the invariant Cantor set Λ is also topologically chaotic. In particular, there is sensitive dependence on initial conditions, since for close-by but different initial states x and y in the Cantor set Λ, applying f_λ a suitable number of times N, $f_\lambda^N(x)$ will be in say I_0, while $f_\lambda^N(y)$ will be in I_1. Hence, nearby initial states in the Cantor set, after some time are separated by some distance C (equal to the distance between I_0 and I_1).

The quadratic map f_λ with $\lambda > 4$ is just a simple example of a topologically chaotic system with an invariant Cantor set with chaotic dynamics. Topologically chaotic systems often possess (infinitely) many chaotic invariant Cantor sets, similar to this example.

2.5   Lyapunov exponent

Chaotic systems are characterized by sensitive dependence upon initial conditions. In a chaotic system, nearby initial states diverge at an exponential rate. On the other hand, in a nonlinear system with bounded time paths, the divergence of time paths cannot go on forever. In nonlinear systems, two time paths that are far apart today may get very close at some future date, thereafter diverging again exponentially for some time, then moving close to each other again, and so on. Chaos is often characterized by an irregular switching between an unstable phase of diverging time paths and a stable phase of converging solutions.

The Lyapunov exponent of a one-dimensional discrete chaotic system, measures the average exponential rate of divergence of nearby initial states. The Lyapunov exponent thus quantifies the sensitive dependence on initial states. In order to formalize this notion, consider a dynamic model $x_{t+1} = f(x_t)$ with two nearby initial states, x_0 and

$x_0 + \delta$. After n time periods, the separation between the two orbits is, to a first-order approximation:

$$\left| f^n(x_0 + \delta) - f^n(x_0) \right| \approx \left| (f^n)'(x_0)\delta \right|.$$

The exponent $\lambda(x_0)$ measuring the average exponential rate of divergence therefore must satisfy

$$\left| f^n(x_0 + \delta) - f^n(x_0) \right| \approx \left| (f^n)'(x_0)\delta \right| = e^{n\lambda(x_0)}\left| \delta \right|,$$

or equivalently

$$e^{n\lambda(x_0)} = \left| (f^n)'(x_0) \right|.$$

The Lyapunov exponent thus satisfies

$$\lambda(x_0) = \frac{1}{n}\ln(\left| (f^n)'(x_0) \right|). \tag{2.10}$$

Using the chain rule for $(f^n)'(x_0)$, and taking the limit $t \to \infty$ we get

$$\lambda(x_0) \equiv \lim_{n\to\infty} \frac{1}{n} \sum_{i=0}^{n-1} \ln(\left| f'(f^i(x_0)) \right|), \tag{2.11}$$

that is, the Lyapunov exponent is the average of the logarithms of the absolute values of the derivative along the orbit.

For an initial state x_0 converging to a steady state, the Lyapunov exponent is the logarithm of the absolute value of the derivative at the steady state. For an initial state x_0 converging to a periodic orbit, with period k, the Lyapunov exponent is the logarithm of the absolute value of the derivative of f^k, at the periodic point, divided by k. Consequently, for an initial state converging to a *stable* steady state or a *stable* k-cycle, the corresponding Lyapunov exponent is *negative*. In contrast, a chaotic time path is characterized by a *positive Lyapunov exponent*, measuring how fast, on average, nearby initial states diverge from each other.

In general, the Lyapunov exponent $\lambda(x_0)$ defined above, depends upon the initial state x_0. However, under fairly general conditions, in chaotic systems such as the quadratic map, the Lyapunov exponent $L = \lambda(x_0)$, is the same "number" for Lebesgue almost all initial states.[9] In that case, we call L the Lyapunov exponent of the system.

It is useful to illustrate this point by a simple chaotic example. Consider the piecewise linear (symmetric) tent map

$$T(x) = \begin{cases} 2x, & 0 \le x \le 1/2, \\ 2(1-x), & 1/2 < x \le 1. \end{cases} \tag{2.12}$$

This piecewise linear map has slopes $+2$ and -2, so that $|T'(x)| = 2$, $x \neq 1/2$. Hence, the Lyapunov exponent, being the average of the logarithms of the absolute values

---

[9] That is, there is only a small, unobservable (zero Lebesgue measure) set of exceptional initial states x_0, for which the Lyapunov exponent $\lambda(x_0) \neq L$.

(a) $f(x) = \lambda x(1-x)$, $x_0 = 0.4$ and $n = 1000$

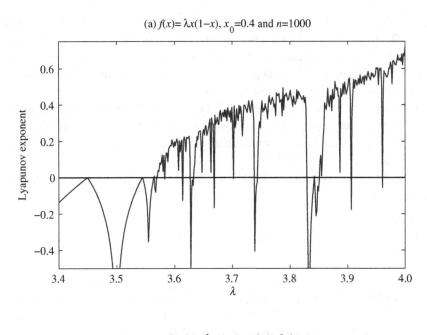

(b) $f(x) = \lambda x(1-x)$ and $x_0 = 0.4$

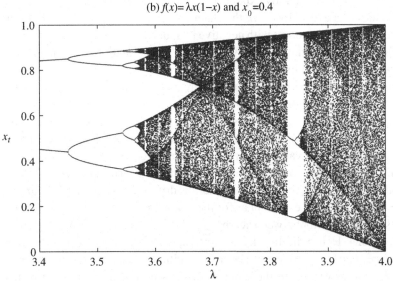

Figure 2.15. Lyapunov exponent L and bifurcation diagram for the quadratic map as a function of the parameter λ. For many parameter values the Lyapunov exponent is positive, indicating chaotic dynamics. The graph of the Lyapunov exponent has infinitely many spikes, when stable cycles occur. At bifurcations of cycles, the Lyapunov exponent touches 0, e.g., when period-doubling bifurcations occur from a stable 2- to a stable 4-cycle, a stable 4- to a stable 8-cycle, or from a stable 3- to a stable 6-cycle. A positive Lyapunov exponent corresponds to chaotic dynamics and sensitive dependence.

of the derivative along an orbit, must be $\lambda(x_0) = \ln(2)$. Does this hold for all points $x_0 \in [0, 1]$? It certainly does not hold for the critical point $x_0 = 1/2$, since the piecewise linear map T is not differentiable at the critical point. For the same reason, it does not hold for points x_0 that are mapped onto the critical point, that is, for points such that $T^k(x_0) = 1/2$, for some $k \geq 1$. This set of exceptional points contains infinitely many points and it is dense in the interval $[0, 1]$. However, this set of exceptional points is countable and therefore it has Lebesgue measure 0. In summary, in this example the Lyapunov exponent is well defined and equal to $L = \ln(2)$, for Lebesgue almost all points x_0.

This brings us to a *numerical definition of chaos*, which is useful from an applications point of view:

Definition 2.5.1. *The dynamics of a difference equation $x_{t+1} = f(x_t)$ is called* **chaotic** *if there exists a set of initial states of positive Lebesgue measure, such that the Lyapunov exponent $\lambda(x_0) > 0$.*

Figure 2.15 shows the Lyapunov exponent L of the quadratic difference equation, together with the bifurcation diagram, as a function of the model parameter λ, $3.4 \leq \lambda \leq 4$. For many λ-values beyond the limiting value $\lambda_\infty \approx 3.57$ of period-doubling bifurcations, the Lyapunov exponent L is positive, and therefore for many λ-values the dynamics is chaotic. However, the chaotic region is interspersed with (infinitely many) small parameter windows with negative Lyapunov exponents, when stable cycles occur. In fact, the graph of the Lyapunov exponent L, as a function of the model parameter λ, is a fractal curve, with infinitely many downward spikes. Notice also that, at bifurcation points, e.g., when period-doubling bifurcations occur from a stable 2- to a stable 4-cycle, from a stable 4- to a stable 8-cycle, or from a stable 3- to a stable 6-cycle, the Lyapunov exponent $L = 0$. This numerical observation is consistent with the theory, since at bifurcation values of k-cycles the corresponding derivative $|(f^k)'(x)| = 1$ and the corresponding Lyapunov exponent therefore equals 0.

The Lyapunov exponent is a measure of the long-term (un)predictability in a chaotic model. For example, for $\lambda = 4$, the quadratic difference equation has Lyapunov exponent $L = \ln(2)$, the same exponent as for the tent map (2.12). This implies that, on average, the separation factor between nearby initial states, after say 10 time periods, is $e^{10 \ln(2)} = 2^{10} = 1024$. Hence, in this chaotic system, the prediction uncertainty after 10 periods is more than 1000 times as big as the initial measurement uncertainty. The larger the Lyapunov exponent, the more difficult (long run) prediction in a chaotic system becomes.

2.6   Chaos and autocorrelations

In previous sections we have seen that simple, deterministic nonlinear models can generate chaotic time paths with "random looking" behavior. These chaotic time series look very unpredictable and, to an outside observer may seem similar to random time series generated by a stochastic process. In particular, chaotic time series may have

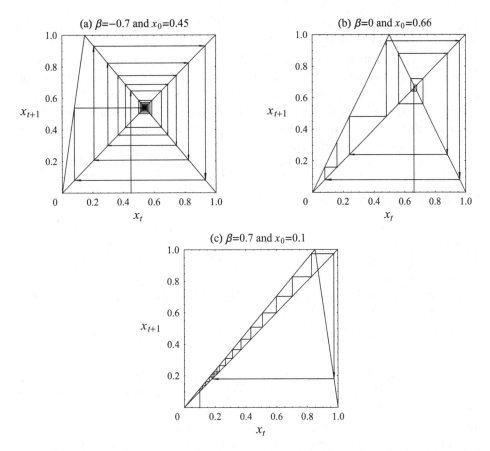

Figure 2.16. Graphs of the asymmetric tent map: (a) $\beta = -0.7$, (b) $\beta = 0$ and (c) $\beta = 0.7$. Typical time series are chaotic, with sample average 0.5 and sample autocorrelation coefficients β^j similar to a stochastic AR(1) process.

zero autocorrelations at all leads and lags. Therefore, from a linear statistical viewpoint, chaos may be indistinguishable from pure white noise.

In this section, by means of a simple example of an asymmetric tent map, we discuss some statistical aspects of chaos, especially sample autocorrelations of chaotic series. As we will see, the autocorrelation functions (ACFs) of asymmetric tent maps exactly coincide with the ACFs of linear stochastic AR(1) processes.

The asymmetric tent map T_β is the continuous, piecewise linear map $T_\beta : [0, 1] \to [0, 1]$ defined as (see Figure 2.16)

$$T_\beta(x) = \begin{cases} \dfrac{2}{1+\beta} x, & 0 \le x \le \dfrac{(\beta+1)}{2}, \\[3mm] \dfrac{2}{1-\beta}(1-x), & \dfrac{\beta+1}{2} < x \le 1, \end{cases} \tag{2.13}$$

where the parameter $-1 < \beta < +1$. Notice first that the asymmetric tent map increases from 0 to 1 on the interval $[0, (\beta+1)/2]$ and then decreases from 1 to 0 on the interval $[(\beta+1)/2, 1]$. Therefore, by the same graphical analysis as for the quadratic map in Figure 2.10 in Subsection 2.4.1, it follows that the dynamics of the asymmetric tent map is "truly" chaotic. Moreover, since the tent map is expanding, with slopes $2/(1+\beta) > 1$ and $-2/(1-\beta) < -1$, it follows immediately that the map T_β cannot have stable steady states or stable cycles and that the Lyapunov exponent is positive.

The dynamics of the piecewise linear tent map

$$x_{t+1} = T_\beta(x_t) \tag{2.14}$$

has the following properties:

1. For any integer $j \geq 1$, T_β has a periodic point of period j; all periodic orbits are unstable.
2. For Lebesgue almost all initial states $x_0 \in [0, 1]$, the time path $\{x_t\}_{t=0}^{\infty}$ is chaotic and dense in the interval $[0, 1]$.
3. For Lebesgue almost all initial states $x_0 \in [0, 1]$, the sample average of the (chaotic) time path is $\bar{x} = \lim_{T \to \infty} \frac{1}{T+1} \sum_{t=0}^{T} x_t = 1/2$.
4. For Lebesgue almost all initial states $x_0 \in [0, 1]$, the sample autocorrelation coefficient at lag j is $\rho_j = \beta^j$.

The first property follows by looking at the graph of the map T_β^j (i.e., the map T_β composed with itself j times). The other three properties are stated without going into the technical details of deriving them.[10] According to the second property the chaotic time paths wander through the interval $[0, 1]$, getting close to every point in the interval, at some time. According to the third property, typically the average of these chaotic series exists and equals $1/2$. Property 4 states that the sample autocorrelation function of a typical chaotic series of T_β is identical to the autocorrelation function of the linear stochastic AR(1) process

$$x_t = \frac{1}{2} + \beta \left(x_{t-1} - \frac{1}{2} \right) + \epsilon_t, \tag{2.15}$$

where ϵ_t is an identically distributed random variable with mean 0.

According to property 4, the sample autocorrelations of the chaotic time series of the asymmetric tent map depend upon the parameter β. Figure 2.16 shows the graphs of T_β, for $\beta = -0.7$, $\beta = 0$ and $\beta = 0.7$. From a graphical analysis, it should be intuitively clear why for a chaotic time series, the autocorrelation coefficient at the first lag must be positive (resp. negative) for $\beta = 0.7$ (resp. $\beta = -0.7$). For $\beta = 0$, a typical chaotic time series has zero sample autocorrelations at all leads and lags, and from a linear statistical viewpoint would be indistinguishable from white noise. More generally, from a linear statistical viewpoint, the deterministically chaotic asymmetric tent map (2.14) is indistinguishable from the stochastic AR(1) processes (2.15).

---

[10] See, e.g., de Melo and van Strien (1993) for an extensive mathematical treatment of 1-D maps. In particular, Property 4 is due to Sakai and Tokumaru (1980).

3 Bifurcations and strange attractors in 2-D systems

In this chapter we discuss some important phenomena arising in nonlinear systems with dimension larger than 1, illustrating most of them by two-dimensional (2-D) systems. Consider a two-dimensional discrete dynamical system

$$(x_{t+1}, y_{t+1}) = F_\lambda(x_t, y_t), \tag{3.1}$$

where F_λ is a nonlinear 2-D (differentiable) map and λ is a parameter. The *orbit* with *initial state* (x_0, y_0) is the set

$$\{(x_0, y_0), (x_1, y_1), (x_2, y_2), ...\} = \{(x_0, y_0), F_\lambda(x_0, y_0), F_\lambda^2(x_0, y_0), ...\}.$$

An orbit thus is a countable set in the $x - y$-plane. Once we know the structure of all possible orbits for all initial states and all parameter values, we can say that the dynamics is completely understood. For example, an orbit may converge to a stable steady state or to a stable k-cycle. However, as we will see, an orbit may converge to a much more complicated set.

This chapter is subdivided into five sections. We start with a simple example of a nonlinear 2-D discrete system, the Hénon map, a 2-D quadratic map, and introduce the notion of strange attractor. In Section 3.2 we discuss bifurcations of 2-D systems, that is, qualitative changes in the dynamics as a model parameter varies. In particular, we discuss the Hopf bifurcation, a bifurcation which cannot occur in 1-D systems, and the subsequent "breaking of an invariant circle" bifurcation route to strange attractors. Section 3.3 focuses on horseshoes, that is, fractal invariant sets with chaotic dynamics. Section 3.4 discusses one of the key features of chaotic systems, namely homoclinic orbits, a notion already introduced by Poincaré. The creation of homoclinic orbits in homoclinic bifurcations is closely related to existence of strange attractors with chaotic dynamics. Finally, in Section 3.5, we discuss the generalization of Lyapunov exponents to two- and higher-dimensional systems.

3.1   The Hénon map

Hénon (1976) introduced the following simple two-dimensional quadratic map:

$$x_{t+1} = 1 - ax_t^2 + y_t,$$
$$y_{t+1} = bx_t,$$
(3.2)

where a and b are parameters. Notice that the special case $b = 0$ yields the 1-D quadratic map $x_{t+1} = 1 - ax_t^2$, so the Hénon map is in fact a 2-D generalization of a 1-D quadratic map. We can write (3.2) as a difference equation $(x_{t+1}, y_{t+1}) = H_{a,b}(x_t, y_t)$, where $H_{a,b}$ is the 2-D map

$$H_{a,b}(x, y) = (1 - ax^2 + y, bx).$$
(3.3)

The map $H_{a,b}$ is called the *Hénon map*.

First we consider the steady states or fixed points of the Hénon map and investigate their stability. A steady state (x, y) of the Hénon map must satisfy the equations

$$1 - ax^2 + y = x,$$
$$bx = y,$$

Substituting the second into the first equation yields

$$ax^2 + (1 - b)x - 1 = 0,$$

with solutions

$$x_{1,2} = \frac{b - 1 \pm \sqrt{(1 - b)^2 + 4a}}{2a}.$$

The steady states are

$$(x_1, y_1) = (\frac{b - 1 + \sqrt{(1 - b)^2 + 4a}}{2a}, bx_1),$$
$$(x_2, y_2) = (\frac{b - 1 - \sqrt{(1 - b)^2 + 4a}}{2a}, bx_2).$$
(3.4)

The stability of the steady states is determined by the eigenvalues of the Jacobian matrix at the steady states. Recall that a steady state is stable if all eigenvalues of the Jacobian matrix at the steady state are inside the unit circle. The Jacobian matrix $J H_{a,b}$ of the Hénon map (6) is given by

$$J H_{a,b}(x, y) = \begin{pmatrix} -2ax & 1 \\ b & 0 \end{pmatrix}.$$
(3.5)

The characteristic equation determining the eigenvalues at the steady states is

$$\lambda^2 + 2ax_i\lambda - b = 0,$$

so the eigenvalues of $J H_{a,b}(x_i, y_i)$ are

$$\lambda_i = -ax_i \pm \sqrt{(ax_i)^2 + b}.$$

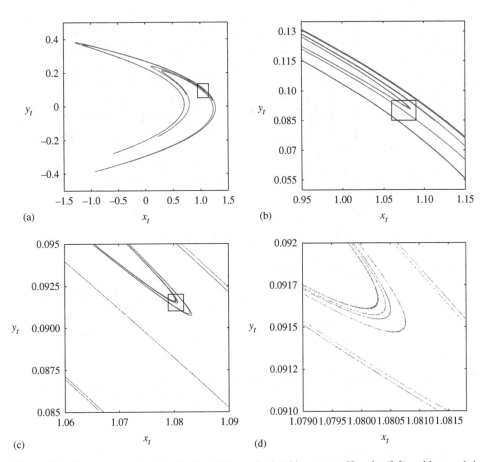

Figure 3.1. The strange attractor for the 2-D quadratic Hénon map $H_{a,b}$ in (3.3), with $a = 1.4$ and $b = 0.3$. (a) 10^6 points of the orbit with initial state $(0,0)$, after a transient of 50 points; (b–d) enlargements of the small boxes in the previous figure, illustrating the fractal, Cantor-like structure of the strange attractor.

Now fix the parameters $a = 1.4$ and $b = 0.3$. A straightforward computation shows that the eigenvalues of $JF(x_1, y_1)$ are $\lambda \approx -1.92$ and $\lambda \approx 0.16$ and the eigenvalues of $JF(x_2, y_2)$ are $\lambda \approx 3.26$ and $\lambda \approx -0.09$. Hence, for $a = 1.4$ and $b = 0.3$ both steady states are *saddle points* and therefore both are *unstable*.

Figure 3.1 shows the long term dynamical behavior of the Hénon map. In Figure 3.1a, 10^6 points of the orbit with initial state $(0,0)$ have been plotted, after a transient of 50 points. Other initial states yield similar pictures. This set is called the *attractor* of the Hénon map, for $a = 1.4$ and $b = 0.3$. An attractor represents the long term dynamical behavior of a system. Figures 3.1b–d show enlargements of each of the small boxes in the previous figure. These enlargements suggest a very complicated geometric structure of the attractor. The attractor does not seem to be a "curve," but rather the enlargements suggest a structure with infinitely many "lines" or "curves" on a finer scale. In fact,

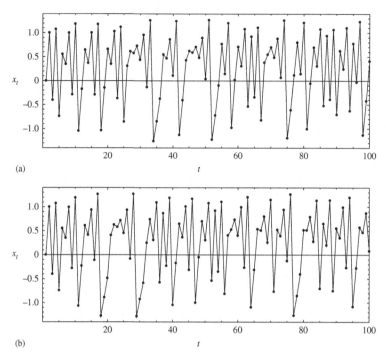

(a)

(b)

Figure 3.2. Chaotic time series and sensitive dependence on initial conditions for the Hénon map $H_{a,b}$ in (3.3), with $a = 1.4$ and $b = 0.3$. (a) Time series with initial state $(x_0, y_0) = (0,0)$, and (b) time series with slightly perturbed initial state $(x_0, y_0) = (0.001, 0)$.

the pictures suggest a fractal, Cantor-like structure: locally, the attractor seems to be the product of a line and a Cantor set. Ruelle and Takens (1971) introduced the name *strange attractor* for such complicated long run dynamical behavior.

The dynamical behavior on the attractor is chaotic, as the orbit jumps irregularly over the strange attractor. Figure 3.2 shows two time series corresponding to the strange attractor, with slightly different initial states. The first time series has initial state $(x_0, y_0) = (0,0)$, while the second time series has initial state $(x_0, y_0) = (0.001, 0)$. Although the initial states are close, the two time series are quite different after some time. In fact, nearby initial states diverge exponentially fast. Hence, the Hénon map exhibits sensitive dependence on initial conditions and the dynamical behavior is chaotic.

Definition of a strange attractor

Loosely speaking, an attractor is a set of points representing the long term dynamical behavior of the system. There are several ways to formalize this notion and several definitions of attractors occur in the literature. One frequently used definition is the following:

Definition 3.1.1. *An attractor of a K-dimensional system $X_{t+1} = F(X_t)$ is a compact (i.e., closed and bounded) set A with the following three properties:*

1. *The set A is invariant, i.e., $F(A) \subset A$.*
2. *There exists an open neighborhood U of A (i.e., $A \subset U$), such that all initial states $X_0 \in U$ converge to the attractor, i.e., for all $X_0 \in U$,*
   $\lim_{n \to \infty} dist(F^n(X_0), A) = 0.$
3. *There exists an initial state $X_0 \in A$ for which the orbit is dense in A.*

The first invariance property says that for an initial state in A, the entire orbit is in A. According to the second property, there is an open set U containing A, such that for initial states in U the orbits settle down to the attractor A. Stated differently, A is attracting all nearby initial states. A set A satisfying only the first two properties is called an *attracting set*. The third property roughly says that there exists at least one orbit visiting all arbitrarily small regions in the attractor A. This third property ensures that A is the smallest set satisfying the first two properties.

The simplest example of an attractor is a stable steady state, where the attractor consists of a single point, attracting all other orbits with initial states in some neighborhood. Another simple example is a stable periodic orbit with period k, in which case the attractor consists of k points. In nonlinear systems, however, much more complicated attractors consisting of infinitely many points and having a complicated fractal structure may arise. These so-called strange attractors arise as limiting sets on which long run chaotic dynamics arises. Again there are several definitions for the notion of strange attractor. We use the following:

Definition 3.1.2. *An attractor A is called a strange attractor of the N-dimensional dynamical system $x_{t+1} = F(x_t)$, if the map F has sensitive dependence w.r.t. the set of initial states converging to A.*

Since the discovery by Hénon of the strange attractor in Figure 3.1 for a simple quadratic map in the late 1970s, it has become clear that many other nonlinear dynamical systems possess strange attractors. In our definition above, we have emphasized the chaotic dynamics and sensitive dependence on initial conditions as the defining characteristics of strange attractors. It should be stressed, however, that many strange attractors share another important characteristic, namely their complicated and intricate fractal structure as illustrated in Figure 3.1.[1]

3.2 Bifurcations

In this section, we focus on bifurcations of 2-D systems, that is, qualitative changes in the dynamical behavior of a one-parameter family F_λ of 2-D maps, as the model parameter

---

[1] The fractal structure of an attractor can be quantified by the so-called (non-integer) fractal dimension of the attractor. For example, the strange attractor of the Hénon map has a fractal dimension $D \approx 1.26$; see Falconer (1990) for an extensive mathematical treatment of fractal geometry and the seminal work of Mandelbrot (1982) concerning the prevalence of fractal shapes in nature.

λ varies. In Chapter 2 on one-dimensional maps, the two most important bifurcations that have been discussed are the tangent and the period-doubling bifurcation. These bifurcations also arise in two-dimensional systems and we start by discussing them briefly in the first subsection. In two- or higher- dimensional systems, the tangent bifurcation is usually called a *saddle-node* bifurcation, for reasons which should become clear shortly. In Subsection 3.2.2, we discuss another important type of bifurcation, the Hopf bifurcation, which cannot arise in 1-D systems. Subsection 3.2.3 describes a bifurcation route to chaos that may arise after a Hopf bifurcation. Finally, Subsection 3.2.4 describes a more advanced degenerate Hopf bifurcation, a so-called codimension two bifurcation. This bifurcation is important, because it gives rise to *coexisting attractors* – a locally stable steady state coexisting with a stable limit cycle (or a more complicated attractor) – an important phenomenon in nonlinear dynamical systems.

3.2.1 Saddle-node and period-doubling bifurcation

We discuss a very simple example which captures the essential features of both the saddle-node and the period-doubling bifurcations for a 2-D map. Consider the map

$$F_\lambda(x,y) = \left(e^x - \lambda, -\arctan\left(\frac{\lambda y}{2}\right) \right). \tag{3.6}$$

Notice that the 2-D map F_λ is in fact a combination of two 1-D maps, since we may write $F_\lambda(x,y) = (f_\lambda(x), g_\lambda(y))$ It is easy to show (by the graph of the corresponding 1-D map) that, as λ increases, the 1-D map

$$f_\lambda(x) = e^x - \lambda \tag{3.7}$$

has a *tangent bifurcation* for $\lambda = 1$ in which two steady states x_1^* and x_2^*, $x_1^* < 0 < x_2^*$, one stable and one unstable, are created. Furthermore, as λ increases, the decreasing 1-D map

$$g_\lambda(y) = -\arctan\left(\frac{\lambda y}{2}\right) \tag{3.8}$$

has a *period-doubling bifurcation* for $\lambda = 2$ in which the steady state $y = 0$ becomes unstable and a stable 2-cycle $\{y_1^*, y_2^*\}$, $y_1^* \le 0 \le y_2^*$ is created. Using these results for the two 1-D maps f_λ and g_λ it follows that the phase portraits of the 2-D map F_λ (or its second iterate F_λ^2) are as shown in Figure 3.3. In particular, we have:

- $0 < \lambda < 1$: F_λ has no fixed points and all points converge to the x-axis and move to the right.
- $\lambda = 1$: F_λ has a unique fixed point $(0,0)$. For each initial state (x_0, y_0) with $x_0 \le 0$, the orbit converges to $(0,0)$; for each initial state (x_0, y_0) with $x_0 > 0$, the orbit moves to the right.
- $1 < \lambda < 2$: F_λ has a two fixed points, one attracting *stable node* $(x_1^*, 0)$ and a *saddle* $(x_2^*, 0)$, where $x_1^* < 0 < x_2^*$ are the fixed points of the 1-D map f_λ. Initial states

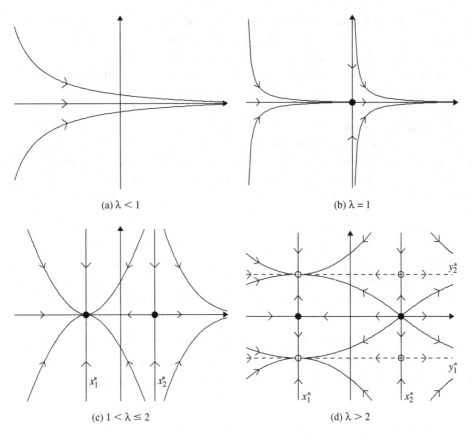

(a) $\lambda < 1$ (b) $\lambda = 1$

(c) $1 < \lambda \leq 2$ (d) $\lambda > 2$

Figure 3.3. Saddle-node bifurcation for $\lambda = 1$ and period-doubling bifurcation for $\lambda = 2$, for the 2-D map F_λ in (3.6). At the saddle-node bifurcation for $\lambda = 1$, a saddle and a node are created. At the simultaneous period-doubling bifurcations of two steady states for $\lambda = 2$, two 2-cycles are created, one stable node and one saddle.

(x_0, y_0) with $x_0 \leq x_2^*$ converge to $(x_1^*, 0)$; initial states (x_0, y_0) with $x_0 > x_2^*$ move to the right.

- $\lambda > 2$: F_λ has two unstable fixed points, one saddle $(x_1^*, 0)$ and one repeller or *unstable node* $(x_2^*, 0)$. In addition F_λ has two 2-cycles, one attracting $\{(x_1^*, y_1^*), (x_1^*, y_2^*)\}$ and one saddle $\{(x_2^*, y_1^*), (x_2^*, y_2^*)\}$, where $\{y_1^*, y_2^*\}$ is the 2-cycle of the 1-D map g_λ. Initial states (x_0, y_0) with $x_0 \leq x_2^*$ converge to the stable 2-cycle $\{(x_1^*, y_1^*), (x_1^*, y_2^*)\}$; initial states (x_0, y_0) with $x_0 > x_2^*$ move to the right.

There are thus two bifurcations occurring in the 2-D family of maps F_λ in (3.6), as λ increases. For $\lambda = 1$ the 2-D map F_λ has a *saddle-node bifurcation* at the fixed point $(0,0)$. At the saddle-node bifurcation value $\lambda = 1$, $DF_\lambda(0,0)$ has an eigenvalue $+1$ and another eigenvalue less than one in absolute value. In the saddle-node bifurcation two steady states are created: a saddle and a node. For $\lambda = 2$, the 2-D map F_λ exhibits two simultaneous *period-doubling* bifurcations, at the two fixed points $(x_1^*, 0)$ and $(x_2^*, 0)$.

In the first, the attracting fixed point $(x_1^*, 0)$ becomes a saddle and a stable 2-cycle is created. At the second period-doubling bifurcation at $\lambda = 2$, the saddle fixed point $(x_2^*, 0)$ becomes an unstable node, and an unstable saddle 2-cycle is created. At the period-doubling bifurcation value $\lambda = 2$, the Jacobian DF_λ, at both fixed points, has an eigenvalue -1 and another eigenvalue not equal to 1.

3.2.2   Hopf bifurcation

The previous example captures the essential features of the saddle-node and the period-doubling bifurcations for 2-D systems. The saddle-node and the period-doubling bifurcations are two important bifurcations occurring in one-parameter families F_λ of 2-D (and also 1-D) systems. The saddle-node bifurcation is characterized by an eigenvalue $\lambda = +1$ of the Jacobian matrix at the steady state, whereas the period-doubling bifurcation is characterized by an eigenvalue $\lambda = -1$ of the Jacobian matrix at the steady state. For one-parameter families of 2-D systems, there is another important third type of bifurcation, the Hopf bifurcation, which cannot occur for families of 1-D maps. The *Hopf bifurcation* is characterized by *two complex eigenvalues crossing the unit circle* as a parameter changes. We discuss the Hopf bifurcation by means of an example.[2]

Example: delayed logistic growth $N_{t+1} = a\,N_t(1 - N_{t-1})$
Introducing an extra time delay into the quadratic (logistic) difference equation $x_{t+1} = ax_t(1 - x_t)$, yields the second-order *delayed logistic difference equation*

$$N_{t+1} = aN_t(1 - N_{t-1}). \tag{3.9}$$

A second-order difference equation can always be translated into a 2-D first-order difference equation. Substituting $x_t = N_{t-1}$ and $y_t = N_t$ we get

$$
\begin{aligned}
x_{t+1} &= y_t, \\
y_{t+1} &= ay_t(1 - x_t).
\end{aligned}
\tag{3.10}
$$

This is a first-order difference equation $(x_{t+1}, y_{t+1}) = F_a(x_t, y_t)$, where F_a is the 2-D map

$$F_a(x, y) = (y, ay(1 - x)), \tag{3.11}$$

with $a \geq 0$ a parameter. First we determine the steady states of the map F_a. The steady states have to satisfy the equations

$$
\begin{aligned}
y &= x, \\
ay(1 - x) &= y.
\end{aligned}
$$

---

[2] Strictly speaking the Hopf bifurcation refers to continuous-time systems, when the real part, $\mathrm{Re}(\lambda)$, of a pair of complex eigenvalues of the Jacobian matrix of a steady state crosses the imaginary axis. A Hopf bifurcation for discrete-time systems is sometimes referred to as a *Neimark-Sacker* bifurcation.

Substituting the first into the second equation yields $ax(1-x)=x$, with solutions $x=0$ and $x=\frac{a-1}{a}$. Hence, the steady states are

$$(x_1,y_1)=(0,0) \quad \text{and} \quad (x_2,y_2)=(\frac{a-1}{a},\frac{a-1}{a}). \tag{3.12}$$

The stability of the steady states is determined by the eigenvalues of the Jacobian matrix at the steady states. The Jacobian matrix JF_a is

$$JF_a(x,y)=\begin{pmatrix} 0 & 1 \\ -ay & a(1-x) \end{pmatrix}. \tag{3.13}$$

The Jacobian matrices at the steady states are then given by

$$JF_a(0,0)=\begin{pmatrix} 0 & 1 \\ 0 & a \end{pmatrix}, \tag{3.14}$$

$$JF_a\left(\frac{a-1}{a},\frac{a-1}{a}\right)=\begin{pmatrix} 0 & 1 \\ 1-a & 1 \end{pmatrix}. \tag{3.15}$$

The eigenvalues of $JF_a(0,0)$ are 0 and a, so $(0,0)$ is a stable node for $0 \le a < 1$ and an unstable saddle point for $a > 1$. The characteristic equation for the eigenvalues of $JF_a(\frac{a-1}{a},\frac{a-1}{a})$ is

$$\lambda^2 - \lambda + a - 1 = 0,$$

so that the eigenvalues are

$$\lambda_1 = \frac{1}{2} - \frac{1}{2}\sqrt{5-4a} \quad \text{and} \quad \lambda_2 = \frac{1}{2} + \frac{1}{2}\sqrt{5-4a}.$$

The eigenvalues λ_1 and λ_2 of $JF_a(\frac{a-1}{a},\frac{a-1}{a})$ satisfy the following properties:

- $0 \le a < 1$: real eigenvalues with $-1 < \lambda_1 < 1 < \lambda_2$, so $(\frac{a-1}{a},\frac{a-1}{a})$ is a saddle.
- $1 < a < \frac{5}{4}$: real eigenvalues with $0 < \lambda_1 < \lambda_2 < 1$, so $(\frac{a-1}{a},\frac{a-1}{a})$ is a stable node.
- $\frac{5}{4} < a < 2$: complex eigenvalues with $\lambda_1\lambda_2 = a - 1 < 1$, so $(\frac{a-1}{a},\frac{a-1}{a})$ is a stable focus.
- $a > 2$: complex eigenvalues with $\lambda_1\lambda_2 = a - 1 > 1$, so $(\frac{a-1}{a},\frac{a-1}{a})$ is an unstable focus.

For $a = 1$ a transcritical bifurcation occurs (see Subsection 2.3.3): the two steady states $(0,0)$ and $(\frac{a-1}{a},\frac{a-1}{a})$ coincide and there is an exchange of stability. From the last two properties above, it follows that the delayed logistic equation exhibits a *Hopf bifurcation* for $a = 2$. As the parameter a increases and passes the bifurcation value 2, the two complex eigenvalues cross the unit circle from inside to outside and the steady state $(\frac{a-1}{a},\frac{a-1}{a})$ loses stability. At the bifurcation value $a = 2$, the eigenvalues of $JF_a(\frac{a-1}{a},\frac{a-1}{a})$ are $\lambda_{1,2} = \frac{1}{2} \pm \frac{1}{2}i\sqrt{3} = \cos\varphi \pm i\sin\varphi$, with $\varphi = \pi/3$, which are exactly on the unit circle.

3.2.3   Breaking of an invariant circle bifurcation route to chaos

What can be said about the dynamical behavior after the Hopf bifurcation, for $a > 2$, when the steady state is unstable? Figure 3.4a shows attractors in the phase space, for increasing a-values after the Hopf bifurcation.

For each a-value, 5000 points have been plotted after a short transient of say 10 periods. For a-values close to 2 ($a = 2.01$, 2.04 and 2.09) the orbit converges to an *attracting invariant "circle"* (a closed curve). As a increases, the invariant circle increases and gets distorted (e.g., $a = 2.16$) and becomes more and more complicated. For $a = 2.27$ it seems that the attractor is not an invariant "circle" anymore, but a more complicated set. In fact, the enlargements in Figures 3.4b-e suggest that we have a strange attractor with a similar fractal structure as in the case of the Hénon map. This bifurcation route to chaos is called the *breaking of an invariant circle*. The smooth invariant circle created in the Hopf bifurcation changes and breaks into a strange attractor in a complicated, infinite sequence of bifurcations, as the parameter a increases.

Figure 3.5 shows some time series corresponding to the attractors in Figure 3.4. For a-values close to 2 ($a = 2.01$, 2.04 and 2.09), the time series are almost periodic with period 6. The time series are not exactly periodic as an orbit seems to densely fill the invariant "circles" in Figure 3.4a. Such an attracting invariant circle with a dense orbit is called a *quasi-periodic attractor*. Quasi-periodic dynamics can be characterized as almost periodic. The orbits never repeat themselves exactly, but there is no sensitive dependence upon initial conditions. Notice that for $a = 2$, the linearized system at the steady state determined by the Jacobian $JF_a(\frac{a-1}{a}, \frac{a-1}{a})$ has period-6 cycles, since the eigenvalues are $\lambda_{1,2} = \frac{1}{2} \pm \frac{1}{2}i\sqrt{3}$. Immediately after the Hopf bifurcation, i.e., for a slightly larger than 2, the dynamics is either periodic or quasi-periodic (with period close to 6). However, as the parameter a further increases ($a = 2.16$ and 2.27), the time series become more complicated and chaos and sensitivity to initial states arise.

Figure 3.6 shows bifurcation diagrams for the delayed logistic equation in (3.10), for $1.95 \le a \le 2.27$ and $2.2 \le a \le 2.27$. After the Hopf bifurcation for $a = 2$, periodic and quasi-periodic dynamics (the dark regions after the Hopf bifurcation) on an invariant circle arise. Quasi-periodic dynamics is interrupted with stable cycles, e.g., a stable 7-cycle around $a = 2.19$. For larger values of a the dynamics becomes chaotic and infinite cascades of period-doubling and period-halving bifurcations occur. For example, around $a = 2.24$ an infinite cascade of period-doubling bifurcations of an 8-cycle can be observed, followed by an infinite cascade of period-halving bifurcations back to a 16-cycle.[3]

Types of local bifurcations

Bifurcations are important in order to understand the transition from simple dynamics to more complicated fluctuations as a model parameter is varied. For one-dimensional systems we have already encountered the period-doubling route to chaos. The strange

---

[3] For more details on the bifurcation routes to chaos in the delayed logistic map, see, e.g., Guckenheimer and Holmes (1983).

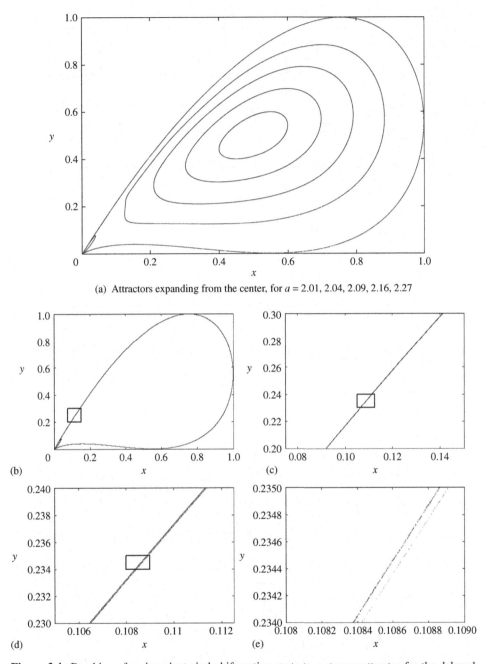

(a) Attractors expanding from the center, for $a = 2.01, 2.04, 2.09, 2.16, 2.27$

Figure 3.4. Breaking of an invariant circle bifurcation route to a strange attractor for the delayed logistic equation in (3.10). (a) Attractors for different a-values. After the Hopf bifurcation at $a = 2$ orbits converge to an invariant circle. As a increases, the invariant circle grows and breaks up into a strange attractor, as illustrated for $a = 2.27$ in (b) and the enlargements of the small boxes in (c–e).

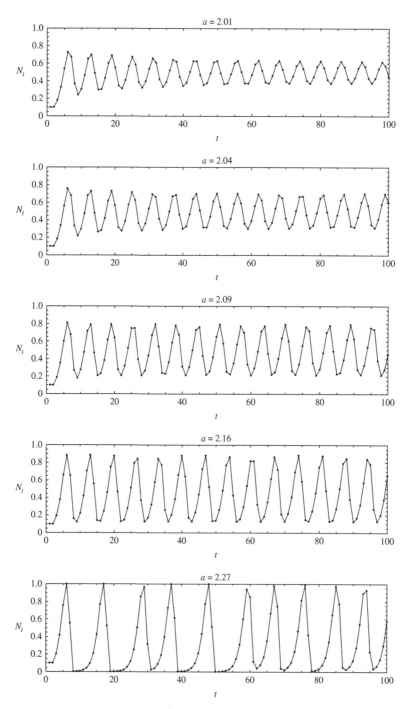

Figure 3.5. Time series for the delayed logistic equation in (3.9) for different values of the parameter a after the Hopf bifurcation for $a = 2$. For a-values close to 2 ($a = 2.01$, 2.04 and 2.09), the time series are quasi-periodic with period close to 6. For higher values of a ($a = 2.16$, 2.27), the dynamics becomes chaotic.

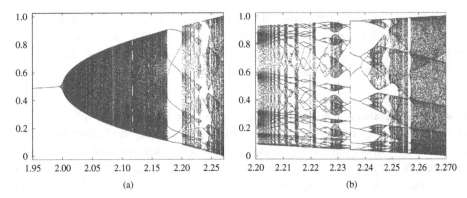

Figure 3.6. Bifurcation diagrams for the delayed logistic equation in (3.10), for $1.95 \le a \le 2.27$ and $2.2 \le a \le 2.27$. (a) A Hopf bifurcation occurs for $a = 2$, after which periodic and quasi-periodic dynamics (the dark regions) on an invariant circle arise. Quasi-periodic dynamics is interrupted with stable cycles, e.g., a stable 7-cycle around $a = 2.19$. (b) For larger values of a the dynamics becomes chaotic and infinite cascades of period-doubling and period-halving bifurcations occur.

attractor in the Hénon family also arises after an infinite cascade of period-doubling bifurcations. In the delayed logistic model we have seen a different route to chaos, the *breaking of an invariant circle*, after the primary Hopf bifurcation.

It is useful to summarize the most important steady state bifurcations in 1-D and 2-D (and higher-dimensional) systems that we have discussed and classify them using the first-order condition, i.e., the corresponding critical eigenvalues of the Jacobian matrix at the steady state (assuming all other eigenvalues are inside the unit circle)[4]:

1. $\lambda = +1$: three types of bifurcations can occur:

   - *saddle-node bifurcation*: two new steady states, a saddle and a node, are created;
   - *pitchfork bifurcation*: one steady state becomes unstable and two new stable steady states are created;
   - *transcritical bifurcation*; two steady states collide and exchange stability.

2. $\lambda = -1$:

   - *period-doubling bifurcation*, the steady state loses stability and a stable 2-cycle is created.

3. a pair of complex eigenvalues λ_1 and λ_2 on the unit circle, i.e., $|\lambda_1 \lambda_2| = 1$:

   - *Hopf bifurcation*, the steady state becomes an unstable focus and an attracting invariant circle is created on which the dynamics is periodic or quasi-periodic.

---

[4] It should be noted that this classification of bifurcations is far from complete. In particular, so far we have not discussed higher-order conditions of bifurcations (but see Subsection 3.2.4). For example, there are different types of period-doubling, pitchfork and Hopf bifurcations, so-called *supercritical* and *subcritical*, depending on higher-order derivatives. The period-doubling, pitchfork and Hopf bifurcations that we have discussed are in fact supercritical, and a new attractor is created (a stable 2-cycle, two stable steady states, an attracting invariant circle). Subcritical bifurcations involve the creation of unstable steady states, unstable periodic orbits or a repelling invariant circle. See Kuznetsov (1995) for a detailed mathematical classification of bifurcations.

It should be clear that the same types of bifurcations can occur for periodic points. This follows by observing that a periodic point with period n is a fixed point (steady state) of the n-th iterate $G = F^n$. In nonlinear dynamic systems, as a model parameter changes, the primary bifurcation often is the onset to a complicated bifurcation route to chaos.

3.2.4   A codimension two bifurcation: degenerate Hopf bifurcation

All local bifurcations encountered in this book so far, such as period-doubling, saddle-node and Hopf bifurcations, are *codimension one* bifurcations, that is, these bifurcations occur generically in nonlinear systems when a single parameter is varied. In this subsection we discuss a more advanced *codimension two* bifurcation, the so-called Chenciner bifurcation (also called degenerate Hopf bifurcation). A codimension two bifurcation is a non-generic phenomenon in a nonlinear system with only one parameter, but it is a generic phenomenon when two parameters can be varied simultaneously. Hence, in a nonlinear system with (at least) two parameters, codimension two bifurcations points are not special, but will be encountered generically in the 2-D parameter space. Moreover, codimension two bifurcation points act as an *organizing center of codimension one bifurcation curves* in the parameter space.

We include a discussion of the more advanced co-dimension two degenerate Hopf bifurcation here, because it gives rise to *coexisting attractors*. In particular, close to a degenerate Hopf bifurcation point, there is an open region in the parameter space for which a locally stable steady state coexists with a stable limit cycle. We will encounter the degenerate Hopf bifurcation in the heterogeneous expectations asset pricing model with evolutionary learning in Chapter 6, and we will identify a region of coexisting attractors – which we call a "volatility clustering region"– in the parameter space (see Subsection 6.6.2, Figure 6.8). Coexistence of a stable steady state and a stable limit cycle provides an endogenous mechanism for volatility clustering, because in the presence of small dynamic noise to the system, the simulated time series jumps irregularly between the basin of attraction of the stable steady state (a phase of low volatility) and the basin of attraction of a surrounding stable limit cycle (a phase of high volatility).

This subsection presents a general discussion of the Chenciner bifurcation by means of the 2-D bifurcation diagram of its *normal form* (see Figure 3.7). The normal form of a bifurcation may be thought of as the simplest model in which the bifurcation occurs.

Supercritical and subcritical Hopf bifurcation

As discussed in Subsection 3.2.2, a steady state loses stability through a Hopf bifurcation when its Jacobian matrix has two eigenvalues on the unit circle with all other eigenvalues inside the unit circle. Depending on higher-order derivatives, there are two different types of Hopf bifurcation:

(i) a *supercritical* Hopf bifurcation, where the stable steady state becomes unstable, and the unstable steady state is surrounded by an *attracting invariant circle* with periodic or quasi-periodic dynamics;

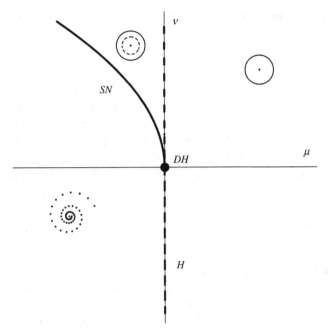

Figure 3.7. Bifurcation diagram of the degenerate Hopf (DH) or Chenciner bifurcation for the normal form (3.18) in the μ-ν plane. The codimension 2 bifurcation point DH is in the origin of the coordinate system. The vertical dashed line $H : \{\mu = 0\}$ is a curve of Hopf bifurcation values, supercritical on one side of the Chenciner point ($\nu < 0$), subcritical on the other ($\nu > 0$). The solid curve SN denotes a curve of saddle-node bifurcations of invariant circles. The region of coexisting attractors, where a stable steady state and a stable limit cycle coexist, separated by an unstable invariant circle, is the region between the curve SN and the positive ν-axes.

(ii) a *subcritical* Hopf bifurcation, where the stable steady state becomes unstable, and the stable steady state is surrounded by a *repelling invariant circle* with periodic or quasi-periodic dynamics.

The so-called normal form of the Hopf bifurcation determines whether it is super- or subcritical. For a given model, the normal form can be obtained by a (sequence of) suitable coordinate transformation(s) around the steady state, restricted to the *center manifold*, which is an invariant manifold through the steady state tangent to the eigenspace spanned by the eigenvectors associated to the complex eigenvalues λ and $\bar{\lambda}$. The normal form of a Hopf bifurcation is a 2-D map describing the dynamics on the center manifold. Although such normal form computations are straightforward, in practical applications they can be quite complicated.[5]

---

[5] For a mathematical treatment of bifurcation theory and details on how to compute center manifolds and normal forms see, for example, Guckenheimer and Holmes (1983) and Kuznetsov (1995). The latter also contains a detailed treatment of the degenerate Hopf or Chenciner bifurcation.

The normal form of the Hopf bifurcation with complex eigenvalues $\lambda = (1+\mu)e^{i\omega}$, written in polar coordinates, has the general form

$$\varphi(r,\vartheta) = (r + \mu r + \nu r^3, \vartheta + \omega + \gamma r^2) + \dots. \tag{3.16}$$

Here the dots denote terms of higher order in r and ϑ. Polar coordinates (r,ϑ) are used to describe points on the 2-D real center manifold W^c. They are chosen such that $r = 0$ corresponds to the steady state of the system. The Hopf bifurcation occurs at $\mu = 0$, for which the complex eigenvalues lie on the unit circle, and ω denotes the angle of the complex eigenvalues. For a generic Hopf bifurcation, the coefficients ν and γ must satisfy the non-degeneracy condition $\nu \neq 0 \neq \gamma$. The non-degeneracy condition $\gamma \neq 0$ ensures that the rotational part of the normal form is not linear. For $\nu < 0$ the Hopf bifurcation is supercritical, whereas for $\nu > 0$ the Hopf bifurcation is subcritical. In applications, the coefficient ν depends upon system parameters and its computation can be quite complicated.

Degenerate Hopf or Chenciner bifurcation

For $\nu = 0$ the Hopf bifurcation becomes degenerate and higher-order terms have to be taken into account in the analysis. This bifurcation is called a *degenerate Hopf* or *Chenciner* bifurcation. The Chenciner bifurcation is a codimension two bifurcation, implying that it is a generic phenomenon in systems with two or more parameters.

The normal form of the Chenciner bifurcation, with complex eigenvalues $\lambda = (1 + \mu)e^{i\omega}$, written in polar coordinates is given by

$$\varphi(r,\vartheta) = \left(r + \mu r + \nu r^3 + \gamma_1 r^5 + \cdots, \vartheta + \omega + \gamma_2 r^2 + \cdots \right). \tag{3.17}$$

Here the dots again denote terms of higher order in r and ϑ. The Chenciner bifurcation occurs at $(\mu,\nu) = (0,0)$, for which the complex eigenvalues lie on the unit circle and the third-order term in the normal form vanishes. The non-degeneracy conditions for the Chenciner bifurcation are in these coordinates $\gamma_1 \neq 0 \neq \gamma_2$. We discuss the case $\gamma_1 < 0$ (which occurs in our application in Chapter 6) and, without loss of generality, we assume that $\gamma_1(0) = -1$. The normal form then simplifies to

$$\varphi(r,\vartheta) = \left(r + \mu r + \nu r^3 - r^5, \vartheta + \omega + \gamma_2 r^2 \right), \tag{3.18}$$

where the higher-order terms are set to zero.

We discuss the structure of the local bifurcation diagram of the Chenciner bifurcation, illustrated in Figure 3.7, using the normal form (3.18). Note that any positive solution r_* to the equation

$$\mu + \nu r^2 - r^4 = 0,$$

or, equivalently, to

$$\left(r^2 - \frac{\nu}{2} \right)^2 = \frac{\nu^2}{4} + \mu, \tag{3.19}$$

corresponds to an *invariant circle* in phase space.

For $\mu > 0$, equation (3.19) has exactly one positive solution. For $\mu = 0$ equation (3.19) has a solution $r_* = 0$. Thus, $\mu = 0$ is a line of Hopf bifurcations, whose type is determined by the sign of ν: for $\nu < 0$, the Hopf bifurcation is supercritical, for $\nu > 0$ it is subcritical.

The number of positive solutions for $\mu < 0$ is determined by the sign of $\nu^2/4 + \mu$: there are two if it is positive, none if it is negative. Finally, for parameters on the curve

$$SN : \frac{\nu^2}{4} + \mu = 0, \tag{3.20}$$

two positive roots of equation (3.19) coincide. The curve SN in (3.20) thus corresponds to parameter values for which a *saddle-node bifurcation of invariant circles* occurs.

A sketch of the complete bifurcation diagram is given in Figure 3.7. Consider a point in parameter space $\{(\mu, \nu)\}$, with $\mu < 0$ and $\nu < 0$. For these parameter values the steady state is locally stable. Now fix ν and increase μ. When crossing the negative ν-axis, for $\mu = 0$, a *supercritical* Hopf bifurcation occurs, that is, a stable invariant circle is created and the steady state becomes unstable. Thus, in the region $\{\mu > 0\}$ a stable limit cycle around an unstable steady state exists. Now fix a parameter value $\nu > 0$ and decrease μ from some positive value. When crossing the positive ν-axis at $\mu = 0$, a *subcritical* Hopf bifurcation occurs in which the steady state becomes stable, an unstable invariant circle emerges out of the steady state, and the stable invariant circle still exists. Decreasing μ further, the unstable and stable circles approach each other and disappear in a *saddle-node bifurcation of invariant circles* when μ crosses the curve SN. Thus, in the region between the positive ν-axes and the curve SN the system has two attractors, a stable steady state and an attracting (large) invariant circle, separated by an unstable invariant circle which forms the boundary between these two attractors.

The local, codimension two Chenciner bifurcation point acts as an *"organizing center"* for the dynamical behavior for nearby parameter values. In particular, existence of a local, codimension two Chenciner bifurcation of the steady state, with the sign restriction $\gamma_1 < 0$ in the normal form (3.17), implies a global, codimension one saddle-node bifurcation of invariant circles and existence of a region of coexisting attractors, where a stable steady state and a stable limit cycle coexist in the parameter space. Close to the Chenciner bifurcation point the dynamics on the stable invariant circle is either periodic or quasi-periodic. When parameters move away from the Chenciner bifurcation point, subsequent bifurcations may lead to more complicated, chaotic dynamics, e.g., a breaking of the invariant circle bifurcation route to strange attractors may arise, similar to what we have seen for the delayed logistic equation. Such a bifurcation route to strange attractors may even arise, while the steady state remains locally stable.

3.3   The horseshoe map

In one-dimensional systems the occurrence of (topological) chaos is relatively easy to show, by investigating the graph of the associated 1-D map and, for example, by using the well-known "Period 3 implies chaos" theorem of Li and Yorke. This result,

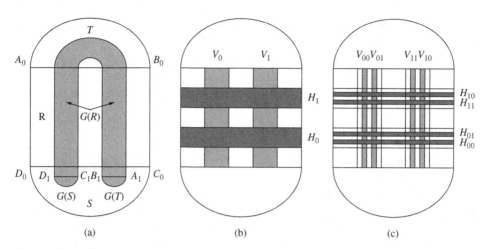

Figure 3.8. Smale's horseshoe map. (a) The region $D = S \cup R \cup T$ is contracted in the horizontal direction, expanded in the vertical direction and folded into a horseshoe-like figure $G(D)$ fitting into D. (b) The horizontal strips H_0 and H_1 are mapped onto the vertical strips V_0 and V_1. (c) The forward invariant set in the region R is a Cantor set of horizontal line segments with topological chaos.

however, only holds for 1-D systems, so it cannot be applied to a 2-D model. In a two-(or higher-) dimensional system there is another way to prove the existence of topological chaos, namely via the existence of so-called horseshoes. The essential features of this rather abstract geometric construction are due to Smale (1963) in the early 1960s. It illustrates that, well before the notion of chaos was introduced in the 1970s, mathematicians were already aware of the possibility of complicated dynamics in planar systems.

Smale's horseshoe construction goes as follows. Consider a rectangular region $R = \overline{A_0 B_0 C_0 D_0}$ together with two semi-disks S and T, as in Figure 3.8. Let $D = S \cup R \cup T$ and define a map G on D by applying the following three consecutive geometric steps (see Figure 3.8a):

1. D is contracted in the horizontal direction by a factor $\leq 1/3$.
2. D is expanded in the vertical direction by a factor 3.
3. The horizontally contracted and vertically expanded figure is folded into a horseshoe-like figure $G(D)$ fitting into D again.

We will say that the map G has a *horseshoe*. The images of the points A_0, B_0, C_0 and D_0 are A_1, B_1, C_1 and D_1, and the images of the semi-disks S and T are small semi-disks contained in S. From the three properties above it follows that there are two horizontal strips H_0 and H_1 in R which are mapped 1-1 onto the two vertical strips $V_0 = G(H_0)$ and $V_1 = G(H_1)$ in R, as in Figure 3.8b. The subregion in R between H_0 and H_1 is mapped into the semi-disk T, while the subregions in R below H_0 and above H_1 are mapped into the semi-disk S.

Since $G(S) \subset S$, and G is contracting on S, it follows that the map G has a unique stable fixed point in S. All points in the semi-disk S therefore converge to this stable steady state. Since the semi-disk T is mapped into S, points in T also converge to the steady state. Moreover, all points in the rectangular region R below H_0, above H_1 and between H_0 and H_1 are mapped into S and T, and therefore converge to the steady state. The question arises: *which points in the rectangular region R never escape from R, and therefore do not converge to the stable fixed point?* Stated differently, what is the *maximal invariant set* Λ in R?

The horizontal strips H_0 and H_1 are exactly those points $X \in R$ for which $G(X) \in R$. Each horizontal strip H_{s_0}, $s_0 = 0$ or 1, contains two smaller horizontal strips $H_{s_0 s_1}$, $s_j = 0$ or 1, $j = 0, 1$, consisting of points X for which both $G(X) \in R$ and $G^2(X) \in R$, with the properties (see Figure 3.8c):

$$G^2(H_{00}) = V_{00} \subset V_0,$$

$$G^2(H_{10}) = V_{01} \subset V_0,$$

$$G^2(H_{01}) = V_{10} \subset V_1,$$

$$G^2(H_{11}) = V_{11} \subset V_1.$$

There are thus four horizontal strips $H_{s_0 s_1}$, $s_j = 0$ or 1, $j = 0, 1$, of points X for which $G^k(X) \in R$ for $k = 0, 1$ and 2. Moreover, for $X \in H_{s_0 s_1}$ we have $G(X) \in V_{s_0}$ and $G^2(X) \in V_{s_1}$. This construction can be repeated. At the n-th stage of the construction we have 2^n horizontal strips $H_{s_0 s_1 \ldots s_{n-1}}$, $s_k = 0$ or 1, $0 \leq k \leq n - 1$, with the following properties:

1. $G^n(H_{s_0 s_1 \ldots s_{n-1}})$ is a vertical strip contained in $V_{s_{n-1}}$ (ensuring that the construction can be repeated);
2. for each $X \in H_{s_0 s_1 \ldots s_{n-1}}$, we have $G^k(X) \in V_{s_k}$, for $0 \leq k \leq n - 1$ (i.e., the symbol s_k encodes whether after k periods the orbit is in V_0 or V_1).

Let Λ_n be the set of points $X \in R$ for which $G^k(x) \in R$ for all $0 \leq k \leq n$. From the above construction and properties 1 and 2, it follows that Λ_n consists of 2^n horizontal strips $H_{s_0 s_1 \ldots s_{n-1}}$. The invariant set Λ^+, i.e., the set of points whose orbit remains in the rectangular region R for all time, is a Cantor set of horizontal line segments. Using the fact that the map G is expanding in the vertical direction, it can be shown that the forward invariant set Λ^+ is a (zero Lebesgue measure) Cantor set of horizontal line segments. The forward invariant set Λ^+ is exactly the set of initial states whose orbits do not converge to the stable steady state in S.

In the same way, it can be shown that the *backward invariant set* Λ^-, that is, the set of points X for which $G^{-n}(X) \in R$ for all $n \in \mathcal{N}$, is a (zero Lebesgue measure) Cantor set of vertical line segments. The maximal invariant set in R, i.e., the set of points that remain in R for both positive and negative time, is then given by $\Lambda = \Lambda^+ \cap \Lambda^-$. The maximal invariant set is thus an intersection of Cantor sets of vertical and horizontal line segments.

We next turn to the forward dynamics on the invariant set Λ. According to property 2 above, the labeling of horizontal strips $H_{s_0 s_1 \ldots s_{n-1}}$ already contains all information concerning the forward dynamics of G. In fact, the forward dynamics of G on the invariant Cantor set Λ can be described by *symbolic dynamics*, similar to the invariant Cantor set of the 1-D quadratic map (see Subsection 2.4.3). In particular, the forward dynamics on the invariant Cantor set Λ has the following properties:

1. Λ contains infinitely many unstable periodic points with different period.
2. Λ contains an uncountable set of aperiodic points (i.e., points whose orbits are not periodic and do not converge to a periodic orbit).
3. The map G has sensitive dependence on initial conditions w.r.t. initial states in Λ, that is, there exists a $C > 0$, such that for all $\bar{x}_0, \bar{y}_0 \in \Lambda$, $\bar{x}_0 \neq \bar{y}_0$,

$$\lim_{n \to \infty} \sup \left| G^n(\bar{x}_0) - G^n(\bar{y}_0) \right| > C.$$

We call such a set Λ a *chaotic invariant set*. The sensitive dependence (property 3) follows from the fact that for any two different initial states X_0 and Y_0 in Λ^+, there exists an $N > 0$ such that $G^N(X_0) \in V_0$ and $G^N(Y_0) \in V_1$ (or the other way around). Note that the chaotic invariant set Λ in Smale's horseshoe is not an attractor, but rather has a saddle structure. Despite the fact that the dynamical behavior on the Cantor set Λ is complicated, for most initial states the long run behavior under the map G is regular: Lebesgue almost all points converge to the stable fixed point of G in the semi-disk S. The points which do not converge to this stable fixed point are precisely the points in the invariant Cantor set Λ, but this Cantor set has Lebesgue measure zero. Hence, the horseshoe map exhibits *topological chaos*. The initial part of many orbits may be erratic, but eventually most orbits settle down to the stable steady state. However, initial states close to the invariant Cantor set will mimic the chaotic dynamics for a long time before settling down to the stable fixed point. Therefore, from an economic applications point of view, topological chaos is important, since the first say 100 points of the erratic part of the time path may be more relevant than its regular part after a long transient.

3.4 Homoclinic orbits

In the previous section, we have seen that if a 2-D map F has a horseshoe then the dynamics is topologically chaotic. At first sight, however, Smale's geometric conditions for having a horseshoe seem rather abstract and special, and may be hard to verify in concrete examples. In this section we will argue that many 2-D maps F (or some iterate F^k) can have horseshoes and exhibit not only topological chaos but also "true chaos" and strange attractors for large sets of parameter values. In fact, any continuous 2-D (or higher-dimensional) map F having a so-called *homoclinic orbit* has (infinitely) many horseshoes and possibly has strange attractors.

Let us first introduce some new notions. Let p be a fixed point of the 2-D map F. The *local stable manifold* and *local unstable manifold* of p are defined as

$$W_{loc}^s(p) = \{x \in U \mid \lim_{n \to \infty} F^n(x) = p\}, \tag{3.21}$$

$$W_{loc}^u(p) = \{x \in U \mid \lim_{n \to -\infty} F^n(x) = p\}, \tag{3.22}$$

where U is some small neighborhood of p. Suppose now that the fixed point p is a saddle point, with eigenvalues $0 < \lambda < 1$ and $\mu > 1$. If the map F is linear, then the (local) stable and unstable manifolds are just the stable and unstable *eigenvectors* E^s and E^u. In general, for a nonlinear map F the local stable manifold W_{loc}^s and the local unstable manifold W_{loc}^u are smooth curves tangent to the stable and unstable eigenvectors of the Jacobian matrix $JF(p)$ (see Figure 3.9a).

The *global stable manifold* and the *global unstable manifold* are now defined as

$$W^s(p) = \bigcup_{n=0}^{\infty} F^{-n}(W_{loc}^s), \tag{3.23}$$

$$W^u(p) = \bigcup_{n=0}^{\infty} F^n(W_{loc}^u). \tag{3.24}$$

For linear maps, the stable and unstable manifolds are simple and coincide with the stable and unstable eigenvectors of a saddle point. For nonlinear maps, however, the stable and unstable manifolds may have intersection points different from p and may be very complicated curves. We now introduce a key notion (see Figure 3.9b):

Definition 3.4.1. *A point q is called a* **homoclinic point** *if $q \neq p$ and q is an intersection point of the stable and unstable manifolds of the saddle point p, that is, $q \in W^s(p) \cap W^u(p)$.*

The notion of homoclinic points was introduced by Poincaré at the end of the nineteenth century, and he realized that a homoclinic point implies very complicated dynamical behavior. Poincaré was working on the dynamics of a three-body system, that is, a system of sun, earth and moon.[6] In order to study the dynamics of this 3-D system of differential equations, Poincaré introduced a 2-D return map G for a suitable plane section, where for each point X in the plane section, $G(X)$ was defined as the next intersection point of the solution of the differential equations with the plane section. Poincaré then showed that the 2-D map G may have homoclinic points, implying complicated dynamics of G and therefore complicated dynamics in the three-body problem. Poincaré thus showed that the motion of sun, earth, and moon need not be periodic, but may become highly irregular and unpredictable. In modern terminology, Poincaré showed that a homoclinic orbit implies chaotic motion and sensitive dependence on

---

[6] Poincaré (1890).

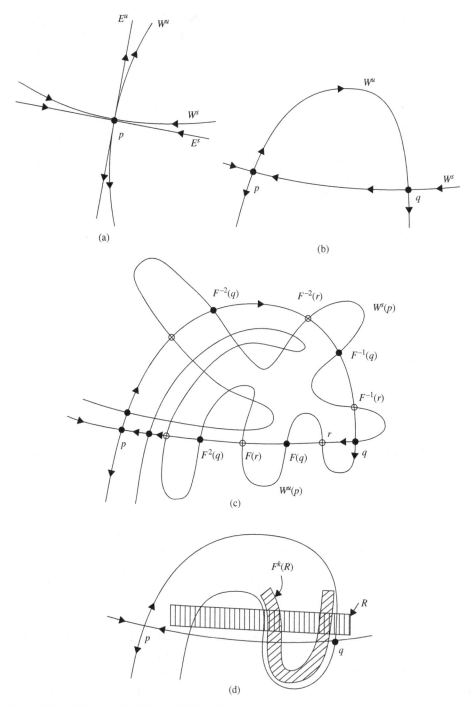

Figure 3.9. (a) The local stable manifold W^s and unstable manifold W^u of a saddle point p are tangent to the stable and unstable eigenvectors E^s and E^u of the Jacobian matrix $JF(p)$. (b) A homoclinic point is an intersection point $q \neq p$ of the stable and unstable manifolds of a saddle point p. (c) A homoclinic point implies *homoclinic tangles*, a complicated global structure of the stable and unstable manifolds. (d) A homoclinic point implies that F^k, for some sufficiently large $k \geq 1$, has a horseshoe and therefore the dynamics is topologically chaotic.

initial conditions. Poincaré's notion of homoclinic orbits turned out to be a key feature of complicated motion and strange attractors and may be seen as an early signature of chaos.

Why does the existence of a homoclinic point imply complicated dynamical behavior? To answer this questions, a first observation is that if q is a homoclinic point then there are infinitely many homoclinic points, since each point $F^n(q)$, $n \in \mathcal{Z}$, is also a homoclinic point (see Figure 3.9c). Hence, the points $F(q)$, $F^2(q)$, $F^3(q)$, etc., are all homoclinic points; since $q \in W^s(p)$, these points approach the saddle point p. Similarly, the points $F^{-1}(q)$, $F^{-2}(q)$, $F^{-3}(q)$, etc., are all homoclinic points; since $q \in W^u(p)$, these points also approach the saddle point p. Consequently, so-called *homoclinic tangles* arise, i.e., wild oscillations of both the stable and unstable manifolds, with infinitely many homoclinic intersections and the stable and unstable manifolds accumulating onto each other (Figure 3.9c). These homoclinic tangles imply sensitive dependence on initial conditions. For example, two different initial states close to a homoclinic point q will be separated along the unstable manifold and lead to very different states after some iterations.

A homoclinic point also implies existence of horseshoes for some iterate F^k, that is, there exists a rectangular region R and an integer k such that the k-th iterate F^k of the map F has a horseshoe. Figure 3.9d indicates such a rectangular region R, suitably chosen close to the stable manifold and homoclinic points. In fact, a homoclinic point implies that there are infinitely many horseshoes and, therefore, infinitely many invariant Cantor sets with chaotic dynamics.

Homoclinic bifurcations

Homoclinic orbits are created in so-called *homoclinic bifurcations*. While homoclinic orbits imply topological chaos, homoclinic bifurcations imply "true chaos" and existence of strange attractors for many parameter values.

Let F_α be a one-parameter family of 2-D maps with a saddle point p_α, which depends upon the parameter α. We define (see Figure 3.10):

Definition 3.4.2. *We say that F_α has a homoclinic bifurcation, associated to the saddle point p_α, at $\alpha = \alpha_0$, if*

1. *for $\alpha < \alpha_0$, $W^s(p_\alpha)$ and $W^u(p_\alpha)$ have no intersection point $q \neq p$;*
2. *for $\alpha = \alpha_0$, $W^s(p_\alpha)$ and $W^u(p_\alpha)$ have a point of homoclinic tangency;*
3. *for $\alpha > \alpha_0$, $W^s(p_\alpha)$ and $W^u(p_\alpha)$ have a transversal homoclinic intersection point.*

We have only discussed homoclinic orbits and homoclinic bifurcations associated to the stable and unstable manifolds of a saddle fixed point p. However, it should be clear that homoclinic bifurcations associated to the stable and unstable manifolds of a periodic saddle point, with period k, can also arise. In the definitions above, one only has to replace F by its k-th iterate F^k.

The saddle-node, the period-doubling and the Hopf bifurcations discussed in Section 3.2 are *local bifurcations* in which a change in the stability of a steady state or

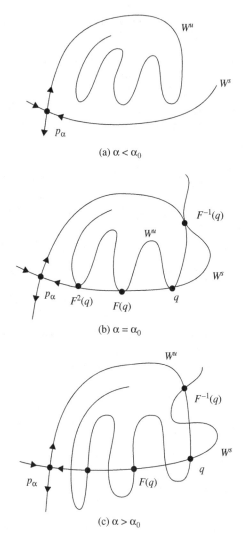

Figure 3.10. Homoclinic bifurcation for $\alpha = \alpha_0$. (a) for $\alpha < \alpha_0$, $W^s(p_\alpha)$ and $W^u(p_\alpha)$ have no intersection point $q \neq p$; (b) for $\alpha = \alpha_0$, $W^s(p_\alpha)$ and $W^u(p_\alpha)$ have a point of homoclinic tangency; where the stable and unstable manifolds are tangent, and (c) for $\alpha > \alpha_0$, $W^s(p_\alpha)$ and $W^u(p_\alpha)$ have a transversal homoclinic intersection point.

a periodic orbit arises. These local bifurcations lead to creation of new periodic orbits near the steady state or near the periodic orbit. A homoclinic bifurcation is a *global bifurcation*, having important consequences for the global dynamical behavior in a model. After a homoclinic bifurcation the global dynamics becomes very complicated. Notice that at a homoclinic bifurcation point, there are infinitely many points of homoclinic tangency. In recent years it has become clear that a one-parameter family F_α of 2-D maps exhibiting homoclinic bifurcations can have strange attractors for a large set of parameter values α. Without going into technical details we state the following important theoretical result[7]:

Theorem 3.4.1. *(Strange attractor theorem)*
In generic one-parameter families F_α exhibiting a homoclinic bifurcation associated to some dissipative period k saddle point p_α, at $\alpha = \alpha_0$, there exists a set of α-values of positive Lebesgue measure, for which F_α has a strange attractor.

This theorem implies chaotic long run dynamical behavior on strange attractors, for a large set of parameter values, in generic systems exhibiting a homoclinic bifurcation. For example, this result explains the occurrence of chaos and strange attractors observed in the computer simulations of the Hénon map and the delayed logistic equation.

3.5   Lyapunov characteristic exponents

In Section 2.5 we introduced the Lyapunov exponent for one-dimensional systems. The Lyapunov exponent measures the average exponential rate of divergence of nearby initial states. A positive Lyapunov exponent implies chaos and sensitive dependence on initial conditions. In this section, we discuss how this notion can be generalized to two- and higher-dimensional systems. Generally, an n-dimensional system has n Lyapunov characteristic exponents, measuring the average rate of divergence and/or convergence in n different directions.

Consider a dynamic model $x_{t+1} = F(x_t)$, where F is an n-dimensional map. Let x_0 be an initial state vector and δ an (small) initial perturbation vector. After n time periods, the separation between the two initial state vectors x_0 and $x_0 + \delta$ is approximately

$$\| F^n(x_0 + \delta) - F^n(x_0) \| \approx \| (D_{x_0} F^n)(\delta) \|,$$

where $D_{x_0} F^n$ is the Jacobian matrix of F^n at x_0, δ is the (normalized) initial perturbation vector and $\| \cdot \|$ denotes the Euclidean distance. Since the Lyapunov exponent is a measure of the average exponential rate of divergence, it is natural to define

$$\lambda(x_0, \delta) = \lim_{n \to \infty} \frac{1}{n} \ln(\| (D_{x_0} F^n)(\delta) \|). \tag{3.25}$$

The Lyapunov exponent $\lambda(x_0, \delta)$ defined above, depends upon both the initial state vector x_0 and the initial perturbation vector δ. The exponent measures the average stretching or contraction of the initial perturbation vector δ, along the orbit with initial state x_0. For a given initial state x_0, there are n different Lyapunov characteristic exponents (LCE) $\lambda_1(x_0) \geq \lambda_2(x_0) \geq \cdots \geq \lambda_n(x_0)$, each measuring an average expansion or contraction in one of the n possible directions.

The main idea is illustrated for a 2-D system in Figure 3.11, showing an initial disk and its first four iterations. The circle surrounding the initial disk is transformed into

---

[7] See Palis and Takens (1993) for technical details and a general mathematical treatment of homoclinic bifurcations and associated strange attractors. In particular, a period k saddle is dissipative if the eigenvalues of the Jacobian $JF^k(p_\alpha)$ satisfy $|\lambda \mu| < 1$.

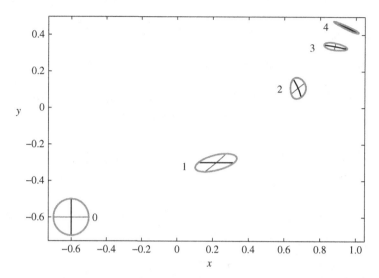

Figure 3.11. In a 2-D system, contraction and expansions occur along different directions. The figure shows an initial disk (marked 0) and its first four iterations (marked 1, 2, 3 and 4). The Lyapunov characteristic exponent λ_1 measures the average (exponential) divergence of the longest axis of the ellipse, while the Lyapunov characteristic exponent λ_2 measures the average (exponential) contraction of the shortest axis of the ellipse.

an ellipse in the first iteration, which becomes more distorted into a long thin ellipse after four iterations. The Lyapunov characteristic exponent λ_1 measures the average divergence of the longest axis of the ellipse, while the Lyapunov characteristic exponent λ_2 measures the average contraction of the shortest axis of the ellipse.

Under fairly general conditions, it holds that for Lebesgue almost all initial perturbation vectors, $\lambda(x_0, \delta) = \lambda_1(x_0)$. Hence, for most initial perturbation vectors the average stretching or contraction equals the *largest Lyapunov characteristic exponent*. If, for Lebesgue almost all initial states x_0 converging to an attractor A, the Lyapunov characteristic exponents $\lambda_1 \geq \lambda_2 \geq \cdots \geq \lambda_n$ are independent of x_0, then we call this set of Lyapunov characteristic exponents the Lyapunov spectrum of the attractor A. Attractors may be characterized according to their Lyapunov spectrum. For a stable steady state or a stable k-cycle all LCEs are negative. For a quasi-periodic attractor, which is topologically equivalent to a circle, $\lambda_1 = 0$, whereas all other LCEs are negative. For a chaotic or a strange attractor, the largest LCE $\lambda_1 > 0$. The largest LCE is a measure of the sensitivity to initial states and the typical long run (un)predictability of the system.

4   The nonlinear cobweb model

In this chapter we discuss price dynamics in *nonlinear* versions of the cobweb or the "hog cycle" model under homogeneous price expectations. The main purpose is to illustrate the role of expectations feedback and bounded rationality in a simple nonlinear economic environment. To keep the analysis as simple as possible, we will work with a linear demand curve, whereas the supply curve will be nonlinear, but monotonically increasing most of the time; in some examples the supply curve will be non-monotonic, backward-bending. We use the nonlinear cobweb model as a didactic tool, because it is one of the simplest dynamic models in economics. It has served as a benchmark model since its introduction in the 1930s[1] and, in particular, it has served as a simple economic environment to discuss expectations feedback. For example, Ezekiel (1938) studied the cobweb model under *naive expectations*, Goodwin (1947) under linear *trend-following* and *contrarian* expectations rules and Nerlove (1958) under *adaptive expectations*. Muth (1961) used the cobweb framework in his seminal paper introducing rational expectations. In this chapter we study the *nonlinear* cobweb model with *homogeneous expectations*, i.e., all producers have the same price expectations. Our main purpose is to illustrate how simple but commonly used expectations rules and bounded rationality in a nonlinear environment may lead to irregular, possibly chaotic price fluctuations. In Chapter 5 we will consider the cobweb model with heterogeneous expectations.

4.1   The cobweb model

The classical cobweb model is a partial equilibrium model describing commodity price fluctuations of a non-storable good, such as corn or hogs, that takes one time period to produce. It is one of the simplest benchmark models in economic dynamics and can be found in many standard textbooks (e.g., Nicholson 1995, pp. 590–594). Producers form price expectations one period ahead and derive their optimal production decision from

---

[1] See, e.g., Ricci (1930; discussing work of H.L. Moore), Schultz (1930), Tinbergen (1930) and Leontief (1934) for early (German) references, surveyed in Waugh (1964). The name cobweb model is due to Kaldor (1934, pp. 134–135), referring to the price–quantity "cobweb" diagrams. Pashigian (1987) gives an overview of "cobweb theorems." Rosser (2000) attributes the first reference to the cobweb model to Cheysson (1887).

expected profit maximization. Given producers' price forecast p_t^e, profit maximizing supply is given by

$$S(p_t^e) = \text{argmax}_{q_t} \{p_t^e q_t - c(q_t)\} = (c')^{-1}(p_t^e). \tag{4.1}$$

The cost function $c(\cdot)$ is assumed to be strictly convex so that the second-order condition for profit maximization is satisfied. The marginal cost function is then invertible and supply is strictly increasing in expected price. The simplest case arises when the cost function is quadratic, $c(q) = q^2/(2s)$, yielding a linear supply curve

$$S(p^e) = sp^e, \qquad s > 0. \tag{4.2}$$

In general a strictly convex cost curve leads to a nonlinear, increasing, supply curve. As an example of a nonlinear supply curve, we will consider an increasing, S-shaped supply curve

$$S(p^e) = b + \tanh\left[\lambda\left(p^e - c\right)\right], \qquad \lambda > 0, \qquad b \geq 1, \qquad c \geq 0, \tag{4.3}$$

where the parameter λ tunes the *nonlinearity* of the supply curve, $b \geq 1$ ensures that production is always non-negative and $c \geq 0$ determines the inflection point of the supply curve.[2]

Consumer demand D depends upon the current market price p_t. The demand curve D can be derived from consumer utility maximization, but for our purposes it is not necessary to specify these preferences explicitly. Throughout the chapter we will simply work with a linearly decreasing demand curve

$$D(p_t) = a - dp_t + \epsilon_t, \qquad a, d > 0, \tag{4.4}$$

where $-d$ is the slope of the demand curve, a determines the demand level and ϵ_t is an independently and identically distributed (IID) stochastic series representing (small) exogenous random demand shocks. With an increasing supply curve and a decreasing demand curve, there is a unique price, denoted by $p = p^*$, where demand and supply intersect. Figure 4.1 illustrates the demand and supply curves for $a = 4.5, b = 1, c = 6$, $d = 0.5$ and $\lambda = 1$.

If beliefs are *homogeneous*, i.e., all producers have identical price expectations p_t^e, market clearing implies

$$D(p_t) = S(p_t^e), \tag{4.5}$$

yielding the realized market equilibrium price

$$p_t = D^{-1}(S(p_t^e)) = \frac{a + \epsilon_t - S(p_t^e)}{d}. \tag{4.6}$$

---

[2] An S-shaped supply curve can, for example, be derived from a fourth- or higher-order polynomial convex cost curve $c(q) = \frac{1}{d+1}(q-1)^{d+1} + q$, where d is an odd integer, e.g., $d = 3$. Optimal supply then becomes $q = S(p^e) = (p^e - 1)^{\frac{1}{d}} + 1$; see Hommes (2000).

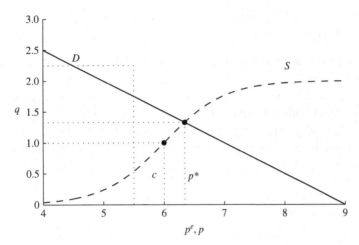

Figure 4.1. Linear demand (4.4) and nonlinear, S-shaped supply curve (4.3) in the cobweb model, with parameters $a = 4.5$, $b = 1$, $c = 6$, $d = 0.5$ and $\lambda = 1$.

The price dynamics in (4.6) thus depends upon the demand and supply curves, but it also depends crucially on the assumed *expectations hypothesis*. A different expectations hypothesis would lead to a completely different dynamical system describing price fluctuations. This is true in general for dynamic economic models: dynamics crucially depends upon the expectations hypothesis. How do producers form these price expectations? We first consider some benchmarks cases, such as naive, rational and adaptive expectations.

4.2 Naive expectations

Before the rational expectations revolution it was common practice to use simple forecasting rules. The simplest case studied in the 1930s, e.g., by Ezekiel (1938), assumes that producers have *naive expectations*, that is, their prediction equals the last observed price: $p_t^e = p_{t-1}$. Under naive expectations, the price dynamics (4.6) reduces to a one-dimensional map

$$p_t = D^{-1}(S(p_{t-1})) = f(p_{t-1}). \tag{4.7}$$

When demand is decreasing and supply is increasing, the map $f = D^{-1}S$ is decreasing. The price dynamics (4.7) then has a unique steady state p^*, at the unique price where demand and supply intersect. According to the well-known *cobweb theorem* (see, e.g., Ezekiel, 1938) the *local stability* of the steady state depends upon the ratio of marginal supply and marginal demand at the steady state p^*. There are essentially two possibilities for the price dynamics:

1. if $-1 < S'(p^*)/D'(p^*)(< 0)$ the steady state p^* is (locally) stable, and prices (in a neighborhood of the steady state) converge to the steady state;

2. if $S'(p^*)/D'(p^*) < -1$ the steady state p^* is (locally) unstable and prices diverge
   from the steady state.

In the case of a nonlinear, bounded supply curve as in (4.3), in case 2 above, when the
steady state is unstable, prices will converge to a *stable 2-cycle*, with regular up and
down oscillations (see Chapter 1, Figure 1.1 for an example). Under naive expectations,
in the cobweb model with nonlinear, but monotonic demand and supply curves, the
price dynamics is always simple: prices either converge to a stable steady state or
prices diverge from the steady state converging to a stable 2-cycle (or to unbounded up
and down oscillations).[3]

4.3   Rational expectations

A well-known argument against simple forecasting rules such as naive expectations is
that they are "irrational" in the sense that they lead to *systematic forecasting errors*. This
argument seems particularly strong in a cobweb model with an unstable steady state
and prices converging to a (noisy) 2-cycle. When producers expect a high (low) price,
they will supply a high (low) quantity and consequently, by the law of demand and
supply, the realized market price will be low (high), contradicting their expectations.
Along a "hog cycle" of up and down price oscillations, expectations are *systematically
wrong*, and forecasting errors are strongly correlated. Smart, rational agents would learn
from their systematic mistakes and revise expectations accordingly, so the argument
goes. Similar considerations led Muth (1961) to introduce *rational expectations*, where
producers' subjective price expectations equal the objective conditional mathematical
expectation of the market price, i.e., $p_t^e = E_t[p_t]$. Using market equilibrium (4.5) with
the linear demand curve (4.4), taking conditional mathematical expectation on both
sides, we can solve for the rational expectations forecast

$$p_t^e = E_t[p_t] = p^*, \tag{4.8}$$

where p^* is the unique price corresponding to the intersection point of demand and
supply. Given producers' rational price forecast $p_t^e = p^*$, the actual law of motion (4.6)
becomes

$$p_t = p^* + \frac{\epsilon_t}{d}. \tag{4.9}$$

The cobweb model has a unique rational expectations equilibrium (REE), given by an
IID process with mean p^*. Along a REE expectations are *self-fulfilling* and producers
make no systematic mistakes, since forecasting errors are uncorrelated. However, in
order to form rational expectations, perfect knowledge of the underlying market equilibrium equations as well as strong computing abilities to compute the equilibrium price
are required. Agents must know the exact demand and supply curves and must be able

---

[3] In general, for nonlinear monotonic demand and/or supply curves a locally stable steady state and a stable
2-cycle (or even multiple stable 2-cycles) may coexist separated by an unstable 2-cycle.

to compute their intersection point p^*. These assumptions are not very realistic in a real complex market environment.

4.4 Naive expectations in a complex market

It is useful at this stage to discuss the role of naive expectations in an example with a strongly nonlinear, backward-bending supply curve. In the case of *non-monotonic* supply and/or demand curves, price dynamics under naive expectations can be complicated and unpredictable. Indeed, with a decreasing demand curve and a non-monotonic supply curve, the cobweb model with naive expectations can generate chaotic price fluctuations.[4] A non-monotonic supply curve has been justified by some kind of "income effect." For example, in an agricultural market at high market prices farmers might decide to work less and consume more leisure instead. Supply then increases at low expected prices, but decreases at high expected prices. At the end of this chapter, in Section 4.8, we will discuss an example of a fishery-harvesting model with a backward-bending supply curve.

Consider the linear demand curve D and the non-monotonic piecewise linear supply curve S

$$D(p) = 1 - p$$

$$S(p^e) = \begin{cases} 2p^e, & \text{if } 0 \le p^e \le 0.5, \\ 2 - 2p^e, & \text{if } 0.5 < p^e \le 1. \end{cases} \tag{4.10}$$

The price dynamics (4.7) under naive expectations is then described by

$$p_{t+1} = T(p_t), \tag{4.11}$$

with T the "upside down" tent map defined as

$$T(x) = \begin{cases} -2x + 1, & \text{if } 0 \le x \le 0.5, \\ 2x - 1, & \text{if } 0.5 < x \le 1. \end{cases} \tag{4.12}$$

The tent map (4.12) is a well-known example of a chaotic system. For Lebesgue almost all initial states $x_0 \in [0, 1]$ the time series $\{T^j(x_0)\}_{j=0}^{\infty}$ is chaotic and has zero autocorrelation coefficients ρ_k at all positive lags k (see Chapter 2, Section 2.6). Hence, (4.11) represents a chaotic cobweb model under naive expectations where, to an outside observer, the chaotic price series appears to be a stochastic random time series.

Figure 4.2 shows a typical chaotic price time series and its sample autocorrelation function (ACF) at the first 20 lags. The chaotic price series is highly irregular and autocorrelations are not significantly different from 0. Hence, prices are uncorrelated and

---

[4] See for example, Artstein (1983), Jensen and Urban (1984), Lichtenberg and Ujihara (1989) and Day and Hanson (1991).

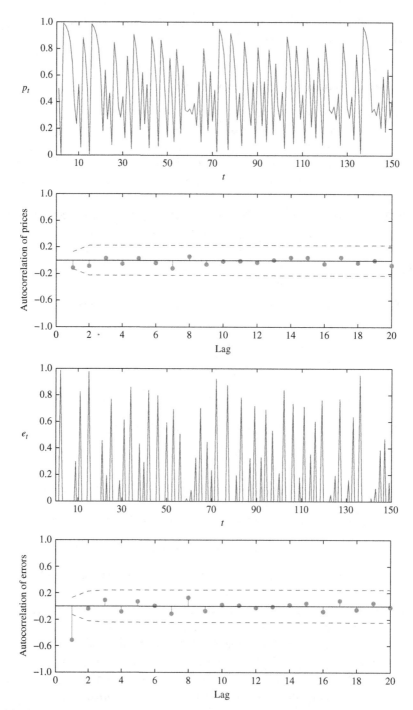

Figure 4.2. Chaotic price dynamics in a cobweb model with a backward-bending supply curve under naive expectations. Top panel: Chaotic price fluctuations with zero ACF (second panel), and corresponding forecasting errors (third panel). Chaotic forecasting errors still have a significant first-order negative autocorrelation coefficient $\beta \approx -0.5$ (bottom panel).

from a linear statistical point of view indistinguishable from white noise. Forecasting errors under naive expectations are given by

$$e_t = p_t - p_t^e = p_t - p_{t-1} = T(p_{t-1}) - p_{t-1}.$$

Figure 4.2 also shows the corresponding time series of expectational errors e_t and its sample ACF at the first 20 lags. Although prices have zero ACF, forecasting errors do not have zero ACF at all lags, but a statistically significant negative autocorrelation coefficient $\rho_1 \approx -0.5$ at the first lag.

This simple example shows that, in a complex nonlinear environment naive expectations does not necessarily lead to easily forecastable prices. Prices may fluctuate irregularly, and naive expectations may be a reasonable strategy that is not easily improved upon. Boundedly rational agents might coordinate on such a simple forecasting rule as a first approximation. In a complex nonlinear world, it is not clear whether and how agents could improve upon such a simple forecasting strategy in the absence of perfect knowledge about the complex market environment.

4.5   Adaptive expectations

Consider another simple and frequently used expectations scheme, *adaptive expectations*, introduced in another classical paper on the cobweb model by Nerlove (1958). Adaptive expectations are given by

$$p_t^e = p_{t-1}^e + w(p_{t-1} - p_{t-1}^e), \qquad 0 \leq w \leq 1. \tag{4.13}$$

The expected price is "adapted" in the direction of the most recently observed actual price p_{t-1}, with expectations weight factor w. Adaptive expectations (4.13) is sometimes referred to as *error correction learning*. An equivalent form for adaptive expectations is

$$p_t^e = (1 - w)p_{t-1}^e + wp_{t-1}, \qquad 0 \leq w \leq 1, \tag{4.14}$$

that is, expected price is a weighted average of the most recently observed actual price and the most recent expected price. Naive expectations are just a special case of adaptive expectations with $w = 1$. Using (4.14) repeatedly, adaptive expectations can be written as a weighted sum, with geometrically declining weights, of all past prices, that is,

$$p_t^e = wp_{t-1} + w(1-w)p_{t-2} + w(1-w)^2 p_{t-3} + \cdots = \sum_{i=1}^{\infty} w(1-w)^{i-1} p_{t-i}. \tag{4.15}$$

Using (4.14) and the market equilibrium condition (4.5), one easily derives that the dynamics of expected prices is described by

$$p_t^e = (1 - w)p_{t-1}^e + wD^{-1}S(p_{t-1}^e). \tag{4.16}$$

The one-dimensional map generating the expected price behavior[5] is

$$f_w(x) = (1 - w)x + wD^{-1}S(x). \qquad (4.17)$$

When demand and supply are *monotonic* (with demand decreasing and supply increasing) the map f_w has a unique fixed point $x = p^*$, at the price p^* where demand and supply intersect. A straightforward computation shows that the steady state $x = p^*$ is locally stable if

$$-\frac{2}{w} + 1 < \frac{S'(p^*)}{D'(p^*)}(< 0). \qquad (4.18)$$

For $w = 1$ (4.18) reduces to the familiar cobweb stability condition $S'(p^*)/D'(p^*) > -1$ under naive expectations. For $0 < w < 1$, the stability condition (4.18) is less stringent and therefore Nerlove (1958) concluded that adaptive expectations has a *stabilizing effect* upon (local) price stability.

Recall that in the case of naive expectations and monotonic (nonlinear) demand and supply curves, prices converge either to a stable steady state or to a stable period two "hog-cycle". The case with adaptive expectations and nonlinear, monotonic demand and supply is much more complicated (and interesting), however. Chiarella (1988), Finkenstädt and Kuhbier (1992) and Hommes (1991a and b, 1994) have shown that *under adaptive expectations chaotic price oscillations can arise even when both demand and supply are monotonic*. An intuitive reason why chaotic price fluctuations can arise, even when demand and supply are monotonic, is the following. When demand is decreasing and supply is increasing, the composite map $D^{-1}S$ is decreasing. The graph of the map f_w in (4.17) is a weighted average of the increasing diagonal $y = x$ and the decreasing graph of the (nonlinear) map $D^{-1}S$. Hence, for $w = 0$, f_0 is increasing while for $w = 1$ (i.e., for naive expectations) the graph of f_1 is decreasing. For *nonlinear*, monotonic demand and supply curves there typically exists an interval of intermediate w-values for which the map f_w is *non-monotonic*. For such w-values chaotic price oscillations may arise. *In a nonlinear world, adaptive expectations may generate chaos.*

Figure 4.3 shows a bifurcation diagram with respect to the expectations weight factor w, with the nonlinear, S-shaped supply curve (4.3). For high values of w, sufficiently close to $w = 1$, prices converge to a stable 2-cycle as in the case of naive expectations; for small values of w, sufficiently close to $w = 0$, prices converge to the RE steady state. For intermediate w-values however, chaotic price oscillations arise; see also Chapter 1, Figure 1.1 for another example. Notice also that, as w decreases from 1 to 0, the *amplitude* of the price oscillations decreases. In a nonlinear cobweb model, adaptive expectations therefore also has a stabilizing effect upon price fluctuations in the sense that its amplitude decreases; however, at the same time the nature of these smaller amplitude price fluctuations may become more and more irregular and lead to close to the steady state chaotic price fluctuations. In the noisy bifurcation diagram in Figure 4.3

---

[5] The dynamics of prices (and quantities) is equivalent to the dynamics of expected prices since $p_t = D^{-1}S(p_t^e)$. However, in order to analyze the dynamical behavior in the case of nonlinear demand and supply curves, it is more convenient to work with the 1-D difference equation for expected prices.

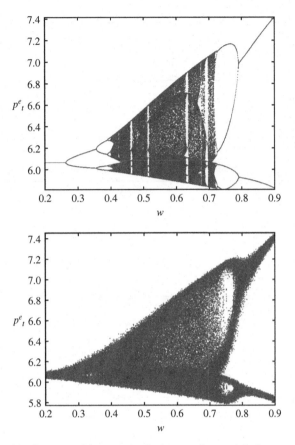

Figure 4.3. Bifurcation diagrams with respect to the expectations weight factor w without noise (top panel) and with small noise (bottom panel), with the other parameters fixed at $a = 7.65, b = 1, c = 6$, $d = 1, \lambda = 10$ and standard deviations of the noise $\sigma = 0.01$ For large values of w, prices converge to a stable 2-cycle with large amplitude. As w decreases, the amplitude of price fluctuations decreases, but at the same time a bifurcation route to chaos occurs. When w becomes very small, chaotic fluctuations are stabilized and prices converge to the REE.

(bottom panel) the overall pattern is similar. Although the detailed bifurcation structure has disappeared in the presence of noise, the regions of the stable steady state (for small values of w), a stable 2-cycle or stable 4-cycle (for high values of w), are clearly visible.[6]

When prices fluctuate chaotically, the corresponding forecasting errors will be highly unpredictable. Will boundedly rational agents be able to detect any structure in these chaotic forecasting errors and improve upon their simple adaptive expectations forecasts?

---

[6] The noisy bifurcation diagram has been created by adding a normally distributed random noise term with standard deviation 0.01 to the dynamics of expected price p_t^e in (4.16), which is equivalent to adding small demand or supply shocks.

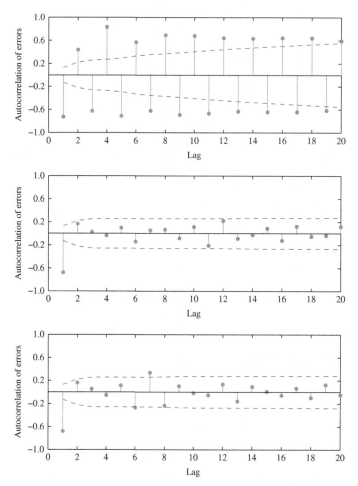

Figure 4.4. Sample autocorrelations of expectational errors under adaptive expectations, with $a = 7.65$, $b = 1$, $c = 6$, $d = 1$ and $\lambda = 10$. (a) $w = 0.71$: chaotic price fluctuations on a 2-piece chaotic attractor. (b)–(c) $w = 0.58$: chaotic price fluctuations on a 1-piece chaotic attractor, (b) without noise and (c) with small noise ($\sigma = 0.01$).

Figure 4.4 illustrates the ACF of forecasting errors for two different values of w. For $w = 0.71$ prices converge to a 2-piece chaotic attractor, jumping irregularly from one interval to another. Although price fluctuations are chaotic, there is still clear structure in the ACF of prices and forecasting errors, with the ACF function exhibiting a significant zig-zag pattern (top panel, Figure 4.4). One would think that boundedly rational agents might recognize this structure and improve their forecasts. This example illustrates that, even when price fluctuations are chaotic, there may still be some regularities that boundedly rational agents might exploit.

Figure 4.4 also illustrates the ACF of forecasting errors for $w = 0.58$, without noise (middle panel) and with noise (bottom panel). For $w = 0.58$ prices are chaotic, jumping irregularly in an interval. There is much less structure in the ACF of prices and forecasting errors and the zig-zag pattern has disappeared. Only the first lag of the ACF function of forecasting errors is significant. For boundedly rational agents it would be hard to improve their forecasts and in a nonlinear world adaptive expectations with chaotic price fluctuations might be a reasonable (long run) boundedly rational equilibrium of aggregate price behavior.

4.6 Linear backward-looking expectations

Any forecast of future prices should be some function of past and current information. In this section, we consider the case where expectations are a function of past prices only. The simplest expectations scheme then arises when the predictor is a *linear* function of a finite number of past prices, that is,

$$p_t^e = w_1 p_{t-1} + w_2 p_{t-2} + \cdots + w_L p_{t-L}, \qquad \sum_{i=1}^{L} w_i = 1, \qquad (4.19)$$

that is, expected price is a weighted average of L past prices. We will refer to the predictor (4.19) as *linear backward-looking expectations (LBE)*; sometimes it is also referred to as *distributed lag* expectations (e.g., Goodwin, 1947). The number of lags L is finite and all coefficients w_i are fixed over time.

Adaptive expectations is a weighted sum, with geometrically declining weights, of all past prices as in (4.15). Since adaptive expectations with nonlinear, monotonic demand and supply curves can lead to chaotic price fluctuations, similar behavior is to be expected with LBE. There are many possibilities for the distribution of weights w_i. In all examples below, we focus on the natural and plausible case where more weight is given to more recent observations, that is $w_i > w_{i+1}, 1 \leq i \leq L - 1$[7,8].

4.6.1 LBE with two lags
In the simplest case with two lags, linear backward-looking expectations are given by

$$p_t^e = w_1 p_{t-1} + w_2 p_{t-2}, \qquad w_1 + w_2 = 1, \qquad (4.20)$$

i.e., expected price is a weighted average of the two most recent observations. Substituting (4.20) into the market equilibrium condition (4.5) we obtain a second-order difference equation for the price behavior:

$$p_t = D^{-1} S(w_1 p_{t-1} + w_2 p_{t-2}). \qquad (4.21)$$

---

[7] The examples in this section are taken from Hommes (1998).

[8] Holmes and Manning (1988) have shown that when expected price is the average of past prices (i.e., all weights w_i are equal) and the number of lags tends to infinity, the steady state is always globally stable. The representation (4.15) for adaptive expectations and the occurrence of chaos shows that this result cannot be true, even with an infinite number of lags, in the natural case when more weight is given to recent observations.

Writing $p_t = y_t$, $p_{t-1} = x_t$ an equivalent two-dimensional difference equation is obtained:

$$x_{t+1} = y_t,$$
$$y_{t+1} = D^{-1} S(w_1 y_t + w_2 x_t). \tag{4.22}$$

For the linear demand curve (4.4) the corresponding two-dimensional map is[9]

$$F(x,y) = (y, [a - S(w_1 y + w_2 x)]/d). \tag{4.23}$$

F has a unique steady state (p^*, p^*), where p^* is the price corresponding to the intersection point of demand and supply. The stability of the steady state is determined by the characteristic equation

$$\lambda^2 + \frac{w_1 S'(p^*)}{d}\lambda + \frac{w_2 S'(p^*)}{d} = 0. \tag{4.24}$$

Figure 4.5 shows how the stability of the steady state depends upon w_1 (with $w_2 = 1 - w_1$) and the ratio $\frac{S'(p^*)}{d}$ of marginal supply and demand at the steady state. Three curves are drawn in the parameter space:

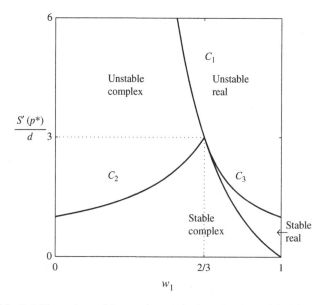

Figure 4.5. Stability regions of the steady state in the cobweb model with LBE with two lags. C_2 is a Hopf bifurcation curve and C_3 a period-doubling bifurcation curve.

---

[9] The reader may easily verify that, when both demand and supply are smooth, monotonic curves, the map F is a diffeomorphism, that is, F is a differentiable 1-1 map with a differentiable inverse F^{-1}.

$$C_1: \quad \frac{S'(p^*)}{d} = \frac{4(1-w_1)}{w_1^2} \qquad \text{Discriminant } D = 0$$

$$C_2: \quad \frac{S'(p^*)}{d} = \frac{1}{1-w_1} \qquad \text{Hopfbifurcation } (H) \qquad (4.25)$$

$$C_3: \quad \frac{S'(p^*)}{d} = \frac{1}{2w_1-1} \qquad \text{Period-doubling } (PD)$$

The curve C_1 consists of parameter values for which the eigenvalues of the Jacobian at the steady state change from real to complex. Along the curve C_2 the product of the eigenvalues of the Jacobian at the steady state equals 1; if in addition, the eigenvalues are complex, they must lie on the unit circle and this part of the curve consists of parameter values for which a Hopf bifurcation of the steady state occurs. Finally, the curve C_3 consists of parameter values for which the Jacobian matrix at the steady state has an eigenvalue -1 (with the other real eigenvalue between -1 and 0). For these parameters a period-doubling bifurcation occurs. The three curves have a common intersection point $(w_1, \frac{S'(p^*)}{d}) = (\frac{2}{3}, 3)$. We conclude that for low values of $\frac{S'(p^*)}{d}$ the steady state price p^* is stable. As $\frac{S'(p^*)}{d}$ increases, the steady state loses stability: for $w_1 < \frac{2}{3}$ through a *Hopf bifurcation* and for $w_1 > \frac{2}{3}$ through a *period-doubling bifurcation*.

In the cobweb model with LBE with two lags, when the steady state becomes unstable, chaos and strange attractors arise. Two different bifurcation routes to chaos can be observed when $\frac{S'(p^*)}{d}$ increases. The first is the well-known *period-doubling route* to chaos. The strange attractors illustrated in the phase diagrams in Figure 4.6 for $w_1 = 0.75$ and $w_2 = 0.25$, arise after an infinite sequence of period-doubling bifurcations. A second route to chaos, the *breaking of an invariant circle*, occurs after the Hopf

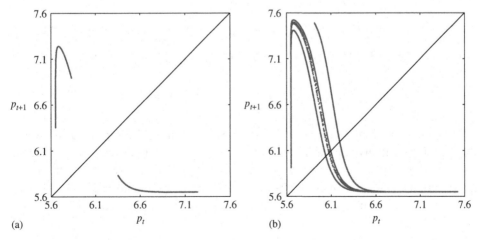

(a)   (b)

Figure 4.6. Strange attractors in the cobweb model with LBE with two lags. (a) $\lambda = 6.5$, two-piece strange attractor; (b) $\lambda = 8$ one-piece strange attractor. Other parameters: $a = 7.65$, $b = 1$, $c = 6$, $d = 1$, $w_1 = 0.75$ and $w_2 = 0.25$.

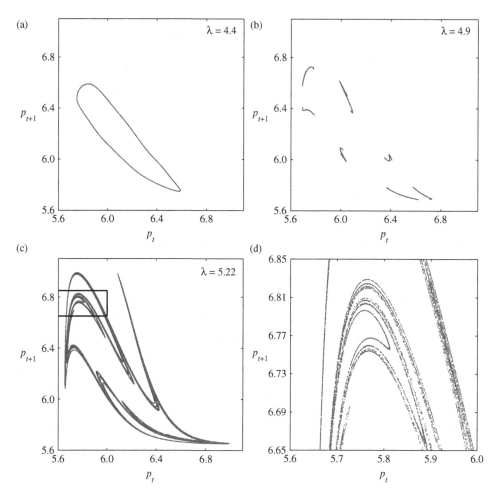

Figure 4.7. Breaking of invariant circle bifurcation route to strange attractors in the cobweb model with LBE with two lags. $a = 7.65$, $b = 1$, $c = 6$, $d = 1$ $w_1 = 0.65$ and $w_2 = 0.35$. (a) $\lambda = 4.4$ quasi-periodic attractor, (b) $\lambda = 4.9$ seven-piece strange attractor, (c) $\lambda = 5.22$ one-piece strange attractor and (d) enlargement of (c).

bifurcation of the steady state (see Chapter 3, Subsection 3.2.3). Figure 4.7 illustrates the breaking of an invariant circle route to chaos for $w_1 = 0.65$ and $w_2 = 0.35$.[10] Just after the Hopf bifurcation the model has an attracting invariant circle with periodic or quasi-periodic price dynamics. As the ratio $\frac{S'(p^*)}{d}$ increases, the invariant circle grows and becomes more and more complicated, turning into a strange attractor through a

---

[10] Many of these strange attractors have a similar geometric structure, which Dee Dechert termed the *high-heeled shoe attractor*.

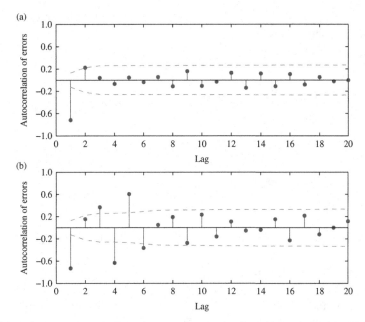

Figure 4.8. Sample autocorrelations of expectational errors in the cobweb model with LBE with two and three lags corresponding to the one-piece strange attractors in Figures 4.6 b and 4.7 c.

complex bifurcation sequence of both period-doubling and homoclinic bifurcations between the stable and unstable manifolds of periodic saddle points.[11,12]

Figure 4.8 illustrates the ACFs of forecasting errors corresponding to the one-piece strange attractors in Figures 4.6b and 4.7c. As in the earlier chaotic example with adaptive expectations, there is not much structure in the ACF of forecasting errors. Only the first lag of the ACF function of forecasting errors is persistently significant. For boundedly rational agents it is not easy to improve upon their simple linear forecasts. In a complex, nonlinear world, backward-looking expectations with only two lags may be a reasonable forecasting strategy as a first approximation.

4.6.2   LBE with many lags

Next consider the case of linear backward-looking expectations with many, that is three or more, lags. Expectations are a weighted sum of L past prices as in (4.19). Substituting this forecasting rule into the market equilibrium condition (4.5) an L-th order difference equation for the price dynamics is obtained:

$$p_t = D^{-1} S(w_1 p_{t-1} + w_2 p_{t-2} + \cdots + w_L p_{t-L}). \qquad (4.26)$$

---

[11] Another economic application of the breaking of an invariant circle route to chaos in a 2-D version of the Overlapping Generations model is given by de Vilder (1996).

[12] For high values of $\frac{S'(p^*)}{d}$ the strange attractor disappears and the price dynamics becomes regular again, converging to a stable-period 3-cycle.

Writing $p_{t-1} = x_{L,t}$, $p_{t-2} = x_{L-1,t}$, ... $p_{t-L} = x_{1,t}$ an equivalent L-dimensional first-order difference equation is written as:

$$x_{1,t+1} = x_{2,t}$$

$$x_{2,t+1} = x_{3,t}$$

$$\cdot$$
$$\cdot \qquad\qquad\qquad\qquad\qquad\qquad\qquad\qquad (4.27)$$
$$\cdot$$

$$x_{L-1,t+1} = x_{L,t}$$

$$x_{L,t+1} = D^{-1} S(w_1 x_{L,t} + w_2 x_{L-1,t} + ... + w_L x_{1,t}).$$

For the linear demand curve (4.4) the corresponding L-dimensional map is[13]

$$F(x_1, x_2, ..., x_L) = (x_2, x_3, ..., \frac{a - S(w_1 x_L + w_2 x_{L-1} + \cdots w_L x_1)}{d}). \qquad (4.28)$$

The unique steady state of F is $\vec{P}^* = (p^*, p^*, ..., p^*)$, with p^* the price corresponding to the intersection point of demand and supply. The characteristic equation for the stability of the steady state is

$$\lambda^N + \frac{w_1 S'(p^*)}{d} \lambda^{N-1} + \cdots + \frac{w_{N-1} S'(p^*)}{d} \lambda + \frac{w_N S'(p^*)}{d} = 0. \qquad (4.29)$$

As for the case of LBE with two lags, it can be shown that when the ratio $\frac{S'(p^*)}{d}$ of marginal demand and supply at the steady state is sufficiently close to 0, the steady state is (locally) stable, whereas for $\frac{S'(p^*)}{d}$ sufficiently large the steady state state is unstable.

As a typical example with three lags, consider the case $w_1 = 0.43$, $w_2 = 0.36$ and $w_3 = 0.21$. For high values of $\frac{S'(p^*)}{d}$ a one-piece strange attractor arises as illustrated in Figure 4.9b. This strange attractor arises after two period-doubling bifurcations of the steady state into a stable 4-cycle, a Hopf bifurcation of the 4-cycle and thereafter the breaking of the four invariant circles into a one-piece strange attractor.

As an example of the LBE case with more than three lags, consider the weights

$$w_i = \frac{2(L+1-i)}{L(L+1)}, \qquad (4.30)$$

where the weights form a declining arithmetic sequence summing to 1.

For large L, the stability region of the steady state becomes larger. More memory stabilizes the system (at least locally). Nevertheless, for sufficiently high values of the ratio $\frac{S'(p^*)}{d}$ the steady state becomes unstable and complicated price dynamics can arise. Figures 4.9c,d show strange attractors for the case $L = 10$ and Figures 4.9e,f for

---

[13] As in the 2-D case, when both demand and supply are smooth, monotonic curves, the map F is a diffeomorphism; see footnote 9.

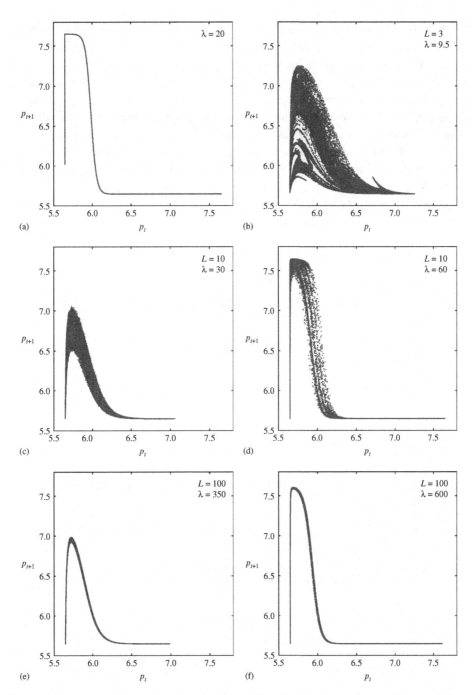

Figure 4.9. Strange attractors in the cobweb model with (a) adaptive expectations and linear backward-looking expectations with various memory (b) $L = 3$, (c-d), $L = 10$ and (e-f) $L = 100$; Parameters: $a = 7.65, b = 1, c = 6, d = 1$. (a) adaptive expectations: $w = 0.75$ and $\lambda = 20$. (b) $L = 3$: $w_1 = 0.43$, $w_2 = 0.36$, $w_3 = 0.21$ and $\lambda = 9.5$. (c)-(d) $L = 10$, with (c) $\lambda = 30$ and (d) $\lambda = 60$. (e)-(f) $L = 100$ with (e) $\lambda = 350$ and (f) $\lambda = 600$.

$L = 100$. These strange attractors arise after an infinite sequence of period-doubling bifurcations, when the parameter λ tuning the nonlinearity of the supply curve increases. Figure 4.9a shows the chaotic attractor in the case of adaptive expectations, where $w_i = w(1-w)^{i-1}$, $i \in \mathcal{N}$, as in (4.15). From Section 4.5 it follows that this attractor is (contained in) a one-dimensional curve, since the cobweb model with adaptive expectations can be reduced to a one-dimensional dynamic system. It is remarkable that the geometric structure of the strange attractors for LBE with $L = 3$, $L = 10$ and $L = 100$ is similar to the one-dimensional chaotic adaptive expectations attractor. Notice, however, that when the number of lags L is large much stronger nonlinearity (i.e., a higher value of λ or the ratio $\frac{S'(p^*)}{d}$) is needed before strange attractors arise.

Figure 4.10 shows ACFs of forecasting errors corresponding to some of the (one piece) strange attractors in Figures 4.9b, 4.9c and 4.9e. There is no clear significant

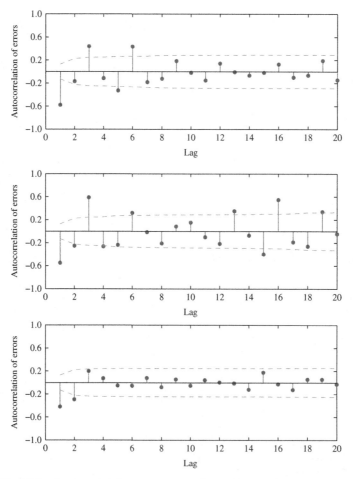

Figure 4.10. ACFs of expectational errors corresponding to the one-piece strange attractors in Figure 4.9b, c and e

pattern in these ACFs, except that the first-order sample autocorrelation is significantly negative.

We now have seen a number of examples with simple forecasting rules, such as adaptive or backward-looking linear expectations, generating chaotic price fluctuations on strange attractors in the cobweb model with *nonlinear, monotonic* demand and supply curves. Agents make mistakes, but even in this simple nonlinear cobweb market the structure in these mistakes may be difficult to detect. This situation may be a reasonable *behavioral rationality* equilibrium in which agents use a simple forecasting rule in a complex, nonlinear environment and it may not be easy for boundedly rational agents to improve their forecast beyond their behavioral linear rule. If agents are more sophisticated statisticians using time series methods, such as linear autocorrelations, they may be able to detect structure in the chaotic forecasting errors. The next section therefore discusses the role of autocorrelations and adaptive learning in expectation rules.

4.7 A behaviorally rational linear forecasting rule

Chaotic time series are highly irregular and may be difficult to distinguish from random time series. For example, a chaotic time series may have zero autocorrelations at all lags and, from a linear statistical perspective, would then be indistinguishable from a purely random time series.

Grandmont (1998) put forward the notion of a *self-fulfilling mistake*, where agents incorrectly believe that the economy follows a stochastic process, whereas the actual dynamics is generated by a deterministic chaotic process which is indistinguishable from the former (stochastic) process by linear statistical tests. In this section we discuss the notion of consistent expectations equilibrium (CEE), introduced in Hommes and Sorger (1998) as a simple example of a self-fulfilling mistake. The concept of CEE was motivated by the fact that piecewise linear asymmetric tent maps can generate deterministic chaotic time series with the same autocorrelations structure as a stochastic AR(1) process (see Chapter 2, Subsection 2.6). Along a (chaotic) CEE agents use a simple linear AR(1) forecasting rule, while the economy follows a nonlinear chaotic asymmetric tent map dynamics with the same autocorrelation structure. We call such an AR(1) rule *behaviorally rational*, because the simple linear rule has an intuitive behavioral interpretation and because it is optimal within the class of simple linear rules.

A CEE may be viewed as an early example of a Restricted Perceptions Equilibrium (RPE), as in Evans and Honkapohja (2001), based on the idea that agents have misspecified beliefs, but within the context of their forecasting model they are unable to detect their misspecification.[14]

---

[14] In a stimulating survey Branch (2006) argues that the RPE is a natural alternative to rational expectations equilibrium because it is to some extent consistent with Muth's original hypothesis of REE while allowing for bounded rationality by restricting the class of the perceived law of motion. Recent extensions and applications

4.7.1 Consistent expectations equilibrium

Assume that all agents believe that prices are generated by a stochastic AR(1) process. Given this perceived law of motion and prices known up to p_{t-1}, the optimal forecast, that is, the prediction for p_t minimizing the mean squared prediction error is

$$p_t^e = \alpha + \beta(p_{t-1} - \alpha), \tag{4.31}$$

where α is the long run average and $\beta \in [-1, 1]$ the first-order autocorrelation of the AR(1) process. Given that agents use the linear forecast (4.31), the *implied actual law of motion* of the cobweb economy becomes

$$p_t = F_{\alpha,\beta}(p_{t-1}) := D^{-1}S(\alpha + \beta(p_{t-1} - \alpha)). \tag{4.32}$$

The (observable) *sample average* of a time series $(p_t)_{t=0}^{\infty}$ is defined as

$$\bar{p} = \lim_{T \to \infty} \frac{1}{T+1} \sum_{t=0}^{T} p_t \tag{4.33}$$

and the (observable) *sample autocorrelation* coefficients are given by

$$\rho_j = \lim_{T \to \infty} \frac{c_{j,T}}{c_{0,T}}, \qquad j \geq 1, \tag{4.34}$$

where

$$c_{j,T} = \frac{1}{T+1} \sum_{t=0}^{T-j} (p_t - \bar{p})(p_{t+j} - \bar{p}), \qquad j \geq 0. \tag{4.35}$$

A consistent expectations equilibrium (CEE) is defined as

Definition 4.7.1. A triple $\{(p_t)_{t=0}^{\infty}; \alpha, \beta\}$, where $(p_t)_{t=0}^{\infty}$ is a sequence of prices and α and β are real numbers, $\beta \in [-1, 1]$, is called a *consistent expectations equilibrium* (CEE) if

1. the sequence $(p_t)_{t=0}^{\infty}$ satisfies the implied actual law of motion (4.32);
2. the sample average $\bar{p}$ in (4.33) exists and is equal to α, and
3. the sample autocorrelation coefficients ρ_j, $j \geq 1$, in (4.34) exist and one of the following is true:
   (a) if $(p_t)_{t=0}^{\infty}$ is a convergent sequence, then $\text{sgn}(\rho_j) = \text{sgn}(\beta^j)$, $j \geq 1$;
   (b) if $(p_t)_{t=0}^{\infty}$ is not convergent, then $\rho_j = \beta^j$, $j \geq 1$.

A CEE is a price sequence together with AR(1) belief parameters α and β, such that expectations are *self-fulfilling* in terms of the *observable* sample average and sample autocorrelations. Along a CEE expectations are thus correct in a linear statistical sense. Hommes and Sorger (1998) showed that, given an AR(1) belief, there are (at least) three different types of CEE:

of CEE include Sögner and Mitlöhner (2002), Tuinstra (2003), Hommes et al. (2013), Branch and McGough (2005), Lansing (2009), Bullard et al. (2008, 2010) and Hommes and Zhu (2012).

- a *steady state CEE* in which the price sequence $(p_t)_{t=0}^{\infty}$ converges to a steady state p^*, with $\alpha = p^*$ and $\beta = 0$;
- a *2-cycle CEE* in which the price sequence $(p_t)_{t=0}^{\infty}$ converges to a period two cycle $\{p_1^*, p_2^*\}$, $p_1^* \neq p_2^*$, with $\alpha = (p_1^* + p_2^*)/2$ and $\beta = -1$;
- a *chaotic CEE* in which the price sequence $(p_t)_{t=0}^{\infty}$ is chaotic, with sample average α and autocorrelations β^j.

A steady state CEE is a REE (at least in the long run) corresponding to some fixed point where demand and supply intersect. A 2-cycle CEE also is a REE, where the price jumps back and forth between two different intersection points of the demand and supply curves. A chaotic CEE is a nonrational equilibrium, where agents believe in a linear stochastic law of motion, while the true law of motion is nonlinear and chaotic. Which of these cases occurs in the cobweb model depends on the implied actual law of motion, i.e., upon the composite mapping $D^{-1}S$ in (4.32), determined by demand and supply curves, and will be discussed below.

4.7.2 Sample autocorrelation (SAC) learning
The notion of CEE involves an AR(1) belief with fixed parameters α and β. Now consider the more flexible situation of *adaptive learning* with agents (slowly) changing their forecasting function over time within the class of AR(1) beliefs, by updating their belief parameters α_t and β_t, as additional observations become available.

There is a large literature on adaptive learning in macroeconomics, see, e.g., Sargent (1993) and Evans and Honkapohja (2001) for extensive discussion and overviews. Adaptive learning is also referred to as *statistical learning*. The underlying assumption is that agents behave like statisticians and estimate the parameters of their forecasting functions from past observations, using standard tools such as (recursive) ordinary least squares. Adaptive learning thus means that parameters in the forecasting function are time varying and are updated by a statistical learning scheme as more observations become available.

A natural and simple learning scheme fitting the framework of CEE is based upon sample average and sample autocorrelation coefficients. For any finite set of observations $\{p_0, p_1, \ldots, p_t\}$ the sample average is

$$\alpha_t = \frac{1}{t+1} \sum_{i=0}^{t} p_i, \qquad t \geq 1, \tag{4.36}$$

and the first-order sample autocorrelation coefficient is

$$\beta_t = \frac{\sum_{i=0}^{t-1}(p_i - \alpha_t)(p_{i+1} - \alpha_t)}{\sum_{i=0}^{t}(p_i - \alpha_t)^2}, \qquad t \geq 1. \tag{4.37}$$

When, in each period, the belief parameters are updated according to (4.36) and (4.37) the (temporary) law of motion (4.32) becomes

$$p_{t+1} = F_{\alpha_t,\beta_t}(p_t) = D^{-1}S(\alpha_t + \beta_t(p_t - \alpha_t)), \qquad t \geq 0. \qquad (4.38)$$

We call the dynamical system (4.36)–(4.38) the actual dynamics with *sample autocorrelation learning* (SAC learning) .[15] The initial state for the system (4.36)–(4.38) can be any triple (p_0, α_0, β_0) with $\beta_0 \in [-1, 1]$.

An important feature of CEE and SAC learning is that both have a simple, intuitive *behavioral interpretation*. In a CEE agents use a linear forecasting rule with two parameters, the mean α and the first-order autocorrelation β. Both can be observed from past observations by inferring the average price level and the (first-order) persistence of the time series. For example, $\beta = 0.5$ means that, on average, prices mean-revert toward their long-run mean by 50 percent. The linear univariate AR(1) rule and the SAC learning process are examples of simple forecasting heuristics that can be used without any knowledge of statistical techniques, simply by observing a time series and roughly "guestimating" its sample average and its first-order persistence coefficient.[16]

4.7.3   Chaotic consistent expectations equilibrium

Which type of CEE exist in the nonlinear cobweb model and to which of them will the SAC learning dynamics converge? Hommes and Sorger (1998) show that in the most relevant case, when demand is decreasing and supply is increasing, the *only* CEE is the RE steady state price p^*. This means that, even when the underlying market equilibrium equations are *not* known, agents will be able to learn and coordinate on the REE price if they learn the correct sample average and sample autocorrelations. Hence, in a nonlinear cobweb economy with monotonic demand and supply, boundedly rational agents should, at least in theory, be able to learn the unique REE from time series observations.[17]

In this section we discuss the possibility of more complicated, 2-cycle and chaotic CEE in the nonlinear cobweb model. Hommes and Sorger (1998) present an example where demand is linear and supply is non-monotonic and piecewise linear. Let demand be given by

$$D(p) = \begin{cases} 9 - p & \text{if } 0 \leq p \leq 9, \\ 0 & \text{if } p > 9, \end{cases} \qquad (4.39)$$

---

[15] Although not identical, SAC learning is closely related to the ordinary least squares (OLS) learning scheme; see the discussion in Hommes and Sorger (1998). A convenient feature of the SAC estimate β_t in (4.37) is that it always lies in the interval $[-1, 1]$, reflecting the fact that the first-order autocorrelation coefficient is not explosive, while the OLS estimate may be outside this interval.

[16] In learning-to-forecast laboratory experiments with human subjects, discussed in Chapter 8, for many subjects forecasting behavior can indeed be described by simple rules, such as a simple AR(1) rule.

[17] For the cobweb model, Bray and Savin (1986) show that OLS learning also converges to the REE steady state, while Arifovic (1994) shows that agents using genetic algorithms can learn the REE steady state. In the laboratory experiments of Hommes et al. (2007), however, prices do not always converge to the REE steady state; see Chapter 8, Section 8.2.

and supply by the piecewise linear curve[18]

$$
S(p) = \begin{cases}
(25/2)p & \text{if } 0 \le p \le 18/25, \\
10 - (25/18)p & \text{if } 18/25 < p \le 18/5, \\
5 + \epsilon[p - (18/5)] & \text{if } p > 18/5.
\end{cases} \tag{4.40}
$$

For these demand and supply curves, the mapping $F = D^{-1}S$ is given by

$$
F(x) = \begin{cases}
9 - (25/2)x & \text{if } 0 \le x \le 18/25, \\
(25/18)x - 1 & \text{if } 18/25 < x \le 18/5, \\
4 - \epsilon[x - (18/5)] & \text{if } 18/5 < x \le 18/5 + 4/\epsilon, \\
0 & \text{if } x > 18/5 + 4/\epsilon.
\end{cases} \tag{4.41}
$$

This example has a chaotic CEE with belief parameters $\alpha = 2$ and $\beta = 4/5$. This follows from the fact that, for $\alpha = 2$ and $\beta = 4/5$, the implied actual law of motion

$$
p_t = F(\alpha + \beta(p_{t-1} - \alpha)) \tag{4.42}
$$

is an upside down asymmetric tent map on the interval $[0,4]$ and with AR(1) coefficient β (see Chapter 2, Section 2.6).

In addition to chaotic CEE, there exist three steady state CEE, corresponding to the three intersection points $p_1^* = 2/3$, $p_2^* = 18/7$, and $p_3^* = (20 + 18\epsilon)/(5 + 5\epsilon)$ of demand D and supply S in (4.39, 4.40) (or equivalently, the fixed points of $F = D^{-1}S$ in (4.41)), and three 2-cycle CEE $\{p_1^*, p_2^*\}$, $\{p_1^*, p_3^*\}$, and $\{p_2^*, p_3^*\}$. To which of these CEE the SAC learning process will converge depends upon the initial states of the learning process.

Figures 4.11 and 4.12 illustrate typical behaviors observed in simulations of the SAC learning dynamics. We observe the following:

- for initial states $p_0 = \alpha_0 \approx p_1^*$, convergence to the steady state CEE p_1^* occurs (Figure 4.11, top panels);
- for initial states $p_0 = \alpha_0 \approx p_2^*$, convergence to the steady state CEE p_1^* occurs after a (possibly long) transient phase with price fluctuations similar to the chaotic CEE with $\alpha = 2$ and $\beta = 4/5$ (Figure 4.11, bottom panels);
- for initial states with $p_2^* < p_0 \ne \alpha_0$ and $\beta_0 = -1$, two possibilities have been observed:

  - first there is a transient phase with prices close to the steady state p_2^*, followed by a second transient phase with price fluctuations similar to the chaotic CEE with $\alpha = 2$ and $\beta = 4/5$, and finally convergence to the steady state CEE p_3^* (Figure 4.12, top panels);
  - there is a transient phase with prices close to the steady state p_2^*, followed by convergence to the 2-cycle CEE $\{p_1^*, p_3^*\}$ (Figure 4.12, bottom panels).

---

[18] See Section 4.8 for an optimal fishery management model of Hommes and Rosser (2001) with a similar, smooth strongly backward-bending supply curve.

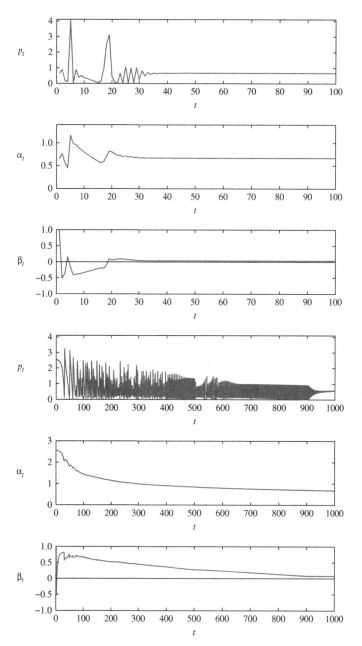

Figure 4.11. SAC learning in the cobweb model with non-monotonic supply curve with parameter $\epsilon = 0$. Three top panels: convergence to steady state CEE p_1^* for initial states $p_0 = 0.65$, $\alpha_0 = 0.65$ and $\beta_0 = 1$; three bottom panels: convergence to steady state CEE p_1^* after long chaotic transient for initial states $p_0 = 2.55$, $\alpha_0 = 2.55$ and $\beta_0 = 1$.

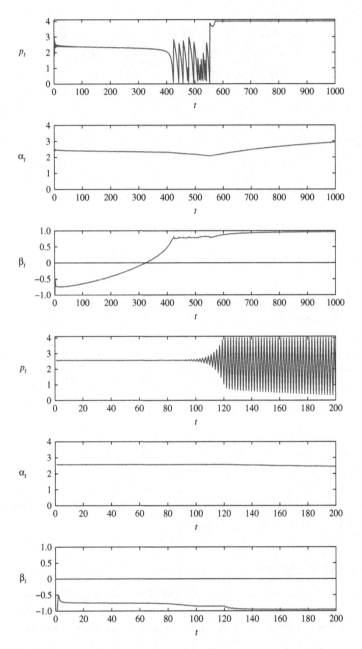

Figure 4.12. SAC learning in the cobweb model with non-monotonic supply curve with parameter $\epsilon = 0$. Three top panels: unstable steady state CEE p_2^*, chaotic transient and convergence to steady state CEE p_3^* for initial states $p_0 = 3$, $\alpha_0 = 2.51$ and $\beta_0 = -1$; three bottom panels: learning to believe in two-cycle CEE $\{(p_1^*, p_3^*)\}$ for initial states $p_0 = 2.6$, $\alpha_0 = 2.57$ and $\beta_0 = -1$.

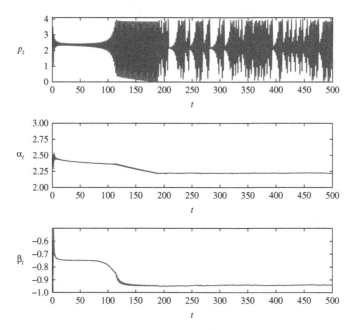

Figure 4.13. Learning to believe in chaos in non-monotonic piecewise linear cobweb model. Belief parameters converge to constant values, i.e., $(\alpha_t, \beta_t) \rightarrow (\alpha^*, \beta^*) \approx (2.22, -0.89)$, but at the same time prices keep fluctuating chaotically with sample mean α^* and sample autocorrelation coefficients $(\beta^*)^k$, as for the corresponding AR(1) model. Initial states are $p_0 = 3.5$, $\alpha_0 = 2.5$ and $\beta_0 = -1$, with $\epsilon = 0.25$.

In the previous example, there exists a chaotic CEE, but it seems to be unstable under SAC learning. By increasing the parameter ϵ an example where a chaotic CEE is stable under SAC learning is obtained, as illustrated in Figure 4.13. The key feature is that learning parameters converge to constants, whereas prices do not converge but fluctuate chaotically, with the correct sample average and sample autocorrelations. We will refer to this situation as *learning to believe in chaos*.

4.8   Learning to believe in chaos

In this section, we discuss another example of a cobweb model with a backward-bending supply curve having its origin in a fishery model. This example serves to illustrate how in a stylized nonlinear environment, "learning to believe in chaos" may arise.[19] That

---

[19] The notion of *learning to believe in chaos* was introduced in Hommes (1998, p. 360), and the first examples were given by Sorger (1998) and Hommes and Sorger (1998). For related work on the instability of OLS learning, see, e.g., Bullard (1994) and Grandmont (1998). Schönhofer (1999) has used the notion of learning to believe in chaos in a somewhat different context, namely when the entire OLS learning process fluctuates chaotically. In Schönhofers' examples belief parameters of the OLS learning scheme do *not* converge, but keep fluctuating chaotically and at the same time, due to inflation, prices diverge to infinity, so that agents are in fact running an OLS regression on a nonstationary time series. Tuinstra and Wagener (2007) consider the same model with heterogeneous expectations, with agents switching between different OLS estimation methods.

is, in an unknown nonlinear environment agents learn the parameters of a simple, linear AR(1) forecasting rule, while the law of motion of the economy is nonlinear and chaotic. In the long run, the sample mean and first-order autocorrelation coefficient of the AR(1) rule correspond to the observed sample mean and first-order autocorrelation of the unknown nonlinear chaotic process. Agents cannot reject the null hypothesis of a stochastic AR(1) process and thus in a linear statistical sense beliefs and realizations coincide.

A chaotic CEE may be seen as an example of an *approximate rational expectations equilibrium* (Sargent, 1999) or a Restricted Perceptions Equilibrium (RPE) (Evans and Honkapohja, 2001, Branch, 2006). Agents have misspecified beliefs, but within the context of their forecasting model they are unable to detect their misspecification, and they learn the optimal misspecified forecasts. We also would like to stress the *behavioral rationality* interpretation of CEE and SAC learning, because the simple AR(1) rule is intuitively plausible and SAC learning may be seen as a learning heuristic through guestimating the sample average and first-order sample autocorrelation.

The Clark–Gordon–Schaefer fishery model

Fisheries have long presented great difficulties of understanding to biologists, economists and policymakers. There have been many collapses of fisheries around the world and serious disputes about their causes. Understanding fisheries involves modeling both the biological aspect as well as the economic aspect and integrating the two in a sound manner, a fusion labeled bioeconomics by Clark (1990).

A number of special peculiarities arise in the case of fisheries. One is that supply curves in fisheries may be backward-bending, one of the few markets where this can happen. Clark (1990) shows that such a backward-bending outcome can occur in an optimally managed fishery without open access, as long as there is a sufficiently high discount rate. We use an optimal control theoretic version of the Gordon–Schaeffer fishery model, following Clark (1990).[20] Let us first introduce some notation. Let x denote population or stock of fish (measured in terms of biomass units), h harvest of fish and $F(x) = \frac{dx}{dt}$ growth of fish population without harvest. The sustained yield, with sustained yield holding if harvesting equals population growth, is given by a logistic function:

$$h = F(x) = rx \left(1 - \frac{x}{k}\right),\tag{4.43}$$

with r the intrinsic growth rate of the fish population and k the ecological carrying capacity for the fishery, that is, the maximum possible steady-state level of x. This yield function admits a level of the stock x at which a maximum sustained yield (MSY) will occur which will be at $x = k/2$.

---

[20] See Hommes and Rosser (2001) for a more detailed discussion and derivation of the model.

The optimal control fish management solution x_δ^* is given by[21]

$$x_\delta^*(p) = \frac{k}{4}\left[1 + \frac{c}{pqk} - \frac{\delta}{r} + \sqrt{\left(1 + \frac{c}{pqk} - \frac{\delta}{r}\right)^2 + \frac{8c\delta}{pqkr}}\,\right]. \qquad (4.44)$$

This optimal solution x_δ^* is usually referred to as the *bioeconomic equilibrium*, and is a function of the discount rate δ, the fish price p, and the other parameters such as the carrying capacity k, the catchability q, the marginal cost of effort c and the growth rate of fish r. The corresponding optimal sustained yield is given by

$$S_\delta(p) = h = F(x_\delta^*(p)). \qquad (4.45)$$

$S_\delta(p)$ in (4.45) is the *discounted equilibrium supply curve*. A straightforward computation shows that, in the limit as the discount rate tends to infinity, the discounted supply curve reduces to the open access supply curve

$$S_\infty(p) = \frac{rc}{pq}\left(1 - \frac{c}{pqk}\right). \qquad (4.46)$$

The reader may easily check that at the minimum price $p_{min} = c/(qk)$ the (discounted) equilibrium supply becomes 0; we will assume that below this minimum price the equilibrium supply equals zero. For consumer demand for fish, we will choose a simple, linear form

$$D(p) = A - Bp. \qquad (4.47)$$

Figure 4.14 shows plots of the equilibrium demand and supply system, for different values of the discount rate δ, with the other parameters of the discounted supply curve fixed at

$$k = 400.000, \quad q = 0.000013, \quad c = 5000 \quad \text{and} \quad r = 0.05,$$

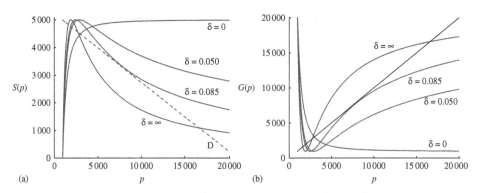

(a)   (b)

Figure 4.14. (a) Demand and discounted equilibrium supply curves S_δ in (4.45), and (b) implied law of motion G_δ in (4.49) under naive expectations for several discount factors δ. As the discount factor δ increases, two additional steady states are created in a tangent bifurcation for $\delta \approx 0.085$.

---

[21] See Clark (1990) for an extensive treatment; see Hommes and Rosser (2001) for a derivation of (4.44).

as suggested for several specific fisheries by Clark (1985, pp. 25, 45 and 48), and the parameters of the demand curve fixed at

$$B = 0.25 \quad \text{and} \quad A = \frac{kr}{4} + \frac{Ac}{qk} = 5240.5.$$

The marginal demand B has been chosen small, to allow for the possibility of multiple equilibria. The constant A has been chosen such that at the minimum price $p_{min} = c/(qk)$ consumer demand would be exactly equal to the maximum sustained yield. This is a convenient way of parameterizing the demand curve in such a way that the price dynamics under adaptive learning will be well defined and remain bounded for all time; other nearby choices of the demand parameters lead to similar results as those presented below.

At the extreme case $\delta = 0$, that is when the sole owner treats the far distant future as equally valuable as today, the supply curve is upward sloping and approaches the maximum sustained yield (MSY), as illustrated in Figure 4.14. For positive values of the discount factor δ, the supply curve (4.45) is backward-bending. This follows easily from the observation that the bionomic equilibrium $x_\delta^*(p)$ is a decreasing function of the fish price p and the population growth map F is non-monotonic. Figure 4.14 shows that, as the discount rate δ increases, the supply curve becomes more backward-bending. The most backwardly bent supply curve corresponds with the totally myopic case of $\delta = \infty$, which corresponds to the open access bionomic equilibrium case and which is associated with overfishing behavior.

Figure 4.14 also contains plots of the (linear) demand curve, illustrating the fact that a backward-bending supply curve together with a sufficiently inelastic demand curve may lead to multiple steady state equilibria even for the static case. In the extreme case $\delta = 0$ there is a unique steady state equilibrium price, whereas at the other extreme $\delta = +\infty$ there are three different steady state equilibria. The two additional steady states are created through a tangent bifurcation at $\delta = \delta^* \approx 0.085$. This shows that in the case of a strongly backward-bending supply curve, increasing demand could lead to a collapse of a fishery and a jump in the equilibrium.

Dynamics under naive expectations
The market equilibrium price at date t is determined by demand and supply, i.e.,

$$D(p_t) = S_\delta(p_t^e), \tag{4.48}$$

with D the consumer demand (4.47) and S_δ the discounted supply curve (4.45). It will be instructive to discuss the case of naive expectations first. Given that producers have naive price expectations, the implied actual law of motion becomes

$$p_t = G_\delta(p_{t-1}) = D^{-1} S_\delta(p_{t-1}) = \frac{A - S_\delta(p_{t-1})}{B}. \tag{4.49}$$

Figure 4.14 shows graphs of the implied actual law of motion G_δ under naive price expectations, for different values of the discount rate. At the extreme case $\delta = 0$, supply is increasing so that the map G_δ is decreasing, and under naive expectations prices diverge from an unstable steady state and converge to a stable 2-cycle. For positive discount rates, beyond a critical price the graph of G_δ is increasing, so that the implied actual law of motion becomes a non-monotonic map. As the discount rate increases, the implied actual law of motion becomes strongly upward sloping for high prices and the price dynamics under naive expectations become more complicated. It is not hard to show by graphical analysis that, e.g., for the tangent bifurcation value $\delta^* \approx 0.085$ the dynamics under naive expectations is (topologically) chaotic. In fact, under naive expectations and with the other parameters fixed as before, complicated dynamics arises for relatively small values of the discount rate, say for $0.02 \le \delta \le 0.085$. For sufficiently high values of the discount rate, e.g., for $\delta \approx 0.1$, naive expectations drives the system to the "bad" stable steady state equilibrium, with a high price and low fish stock.

Let us now discuss what would happen under rational expectations (perfect foresight). Recall that there is a critical parameter value $\delta^* \approx 0.085$ for which a tangent bifurcation occurs at which the number of steady states changes from one, to two steady states at the bifurcation value and three steady states beyond the bifurcation value. For small discount rates $0 \le \delta \le \delta^*$ the unique steady state solution $p_t \equiv p_1^*$, for all t, is the only rational expectations equilibrium (REE). For large discount rates $\delta > \delta^*$, three different steady states p_i, $i = 1, 2$ or 3, coexist, and there are multiple stationary REE. For example, three constant steady state REE exist, where $p_t \equiv p_i$, for all t, and i is fixed at 1, 2 or 3. In addition, however, infinitely many non-constant REE exist, since any solution $p_t = p_i^*$, for all t, and i switching between 1,2 and 3, is a REE. For high discount rates infinitely many REE coexist, for which prices are switching arbitrarily between the three different steady state price levels p_i^*, with the fish stock switching between the corresponding high and low levels.

What happens when agents are boundedly rational and do not have exact knowledge about underlying market equilibrium equations? Would boundedly rational agents be able to learn the "good" steady state equilibrium with low prices and high fish stock? Would boundedly rational agents be able to discover regularities in their forecasting errors under naive expectations and change expectations accordingly? In the simple case of convergence to a stable period-2 price cycle agents should, at least in theory, be able to learn from their systematic forecasting errors and improve their forecasts. But what about the case of chaotic equilibrium price fluctuations? Are boundedly rational agents able to learn in a chaotic environment and detect regularities from time series observations to improve their forecasts?

Figure 4.15 shows a chaotic price series under naive expectations and the corresponding chaotic forecasting errors, for $\delta = 0.02$. It also illustrates the ACF of the forecasting errors, with the first lags being highly significant. In particular, the chaotic forecasting errors have a strongly significant negative first-order autocorrelation coefficient $\rho_1 \approx -0.646$. Boundedly rational agents might try to improve their forecast accuracy by using a simple linear AR(1) rule with a negative first-order coefficient, and try to optimize the forecast parameters by adaptive learning as additional observations become available.

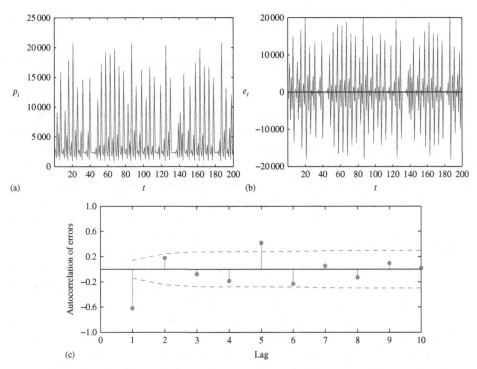

Figure 4.15. (a) Chaotic prices and (b) corresponding forecasting errors under naive expectations for $\delta = 0.02$. The chaotic forecasting errors exhibit significant autocorrelations (c), especially a negative first-order autocorrelation coefficient.

Sample autocorrelation (SAC) learning

When, in each period, the belief parameters are updated according to their sample average (4.36) and their first-order sample autocorrelation in (4.37), the (temporary) law of motion (4.49) becomes

$$p_{t+1} = G_{\alpha_t,\beta_t}(p_t) = G(\alpha_t + \beta_t(p_t - \alpha_t)), \qquad t \geq 0. \tag{4.50}$$

The dynamical system (4.36), (4.37) and (4.50) describes the price dynamics under sample autocorrelation (SAC) learning.

Learning to believe in chaos

In our simulations of the SAC learning process (4.36), (4.37) and (4.50), with $G \equiv G_\delta = D^{-1} S_\delta$ we have observed three typical outcomes:

- convergence to the "good" steady state equilibrium with a low price and a high fish stock;
- convergence to the "bad" steady state equilibrium with a high price and a low fish stock;

- convergence to a chaotic CEE, with prices and fish stock irregularly jumping between low and high values.

Simulations of the SAC learning dynamics suggest that for low values of the discount rate convergence to the "good" equilibrium steady state is the most likely outcome of the SAC learning process, whereas for high values of the discount rate convergence to the "bad" steady state is most likely. For intermediate discount rates the outcome of the learning process is uncertain and in general depends on the initial states, i.e., on the initial belief parameters α_0, β_0 and the initial fish stock x_0. The system may settle down to either the "good" or the "bad" steady state, possibly after a long (chaotic) transient. However, it may also happen that belief parameters α_t and β_t converge to constants α^* and β^* while prices never converge to a steady state (or to a cycle), but keep fluctuating chaotically, as illustrated in Figure 4.16 for $\delta = 0.1$. This situation is referred to as *learning to believe in chaos* and it seems to occur with positive probability, that is, for an open set of initial states (x_0, α_0, β_0). Learning to believe in chaos means that the SAC learning dynamics converges to a chaotic system, when α_t and β_t have converged to constants α^* and β^*, while prices keep fluctuating chaotically. Figure 4.16 shows an example with the learning parameters (α_t, β_t) converging to $(\alpha^*, \beta^*) \approx (5478, -0.90)$ and permanent chaotic price fluctuations with sample average α^* and strongly negative first-order autocorrelation coefficient β^*.

Recall that our boundedly rational agents have no knowledge about underlying market equilibrium equations, and therefore do not know the implied actual law of motion. They only observe time series and use linear statistical techniques. Would they be satisfied with their linear forecasting rules and stick to their AR(1) belief? Figure 4.16e shows that the forecasting errors under SAC learning are uncorrelated. As a next step, one could do statistical hypothesis testing of the linear forecasting rule. Would boundedly rational agents be able to reject their stochastic AR(1) belief or perceived law of motion by linear statistical hypothesis testing? Hommes and Rosser (2001) show that careful statistical hypothesis testing may reject the null of a stochastic AR(1) perceived law of motion.

But now let us investigate the effect of noise upon the learning dynamics. SAC learning with additive dynamic noise is given by (4.36), (4.37), as before, and adding a noise term to the implied actual law of motion, i.e.,

$$p_{t+1} = G_{\delta, \alpha_t, \beta_t}(p_t) = G_\delta(\alpha_t + \beta_t(p_t - \alpha_t)) + \epsilon_t, \qquad t \geq 0, \qquad (4.51)$$

where ϵ_t is an independently identically distributed (IID) random process and $G_\delta = D^{-1}S_\delta$ in (4.49) as before. Notice that the noise is not merely observational noise, but dynamic noise affecting the dynamic law of motion in each period of time. Figure 4.17 illustrates a typical example, with ϵ_t drawn from a uniform distribution over the interval $[-500, +500]$;[22] for this choice of the noise process, the signal-to-noise ratio, as measured by the ratio σ_p/σ_ϵ of standard deviations of the noise-free price series to the

---

[22] The basin of attraction of chaotic motion is bounded above by $p = \bar{p} \approx 9290$. Adding noise to the system may therefore lead to prices diverging away from the chaotic region, and lock into the "bad" steady state equilibrium

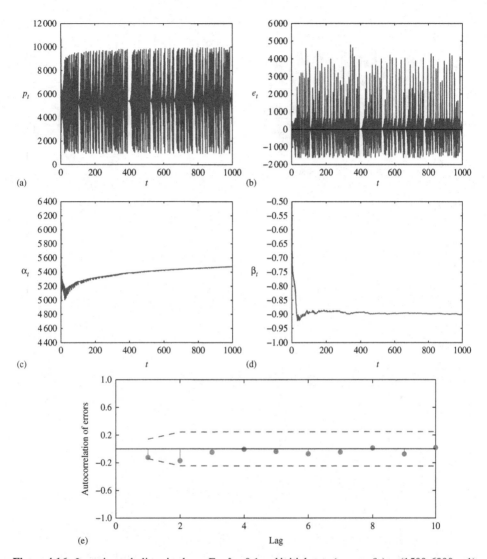

Figure 4.16. Learning to believe in chaos. For $\delta = 0.1$ and initial state $(p_0, \alpha_0, \beta_0) = (1500, 6000, -1)$ in the SAC learning process, prices fluctuate chaotically (a), while belief parameters α_t (c) and β_t (d) converge to constants $\alpha^* \approx 5478$ and $\beta^* \approx -0.90$. Forecasting errors (b) are chaotic unpredictable, with amplitude much smaller than under naive expectations (cf. Figure 4.15). The ACF of forecasting errors (e) shows that errors are uncorrelated.

noise, is about 5. Surprisingly, even in the presence of dynamic noise, the SAC learning dynamics still settles down to a (noisy) chaotic CEE as illustrated in Figure 4.17. The

with a high price. In the simulations with noise we have therefore chosen a bounded noise process and imposed an upper bound on (noisy) prices of 10 000. This upper bound for prices is not inconsistent with the AR(1) forecasting rule, because it always predicts a price well below this upper bound.

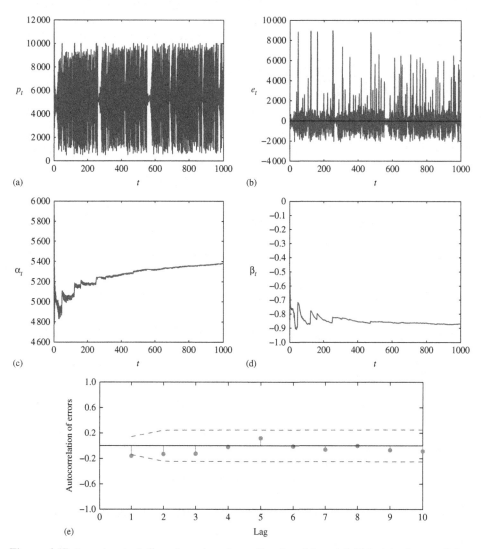

Figure 4.17. Learning to believe in noisy chaos. For $\delta = 0.1$ and initial state $(p_0, \alpha_0, \beta_0) = (1500, 6000, -1)$. In the presence of noise, SAC learning converges to a (noisy) chaotic CEE, with chaotic price fluctuations (a) and at the same time convergence of the belief parameters α_t (c) and β_t (d). Forecasting errors (b) are (noisy) chaotic and seemingly unpredictable. The ACF of forecasting errors (e) shows that errors are uncorrelated. The null hypothesis that prices follow an AR(1) processes cannot be rejected.

noisy chaotic series has an autocorrelation pattern very similar to that of an AR(1) process with strongly negative first-order autocorrelation. Hommes and Rosser (2001) show that in the presence of noise, the null hypothesis that prices follow a stochastic AR(1) process cannot be rejected, not even at the 10% level. *Learning to believe in noisy chaos* is thus a possibility which is not rejected by linear statistical theory.

A chaotic CEE may be seen as an *approximate rational expectations equilibrium,* where agents use an optimal linear predictor to forecast an unknown nonlinear actual law of motion. We have shown that such equilibria are persistent with respect to dynamic noise. In fact, the presence of noise may increase the probability of convergence to such learning equilibria. Agents are using a simple, but misspecified model to forecast an unknown, complicated actual law of motion. Without noise, boundedly rational agents using time series analysis might be able to detect the misspecification and improve their forecast model. In the presence of dynamic noise, however, misspecification becomes harder to detect and boundedly rational agents using linear statistical techniques can do no better than stick to their optimal, simple linear model of the world. Moreover, the SAC learning process has an intuitive behavioral interpretation, so that this equilibrium qualifies as behaviorally rational.

5 The cobweb model with heterogeneous expectations

In the previous chapter we have focused on a representative behaviorally rational agent in the nonlinear cobweb model. But why would all agents have the same individual expectations? Agents are heterogeneous and laboratory experiments have shown that, even when facing the same information, individuals may disagree and take different strategic consumption, production or investment decisions. In a complex market environment it seems more appropriate to model agents as *boundedly rational* and *heterogeneous*, using different types of strategies. In this chapter, therefore, we study the cobweb model with heterogeneous expectations. The cobweb model provides a simple framework to study the *interactions of heterogeneous expectation rules* and the aggregate behavior resulting from these interactions.

Models with heterogeneous agents are becoming increasingly popular. In particular, in finance models with fundamentalists and chartists have received much attention. Examples include Zeeman (1974), Frankel and Froot (1986), Day and Huang (1990), DeLong et al. (1990a and b), Kirman (1991), Lux (1995), Brock and Hommes (1998) and DeGrauwe and Grimaldi (2006); see the reviews of Hommes (2006) and LeBaron (2006) with many more references.

While heterogeneity in expectations seems plausible in complex systems, it also raises an immediate problem: which of the infinitely many possible rules will boundedly rational agents choose? How will individual heterogeneous agents learn and adapt their behavior as aggregate market behavior evolves?

The chapter starts with a general framework for heterogeneous expectations proposed in Brock and Hommes (1997a), where agents switch between different expectations rules based upon their relative performance. The class of forecasting rules is thus disciplined by *evolutionary selection* and *reinforcement learning*.

A general theme of this chapter is the interaction between rules with different degrees of sophistication and the resulting aggregate behavior. Simple rules, such as naive or adaptive expectations, are freely available, but more sophisticated rules such as fundamental rules or rational expectations require information-gathering costs. A general result is that evolutionary selection between freely available forecasting heuristics and costly sophisticated rules leads to complicated dynamical behavior. In fact, evolutionary interaction between cheap free riding and costly sophisticated prediction is closely linked to Poincaré's homoclinic orbits and its associated complicated, chaotic behavior.

We discuss a number of stylized 2-type examples, starting with the case of costly rational versus freely available naive expectations in Section 5.2. This case may be seen as a stylized example, with rational expectations representing the most sophisticated strategy that can only be obtained at some costs and naive expectations representing the simplest forecasting heuristic. The evolutionary interaction between these strategies may lead to very complicated aggregate price behavior. Section 5.3 considers the interaction of different linear forecasting heuristics, with fundamentalists versus naive expectations and a contrarian strategy versus naive expectations as simple 2-type examples. Finally, in Section 5.4, we combine evolutionary selection and reinforcement learning with adaptive learning, and study the 2-type example with costly sample autocorrelation learning versus freely available naive expectations. This example exhibits very complicated dynamical behavior and shows how an increase of *individual behavioral rationality* leads to more complex aggregate behavior in expectations feedback systems.

5.1 Heterogeneous expectations

A general idea, put forward in Brock and Hommes (1997a), is that agents choose between different types of expectations rules varying in the degree of rationality, ranging from very simple to highly sophisticated. More sophisticated rules require more effort, for example in terms of information gathering, and are therefore costly compared to simple, rule of thumb forecasting rules, that are freely available to everyone. Agents switch between different expectations rules driven by *evolutionary selection* or *reinforcement learning* according to the principle that agents tend to switch to more successful rules. Evolutionary selection and reinforcement learning are therefore the main forces to discipline a potentially large population of forecasting strategies.

Recall that the cobweb model describes price fluctuations in an independent market for a non-storable consumption good that takes one time period to produce. As before, we assume that demand is linearly decreasing and given by

$$D(p_t) = a - dp_t, \qquad d > 0. \tag{5.1}$$

In a heterogeneous expectations cobweb framework, producers can choose between different forecasting rules $p_{ht}^e = f_h(\cdot)$, where $f_h(\cdot)$, $1 \le h \le H$, is some forecasting function based upon past information. The fractions n_{ht} of producers using predictor f_h at date t, will be updated over time based upon a publicly available evolutionary fitness or performance measure, for example given by realized net profits, associated to each predictor.

Supply of producer type h is a function of producer's expected price, p_{ht}^e, derived from expected profit maximization:

$$S(p_{ht}^e) = \mathrm{argmax}_{q_t} \{p_{ht}^e q_t - c(q_t)\} = (c')^{-1}(p_{ht}^e), \qquad (5.2)$$

where $c(\cdot)$ is the producer's cost function. To keep the model as simple as possible, in this chapter the cost function is assumed to be quadratic, $c(q) = q^2/(2s)$, for all producer types, so that supply is linear:

$$S(p_{ht}^e) = s p_{ht}^e, \qquad s > 0. \qquad (5.3)$$

Market equilibrium in the cobweb model with heterogeneous expectations is determined by

$$D(p_t) = \sum_{h=1}^{H} n_{ht} S(p_{h,t}^e), \qquad (5.4)$$

where p_{ht}^e, $1 \le h \le H$, represents the price forecast of producer type h and n_{ht} is the (time-varying) fraction of agents using strategy h at the beginning of period t. To keep the model as simple as possible, throughout this chapter we assume linear demand and supply, so that heterogeneous expectations market equilibrium simplifies to

$$a - d p_t = \sum_{h=1}^{H} n_{ht} s p_{ht}^e. \qquad (5.5)$$

The *only* nonlinearity in (5.5) arises through the time-varying fractions n_{ht} measuring the impact of strategy h at time t.[1] In fact, restricting the forecasting rules to *linear* rules, the dynamic system (5.5) is a linear model with time-varying coefficients determined by the impact of each of the rules at date t.

5.1.1 Evolutionary selection and reinforcement learning

The evolutionary part of the model describes how beliefs are updated over time, that is, how the fractions n_{ht} of trader types evolve over time. Fractions are updated according to an *evolutionary fitness* or *performance measure*. Rules with better performance will attract more followers. The fitness measures of all forecasting strategies are publicly available, but subject to noise. Fitness is derived from a random utility model and given by

$$\tilde{U}_{ht} = U_{ht} + \epsilon_{iht}, \qquad (5.6)$$

where U_{ht} is the *deterministic part* of the fitness measure and the noise term ϵ_{iht} represents individual agents' errors. Assuming that the noise ϵ_{iht} is IID across individual

---

[1] Goeree and Hommes (2000) show that, for nonlinear (but monotonic) demand and supply curves in a heterogeneous expectations cobweb model with rational versus naive expectations, the dynamical behavior is very similar.

agents and across types $h = 1, ..., H$ and drawn from a double exponential distribution, in the limit as the number of agents goes to infinity, the probability that an agent chooses strategy h is given by the well-known *discrete choice model* with multinomial logit probabilities (or "Gibbs" probabilities)[2]

$$n_{ht} = \frac{e^{\beta U_{h,t-1}}}{Z_{t-1}}, \qquad Z_{t-1} = \sum_{h=1}^{H} e^{\beta U_{h,t-1}}, \tag{5.7}$$

where Z_{t-1} is a normalization factor, so that the fractions n_{ht} add up to 1. The crucial feature of (5.7) is that the higher the fitness of trading strategy h, the more traders will select strategy h. The parameter β in (5.7) is called the *intensity of choice*, measuring how sensitive the mass of traders is to selecting the optimal prediction strategy. The intensity of choice β is inversely related to the variance of the noise terms ϵ_{iht}. One extreme case, $\beta = 0$, corresponds to infinite variance noise, so that differences in fitness cannot be observed and all fractions (5.7) will be fixed over time and equal to $1/H$. The other extreme case, $\beta = +\infty$, corresponds to the case without noise, so that the deterministic part of the fitness can be observed perfectly and in each period, *all* traders choose the optimal forecast. An increase in the intensity of choice β represents an increase in the degree of rationality w.r.t. evolutionary selection of trading strategies.

The timing of the coupling between the market equilibrium equation (5.4) or (5.5) and the evolutionary updating of strategies (5.7) is important. The market equilibrium price p_t in (5.4) depends upon the fractions n_{ht} of the different strategies at the beginning of period t. The notation in (5.7) stresses that these fractions n_{ht} depend upon *past* fitness $U_{h,t-1}$, which in turn depends upon *observable* information, such as past prices $p_{t-1}, p_{t-2}, p_{t-3}, ...$ (see below). After the equilibrium price p_t has been determined, it will be used in the evolutionary updating of beliefs and determining the new fractions $n_{h,t+1}$. These new fractions $n_{h,t+1}$ will then determine a new equilibrium price p_{t+1}, and so on. We will refer to the dynamical system (5.4–5.7) as an *adaptive belief system* (ABS) describing how market equilibrium prices and fractions of different trading strategies coevolve over time.[3]

A natural candidate for evolutionary fitness is a weighted average of *realized profits*. For the cobweb model with a linear supply curve (5.3) (or equivalently a quadratic cost function) realized profit by forecasting strategy h in period t is given by

$$\pi_{ht} = p_t S(p_{ht}^e) - c(S(p_{ht}^e)) = \frac{s}{2} p_{ht}^e (2p_t - p_{ht}^e). \tag{5.8}$$

---

[2] See Manski and McFadden (1981) and Anderson et al. (1993) for an extensive treatment of discrete choice models and their applications in economics.

[3] The notion of adaptive belief system was introduced in Brock and Hommes (1998), who applied the evolutionary selection framework to an asset pricing model with heterogeneous beliefs; Brock and Hommes (1997a) used the notion of *adaptive rational equilibrium dynamics* (ARED) for the dynamics in the heterogeneous expectations cobweb model.

The *fitness measure* or *performance measure* for strategy h is a weighted average of realized profits given by

$$U_{ht} = wU_{h,t-1} + (1-w)\pi_{h,t} - C_h, \tag{5.9}$$

where $0 \le w \le 1$ is a *memory* parameter and C_h represents the average costs per time period for obtaining predictor h. For a simple habitual rule of thumb predictor, such as naive or adaptive expectations, these costs C_h will be zero, whereas for more sophisticated predictors such as fundamentalists beliefs, based on fundamental analysis, or rational expectations, costs C_h may be positive. The memory parameter w measures how fast past realized fitness is discounted for strategy selection.[4]

The strategy-switching model (5.7) assumes *synchronous* updating of strategies, that is, in each period *all* agents update their strategies. In the more general case of *asynchronous updating* in each period only a fraction $1 - \delta$ of agents, distributed randomly among agents of both types and independently across time, are assumed to reconsider their strategy on the basis of the most recent information available. The remaining fraction δ stick to their current strategy and therefore, asynchronous updating represents the realistic feature of inertia in strategy decisions. The corresponding dynamics of the fractions is given by a modified version of the discrete choice, logit probabilities[5]:

$$n_{jt} = (1-\delta)\frac{e^{\beta U_{j,t-1}}}{Z_{t-1}} + \delta n_{j,t-1}, \tag{5.10}$$

where $Z_{t-1} = \sum_h e^{\beta U_{h,t-1}}$ is a normalization factor as before. For $\delta = 0$, we are back in the case of synchronous updating, where for a high value of the intensity of choice almost all agents switch to the best strategy. For $\delta > 0$ strategy updating is more gradual. For $\beta = 0$ all fractions become equal to $1/H$, whereas for the other extreme $\beta = \infty$, in each period *all* producers who update in that period (i.e., a fraction $1 - \delta$) switch to the optimal predictor. Hence, the higher the intensity of choice, the more rational agents are in the sense that they switch more quickly to the best strategy in terms of past performance.

5.2 Rational versus naive expectations

In this section we discuss a simple but typical example of the cobweb model with two forecasting strategies, as introduced in Brock and Hommes (1997a): rational versus naive expectations. Agents can either buy the most sophisticated forecast, rational expectations (perfect foresight), at positive per period information costs $C \ge 0$, or freely obtain the simple, naive forecast that simply uses the last observed price. The

---

[4] Brock and Hommes (1997a, 1998) used a slightly different fitness measure, namely $U_{ht} = wU_{h,t-1} + \pi_{h,t} - C_h$, so that the case $w = 1$ corresponds to accumulated profits or wealth; see Hommes et al. (2012) for an extensive discussion and an analysis of how memory affects the (in)stability of evolutionary selection.

[5] Asynchronous updating in the multinomial logit model has been studied by Diks and van der Weide (2005) and Hommes, Huang and Wang (2005a).

two forecasting rules are given by[6]

$$p_{1t}^e = p_t, \tag{5.11}$$

$$p_{2t}^e = p_{t-1}. \tag{5.12}$$

Recall that, if all producers have rational expectations or perfect foresight the price dynamics in the cobweb model becomes extremely simple: $p_t = p^*$ in all periods, where p^* is the (unique) price corresponding to the intersection of demand and supply (see Chapter 4, Section 4.3). If, on the other hand, all producers use the naive predictor, the price dynamics is given by $p_t = D^{-1}(S(p_{t-1}))$ (see Chapter 4, Section 4.2). If demand D is decreasing and supply S is increasing, price dynamics in the cobweb model with naive expectations is simple. If $-1 < S'(p^*)/D'(p^*) < 0$ prices converge to the stable steady state p^*; otherwise, prices diverge away from the steady state and either converge to a (stable) 2-cycle or exhibit unbounded up and down oscillations.

Market equilibrium in the cobweb model with rational versus naive expectations and linear demand and supply, as in (5.1) and (5.3), is given by

$$a - dp_t = n_t^R s p_t + n_t^N s p_{t-1}, \tag{5.13}$$

where n_t^R and n_t^N denote the fractions of producers using the rational respectively naive predictor, at the beginning of period t. Producers using the rational expectations predictor have perfect foresight. Therefore rational agents must have perfect knowledge about the market equilibrium equation (5.13). In particular, rational agents are aware that there are nonrational agents in the market and they have perfect knowledge about the beliefs of all other (nonrational) agents and know exactly how many agents are using nonrational forecasting strategies. In a heterogeneous world perfect rationality is therefore even more demanding than in a homogeneous world. When all agents are the same, rationality means common knowledge of rationality and the assumptions that all agents act rationally. In a heterogeneous world, rational agents must perfectly forecast the behavior of *all* other types of nonrational agents. Assuming that a fraction of agents has rational expectations in a real, heterogeneous market therefore seems highly unrealistic. Nevertheless from an economic theory viewpoint it is appealing to study the interactions between rational and nonrational individual strategies and how this interaction affects aggregate market behavior. Our simple 2-type example represents interaction of the most sophisticated, perfectly rational forecasting strategy with perhaps the simplest, naive forecasting strategy. Rationality, however, is not for free, and the difference C between the per period information costs for rational and naive expectations represents an extra effort producers incur in order to acquire this perfect knowledge. The market clearing equation (5.13) can be solved explicitly for the

---

[6] Lasselle et al. (2005) provides an example with rational versus adaptive expectations, while Goldbaum (2005) and Dudek (2010) consider rational selection over expectations rules when information is costly.

equilibrium price:

$$p_t = \frac{a - n_t^N s p_{t-1}}{d + n_t^R s}. \tag{5.14}$$

The cobweb model with rational versus naive expectations may be seen as an analytically tractable, stylized two-predictor model in which rational expectations represents a costly sophisticated and stabilizing predictor, and naive expectations represent a cheap "forecasting heuristic" but potentially destabilizing prediction strategy. It is interesting to note that other two-predictor cases, such as fundamentalists (expecting prices to return to the rational expectations fundamental steady state price p^*) versus naive expectations yield similar results (see Subsection 5.3.1).

To complete the model, we have to specify how the fractions of traders using rational respectively naive expectations evolve over time. As discussed above, these fractions are updated according to a publicly available "performance" or "fitness" measure associated to each predictor. Here, we take the most recent realized net profit as the performance measure for predictor selection.[7] For the rational expectations forecasting strategy (5.11) and linear supply (5.3), realized profit in period t is given by

$$\pi_t^R = p_t S(p_t) - c(S(p_t)) = \frac{s}{2} p_t^2. \tag{5.15}$$

The *net* realized profit for rational expectations is thus given by $\pi_t^R - C$, where C is the per period information cost that has to be paid for obtaining the perfect forecast. For the naive predictor (5.12) and linear supply (5.3) the realized net profit in period t is given by

$$\pi_t^N = p_t S(p_{t-1}) - c(S(p_{t-1})) = \frac{s}{2} p_{t-1}(2p_t - p_{t-1}). \tag{5.16}$$

In the model with synchronous updating (i.e., $\delta = 0$ in 5.10) and two types, the fractions are determined by the logit discrete choice model probabilities (5.7). The fraction of agents using the rational expectations predictor in period t equals

$$n_t^R = \frac{e^{\beta(\pi_{t-1}^R - C)}}{e^{\beta(\pi_{t-1}^R - C)} + e^{\beta \pi_{t-1}^N}}, \tag{5.17}$$

and the fraction of agents choosing the naive predictor in period t is

$$n_t^N = 1 - n_t^R. \tag{5.18}$$

The key feature of this evolutionary predictor selection is that agents are boundedly rational, in the sense that most agents use the predictor that has higher fitness. Indeed, from (5.17–5.18) we have $n_t^R > n_t^N$ whenever $\pi_{t-1}^R - C > \pi_{t-1}^N$. Hence, the optimal

---

[7] The case where the performance measure is realized net profit in the most recent past period, leads to a two-dimensional dynamic system. The more general case, with a weighted sum of past net realized profits as the fitness measure, leads to a higher-dimensional system. In this more general higher-dimensional case, however, numerical simulations suggest similar dynamical behavior.

predictor is chosen with higher probability. The *intensity of choice* β measures how fast producers switch to the best prediction strategies. In the extreme case $\beta = 0$ both fractions are fixed over time and equal to $1/2$. In the other extreme case $\beta = \infty$ – the *neoclassical limit* in which agents are unboundedly rational – *all* producers choose the optimal predictor in each period. Hence, the higher the intensity of choice the more rational, as measured by evolutionary fitness, agents are in choosing their prediction strategies. The neoclassical limit case $\beta = \infty$ will play an important role in the analysis of the dynamical behavior.

We recall the timing of predictor selection in (5.17). In (5.14) the current fractions n_t^R and n_t^N determine the new equilibrium price p_t. This new equilibrium price p_t is used in the fitness measures (5.15) and (5.16) for predictor choice and the new fractions n_{t+1}^R and n_{t+1}^N are updated according to (5.17) and (5.18). These new fractions then determine the next equilibrium price p_{t+1}, etc. In the ABS equilibrium prices and fractions of strategies thus coevolve over time.

It will be convenient to define the difference m_t of the two fractions:

$$m_t \equiv n_t^R - n_t^N. \tag{5.19}$$

$m_t = -1$ corresponds to all producers being naive, whereas $m_t = +1$ means that all producers have rational expectations in period t. The evolution of the equilibrium price, p_t, and the difference of fractions, m_t, is summarized in the following two-dimensional, nonlinear dynamical system

$$p_t = \frac{a - n_t^N s p_{t-1}}{d + n_t^R s} = \frac{2a - (1 - m_t) s p_{t-1}}{2d + (1 + m_t) s}, \tag{5.20}$$

$$m_{t+1} = \tanh\left(\frac{\beta}{2}\left(\pi_t^R - \pi_t^N - C\right)\right). \tag{5.21}$$

For a linear supply curve, using (5.15) and (5.16), the difference in realized profits between rational and naive agents simplifies to

$$\pi_t^R - \pi_t^N = \frac{s}{2}(p_t - p_{t-1})^2, \tag{5.22}$$

that is, the difference in realized profits is proportional to the squared prediction error of the naive forecast. In the case of linear demand and supply the system becomes[8]

$$p_t = \frac{2a - (1 - m_t) s p_{t-1}}{2d + (1 + m_t) s}, \tag{5.23}$$

$$m_{t+1} = \tanh\left(\frac{\beta}{2}\left[\frac{s}{2}(p_t - p_{t-1})^2 - C\right]\right). \tag{5.24}$$

---

[8] Eqs. (5.20, 5.21) represent a 2-D system $(p_t, m_{t+1}) = F(p_{t-1}, m_t)$. Brock and Hommes (1997a) use a slightly different notation $\tilde{m}_t = m_{t+1}$ and work with the 2-D system $(p_t, \tilde{m}_t) = F(p_{t-1}, \tilde{m}_{t-1})$. Throughout this book we consistently use the same notation in Chapter 5 for the cobweb model and Chapter 6 for the asset pricing model, with fractions n_{ht} depending upon past fitness $U_{h,t-1}$ (as in Eq. 5.7) and fitness $U_{h,t-1}$ depending upon prices $p_{t-1}, p_{t-2}, \cdots$, etc.

The reader may easily verify that the model has a unique steady state $(p^*, m^*) = (a/(d+s), \tanh(-\beta C/2))$. Notice that $p^* = a/(d+s)$ is exactly the rational expectations price where demand and supply intersect. It will be convenient to rewrite (5.23–5.24) in *deviations from the steady state* price, $x_t = p_t - p^*$, yielding[9]

$$x_t = \frac{-(1-m_t)s x_{t-1}}{2d + (1+m_t)s}, \tag{5.25}$$

$$m_{t+1} = \tanh(\frac{\beta}{2}[\frac{s}{2}(x_t - x_{t-1})^2 - C]). \tag{5.26}$$

In the sequel we use the shorthand notation $(x_t, m_{t+1}) = F_\beta(x_{t-1}, m_t)$ for the model (5.25–5.26). We are especially interested in how the dynamics depends upon the "degree of rationality," that is, how the dynamics changes as the intensity of choice β to switch forecasting strategies, increases.

5.2.1   Local (in)stability of the steady state

We will now discuss the dynamical behavior of prices and fractions of rational and naive agents. We start with the stability conditions for the steady state. Recall that the model has a unique steady state $(p^*, m^*) = (a/(d+s), \tanh(-\beta C/2))$, with $p^* = a/(d+s)$ the price where demand and supply intersect. For $C = 0$, i.e., when there are no costs for rational expectations, $m^* = 0$, so that at the steady state the fractions of the two types are equal. Half of the population uses rational and the other half naive expectations, and at the steady state both rules yield identical forecasts $p_1^e = p_2^e = p^*$. In contrast, when information costs for rational expectations are strictly positive, i.e., for $C > 0$, we have $m^* < 0$, so that at the steady state most agents adopt the naive forecasting rule. This is intuitively clear, because at the steady state both forecasting rules yield identical forecasts and most agents then prefer the cheap, naive forecast.

The stability properties of the steady state depend on the slopes of supply and demand at the steady state price p^*. A straightforward computation shows that the eigenvalues of the Jacobian matrix of (5.23–5.24) at the steady state are $\lambda_1 = 0$, and

$$\lambda_2 = \frac{(1-m^*) S'(p^*)}{2 D'(p^*) - (1+m^*) S'(p^*)} = \frac{-(1-m^*)s}{2d + (1+m^*)s} < 0. \tag{5.27}$$

Since $|m^*| \leq 1$, $S'(p^*)/D'(p^*) = -s/d < \lambda_2 < 0$. Hence, if the traditional cobweb stability condition $|S'(p^*)/D'(p^*)| = |s/d| < 1$ holds, implying that the model is stable under naive expectations, then in the cobweb model with rational versus naive expectations and linear demand and supply, the steady state is (globally) stable, for all β. Prices always converge to p^*, and the difference of fractions converges to m^*. To allow for the possibility of an unstable steady state and endogenous price fluctuations in the heterogeneous expectations model, from now on we assume:

---

[9] Notice that (5.25) is equivalent to fixing $a = 0$ in (5.23), so that $p^* = 0$. In fact, working in deviations from the steady state just means choosing the steady state price as the origin.

Assumption U. *The market is locally unstable when all producers are naive, that is,* $S'(p^*)/D'(p^*) = -s/d < -1.$

The stability properties of the steady state are summarized as follows:

Proposition 5.2.1. *Under assumption U, the cobweb model with rational versus naive expectations satisfies:*

(i) *when there are no information costs, i.e., $C = 0$, the steady state is globally stable for all β,*

(ii) *when information costs are strictly positive ($C > 0$), there exists a critical value β_1 such that the steady state is (globally) stable for $0 \leq \beta < \beta_1$ and unstable for $\beta > \beta_1$. At $\beta = \beta_1$ the second eigenvalue satisfies $\lambda_2 = -1$, and F_β in (5.23–5.24) exhibits a period-doubling bifurcation.*

The intuition behind the (local) stability of the steady state is easily explained. For $C = 0$, the steady state difference in fractions $m^* = 0$ and the eigenvalue in (5.27) satisfies $-1 < \lambda_2 < 0$, implying that the steady state is locally stable. Global stability follows by observing that, for $C = 0$ we have $m_t \geq 0$, for all $t \geq 1$, and then using (5.25), x_t must converge to 0, or equivalently, prices always converge to their steady state value and consequently the difference in fractions m_t converges to 0. The second part of the proposition follows by observing from (5.27) that the eigenvalue $\lambda_2 = -1$, when the steady state difference in fractions $m^* = \bar{m} = -d/s$. Assumption U implies that $-1 < \bar{m} = -d/s < 0$. As the intensity of choice β increases from 0 to $+\infty$ the steady state difference in fractions m^* decreases from 0 to -1 and, for some critical value $\beta = \beta_1$ we have $m^* = \bar{m}$, an eigenvalue $\lambda_2 = -1$ and the corresponding period-doubling bifurcation.[10]

5.2.2 A rational route to randomness

According to Proposition 5.2.1, when information costs C for rational expectations are strictly positive, the steady state $(p^*, m^*) = (p^*, \tanh(-\beta C/2))$ becomes unstable as the intensity of choice β increases. In the following subsections we investigate the dynamics for large values of the intensity of choice. A convenient feature of the multinomial logit model is that the neoclassical limit, that is, the case $\beta = \infty$, can be easily analyzed and such an analysis provides important economic intuition about the dynamics for large values of the intensity of choice.

For $\beta = \infty$ and $C > 0$, the steady state difference in fractions $m^* = \tanh(-\beta C/2) = -1$, that is, at the steady state all agents use the cheap, naive forecasting rule. Furthermore, for $\beta = \infty$ in each period *all* agents choose the optimal predictor, that is, in each period $t \geq 1$ either all agents are rational or all agents are naive. In fact, for $\beta = \infty$ the

---

[10] See Brock and Hommes (1997a, p. 1090) for the proof that a (stable) 2-cycle is created at $\beta = \beta_1$.

switching between forecasting strategies (5.24) simplifies to

$$m_{t+1} = \begin{cases} +1 & \text{if } \pi_t^R - \pi_t^N = \dfrac{s}{2}(p_t - p_{t-1})^2 > C, \\[2mm] -1 & \text{if } \pi_t^R - \pi_t^N = \dfrac{s}{2}(p_t - p_{t-1})^2 \le C. \end{cases} \qquad (5.28)$$

Stated differently, as long as the squared prediction error from naive expectations is sufficiently small compared to the per period information costs for rational expectations, i.e., as long as $(p_t - p_{t-1})^2 \le 2C/s$, all agents stick to the simple, cheap forecasting strategy. As long as all agents are naive, the cobweb price dynamics is governed by a linear unstable oscillation around the steady state price p^*, and prices diverge from their steady state value oscillating with increasing amplitude. The squared forecasting error from naive expectations will therefore increase, and at some point the errors must exceed the critical level $2C/s$, and all agents will then switch to rational expectations. When all producers become rational in period t, next period's price $p_{t+1} = p^*$ and the price immediately jumps back to the steady state price. These simple observations prove that, when information gathering is costly the neoclassical limiting case has homoclinic orbits:

Proposition 5.2.2. *Consider the neoclassical limit system with an infinite intensity of choice, $\beta = \infty$, and positive information cost $C > 0$. All time paths in the system (5.23–5.24) converge to the steady state $S = (p^*, -1)$. In particular, under assumption U, the steady state is a locally unstable saddle point, but at the same time it is globally stable. Consequently the system has homoclinic orbits.*

Now suppose we add a small amount of noise to the neoclassical limit system, by adding a small random shock (e.g., a demand shock) in each period to the equilibrium pricing equation (5.23). Alternatively, suppose the intensity of choice is finite, but large. In both scenarios, essentially the same story as above applies, with the only difference that when (almost) all agents switch to rational expectations the system will not be driven exactly onto the steady state, but only very close to it. With prices close to the steady state value, almost all agents will switch back to the cheap, naive forecasting rule and prices will start to oscillate and diverge, and the story repeats. The noisy neoclassical limit as well as the case with a high but finite intensity of choice are thus characterized by an irregular switching between an unstable phase in which almost all agents are naive and prices diverge from the steady state, and a stable phase in which almost all agents switch to become rational and prices return close to the steady state.

Brock and Hommes (1997a) have shown that for high values of the intensity of choice, the dynamical behavior of the system becomes chaotic with prices and fractions moving on a strange attractor. Figure 5.1 shows an example of a strange attractor, with corresponding chaotic time series of prices p_t and fractions n_t^R of rational producers. Numerical simulations suggest that for (almost) all initial states (p_0, m_0) the orbit converges to this strange attractor.

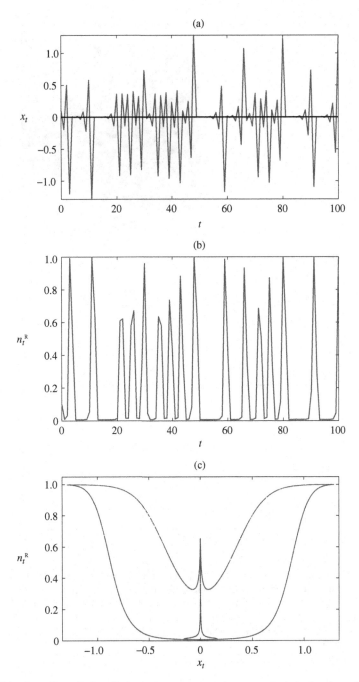

Figure 5.1. Complicated, chaotic dynamics on a strange attractor in the cobweb model with rational versus naive expectations when the intensity of choice β is high. (a) Chaotic time series of prices (in deviations from the steady state); (b) corresponding chaotic time series of fractions of rational agents; and (c) corresponding strange attractor in the (p, n^R)-phase space. Parameters are $\beta = 5$, $a = 0, d = 0.5, s = 1.35$ and $C = 1$.

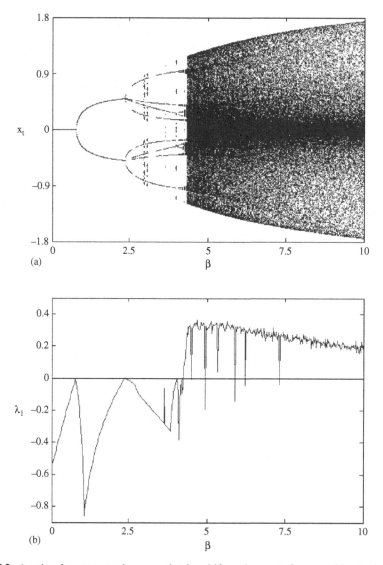

Figure 5.2. A rational route to randomness, that is, a bifurcation route from a stable steady state for small values of the intensity of choice β to chaotic price fluctuations for high values of the intensity of choice. (a) Bifurcation diagram w.r.t. the intensity of choice. The first bifurcation (for $\beta \approx 0.77$) is a period-doubling bifurcation. After the second bifurcation two stable 4-cycles coexist. Largest Lyapunov exponent as a function of the intensity of choice. Parameters are $a = 0$, $d = 0.5$, $s = 1.35$ and $C = 1$, $0 \leq \beta \leq 10$.

Figure 5.2 illustrates the *rational route to randomness*, that is, the bifurcation route from a stable steady state for low values of the intensity of choice to the complicated, chaotic dynamical behavior for high values of the intensity of choice. The primary bifurcation toward instability is a period-doubling bifurcation for $\beta \approx 0.77$, in which the steady state becomes unstable and a stable 2-cycle is created. As the intensity of choice increases, subsequent bifurcations occur and the dynamical behavior becomes more and more complicated. The plot of the largest Lyapunov exponent in Figure 5.2 shows that for large values of the intensity of choice the largest Lyapunov exponent becomes positive and therefore the dynamics becomes chaotic.

For a high intensity of choice price fluctuations are characterized by an irregular switching between a stable phase, with prices close to the steady state, and an unstable phase with fluctuating prices, as illustrated in Figure 5.1. There is a simple economic intuition explaining the switching behavior when the intensity of choice is large. Suppose we take an initial state close to the (locally unstable) steady state. Most agents will use the cheap, naive forecasting rule, because it does not pay to buy a costly, sophisticated forecasting rule that yields an almost identical forecast. With most agents using the cheap, naive predictor, prices diverge from the steady state and start oscillating, forecasting errors of the naive predictor, increase and consequently net realized profits from the naive predictor decrease. At some point these errors become so large that it becomes profitable to buy the rational expectations forecast instead, and when the intensity of choice to switch predictors is high, most agents will then switch to rational expectations. When almost all agents switch to rational expectations, prices are driven back close to the steady state, and the story then repeats. Irregular, chaotic price fluctuations thus result from a (boundedly) rational choice between cheap "free riding" and costly sophisticated prediction. In fact, the above economic mechanism already suggests that, for a large intensity of choice, the cobweb model with rational versus naive expectations will be close to a homoclinic orbit associated to the unstable, saddle point steady state.

5.2.3 Saddle point instability and homoclinic orbits

A key feature of chaotic dynamical behavior is the existence of so-called *homoclinic points*. This concept was introduced by Poincaré (1890), more than a century ago. In this subsection, we will discuss how boundedly rational evolutionary switching between a costly, sophisticated, stabilizing predictor (such as rational expectations) and a cheap, simple, destabilizing predictor (such as naive expectations) leads to saddle point instability of the steady state and homoclinic orbits and their associated complicated dynamical behavior; see Chapter 3, Section 3.4 for theoretical background.

Consider the (two-dimensional) cobweb model with rational versus naive expectations in (5.25–5.26). As the intensity of choice to switch strategies increases, the steady state S loses its stability and becomes a saddle point. In deviations x from the steady state price p^*, the steady $S = (0, m^*) = (0, \tanh(-\beta C/2))$. Recall the notions of the *stable manifold* and the *unstable manifold* of the steady state defined as

$$
W^s(S) = \left\{ (x,m) \mid \lim_{n \to \infty} F^n_\beta(x,m) = S \right\},
$$
$$
W^u(S) = \left\{ (x,m) \mid \lim_{n \to -\infty} F^n_\beta(x,m) = S \right\}.
$$

(5.29)

The stable manifold is the set of points which converge to the saddle point steady state, while the unstable manifold is the set of points "moving away" from the steady state, or more precisely the set of points converging to the steady state backward in time. A *transversal homoclinic point* $Q \neq S$, associated to the saddle steady state S, is an intersection point of the stable and unstable manifold of S. Poincaré showed that the existence of a homoclinic intersection implies that the geometric structure of both the stable and unstable manifold is very complicated, and that the system exhibits some form of sensitive dependence on initial conditions. In modern terminology, a system having a homoclinic point is chaotic.

The stable and the unstable manifolds of the steady state play a crucial role for understanding the global characteristics of the evolutionary dynamics in the cobweb model with rational versus naive expectations. Using (5.25–5.26), the reader may easily verify that all points $(0, m)$ are mapped exactly onto the steady state $(0, m^*)$ in the next period. This implies that the steady state S has an eigenvalue 0 and the stable manifold of the steady state S must contain the vertical line segment $p = p^*$, or in deviations from the steady state, the vertical segment $x = 0$. Figure 5.3 illustrates the geometric shape of the unstable manifold of the steady state for increasing values of the intensity of choice β. Recall that, for $\beta > \beta_1$, the steady state is locally unstable and has a second eigenvalue $\lambda_2 < -1$. Therefore, the unstable manifold consists of two different branches, each branch spiraling around one of the two points of the period-2 orbit, as illustrated in Figure 5.3. For $\beta = 2$, the two branches of the unstable manifold of the steady state spiral toward the two points of the stable 2-cycle. As β increases, the 2-cycle becomes unstable and for $\beta = 3$ the two branches of the unstable manifold of the steady state accumulate around two "invariant circles" created after the secondary bifurcation at which the 2-cycle becomes unstable. When the intensity of choice becomes larger (e.g., $\beta = 4$), the branches of the unstable manifold grow and move closer to the vertical line segment $x = 0$ of the stable manifold. In Figure 5.3, for $\beta = 5$, $\beta = 6$ and $\beta = 10$, the unstable manifold of the steady state cannot be distinguished from the vertical segment $x = 0$, which is part of the stable manifold of the steady state. For β large, the cobweb model with evolutionary switching between costly rational and free naive expectations is therefore close to having a homoclinic orbit.

This geometric explanation of the dynamical complexities of the evolutionary switching dynamics, based upon the shape of the unstable manifold of the saddle point steady state, bears a close similarity to the economic mechanism underlying complicated price fluctuations. On the one hand, for high values of the intensity of choice the system is driven toward the steady state by a "far from equilibrium" stabilizing force when most agents switch to rational expectations. On the other hand, once prices are close to their steady state, due to information-gathering costs for rational expectations most agents switch to cheap naive expectations, and this "close to equilibrium destabilizing force" causes market instability and diverging prices. Price fluctuations on the strange attractors are thus characterized by an irregular switching between a "close to equilibrium" destabilizing force of cheap free riding and a "far from equilibrium" stabilizing force of costly, but sophisticated prediction.

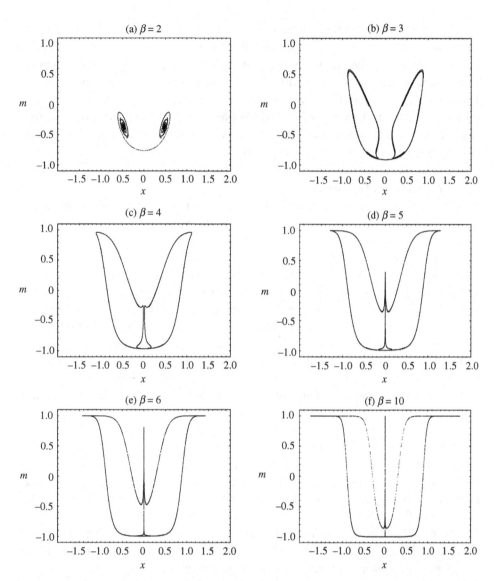

Figure 5.3. The unstable manifold of the steady state, for different values of the intensity of choice β. The stable manifold contains the vertical line segment $p = p^*$, or in deviations from steady state, the vertical segment $x = 0$. The two branches of the unstable manifold spiral around the two points of the (un)stable 2-cycle. As the intensity of choice increases, these branches grow and the unstable manifold moves closer to the vertical line segment $x = 0$ contained in the stable manifold. For large β-values the cobweb model with evolutionary switching between costly rational and free naive expectations is therefore close to a homoclinic tangency between the stable and the unstable manifolds of the steady state. Other parameters: $a = 0$, $d = 0.5$, $s = 1.35$ and $C = 1$.

Brock and Hommes (1997a, Theorem 3.3, p. 1079) showed that if the cobweb model is unstable under naive expectations and if information-gathering costs for rational expectations are positive, for large values of the intensity of choice the cobweb model with rational versus naive expectations has *strange attractors* with chaotic dynamics. These results were obtained by applying the mathematical theory of homoclinic bifurcations (see Palis and Takens 1993, and Chapter 3, Section 3.4), implying that for a large set of parameter values (i.e., a set of positive Lebesgue measure) the evolutionary switching system converges to a strange attractor.[11]

5.2.4   Coexistence of attractors

A careful reader may have observed some "peculiar" behavior in the bifurcation diagram w.r.t. the intensity of choice in Figure 5.2 after the secondary bifurcation when the 2-cycle becomes unstable and a stable 4-cycle arises. The secondary bifurcation is not a regular period-doubling bifurcation but a so-called 1:2-strong resonance Hopf bifurcation of the 2-cycle in which two stable 4-cycles are created.[12]. Immediately after the secondary bifurcation, the system has two *coexisting attractors* (two stable 4-cycles). As can be seen from the bifurcation diagram in Figure 5.2, the time path sometimes converges to say the first and other times to the second stable 4-cycle, as the intensity of choice β increases.

It should be stressed that coexisting attractors is nothing special, but simply a generic possibility for nonlinear system. A nonlinear system can exhibit *path dependence* with different coexisting types of long run dynamical behavior. The long run dynamical behavior then depends upon the initial state of the system.[13]

As noted above, when there are multiple, coexisting attractors, the long run dynamical behavior depends on the initial state. The *basin of attraction* of an attractor is the set of initial conditions converging to that attractor. Figure 5.4 illustrates the basins of attraction of the two coexisting stable 4-cycles for $\beta = 2.74$ and $\beta = 3$ respectively. Dark points converge to one stable 4-cycle, while light points converge to the other (symmetrically opposite) stable 4-cycle. Figure 5.4 illustrates that the *basin boundary*, i.e., the boundary between the dark and light basins of attraction, may be a very complicated set having a fractal structure. When the basin boundary has a fractal structure, it becomes more difficult to predict the long run outcome of the system.

Coexisting attractors are important in economics, because adding (small) exogenous shocks to a nonlinear system may cause the solution to jump from one basin of attraction

---

[11] In the cobweb model with costly rational expectations versus naive expectations, the stable and unstable manifolds of the *steady state* never intersect transversally. Brock and Hommes (1997a, pp. 1077–1079) showed, however, that the fourth iterate, F_β^4, of the 2-D map exhibits transversal intersections of stable and unstable manifolds, implying that the system has 4-cycles with a saddle structure with transversal intersections between the corresponding stable and unstable manifolds of these 4-cycles.

[12] Close to the bifurcation value β_2, the eigenvalues of the Jacobian matrix JF^2 at the 2-cycle are complex, while at the bifurcation value β_2 both eigenvalues equal -1; see Brock and Hommes (1997a, pp. 1080–1081, Theorem 3.4.)

[13] In fact, simple nonlinear systems can have infinitely many stable cycles with different periods, a feature known as the Newhouse phenomenon, see, e.g., Palis and Takens (1993).

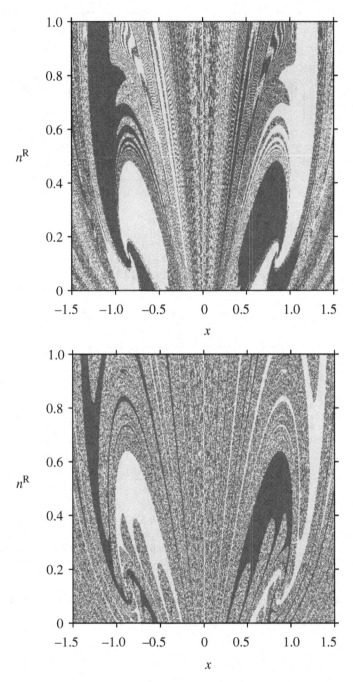

Figure 5.4. Basins of attraction of two coexisting stable 4-cycles, with fractal basin boundaries for $\beta = 2.74$ (top) and $\beta = 3$ (bottom), with other parameters fixed at $a = 0$, $b = 0.5$, $s = 1.35$ and $C = 1$. The horizontal axis shows the deviation x from the steady state price and the vertical axis the fraction n^R of rational agents. Dark respectively light points correspond to initial states converging to different stable 4-cycles. For each initial state a transient time of 1000 has been used, the resolution is 1000×1000 and convergence distance $\epsilon = 0.001$.

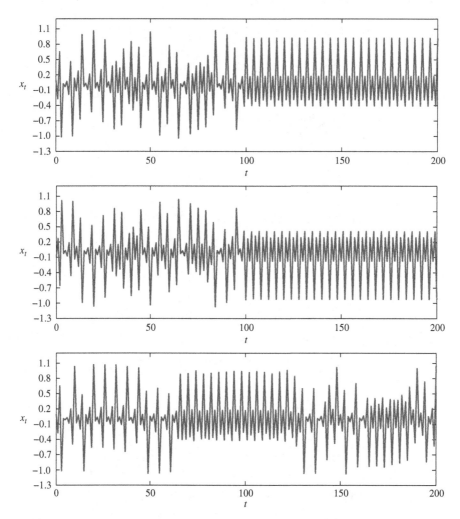

Figure 5.5. Two coexisting stable 4-cycles for $a = 0$, $d = 0.5$, $s = 1.35$, $C = 1$ and $\beta = 3.8$. Without noise a typical price time path converges to one of the two stable 4-cycles; $(p_0, m_0) = (0.1, -1)$ (a) and $(p_0, m_0) = (-0.1, -1)$ (b). In the presence of small noise added to the rational expectations forecast (c) prices jump irregularly between the two basins of attraction of the two stable 4-cycles.

to another, thus leading to irregular fluctuations. Figure 5.5 illustrates a simulation with small noise for $\beta = 3.8$.

5.3   Competing linear forecasting rules

The cobweb model with costly rational expectations versus free naive expectations should be viewed as a stylized example, with rational expectations representing a costly, sophisticated stabilizing forecasting rule and naive expectations a freely available simple, but possibly destabilizing, forecasting rule. Rational agents have perfect knowledge about market equilibrium equations and, in particular, about the beliefs of other, non-rational agents. While this case is theoretically appealing, it seems highly unrealistic in real markets that some agents have (perfect) detailed information about the beliefs of other agents. Therefore, in this section we consider two other, perhaps more realistic 2-type examples, where agents only use information extracted from observable quantities, such as prices. As a starting point of the discussion, we consider the interaction of two simple linear predictors and the resulting aggregate price behavior. Two important examples will be discussed, the case of *fundamentalists* versus naive expectations and the case of *contrarians* versus naive expectations.

Consider the two linear AR(1) prediction rules

$$p^e_{jt} = \alpha_j + \beta_j p_{t-1}, \qquad j = 1, 2, \tag{5.30}$$

with fixed parameters α_j and β_j. As before, we assume that supply is *linear* as in (5.3), with corresponding cost function $c(q) = q^2/(2s)$. The market clearing price in the cobweb model with linear demand and supply and two trader types with linear predictors is determined by[14]

$$a - dp_t = n_{1t}s(\alpha_1 + \beta_1 p_{t-1}) + n_{2t}s(\alpha_2 + \beta_2 p_{t-1}), \tag{5.31}$$

where n_{1t} and n_{2t} denote the fractions of agents using the linear forecasting rules 1 and 2 in (5.30). As before, these fractions will be updated according to an evolutionary fitness measure based on past realized profits. Realized profit in period t for traders using forecast p^e_{jt} is given by

$$\pi_{jt} = sp_t p^e_{jt} - \frac{s}{2}(p^e_{jt})^2. \tag{5.32}$$

The fitness measure is given by

$$U_{jt} = wU_{j,t-1} + (1-w)\pi_{jt} - C_j, \tag{5.33}$$

where w is a memory parameter and C_j represents the average costs per time period for obtaining forecast p^e_{jt}. For a simple habitual rule of thumb predictor, such as naive or adaptive expectations, these costs C_j will be zero, whereas for more sophisticated predictors such as fundamentalists beliefs, based on fundamental analysis, information-gathering costs C_j may be positive.

We consider the more general case of *asynchronous* strategy updating, as introduced in Section 5.1. Per time unit only a fraction $1 - \delta$ of agents update their strategy on the basis of the most recent available information, while the remaining fraction δ stick to their current strategy. The corresponding dynamics of the fractions is given by

$$n_{jt} = (1-\delta)\frac{e^{\beta U_{j,t-1}}}{Z_{t-1}} + \delta n_{j,t-1}, \tag{5.34}$$

---

[14] In our simulations we will continue to work in deviations $x_t = p_t - p^*$ from the fundamental RE steady state price p^*. This is equivalent to setting the parameter $a = 0$, so that the RE steady state $p^* = a/(d+s) = 0$.

where $Z_{t-1} = \sum_h e^{\beta U_{h,t-1}}$ is a normalization factor. For $\delta = 0$, we are back in the case of synchronous updating.

5.3.1 Fundamentalists versus naive expectations

The linear predictors (5.29) specialize to the case of fundamentalists versus naive expectations when $\alpha_1 = p^* = a/(d+s)$ (the steady state price), $\beta_1 = 0$, $\alpha_2 = 0$ and $\beta_2 = 1$:

$$p^e_{1t} = p^* = \frac{a}{d+s}, \tag{5.35}$$

$$p^e_{2t} = p_{t-1}. \tag{5.36}$$

Fundamentalists always predict the steady state price p^*, where demand and supply intersect. Hence, if all agents would be fundamentalists, the realized market price would immediately jump to the rational expectations price p^*. In a heterogeneous world, fundamentalists are not perfectly rational however, because they do not take into account that there are nonrational (in this example naive) agents in the market. Fundamentalists act "as if" all other agents are rational. A fundamentalists strategy, however, requires structural knowledge of the economy and information about "economic fundamentals," and therefore we assume positive information-gathering costs for fundamentalists. In the cobweb model the fundamental forecast requires structural knowledge of demand and supply curves in order to compute the fundamental steady state price p^*. While a fundamentalist strategy may not be perfectly rational in a heterogeneous world, it may be more realistic, because it does not require (perfect) knowledge of the behavior, in particular the beliefs, of other agents in the market.

Figure 5.6 shows attractors for different values of the intensity of choice β and some corresponding time series. The bifurcation diagram and largest LE plot in Figure 5.7 illustrate a rational route to randomness, i.e., a bifurcation route from simple to complicated, chaotic dynamics as the intensity of choice increases. The time series of prices and fractions illustrate that the market switches between periods of low volatility, with prices close to the fundamental price, and high volatility, with irregularly fluctuating prices. Prices diverge slowly from the fundamental steady state price, as long as most agents use the simple, freely available naive forecast. When forecasting errors increase, it becomes worthwhile to buy the sophisticated fundamental forecast, and more agents start switching to the fundamental forecast, thus stabilizing price fluctuations. Due to the *asynchronous* updating of strategies, agents switch more gradually between strategies, and the time series of fractions of fundamentalists shows much more persistence than in the case with synchronous updating. Figure 5.6 (bottom panel) also illustrates the *sample average* and the *first order sample autocorrelation (SAC)* of the price series. The sample average quickly settles down to a value close to 0,[15] whereas the SAC is strongly negative, converging to approximately. -0.85.

---

[15] Recall that the simulations are in deviations $x_t = p_t - p^*$ from the fundamental price, so that the sample average of prices converges to its fundamental value.

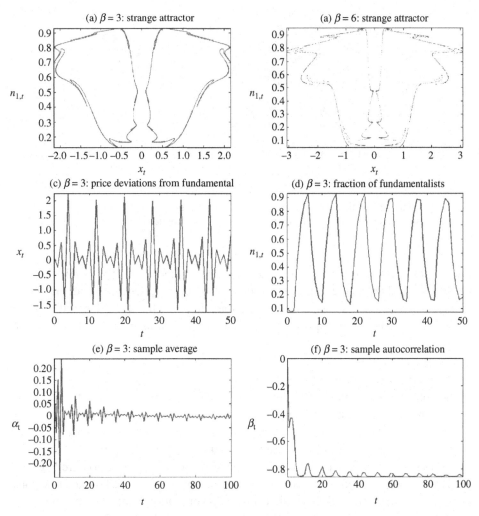

Figure 5.6. Fundamentalists versus naive expectations with asynchronous updating. Strange attractors and time series for different β-values, with other parameters fixed at $a = 0$, $d = 0.5$, $s = 1.35$, $\delta = 0.5$, $w = 0$, $\alpha_1 = 0$, $\beta_1 = 0$, $C_1 = 1$, $\alpha_2 = 0$, $\beta_2 = 1$ and $C_2 = 0$. Although price fluctuations are chaotic, there is still much linear autocorrelation structure. Sample average of prices converge to the fundamental value, while sample autocorrelations converge to -0.85, indicating significantly negative first-order autocorrelation.

The rational route to randomness observed in the case of costly fundamentalists versus naive expectations follows the same economic intuition as the 2-type case with costly rational versus naive expectations. Close to the steady state the majority of agents adopts the cheap naive rule and the system destabilizes. As price fluctuations increase, forecasting errors from naive expectations increase and it becomes worthwhile to buy the more sophisticated fundamental forecast. If the intensity of choice is high, many agents start switching to the fundamental strategy, stabilizing fluctuations and driving

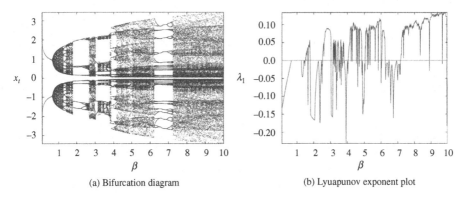

(a) Bifurcation diagram   (b) Lyuapunov exponent plot

Figure 5.7. Fundamentalists versus naive expectations: a rational route to randomness, that is, a bifurcation route to chaos, as the intensity of choice increases. Parameters are $a = 0, d = 0.5, s = 1.35$, $\delta = 0.5, w = 0, \alpha_1 = 0, \beta_1 = 0, C_1 = 1, \alpha_2 = 0, \beta_2 = 1$ and $C_2 = 0$.

prices back close to the steady state, and the story repeats.[16] It is remarkable that both the geometric shape of the strange attractor and the chaotic price time series are similar to the case of rational versus naive expectations. In particular, for β large, the system is close to a homoclinic tangency, as suggested in the strange attractor for $\beta = 6$ in Figure 5.6.[17]

5.3.2 Contrarians versus naive expectations
In the cobweb model with fundamentalists versus naive expectations, the price time series exhibit strong first-order negative autocorrelations, even when the dynamics is chaotic. In the chaotic example in Figure 5.6, for $\beta = 3$, the sample autocorrelations of prices converges to a negative value around -0.85. An agent who behaves as a time series econometrician would easily detect this strong negative autocorrelation and adapt her forecasts. Even without the use of any statistical software, a boundedly rational agent might detect strong negative first-order autocorrelation, simply by observing that positive (negative) price deviations from the average are always followed by negative (positive) price deviations. What would happen if agents recognize this structure by observing realized market prices and adapt their behavior?

Consider a group of *contrarians*, who recognize that there is negative first-order auto-correlation in realized prices and adapt their forecast by predicting that next period's deviation from the fundamental price will be on the opposite side of the steady state. If we continue to assume that agents are boundedly rational and only use simple

---

[16] A difference with the case of rational versus naive, is that, with fundamentalists versus naive, the system may be (locally) unstable even when there are no information costs for fundamentalists (i.e., $C = 0$). This follows immediately by observing that at the steady state fundamentalists and naive prediction rules yield the same steady state forecast p^* and therefore the system will be locally unstable when the slopes of demand and supply satisfy $|s/d| > 2$. In contrast, the two-type case with rational versus naive expectations is always globally stable when there are no information costs for rational agents.

[17] See the original working paper Brock and Hommes (1995) for more details concerning the case of fundamentalists versus naive expectations.

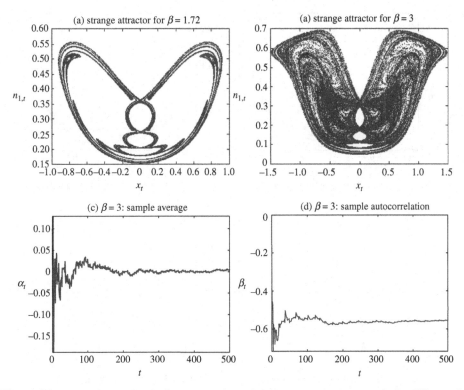

Figure 5.8. Contrarians versus naive expectations. Strange attractors (top panel) for different β-values, with other parameters fixed at: $a = 0$, $d = 0.5$, $s = 1.35$, $\delta = 0.5$, $w = 0$, $\alpha_1 = 0$, $\beta_1 = -0.85$, $C_1 = 1$, $\alpha_2 = 0$, $\beta_2 = 1$ and $C_2 = 0$. Bottom panel: Time series of sample average and (first-order) sample autocorrelation converge. Compared to fundamentalists, contrarians weaken the negative first-order autocorrelations in prices, and in the long run sample autocorrelations converge to -0.57.

linear forecasting rules, it is natural to replace the fundamental forecast by a *linear contrarian rule*

$$p_{1t}^e = p^* + \beta_1(p_{t-1} - p^*), \qquad -1 < \beta_1 < 0. \tag{5.37}$$

Figure 5.8 illustrates an example with $\beta_1 = -0.85$ (with the other parameters as in Figure 5.6), that is, contrarians recognizing the first-order autocorrelation structure present in the previous example. Interestingly, the structure of the strange attractors in Figure 5.8 is much more complicated than in the case of fundamentalists versus naive in Figure 5.6. In particular, the left and the right parts of the attractors in Figure 5.6 are separated, while they "melt together" in Figure 5.8. This more complicated structure is also reflected by the fact that, due to the presence of contrarians, the negative autocorrelation in prices becomes weaker, as the first-order sample autocorrelation $\rho_t \to -0.57$ (instead of -0.85).

Apparently, by increasing the level of "rationality" of the boundedly rational agents, that is, assuming that their linear forecasting rule takes observed (negative)

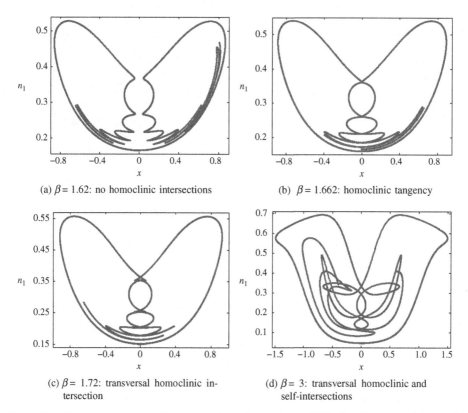

(a) $\beta = 1.62$: no homoclinic intersections

(b) $\beta = 1.662$: homoclinic tangency

(c) $\beta = 1.72$: transversal homoclinic intersection

(d) $\beta = 3$: transversal homoclinic and self-intersections

Figure 5.9. Contrarians versus naive expectations. Unstable manifolds for different β-values, with other parameters fixed at: $a = 0$, $d = 0.5$, $s = 1.35$, $\delta = 0.5$, $w = 0$, $\alpha_1 = 0$, $\beta_1 = -0.85$, $C_1 = 1$, $\alpha_2 = 0$, $\beta_2 = 1$ and $C_2 = 0$. As β increases a homoclinic bifurcation occurs for $\beta = 1.662$, where the unstable manifold of the steady state becomes tangent to the stable manifold (the vertical segment $x = 0$).

autocorrelations into account, the exploitable/forecastable structure in the chaotic price series becomes weaker. Figure 5.9 shows the unstable manifolds of the steady state for increasing values of the intensity of choice β. The reader may easily check that the stable manifold of the steady state contains the vertical line segment $p = p^*$, or equivalently in deviations, the segment $x = 0$. For $\beta \approx 1.662$ a transversal intersection between the stable and the unstable manifolds of the steady state occurs (with infinitely many points of homoclinic tangency). For $\beta > 1.662$ the structure of the unstable manifold of the steady state becomes very complicated, with (infinitely) many homoclinic points (intersections with the stable manifold) and (infinitely) many self-intersections.[18] In summary, in the case of contrarians versus naive expectations, a more complex rational route to randomness occurs characterized by homoclinic bifurcations associated to the unstable saddle-point fundamental steady state, with a more complex fractal structure of the strange attractor and highly unpredictable price fluctuations.

---

[18] Self-intersections of the unstable manifold arise for our two-dimensional map, because it is *non*-invertible.

5.4   Evolutionary selection and adaptive learning

In this subsection, we combine *evolutionary selection* among different types/classes of forecasting rules and adaptive learning of the parameters within (one of) the classes of rules. In the previous 2-type example we have seen that the presence of contrarians in a heterogeneous market weakens the first-order autocorrelations in aggregate price behavior. A careful time series econometrician might note, however, that contrarian behavior is still (somewhat) *inconsistent* with realized prices, because contrarians expect strong negative autocorrelation $\beta_2 = -0.85$, while realized prices exhibit weaker first-order sample autocorrelations, with $\beta_t \approx -0.57$. It seems natural to take the analysis one step further and introduce a type of agent with *adaptive learning* within the class of linear AR(1) rules, that is, to introduce adaptive learning in order to optimize the parameters of the linear forecasting rule. Contrarians are replaced by a more sophisticated linear forecasting rule with time-varying parameters:

$$p_{1t}^e = \alpha_{t-1} + \beta_{t-1}(p_{t-1} - \alpha_{t-1}), \tag{5.38}$$

where α_t and β_t are determined through sample autocorrelation (SAC) learning (as in Chapter 4, Subsection 4.7.2)

$$\alpha_t = \frac{1}{t+1} \sum_{i=0}^{t} p_i, \qquad t \geq 1 \tag{5.39}$$

$$\beta_t = \frac{\sum_{i=0}^{t-1}(p_i - \alpha_t)(p_{i+1} - \alpha_t)}{\sum_{i=0}^{t}(p_i - \alpha_t)^2}, \qquad t \geq 1. \tag{5.40}$$

SAC learning means that type 1 agents are learning the parameters of their linear forecasting rule by the long run sample average α_t and the first-order autocorrelation β_t of prices. Introducing adaptive learning widens the range of forecasting rules to include all linear AR(1) rules. The sophisticated agent type 1 tries to learn an optimal linear rule through adaptive learning, within a heterogeneous agent environment.[19] We stress that these linear rules and the SAC learning process have a simple *behavioral interpretation*. While (5.39) and (5.40) give exact expressions for the updated parameters in the SAC adaptive-learning process, the sample average and first-order sample autocorrelation also may be "guestimated" from a (short run) average price level and the observed (short run) persistence or anti-persistence in the price series.

Figure 5.10 illustrates the dynamics in the 2-type model with costly SAC learning versus naive expectations. In the long run, agents *learn to be contrarians*, as the sample

---

[19] There are a few other recent examples studying heterogeneous agent models with adaptive learning. Branch and Evans (2006) studied a related cobweb model with two types of agents, both using OLS learning of a misspecified model, and allowing for endogenous, evolutionary switching between the two predictors. DeGrauwe and Markiewicz (2012) compare evolutionary learning and adaptive (or statistical) learning in an asset pricing framework, and investigate how these different learning schemes replicate the stylized facts (disconnect puzzles, excess volatility) in exchange rates. See also Hommes (2009) for a discussion and examples in the cobweb framework.

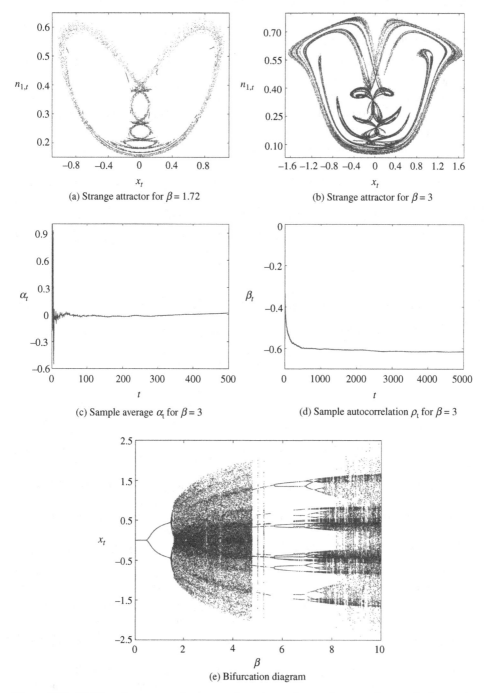

(a) Strange attractor for $\beta = 1.72$

(b) Strange attractor for $\beta = 3$

(c) Sample average α_t for $\beta = 3$

(d) Sample autocorrelation ρ_t for $\beta = 3$

(e) Bifurcation diagram

Figure 5.10. SAC learning versus naive expectations. Agents learn to be contrarians, as the first-order autocorrelation coefficient converges, $\beta_t \rightarrow -0.62$. The bifurcation diagram shows a rational route to randomness, as the intensity of choice β increases. Parameters $a = 0$, $d = 0.5$, $s = 1.35$, $\delta = 0.5$, $w = 0$, $C_1 = 1$, $\alpha_2 = 0$, $\beta_2 = 1$ and $C_2 = 0$.

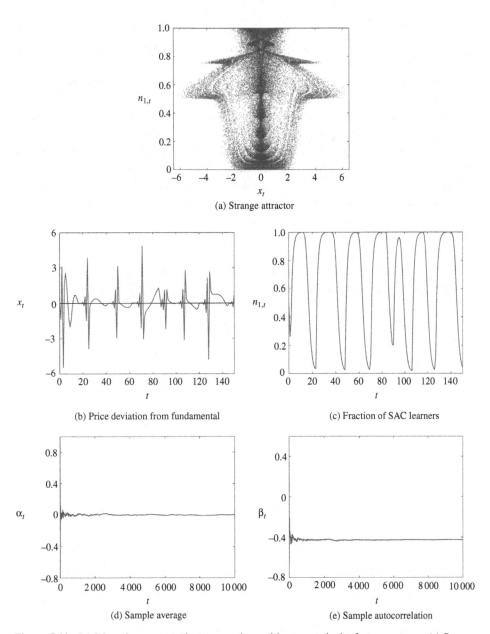

Figure 5.11. SAC learning versus naive expectations with memory in the fitness measure; (a) Strange attractor, (b–e) time series of prices p_t (deviations from fundamental), fraction n_{1t} of SAC learners, sample average α_t and sample autocorrelation coefficient β_t. With more memory in the fitness measure ($w = 0$), the remaining autocorrelation in prices is weaker ($\beta_t \to -0.43$). Parameters: $\beta = 10$, $a = 0$, $d = 0.5$, $b = 1.35$, $\delta = 0.5$, $w = 0.9$, $C_1 = 1$, $\alpha_2 = 0$, $\beta_2 = 1$ and $C_2 = 0$.

average price converges to the fundamental steady state (or equivalently, the sample average deviation converges to 0) and the first-order sample autocorrelation $\beta_t \to -0.62$, consistent with the observed SAC in realized prices. SAC learners therefore learn the correct fundamental steady state price level and the correct first-order sample autocorrelation of realized prices.

In the previous example there is still fairly strong negative first-order autocorrelation in prices, but other examples can be found with less autocorrelations. Figure 5.11 illustrates another example with memory in the fitness measure ($w = 0.9$), where the (first-order) autocorrelation in prices becomes weaker ($\beta_t \to -0.43$).

Although the linear rule in these examples is misspecified, these agents are *behaviorally rational* in a complex heterogeneous expectations environment. The linear rule has a simple behavioral interpretation, as a contrarian rule; the SAC learning has a simple behavioral interpretation, as learning of the anchor (the sample average) and the anti-persistence coefficient of prices (the first-order autocorrelation); and the rule is optimal within the class of misspecified linear rules. In a complex heterogeneous environment it is not easy to improve upon behaviorally rational rules.

6   An asset pricing model with heterogeneous beliefs

In this chapter we present a financial market application of the heterogeneous expectations evolutionary switching framework of Brock and Hommes (1997a). This application has been termed *adaptive belief systems (ABS)*, with beliefs and prices coevolving over time, and was introduced in Brock and Hommes (1998). An ABS is in fact a standard discounted value asset pricing model derived from mean-variance maximization, extended to the case of *heterogeneous expectations*.[1]

The chapter is organized as follows. After introducing some basic assumptions of the model, we discuss the benchmark case of rational expectations and derive the fundamental price. In the following three sections, we then introduce heterogeneous beliefs, evolutionary selection of beliefs and the forecasting strategies. Section 6.5 discusses three typical few type examples: a 2-type example with costly fundamentalists versus chartists, a 3-type example with fundamentalists versus optimists and pessimists and a 4-type example with fundamentalists, biased traders and trend followers. All examples exhibit rational routes to randomness, that is, bifurcation routes to cycles and/or chaos as traders become more sensitive to differences in strategy performance. All examples illustrate how non-fundamental traders may survive evolutionary competition and that markets are characterized by bubble and crash dynamics. Section 6.6 discusses another 2-type example with fundamentalists versus conditional trend followers, who condition their trend-following strategy upon deviations from the fundamental. This example exhibits coexisting attractors, as a stable fundamental steady state may coexist with a stable limit cycle or even a strange attractor. In the presence of small noise, the model then exhibits clustered volatility, with irregular switching between close to the fundamental price fluctuations with fundamentalists dominating the market and phases of large price swings amplified by trend followers. Finally, Section 6.7 discusses the case with many different trading strategies and presents the notion of *large type limit*, a simple low-dimensional system approximating an evolutionary market with many trader types.

---

[1] Here, we will focus on simple, stylized examples. Many extensions of ABS have been proposed in the literature. See Hommes (2001, 2006), Hommes and Wagener (2009) and Chiarella et al. (2009), for extensive overviews of the literature.

The model

Agents can invest either in a risk free asset or in a risky asset. The risk free asset is perfectly elastically supplied and pays a fixed rate of return r; the risky asset, for example a large stock or a market index, pays an uncertain dividend. Let p_t be the price per share (ex-dividend) of the risky asset at time t, and let y_t be the stochastic dividend process of the risky asset. Wealth dynamics is given by

$$\mathbf{W}_{t+1} = (1+r)W_t + (\mathbf{p}_{t+1} + \mathbf{y}_{t+1} - (1+r)p_t)z_t, \tag{6.1}$$

where bold face variables denote random variables at date $t+1$ and z_t denotes the number of shares of the risky asset purchased at date t. Let E_t and V_t denote the conditional expectation and conditional variance based on a publicly available information set such as past prices and past dividends. Let E_{ht} and V_{ht} denote the "beliefs" or forecasts of trader type h about conditional expectation and conditional variance. Agents are assumed to be myopic mean-variance maximizers so that the demand z_{ht} of type h for the risky asset solves

$$\max_{z_t} \left\{ E_{ht}[\mathbf{W}_{t+1}] - \frac{a}{2} V_{ht}[\mathbf{W}_{t+1}] \right\}, \tag{6.2}$$

where a is the risk aversion parameter. The demand z_{ht} for risky assets by trader type h is then

$$z_{ht} = \frac{E_{ht}[\mathbf{p}_{t+1} + \mathbf{y}_{t+1} - (1+r)p_t]}{a V_{ht}[\mathbf{p}_{t+1} + \mathbf{y}_{t+1} - (1+r)p_t]} = \frac{E_{ht}[\mathbf{p}_{t+1} + \mathbf{y}_{t+1} - (1+r)p_t]}{a\sigma^2}, \tag{6.3}$$

where the conditional variance $V_{ht} = \sigma^2$ is assumed to be equal and constant for all types. This simplifying assumption is made for analytical tractability of the heterogeneous expectations model, but it is supported by the observation that in real markets there seems to be more agreement about the variance than about the mean.[2] Let z^s denote the supply of outside risky shares per investor, assumed to be constant, and let n_{ht} denote the fraction of type h at date t. Equilibrium of demand and supply yields

$$\sum_{h=1}^{H} n_{ht} \frac{E_{ht}[\mathbf{p}_{t+1} + \mathbf{y}_{t+1} - (1+r)p_t]}{a\sigma^2} = z^s, \tag{6.4}$$

where H is the number of different trader types. Brock and Hommes (1998) focus on the special case of zero supply of outside shares, i.e., $z^s = 0$, for which the market

---

[2] The observation that estimation of the variance or covariance from observed financial returns series is more accurate than estimation of the mean dates back to Merton (1980, see especially Appendix A). The ARCH/GARCH literature has shown that, under regularity conditions, conditional variance is easier to estimate than conditional mean, see, e.g., Bollerslev et al. (1994, especially Section 4). Gaunersdorfer (2000) studied the asset pricing model with heterogeneous expectations and homogeneous but time-varying beliefs about variances and shows that the results are quite similar to those for constant variance discussed here.

equilibrium pricing equation becomes[3]

$$(1+r)p_t = \sum_{h=1}^{H} n_{ht} E_{ht}[\mathbf{p}_{t+1} + \mathbf{y}_{t+1}].$$ (6.5)

6.1 The homogeneous benchmark with rational agents

Let us first discuss the rational representative agent benchmark. In a world where all traders are identical and expectations are *homogeneous* the arbitrage market equilibrium equation (6.5) simplifies to

$$(1+r)p_t = E_t[\mathbf{p}_{t+1} + \mathbf{y}_{t+1}],$$ (6.6)

where E_t denotes the common conditional expectation at the beginning of period t, based on a publicly available information set I_t such as past prices and dividends, i.e., $I_t = \{p_{t-1}, p_{t-2}, ...; y_{t-1}, y_{t-2}, ...\}$. The arbitrage market equilibrium equation (6.6) states that today's price of the risky asset must be equal to the sum of tomorrow's expected price and expected dividend, discounted by the risk free interest rate. It is well known that, using the arbitrage equation (6.6) repeatedly and assuming that the *transversality condition*

$$\lim_{t \to \infty} \frac{E_t[\mathbf{p}_{t+k}]}{(1+r)^k} = 0$$ (6.7)

holds, the price of the risky asset is uniquely determined by

$$p_t^* = \sum_{k=1}^{\infty} \frac{E_t[\mathbf{y}_{t+k}]}{(1+r)^k}.$$ (6.8)

The price p_t^* in (6.8) is called the fundamental rational expectations (RE) price, or the *fundamental price* for short. The fundamental price is fully determined by economic fundamentals and given by the discounted sum of expected future dividends; it is the price that would prevail in an efficient market populated only with rational traders. In general, the properties of the fundamental price p_t^* depend upon the stochastic dividend process y_t. In this chapter, we focus on the case of an IID dividend process y_t, with constant mean $E[y_t] = \bar{y}$. However, any other random dividend process y_t may be substituted in what follows.[4] For an IID dividend process y_t with constant mean, the

---

[3] Brock (1997) motivates this special case by introducing a risk-adjusted dividend $y_{t+1}^{\#} = y_{t+1} - a\sigma^2 z^s$ and obtains the market equilibrium equation (6.5). In general however, the equilibrium equation (6.5) ignores a risk premium $a\sigma^2 z^s$ for investors holding the risky asset. Since dividends and a risk premium affect realized profits and wealth, in general they will affect the fractions n_{ht} of trader type h. The question how exactly the risk premium affects evolutionary competition could, for example, be studied by taking z^s as a bifurcation parameter. The market equilibrium equation (6.5) in fact represents the case of risk neutral investors.

[4] Brock and Hommes (1997b), for example, discuss a nonstationary example, where the dividend process is a geometric random walk. In Chapter 7 we discuss the estimation of a simple 2-type model on yearly S&P 500 data of Boswijk et al. (2007), who use a stochastic dividend process with a constant growth rate.

fundamental price is constant and given by

$$p^* = \sum_{k=1}^{\infty} \frac{\bar{y}}{(1+r)^k} = \frac{\bar{y}}{r}. \tag{6.9}$$

There are two crucial (unrealistic) assumptions underlying the derivation of the RE fundamental price. The first is that expectations are *homogeneous*, all traders are *rational* and it is *common knowledge* that all traders are rational. In such an ideal, simple, homogeneous, perfectly rational world the fundamental price can be derived from economic fundamentals. Conditions under which a RE price can be derived can be relaxed, to include for example noise traders or limited heterogeneity of information. In real markets, however, typically there is strong disagreement about what the "true fundamental" price should be. In a complex world where traders are *heterogeneous* and have different beliefs or expectations about future prices and/or future dividends, the derivation of a RE fundamental price requires perfect knowledge about the *beliefs* of *all* other traders. In real markets, understanding the beliefs and strategies of all other, competing traders is virtually impossible, and therefore in a complex heterogeneous world derivation of the RE fundamental price becomes practically impossible.

The second crucial assumption underlying the derivation of the fundamental price is the transversality condition (6.7), requiring that the long run growth rate of prices is smaller than the risk free growth rate r. In fact, in addition to the fundamental solution (6.8), so-called *rational bubble solutions* of the form

$$p_t = p_t^* + (1+r)^t (p_0 - p_0^*), \tag{6.10}$$

also satisfy the arbitrage equation (6.6). Along these bubble solutions (6.10), traders have rational expectations. A simple way to see this is to introduce the deviation from the fundamental price, $x_t = p_t - p_t^*$, and to rewrite (6.6) in terms of deviations to obtain

$$(1+r)x_t = E_t[x_{t+1}]. \tag{6.11}$$

It is then immediately clear that the belief

$$E_{ht}[x_{t+1}] = (1+g)^2 x_{t-1} \tag{6.12}$$

is a self-fulfilling belief when $g = r$. Hence, when all agents believe that the deviation from the fundamental grows at a rate $1+r$, this belief becomes self-fulfilling and leads to a rational bubble solution (6.10). These explosive rational bubble solutions, however, do *not* satisfy the transversality condition (6.7). In a perfectly rational world, traders realize that exploding bubbles cannot last forever and therefore they will never get started and the finite fundamental price p_t^* will prevail in the market.

In summary, in a perfectly rational world, all traders will coordinate to believe that the value of a risky asset equals its fundamental price forever. Changes in asset prices are solely driven by unexpected changes in dividends and random "news" about economic fundamentals. In contrast, in a heterogeneous world the situation will be quite different. In fact, we will see that evolutionary forces may lead to endogenous switching between temporary almost self-fulfilling bubble solutions irregularly interrupted by sudden market crashes back (close) to the fundamental price.

6.2 Heterogeneous beliefs

In the asset pricing model with heterogeneous beliefs, market equilibrium in (6.5) states that the price p_t of the risky asset equals the discounted value of tomorrow's expected price plus tomorrow's expected dividend, *averaged over all different trader types*. We shall now be more precise about traders' expectations (forecasts) about future prices and dividends and in which sense these beliefs will be heterogeneous. It will be convenient to work with

$$x_t = p_t - p_t^*, \tag{6.13}$$

the *deviation* from the fundamental price. We make the following assumptions about the beliefs of trader type h:

B1 $V_{ht}[\mathbf{p}_{t+1} + \mathbf{y}_{t+1} - (1+r)p_t] = V_t[\mathbf{p}_{t+1} + \mathbf{y}_{t+1} - (1+r)p_t] = \sigma^2$, for all h,t.
B2 $E_{ht}[\mathbf{y}_{t+1}] = E_t[\mathbf{y}_{t+1}]$, for all h,t.
B3 All beliefs $E_{ht}[\mathbf{p}_{t+1}]$ are of the form

$$E_{ht}[\mathbf{p}_{t+1}] = E_t[\mathbf{p}_{t+1}^*] + f_h(x_{t-1}, ..., x_{t-L}), \qquad \text{for all } h,t. \tag{6.14}$$

According to assumption B1 beliefs about conditional variance are equal and constant for all types, as already discussed above.[5] Assumption B2 states that expectations about future dividends $\mathbf{y}_{t+1}$ are the same for all trader types and equal to the conditional expectation. This assumption seems reasonable, since dividends are an *exogenous* stochastic process which can be observed and learned by individual agents. All traders thus have correct beliefs about dividends and are able to derive the fundamental price p_t^* in (6.8) that would prevail in a perfectly rational world. While expectations on dividends are homogenous, we assume *heterogeneous expectations about prices*. These heterogeneous individual beliefs about prices endogenously affect realized market prices. According to assumption B3, traders believe that in a heterogeneous world prices may *deviate* from their fundamental value p_t^* by some function f_h depending upon past deviations from the fundamental. Each forecasting rule f_h represents a *model of the market* according to which type h believes that prices will deviate from the commonly shared fundamental price. For example, a forecasting strategy f_h may correspond to a technical trading rule, based upon short run or long run moving averages, of the type used in real markets. It should be stressed that assuming a commonly shared belief of the fundamental price in B3 is without loss of generality, but only serves as a convenient mathematical way of formulating the model with arbitrary heterogeneous beliefs in terms of deviations of a benchmark fundamental.

[5] See footnote 2.

We will use the short hand notation

$$f_{ht} = f_h(x_{t-1}, ..., x_{t-L}),$$ (6.15)

for the forecasting strategy employed by trader type h. A convenient consequence of assumptions B1–B3 concerning traders' beliefs is that the heterogeneous agent market equilibrium equation (6.5) can be reformulated in *deviations from the benchmark fundamental*. In particular, substituting the price forecast (6.14) in the market equilibrium equation (6.5) and using the facts that the fundamental price p_t^* satisfies $(1+r)p_t^* = E_t[p_{t+1}^* + y_{t+1}]$ and the price $p_t = x_t + p_t^*$ yields the equilibrium equation in deviations from the fundamental:

$$(1+r)x_t = \sum_{h=1}^{H} n_{ht} E_{ht}[\mathbf{x}_{t+1}] \equiv \sum_{h=1}^{H} n_{ht} f_{ht},$$ (6.16)

with $f_{ht} = f_h(x_{t-1}, ..., x_{t-L})$. A convenient feature of our model formulation in terms of deviations from a benchmark fundamental is that, in this general setup, the benchmark rational expectations asset pricing model is *nested* as a special case, with all forecasting strategies $f_h \equiv 0$. In this way, the adaptive belief systems can be used in empirical and experimental testing whether asset prices deviate significantly from the benchmark fundamental.

6.3 Evolutionary dynamics

The evolutionary part of the model describes how beliefs are updated over time, that is, how the fractions n_{ht} of trader types in the market equilibrium equation (6.16) evolve over time. Fractions are updated according to an *evolutionary fitness* or *performance measure*, as discussed in Chapter 5, Section 5.1. For the convenience of the reader, we briefly recall the main features of the reinforcement learning and strategy switching. The fitness measures of all trading strategies are publicly available, but subject to noise. Fitness is derived from a random utility model and given by

$$\tilde{U}_{ht} = U_{ht} + \epsilon_{iht},$$ (6.17)

where U_{ht} is the *deterministic part* of the fitness measure and ϵ_{iht} represents noise. Assuming that the noise ϵ_{iht} is IID across individual agents i and across types $h = 1, ..., H$, drawn from a double exponential distribution, in the limit as the number of agents goes to infinity, the probability that an agent chooses strategy h is given by the *multinomial discrete choice model*[6]

$$n_{ht} = \frac{e^{\beta U_{h,t-1}}}{Z_{t-1}}, \qquad Z_{t-1} = \sum_{h=1}^{H} e^{\beta U_{h,t-1}},$$ (6.18)

---

[6] In this chapter we only consider the case of synchronous strategy updating; see Section 5.1 for the more general case of asynchronous updating.

where Z_{t-1} is a normalization factor in order for the fractions n_{ht} to add up to 1. The key feature of (6.18) is that more successful strategies attract more followers, with the *intensity of choice* parameter β measuring how quickly agents switch to more successful strategies. At one extreme, $\beta = 0$, there is no switching and all fractions are fixed and equal to $1/H$; at the other extreme, $\beta = +\infty$, *all agents* switch immediately to the best strategy. The timing of the coupling between the market equilibrium equation (6.5) or (6.16) and the evolutionary selection of strategies (6.18) is important. The market equilibrium price p_t in (6.5) depends upon the fractions n_{ht}. The notation in (6.18) stresses the fact that these fractions n_{ht} depend upon *past fitness* $U_{h,t-1}$, which in turn depend upon past prices p_{t-1} and dividends y_{t-1} in periods $t-1$ and further in the past. After the equilibrium price p_t has been revealed by the market, it will be used in evolutionary updating of beliefs and determining the new fractions $n_{h,t+1}$. These new fractions $n_{h,t+1}$ will then determine a new equilibrium price p_{t+1}, and so on. In the ABS, market equilibrium prices and fractions of different trading strategies thus coevolve over time.

A natural candidate for evolutionary fitness is accumulated *realized profits*, as given by

$$U_{ht} = (p_t + y_t - Rp_{t-1})\frac{E_{h,t-1}[\mathbf{p}_t + \mathbf{y}_t - Rp_{t-1}]}{a\sigma^2} - C_h + wU_{h,t-1}, \qquad (6.19)$$

where $R = 1 + r$ is the gross risk free rate of return, C_h represents an average per period *cost* of obtaining forecasting strategy h and $0 \le w \le 1$ is a *memory* parameter measuring how fast past realized fitness is discounted for strategy selection. The cost C_h for obtaining forecasting strategy h will be zero for simple, habitual rule of thumb forecasting rules, but may be positive for more sophisticated forecasting strategies. For example, costs for forecasting strategies based upon economic fundamentals may be positive, representing investors' effort for information gathering and market research, whereas costs for (simple) technical trading rules may be (close to) zero. The first term in (6.19) represents last period's realized profit of type h given by the realized excess return of the risky asset over the risk free asset times the demand for the risky asset by traders of type h. In the extreme case with no memory, i.e., $w = 0$, fitness U_{ht} equals net realized profit in the previous period, whereas in the other extreme case with infinite memory, i.e., $w = 1$, fitness U_{ht} equals total wealth as given by accumulated realized profits over the entire past. In the intermediate case, the weight given to past realized profits decreases exponentially with time.[7]

Fitness can be rewritten in deviations from the fundamental as

$$U_{ht} = (x_t - Rx_{t-1})(\frac{f_{h,t-1} - Rx_{t-1}}{a\sigma^2}) - C_h + wU_{h,t-1}. \qquad (6.20)$$

---

[7] In this chapter, we focus on the simple case without memory, i.e., $w = 0$. See Hommes et al. (2012) for an investigation and discussion how memory in the evolutionary fitness measure affects the dynamical behavior.

Risk adjusted profits as fitness measure

Although realized net profits are a natural candidate for evolutionary fitness, this fitness measure does *not* take into account the *risk* taken at the moment of the investment decision. In fact, given that investors are risk averse mean-variance maximizers maximizing their expected utility from wealth (6.2), another natural candidate for fitness is the *risk adjusted profit*. Using the notation $R_t = p_t + y_t - Rp_{t-1}$ for realized excess return, the realized risk adjusted profit for strategy h in period t is given by

$$\pi_{ht} = R_t z_{h,t-1} - \frac{a}{2}\sigma^2 z_{h,t-1}^2, \tag{6.21}$$

where $z_{h,t-1} = E_{h,t-1}[R_t]/(a\sigma^2)$ is the demand by trader type h as in (6.3). Notice that maximizing expected utility from wealth in (6.2) is equivalent to maximizing expected utility from profits in (6.21). A risk adjusted fitness measure based on (6.21) is thus consistent with the investors' demand function derived from mean-variance maximization of expected wealth. The fitness measure (6.19) based upon realized profits does not take into account the variance term in (6.21), capturing the investors' risk taken before obtaining that profit. On the other hand, in real markets realized net profits or accumulated wealth may be what investors care about most, and the non-risk adjusted fitness measure (6.19) may thus be important in financial practice.

The expression for risk adjusted profit fitness can be simplified and turns out to be equivalent, up to a constant factor, to minus squared prediction errors. In order to see this, we will subtract off the realized risk adjusted profit π_{Rt} obtained by rational (perfect foresight) traders from (6.21). The risk adjusted profit π_{Rt} by rational agents is given by

$$\pi_{Rt} = R_t \frac{R_t}{a\sigma^2} - \frac{a}{2}\sigma^2 \frac{R_t^2}{a^2\sigma^4} = \frac{R_t^2}{2a\sigma^2}. \tag{6.22}$$

Since π_{Rt} is independent of h, subtracting this term from (6.21) will not affect the maximization of expected utility by trader type h. Notice also that, subtracting this term from (6.21) will not affect the fractions n_{ht} of trader type h, since the discrete choice probabilities (6.18) are independent of the level of the fitness. Using $z_{h,t-1} = E_{h,t-1}[R_t]/(a\sigma^2)$ a simple computation shows that

$$\pi_{ht} - \pi_{Rt} = -\frac{1}{2a\sigma^2}(R_t - E_{h,t-1}[R_t])^2$$

$$= -\frac{1}{2a\sigma^2}(p_t - E_{h,t-1}[p_t] + \delta_{y,t})^2 \tag{6.23}$$

$$= -\frac{1}{2a\sigma^2}(x_t - E_{h,t-1}[x_t] + \delta_t)^2,$$

where $\delta_{y,t} = y_t - E_{t-1}[y_t]$ and $\delta_t = p_t^* + y_t - E_{t-1}[p_t^* + y_t]$ are both MDS sequences.[8] The fitness measure risk adjusted profits is thus, up to a constant factor and an MDS

---

[8] In the special case of an IID dividend process $y_t = \bar{y} + \epsilon_t$ and corresponding constant fundamental price $p^* = \bar{y}/r$, we have $\delta_{y,t} = \delta_t = \epsilon_t$.

sequence, equivalent to minus squared forecasting errors. The risk adjusted fitness measure is now formally defined as

$$V_{ht} = -\frac{1}{2a\sigma^2}(p_t - E_{h,t-1}[\mathbf{p}_t] + \delta_{y,t})^2 - C_h + wV_{h,t-1}, \tag{6.24}$$

or, in deviations from the fundamental,

$$V_{ht} = -\frac{1}{2a\sigma^2}(x_t - E_{h,t-1}[\mathbf{x}_t] + \delta_t)^2 - C_h + wV_{h,t-1}. \tag{6.25}$$

The random term δ_t or $\delta_{y,t}$ enters because the dividend process is stochastic, and thus again represents intrinsic uncertainty about economic fundamentals

6.4 Forecasting rules

To complete the model we have to specify the class of forecasting rules. Brock and Hommes (1998) investigated evolutionary competition between *simple linear* forecasting rules with only *one lag*, i.e.,

$$f_{ht} = g_h x_{t-1} + b_h. \tag{6.26}$$

It can be argued that, for a forecasting strategy to have any impact in real markets, it has to be simple. For a complicated forecasting rule it seems unlikely that enough traders will coordinate on that particular rule so that it affects market equilibrium prices. In contrast, a simple forecasting rule such as trend extrapolation may attract many followers simultaneously when such a pattern is recognized. Although the linear forecasting rule (6.26) is extremely simple, it represent a number of important cases. For example, when both the trend parameter and the bias parameter $g_h = b_h = 0$ the rule reduces to the forecast of *fundamentalists*, i.e.,

$$f_{ht} \equiv 0, \tag{6.27}$$

believing that the market price will be equal to the fundamental price p^*, or equivalently that the deviation x from the fundamental will be 0. Other important cases covered by the linear forecasting rule (6.26) are the pure *trend followers*

$$f_{ht} = g_h x_{t-1}, \qquad g_h > 0, \tag{6.28}$$

and the pure *biased belief*

$$f_{ht} = b_h. \tag{6.29}$$

Notice that the simple pure bias forecast (6.29) represents *any* positively or negatively biased forecast of next periods price that traders might have. Another simple and plausible rule that will be considered below is (formulated in prices):

$$p_{t+1}^e = p_{t-1} + g(p_{t-1} - p_{t-2}), \tag{6.30}$$

extrapolating the last observed price change from the last observed price. This *trend-following forecasting rule* has been frequently observed in learning-to-forecast experiments in the laboratory; see Chapter 8.

Instead of simple habitual rule of thumb forecasting rules, some economists prefer the rational, *perfect foresight* forecasting rule

$$f_{ht} = x_{t+1}. \tag{6.31}$$

The perfect foresight forecasting rule (6.31) assumes perfect knowledge of the heterogeneous market equilibrium equation (6.5), and in particular perfect knowledge about the beliefs of *all* other traders. Although a model where at least part of the agents have perfect foresight certainly has theoretical appeal, its practical relevance in a complex heterogeneous world should not be overstated, because assuming knowledge about other agents' beliefs seems highly unrealistic in real markets.[9]

6.5   Simple examples

This section presents simple, stylized examples of adaptive belief systems (ABS), with two, three resp. four competing *linear* forecasting rules (6.26), where the parameter g_h represents a perceived *trend* in prices and the parameter b_h represents a perceived upward or downward *bias*. In deviations from the fundamental, the ABS is of the form:

$$(1+r)x_t = \sum_{h=1}^{H} n_{ht}(g_h x_{t-1} + b_h) + \epsilon_t, \tag{6.32}$$

$$n_{h,t} = \frac{e^{\beta U_{h,t-1}}}{\sum_{h=1}^{H} e^{\beta U_{h,t-1}}}, \tag{6.33}$$

$$U_{h,t-1} = (x_{t-1} - Rx_{t-2})\left(\frac{g_h x_{t-3} + b_h - Rx_{t-2}}{a\sigma^2}\right) + wU_{h,t-2} - C_h, \tag{6.34}$$

where ϵ_t is a small noise term. This noise term could represent a shock to economic fundamentals or, for example, random outside supply of the risky asset or a small fraction of noise traders added to the market equilibrium equation (6.4). In order to keep the analysis of the dynamical behavior tractable, Brock and Hommes (1998) focused on the case where the memory parameter $w = 0$, so that evolutionary fitness is given by last period's realized profit. In the case without memory, i.e., $w = 0$, and

---

[9] In Chapter 5, Section 5.2 we discussed the cobweb model with rational (perfect foresight) versus naive expectations, as in Brock and Hommes (1997a). The cobweb model with rational versus naive remains tractable, because it can be solved explicitly for the unique market equilibrium price (5.14). In general, however, including one type of agents with rational expectations or perfect foresight in a *temporary equilibrium* model with heterogeneous beliefs such as the asset pricing market equilibrium equation in (6.16) leads to an *implicitly defined* dynamical system with x_t on the LHS and x_{t+1} and, e.g., $x_{t-1}, x_{t-2}, \ldots$ on the RHS. Typically such implicitly defined evolutionary systems cannot be solved explicitly and they are difficult to handle analytically or even to run forward computer simulations, because typical solutions are explosive saddle point solutions. See Brock et al. (2009) for an extension of the asset pricing model with heterogeneous beliefs including a perfectly rational trader type and futures markets represented by Arrow securities.

(linear) forecasting rules with only one lag as in (6.26), substituting (6.33) and (6.34) into (6.32) yields a third-order system

$$x_t = \varphi(x_{t-1}, x_{t-2}, x_{t-3}),$$ (6.35)

or equivalently a 3-D dynamical system, whose local stability properties are relatively easy to analyze.[10] Here, we review simple examples with two, three and four forecasting rules discussing the most important bifurcation routes to complicated dynamics; for a more detailed mathematical analysis, the interested reader is referred to Brock and Hommes (1998). A common feature of all examples is that, as the intensity of choice to switch prediction or trading strategies increases, the fundamental steady state becomes (locally) unstable and non-fundamental steady states, cycles or even chaos arise.

6.5.1 Costly fundamentalists versus trend followers
The simplest example of an ABS only has *two* trader types, with forecasting rules

$$f_{1t} = 0, \qquad\qquad\qquad \text{fundamentalists} \qquad (6.36)$$
$$f_{2t} = g x_{t-1}, \qquad g > 0, \qquad \text{trend followers} \qquad (6.37)$$

The first type are fundamentalists predicting that the price will be equal to its fundamental value (or equivalently that the deviation will be zero). The second type are pure trend followers predicting that prices will rise (or fall) by a constant rate. In this example, the fundamentalists have to pay a fixed per period positive cost C for information gathering; in all other examples below, information costs will be set to zero for all trader types.

A straightforward computation shows that the fundamental price $p = p^*$, or equivalently the zero deviation $x^* = 0$, is a steady state, with steady state fractions of fundamentalists and trend followers given by

$$n_1^* = \frac{e^{-\beta C}}{1 + e^{-\beta C}}, \qquad n_2^* = \frac{1}{1 + e^{-\beta C}}. \qquad (6.38)$$

For $\beta = 0$ these fractions are equal, $n_1^* = n_2^* = 0.5$. As β increases, the steady state fraction of trend followers, n_2^*, increases (because of the information costs for fundamentalists) and approaches 1 as β tends to infinity. For small values of the trend parameter, $0 \leq g < 1 + r$, the fundamental steady state is always stable. For larger values of the trend parameter, $g > 1 + r$, trend followers can *destabilize* the system, when the intensity of choice to switch strategies becomes high. This is intuitively clear, since the steady fraction of trend followers approaches 1 as β increases and, if $g > 1 + r$, the fundamental steady state then becomes unstable at some critical β value.

The bifurcation diagram in Figure 6.1 illustrates the typical dynamical behavior for increasing values of the intensity of choice. For low values of the intensity of choice,

---

[10] Hommes et al. (2012) study the effect of the memory parameter w upon the dynamical behavior. For $0 < w < 1$, the dimension of the system increases, since the fitness U_{ht} of each strategy has to be included as a state variable.

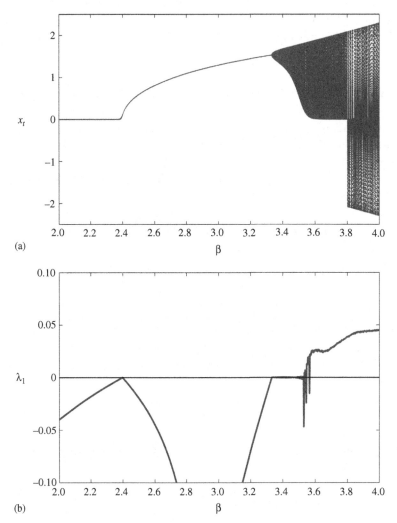

(a)

(b)

Figure 6.1. Bifurcation diagram (a) and largest Lyapunov exponent plot (b) for 2-type asset pricing model with costly fundamentalist versus trend followers. In both plots the model is buffeted with very small noise ($SD = 10^{-6}$ for the noise term ϵ_t in (6.32)), to avoid that for large β-values the system gets stuck in the locally unstable fundamental steady state. Parameters are $g = 1.2$, $R = 1.1$, $C = 1$ and $2 \leq \beta \leq 4$. A pitchfork bifurcation of the fundamental steady state, in which two stable non-fundamental steady states are created (only one is visible), occurs for $\beta \approx 2.37$. The non-fundamental steady states become unstable due to a Hopf bifurcation for $\beta \approx 3.33$, and (quasi-)periodic dynamics arises. For large values of β the largest Lyapunov exponent becomes positive, indicating chaotic price dynamics.

the fundamental steady state is stable and both types of traders coexist in the market. As the intensity of choice increases, the fundamental steady state becomes unstable due to a *pitchfork bifurcation* in which two additional non-fundamental steady states $-x^* < 0 < x^*$ are created. The evolutionary ABS may converge to the positive (i.e.,

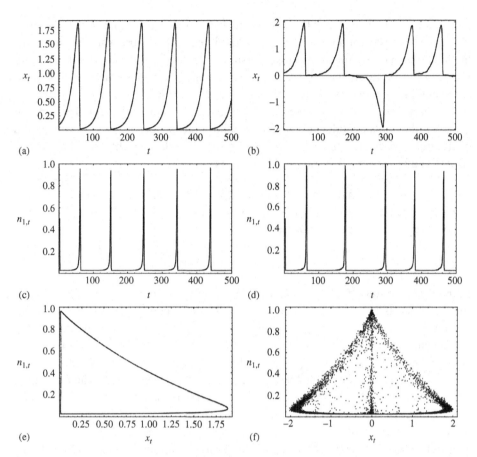

Figure 6.2. Time series of prices and fractions and attractors in the phase space for 2-type asset pricing model with costly fundamentalist versus trend followers. The left panel shows chaotic dynamics without noise and the right panel illustrates the model buffeted with small noise (SD = 0.01 of noise term ϵ_t in [6.32]). Without noise (left panel) the system settles down to the attractor with prices above the fundamental value. Prices exhibit temporary bubbles when the market is dominated by trend followers and sudden crashes when the market becomes dominated by fundamentalists. In the presence of (small) noise, the system switches back and forth between the two coexisting attractors with prices exhibiting bubbles and crashes jumping between above and below fundamental values. Parameters are $\beta = 3.6$, $g = 1.2$, $R = 1.1$ and $C = 1$.

above fundamental) non-fundamental steady state, to the negative (i.e., below fundamental) non-fundamental steady state, or, in the presence of noise, switch back and forth between the high and the low steady state. As the intensity of choice increases further, the two non-fundamental steady states also become unstable due to a secondary Hopf bifurcation, and more complicated dynamics arises as illustrated in Figures 6.1 and 6.2. After the Hopf bifurcation coexisting invariant circles around each of the two non-fundamental steady states arise with stable limit cycles and quasi-periodic attractors. The evolutionary ABS may cycle around the positive unstable non-fundamental steady state, cycle around the negative unstable non-fundamental steady state or, driven by the noise, switch back and forth between cycles around the high and the low steady states. The largest Lyapunov exponent plot in Figure 6.1b illustrates that the asset pricing model with costly fundamentalists versus cheap trend followers exhibits a *rational route to randomness*, that is, a bifurcation route to chaos (with positive largest Lyapunov exponent) as the intensity of choice to switch strategies increases.

It is useful to discuss the case $\beta = +\infty$. It can be shown that for $\beta = +\infty$ and $g > 1+r$, the fundamental steady state is a saddle point and, depending on the magnitude of the trend parameter, there are two possibilities for the unstable manifold $W^u(E)$ (Brock and Hommes, 1998, Lemma 4, p. 1251):

1. if $g > (1+r)^2$, then the unstable manifold $W^u(E)$ equals the (unbounded) unstable eigenvector, and typical solutions are exploding and diverging to infinity with trend followers dominating the market;
2. if $1+r < g < (1+r)^2$, then the unstable manifold $W^u(E)$ is bounded; all time paths converge to the (locally) unstable saddle point fundamental steady state.

In the first case trend followers extrapolate strongly and always make higher profits, causing price bubbles to diverge to infinity. In the second case, for $\beta = +\infty$ and $1+r < g < (1+r)^2$, the system has a *homoclinic orbit*. For an initial state close to the fundamental steady state, prices start following a temporary bubble, with all agents being trend followers, until all agents switch to the fundamental strategy, causing prices to converge to the (unstable) saddle point fundamental steady state.[11] The fact that the system has a homoclinic orbit for $\beta = +\infty$ suggests that the dynamics is complicated, and chaotic, for large values of the intensity of choice.

The dynamics of this simple 2-type example, with fundamentalists versus trend followers, sheds interesting light on the discussion about the "Friedman hypothesis." Milton Friedman has been one of the strongest advocates of a rational agent approach to economics, arguing that the behavior of consumers, firms and investors can be described "as if" they behave rationally. The Friedman hypothesis is essentially an evolutionary argument stating that non-rational agents will not survive evolutionary competition because they will lose money against rational traders and will therefore be driven out of the market. Our simple 2-type example may be seen as a counterexample to the Friedman hypothesis, in which costly (rational) fundamentalists cannot drive out speculative trend followers, who survive evolutionary competition driven by short run profits. The survival of trend followers in our evolutionary adaptive learning system causes persistent price deviations from the fundamental with temporary bubbles and sudden market crashes.

---

[11] In the representative rational agent benchmark, profits of the rational agents equal 0 (cf. the expression of profits in (6.20) and evaluate at the fundamental steady state, i.e., for $x = 0$). In our 2-type model, for $\beta = +\infty$ and $1+r < g < (1+r)^2$, close to the fundamental steady state profits of trend followers will be slightly negative (i.e., slightly smaller than profits in a perfectly rational world), but profits of fundamentalists are negative due to information-gathering costs. As price follows a temporary bubble, for $1+r < g < (1+r)^2$, profits of trend followers become more negative and at some point it becomes profitable to switch to the costly fundamental strategy and price jumps to its fundamental value.

6.5.2   Fundamentalists versus optimists and pessimists

In the 2-type asset pricing model with fundamentalists versus trend followers in the previous subsection as well as in the cobweb model with rational versus naive expectations in Chapter 5, Section 5.2, rational routes to randomness occur due to information-gathering costs for the more sophisticated rational or fundamental forecasting strategy. This subsection discusses a simple ABS example with *three* trader types *without* any information-gathering costs. The forecasting rules are

$$f_{1t} = 0, \qquad\qquad\qquad\qquad \text{fundamentalists} \qquad\qquad (6.39)$$

$$f_{2t} = b, \qquad b > 0, \qquad \text{positive bias (optimists)} \qquad (6.40)$$

$$f_{3t} = -b, \qquad -b < 0, \qquad \text{negative bias (pessimists).} \qquad (6.41)$$

The first type are fundamentalists again, but there will be *no* information costs for fundamentalists (or other types). The second and third types have a purely *biased* belief, expecting a constant price above respectively below the fundamental price. Type 2 are optimistic traders, while type 3 are pessimistic.

Since the optimist and pessimists are symmetrically opposite, using (6.32) it is easy to check that the fundamental price (i.e., $x^* = 0$) is a steady state. The bifurcation diagram in Figure 6.3 shows that the fundamental steady state is stable for low values of the intensity of choice. As the intensity of choice increases, the fundamental steady becomes unstable due to a *Hopf bifurcation* and the dynamics of the ABS is characterized by cycles around the unstable steady state. The plot of the largest Lyapunov exponent in Figure 6.3 (b) shows that after the Hopf bifurcation, the system does *not* become chaotic, but cycles and quasi-periodic dynamics arise with largest Lyapunov exponent (close to) 0.

This example shows that, even when there are *no* information costs for fundamentalists, they cannot drive out other trader types with optimistic and pessimistic opposite biased beliefs. In the evolutionary ABS with high intensity of choice, fundamentalists and biased traders coexist with their fractions varying over time and prices cycling around the unstable fundamental steady state, as illustrated in Figure 6.4. Along the cycles, the fraction of fundamentalists remains relatively low and the market is interchagably dominated by optimists and pessimists. Brock and Hommes (1998, p. 1259, Lemma 9) show that for $\beta = +\infty$ the 3-type ABS converges to a (globally) stable cycle of period 4, with the market dominated by optimistic traders for two periods, thereafter dominated by pessimists for two periods, and so on. Average profits along this 4-cycle are equal for all three trader types. Hence, if the initial wealth is equal for all three types, then in this evolutionary system in the long run accumulated wealth will be equal for all three types. This is another counterexample to the Friedman hypothesis that smart fundamental traders will automatically drive out simple habitual rule of thumb speculative traders. In the current example, even without any information-gathering costs fundamental traders cannot drive out optimistic and pessimistic speculative traders in evolutionary competition driven by profitability. Optimists and pessimists survive evolutionary competition in the long run and cause excess volatility in asset prices.

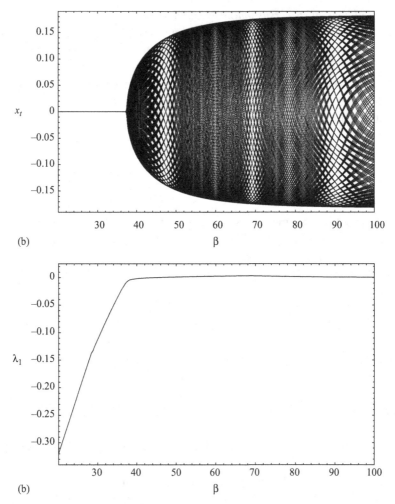

Figure 6.3. Bifurcation diagram (a) and largest Lyapunov exponent plot (b) for 3-type asset pricing model with fundamentalists versus optimists and pessimists. In both plots the model is buffeted with very small noise ($SD = 10^{-6}$ for the noise term ϵ_t in (6.32)), to avoid that for large β-values the system gets stuck in the locally unstable steady state. Belief parameters are $g_1 = 0$, $b_1 = 0$; $g_2 = 0$, $b_2 = 0.2$ and $g_3 = 0$, $b_3 = -0.2$; other parameters are $r = 0.1$, $20 \leq \beta \leq 100$, $w = 0$ and $C_h = 0$ for all $1 \leq h \leq 3$. The 3-type model with fundamentalists versus opposite biases exhibits a Hopf bifurcation for $\beta \approx 37.4$. For large values of β periodic and quasi-periodic dynamics occurs, but chaos with positive largest Lyapunov exponent does not arise.

In this simple 3-type example cycles occur, but chaos does not arise, since the largest Lyapunov exponent always remains non-positive. In the three type example with fundamentalists versus optimists and pessimists, even in the presence of (small) noise, price fluctuations will be fairly regular and therefore returns will be predictable. One might therefore argue that this example is not "evolutionary stable" and other types might

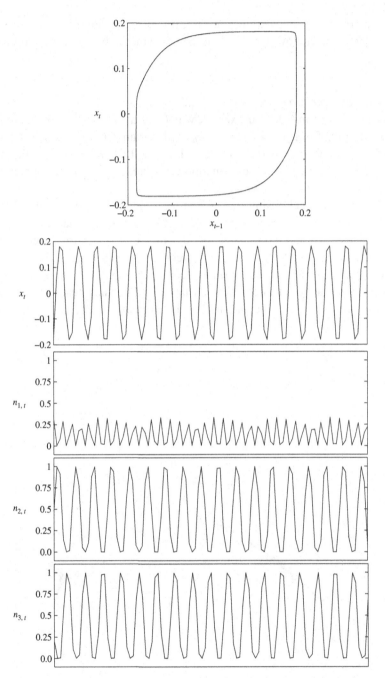

Figure 6.4. Time series and phase plots for 3-type asset pricing model with fundamentalists versus optimists and pessimists. A quasi-periodic attractor (top panel) with quasi-periodic fluctuations in prices and fractions. Belief parameters are $g_1 = 0$, $b_1 = 0$; $g_2 = 0$, $b_2 = 0.2$ and $g_3 = 0$, $b_3 = -0.2$; other parameters are $r = 0.1$, $\beta = 100$, $w = 0$ and $C_h = 0$ for all $1 \leq h \leq 3$ For large values of β periodic and quasi-periodic dynamics occurs, but chaos does not arise.

enter the market. The predictability in asset prices will disappear, or at least become much harder to detect, however, when we combine biased beliefs with trend-following strategies.

6.5.3 *Fundamentalists versus trend and bias*

The third example of an ABS is an example with *four* trader types, with linear forecasting rules (6.26) of the form $f_{ht} = g_h x_{t-1} + b_h$, with parameters $g_1 = 0$, $b_1 = 0$; $g_2 = 0.9$, $b_2 = 0.2$; $g_3 = 0.9$, $b_3 = -0.2$ and $g_4 = 1 + r = 1.01$, $b_4 = 0$. The first type are fundamentalists again, without information costs, and the other three types follow a simple linear forecasting rule with one lag.

The reader may check, using (6.32), that the fundamental price (i.e., $x^* = 0$) is a steady state. For low values of the intensity of choice, the fundamental steady state is stable. Figures 6.5 and 6.6 illustrate the dynamical behavior for different values of the intensity of choice. As the intensity of choice increases, as in the 3-type example before, the fundamental steady state becomes unstable due to a *Hopf bifurcation* and a stable invariant circle around the unstable fundamental steady state arises, with periodic or quasi-periodic fluctuations. As the intensity of choice further increases,

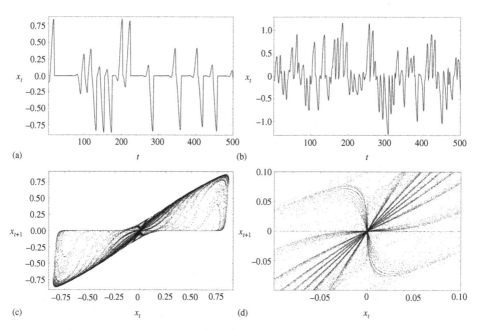

Figure 6.5. Chaotic (a) and noisy chaotic (b) time series of asset prices in adaptive belief system with four trader types. Strange attractor (c) and enlargement of strange attractor (d). Asset prices exhibit temporary bubbles and sudden market crashes. In the presence of small noise, the timing of the bubbles and crashes becomes difficult to predict. Belief parameters are $g_1 = 0$, $b_1 = 0$; $g_2 = 0.9$, $b_2 = 0.2$; $g_3 = 0.9$, $b_3 = -0.2$ and $g_4 = 1 + r = 1.01$, $b_4 = 0$; other parameters are $r = 0.01$, $\beta = 90.5$, $w = 0$ and $C_h = 0$ for all $1 \leq h \leq 4$.

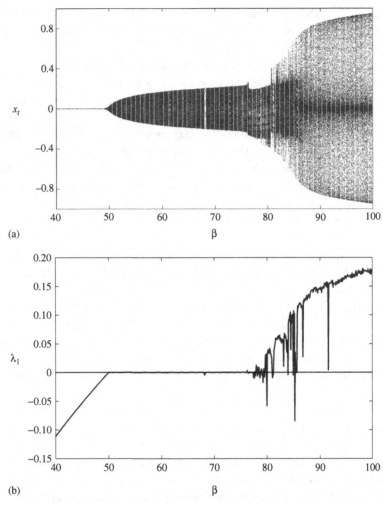

Figure 6.6. Bifurcation diagram (a) and largest Lyapunov exponent plot (b) for 4-type asset pricing model. In both plots the model is buffeted with very small noise ($SD = 10^{-6}$ for noise term ϵ_t in (6.32)), to avoid that for large β-values the system gets stuck in the locally unstable fundamental steady state. Belief parameters are $g_1 = 0$, $b_1 = 0$; $g_2 = 0.9$, $b_2 = 0.2$; $g_3 = 0.9$, $b_3 = -0.2$ and $g_4 = 1 + r = 1.01$, $b_4 = 0$; other parameters are $r = 0.01$, $40 \leq \beta \leq 100$, $w = 0$ and $C_h = 0$ for all $1 \leq h \leq 4$. The 4-type model with fundamentalists versus trend followers and biased beliefs exhibits a Hopf bifurcation for $\beta = 50$. A rational route to randomness occurs, with positive largest Lyapunov exponents, when the intensity of choice becomes large.

the invariant circle breaks into a strange attractor with chaotic fluctuations, as illustrated in Figure 6.5. In the evolutionary ABS fundamentalists and chartists coexist with their fractions varying over time and prices moving chaotically around the unstable fundamental steady state. The bifurcation diagram in Figure 6.6 (a) shows that in this

4-type example with fundamentalists versus trend followers and biased beliefs a rational route to randomness occurs, with a positive largest Lyapunov exponent for large values of β (Figure 6.6(b)).

The (noisy) chaotic price fluctuations are characterized by an irregular switching between phases of close-to-the-fundamental-price fluctuations, phases of "optimism" with prices following an upward trend, and phases of "pessimism," with sudden market crashes, as illustrated in Figure 6.5. Asset returns have close to zero autocorrelations and are therefore difficult to predict. Recall from Subsection 6.1 that, in addition to the benchmark fundamental price, the asset pricing model with homogeneous beliefs has rational bubble solutions of the form (6.10), growing at the risk free rate. One might say that in the ABS prices are characterized by an evolutionary switching between the fundamental value and temporary speculative bubbles. In the purely deterministic chaotic case, the timing and the direction of the temporary bubbles seem hard to predict. However, once a bubble has started, in the deterministic case, the length of the bubble seems to be predictable in most of the cases. In the presence of noise, however, as illustrated in Figure 6.5b, the timing, the direction and the length of the bubble all seem hard to predict.

In order to illustrate the (un)predictability of this simple nonlinear adaptive belief system further, we use the so-called *nearest neighbor forecasting method* to predict the returns, at lags 1 to 20 for the purely deterministic chaotic ABS as well as for several noisy chaotic return time series. The results are illustrated in Figure 6.7.[12] Nearest neighbor forecasting is a method of analogs; it looks for patterns in the time series in the past which resemble the most recent pattern, and then computes as its forecast the average value following all nearby past patterns. It follows from Takens' embedding theorem that this method yields good forecasts for deterministic chaotic systems.[13] Figure 6.7 shows that the nearest neighbor forecasting method works well in the deterministic chaotic case (bottom graph), with forecasting errors much smaller than simply predicting by the sample average. However, as the noise level increases, the graphs in Figure 6.7 move upward, implying that the forecasting performance of the nearest neighbor method quickly deteriorates at all lags. Hence, in the simple nonlinear evolutionary ABS, in the presence of noise it is hard to make good forecasts of future returns. The very simple 4-type nonlinear ABS with small noise (equivalent to a small fraction of noise traders) thus already captures some of the intrinsic unpredictability of asset returns also present in real markets.

This 4-type example ABS shows that, even when there are *no* information costs for fundamentalists, they cannot drive out other simple trader types such as trend followers and fail to stabilize price fluctuations toward its fundamental value. As in the 3-type case, the opposite biases create cyclic behavior and the additional trend extrapolation rules turn these cycles into unpredictable chaotic price fluctuations and create a complex

---

[12] I am grateful to Sebastiano Manzan for computing and providing this figure.

[13] See Kantz and Schreiber (1997) for an extensive treatment of nonlinear time series analysis and nonlinear forecasting techniques such as nearest neighbor.

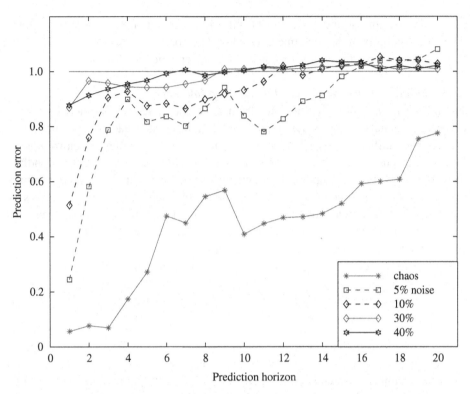

Figure 6.7. Forecasting errors for nearest neighbor method applied to chaotic returns series (lowest graph) as well as noisy chaotic returns series, for time horizons 1−20 and for different noise levels, in ABS with four trader types. All returns series have close to zero autocorrelations at all lags. The benchmark case of prediction by the mean is represented by the horizontal line at the normalized prediction error 1. Nearest neighbor forecasting applied to the purely deterministic chaotic series leads to much smaller forecasting errors (lowest graph), with very small errors at horizons 1−5 and steadily increasing forecasting errors as the time horizon increases. A noise level of say 10% means that the ratio of the variance of the noise term ϵ_t and the variance of the deterministic price series is 1/10. As the noise level slowly increases, the graphs shift upward as forecast errors increase. Small dynamic noise thus quickly deteriorates the forecasting performance in this simple nonlinear ABS.

environment in which trend-following behavior survives profit-driven evolutionary competition and predictable patterns in asset returns are hard to find.

6.6 An example with coexisting attractors

Nonlinear systems may exhibit *path dependence*, i.e., the long run behavior of the system may depend on the initial state. In this section we discuss a simple 2-type example ABS in which different types of attractors coexist.[14] In particular, in this 2-type example ABS a stable fundamental steady state may coexist with a stable limit

---

[14] This subsection is based on Gaunersdorfer et al. (2008), where a more detailed mathematical analysis can be found.

cycle or even with a strange attractor. This illustrates an important feature of nonlinear ABS: local stability of the fundamental steady state does not imply global stability and leaves open the possibility of *far from steady state* endogenous fluctuations.

6.6.1 Fundamentalists versus conditional trend followers

The model in this subsection deviates from the earlier asset pricing model with heterogeneous beliefs in two ways. Firstly, a different evolutionary fitness measure is used, namely utility from realized profits or equivalently risk-adjusted realized profits (instead of non-risk adjusted realized profits). Secondly, technical traders condition their forecasting behavior upon price deviations from the RE fundamental benchmark, that is, the fraction of technical traders will decrease when the asset prices moves too far away from the fundamental price. In some sense, this introduces a nonlinearity in the forecasting strategy. We refer to this type of traders as *conditional trend followers*. Both deviations are discussed in more detail below.

We first formulate the model in terms of prices. Consider two belief types,

$$
\begin{aligned}
p^e_{1,t+1} &= p^* + v(p_{t-1} - p^*), & 0 \le v \le 1 \\
p^e_{2,t+1} &= p_{t-1} + g(p_{t-1} - p_{t-2}), & g \in \mathbb{R}.
\end{aligned}
\tag{6.42}
$$

Type 1 are fundamentalists, believing that next period's price will move in the direction of the fundamental price p^* by a factor v. In the special case $v = 0$, as discussed in earlier examples, fundamentalists believe that the price jumps immediately to the fundamental price. When v is close to 0 (1) fundamentalists believe the price to move quickly (slowly) toward its fundamental value p^*. Trader type 2 are technical traders or chartists, using a simple trend extrapolating rule with the last observed price as an anchor and extrapolating the last observed price change. This rule has been observed frequently in learning-to-forecast laboratory experiments with human subjects (see Chapter 8). If $g > 0$ these traders are trend followers expecting price changes to continue in the same direction; if $g < 0$ they are contrarians expecting a reversal of the latest price change. With two trader types, the equilibrium dynamics (6.5) reads as

$$
Rp_t = \sum_{h=1}^{2} n_{ht} p^e_{h,t+1} + \bar{y},
\tag{6.43}
$$

where $\bar{y}$ is the mean dividend as before.

Fractions n_{ht} are updated according to past performance, conditioned upon the deviation of actual prices from the fundamental value. The evolutionary selection part of the updating rules uses the discrete choice model as before:

$$
\hat{n}_{ht} = \frac{e^{\beta U_{h,t-1}}}{Z_{t-1}}, \qquad Z_{t-1} = \sum_{h} e^{\beta U_{h,t-1}},
\tag{6.44}
$$

where U_{ht} is the fitness measure. Here we take as the fitness measure the *risk adjusted* realized profits, which takes into account the risk taken at the time when the investment was made. Risk adjusted realized profit in period t is given by

$$\pi_{ht} = R_t z_{h,t-1} - \frac{a}{2}\sigma^2 z_{h,t-1}^2, \tag{6.45}$$

where $z_{h,t-1}$ is the demand for the risky asset by trader type h as before. Notice that maximizing expected wealth in (6.2) is equivalent to maximizing expected utility from profits in (6.45). A straightforward computation shows that the risk adjusted profits fitness measure is equivalent to[15]

$$U_{ht} = -\frac{1}{2a\sigma^2}(p_t - p_{ht}^e)^2 + wU_{h,t-1}, \tag{6.46}$$

where the parameter $0 \le w \le 1$ represents "memory strength" of the fitness measure. Here we set $w = 0$.[16]

In the second step of the updating of fractions *conditioning on deviations from the fundamental* by the technical traders is modeled as

$$n_{2t} = \hat{n}_{2t} \exp[-(p_{t-1} - p^*)^2/\alpha], \qquad \alpha > 0,$$
$$n_{1t} = 1 - n_{2t}. \tag{6.47}$$

According to (6.47) the fraction of technical traders decreases more as prices deviate further from their fundamental value p^*. This is motivated by the fact that technical traders are conditioning their charts upon price deviations from the fundamental, as done, for example, in the simulations of the more complicated Santa Fe agent-based artificial stock market model in Arthur et al. (1997b) and LeBaron et al. (1999). One may interpret the term $-(p_{t-1} - p^*)^2/\alpha$ as a penalty term in the fitness measure of technical traders. This penalty term ensures that speculative bubbles cannot last forever, but that at some point when prices have moved far away from the fundamental value more and more trend followers start to believe that the bubble will end and therefore switch to the fundamentalist strategy, the fraction of fundamentalists will increase and prices will stabilize. The penalty term ensures that price deviations from the fundamental remain bounded.[17] Notice that, as before, fractions in period t depend on *observed* prices up to the end of period $t - 1$, $p_{t-1}, p_{t-2}, \ldots$.

As before, it will be convenient to introduce the deviation from the fundamental price,

$$x_t = p_t - p^*.$$

---

[15] See Section 6.3. Numerical simulations in Gaunersdorfer and Hommes (2007) show that the dynamics of the model with realized profits as the fitness measure is very similar to the results presented here.

[16] Gaunersdorfer et al. (2008) also consider the more general case with memory.

[17] Hommes (2001) gives an interpretation of this "penalty term" as a transversality condition in a heterogeneous world, where temporary speculative bubbles are allowed but price deviations from the fundamental remain bounded.

In the case without memory ($w = 0$), we obtain a fourth-order or equivalently 4-D system of the form

$$x_t = \varphi(x_{t-1}, x_{t-2}, x_{t-3}, x_{t-4})$$
$$= \left[\frac{1}{R}\left((1 - n_{2t})vx_{t-1} + n_{2t}(x_{t-1} + g(x_{t-1} - x_{t-2}))\right),\right. \tag{6.48}$$

where n_2 is given by

$$n_{2t} = e^{-x_{t-1}^2/\alpha} \frac{e^{\beta u_{2,t-1}}}{e^{\beta u_{1,t-1}} + e^{\beta u_{2,t-1}}}, \tag{6.49}$$

and

$$u_{1,t-1} = -\frac{1}{2a\sigma^2}(x_{t-1} - vx_{t-3})^2,$$
$$u_{2,t-1} = -\frac{1}{2a\sigma^2}(x_{t-1} - x_{t-3} - g(x_{t-3} - x_{t-4}))^2. \tag{6.50}$$

It is easy to show that the fundamental steady state $x^* = 0$ is the unique steady state of the system. A straightforward computation gives the characteristic equation governing the stability of the fundamental steady state:

$$p(\lambda) = \lambda^2\left(\lambda^2 - \frac{1 + g + v}{2R}\lambda + \frac{g}{2R}\right). \tag{6.51}$$

Thus, the eigenvalues of the Jacobian are 0 (with multiplicity 2) and the roots λ_1, λ_2 of the quadratic polynomial in the last bracket. The reader may easily verify that an eigenvalue $\lambda = +1$ cannot arise (because $0 \le v \le 1$) and that an eigenvalue $\lambda = -1$ occurs when

$$g = g_{PD} = -\frac{1}{2}(v + 2R + 1). \tag{6.52}$$

Notice that the *period-doubling bifurcation* value $g_{PD} < 0$, so that a period-doubling bifurcation only occurs in the presence of contrarians, who expect a reversal of the latest price change. Since $v \ge 0$ and $R > 1$ it follows that $g_{PD} < -1.5$ so that only strong contrarian behavior can destabilize the fundamental steady state. Finally, using the characteristic equation (6.51) it follows that a *Hopf bifurcation*, with complex eigenvalues crossing the unit circle, occurs when

$$g = g_H = 2R. \tag{6.53}$$

The Hopf bifurcation value $g_H > 0$ and is thus caused by trend extrapolating behavior. Since $R > 1$ it follows that $g_H > 2$, implying that only strong trend extrapolators can destabilize the fundamental steady state.[18] In the next section we show, however, that

---

[18] Gaunersdorfer (2001) introduces positive information-gathering costs for fundamentalists. When fundamentalists beliefs are costly compared to simple technical trading rules, the period-doubling and Hopf bifurcation values move closer to 1 and a period-doubling bifurcation may already occur for $g_{PD} \approx -1$ and a Hopf bifurcation already for $g_H \approx 1$.

even for intermediate trend-following parameters $1 < g < 2$ – although the fundamental steady state is locally stable – the evolutionary ABS can have a coexisting stable limit cycle or even a coexisting strange attractor.

6.6.2 A locally stable steady state and coexisting cycles and chaos

This subsection investigates the onset of instability in our simple 2-type ABS. In particular, we investigate the following question: *what is the set of parameter values for which prices in the heterogeneous agent model with evolutionary learning do not necessarily converge to the fundamental steady state?* It turns out that, even when the fundamental steady state is *locally stable*, prices do not always converge to their fundamental value, but may settle down to a "far from equilibrium" coexisting stable limit cycle or even to a strange attractor. In particular, a *degenerate Hopf bifurcation* or *Chenciner bifurcation* plays an important role in the onset of instability and the possibility of coexisting attractors.

Recall from Chapter 3, Subsection 3.2.4, that the Chenciner bifurcation is a codimension 2 bifurcation. The reader should check the 2-D μ–ν bifurcation diagram of the normal form of the Chenciner bifurcation (Figure 3.7 in Subsection 3.2.4. Figure 6.8 (a) shows the bifurcation diagram around the Chenciner bifurcation point in the 2-D g–ν parameter plane, with all other parameters fixed, in the 2-type ABS with conditional trend followers versus fundamentalists. The Chenciner bifurcation point, lying on the Hopf bifurcation manifold H (the vertical line $g = 2R$), is labeled DH, whereas the curve labeled SN is the saddle node bifurcation curve of invariant circles.

To the left of the Hopf bifurcation curve, $g = 2R$, the fundamental steady state is *locally stable*. Below the Chenciner bifurcation point the Hopf bifurcation is supercritical; above the Chenciner bifurcation point the Hopf bifurcation is subcritical. Numerical simulations suggest that on the left-hand side of or below the curve SN, the fundamental steady state is *globally stable*. When crossing the curve SN from left to right, a pair of invariant circles, one stable and one unstable, are created in a saddle-node bifurcation of invariant curves. The unstable invariant circle separates the stable fundamental steady state from the stable invariant circle. In the region above the curve SN and to the left of the Hopf bifurcation curve H a second attractor (a stable limit cycle, or possibly a more complicated, chaotic attractor) coexists with the locally stable fundamental steady state. In this *coexisting attractors* region of the parameter space, the long run behavior of the system thus depends on the initial state.

The curve SN thus marks the *onset of instability*. To the right of this curve, prices do not necessarily converge to the locally stable fundamental steady state but may converge to a stable limit cycle or to a more complicated, chaotic attractor. The enlargement in Figure 6.8b shows that, as the intensity of choice β to switch strategies increases, the curve SN moves to the left and approaches the vertical line $g = 1$. This implies that, although the fundamental steady state remains locally stable, for high values of the intensity of choice β, (global) instability sets in already for trend parameters g close to 1.

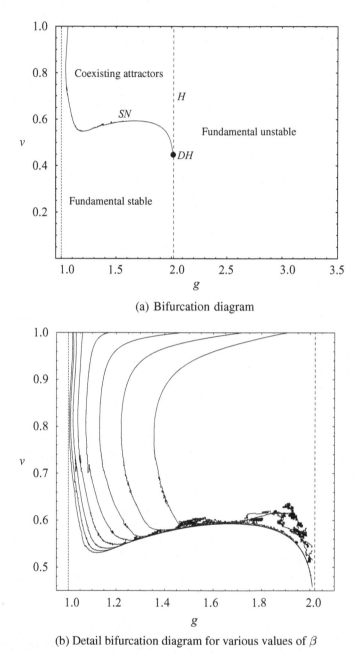

(a) Bifurcation diagram

(b) Detail bifurcation diagram for various values of β

Figure 6.8. (a) Bifurcation diagram of the Chenciner bifurcation in the g–v plane for $\beta = 1000$, $R = 1.01$ and $\alpha = 10$. At the point labeled DH ($g = 2R = 2.02$ and $v \approx 0.45$) a degenerate Hopf or Chenciner bifurcation occurs. This point lies on the Hopf bifurcation line $\{g = 2R\}$, labeled H. From the point DH a curve SN emanates corresponding to the saddle-node bifurcation curve of invariant circles. The area between the curves SN and H is the "volatility clustering region" with a second attractor (a stable limit cycle or a strange attractor) coexisting with the locally stable fundamental steady state. (b) The curve SN, corresponding to the saddle-node bifurcation of the invariant circle, for different values of the intensity of choice $\beta = 10^{i/2}$, $i = 2, \ldots, 8$. The curve SN moves to the left and approaches the vertical line $g = 1$, as the intensity of choice increases from $\beta = 10$ to $\beta = 10\,000$.

The saddle-node bifurcation of invariant circles along the curve SN is a "global" phenomenon. Invariant circles are "global" objects, and the saddle-node bifurcation of invariant curves occurs "far from the steady state." Except in a small neighborhood of the Chenciner bifurcation point, no analytic information can be obtained about the location of the bifurcation curve SN. The sketch of the location of SN in Figure 6.8 has been obtained as follows. For fixed values of β and v, plots of the phase space have been inspected numerically for a range of g-values. The lowest value of g (to a precision of 0.001) for which an attractor other than the fundamental steady state existed, has been termed the (approximate) saddle-node bifurcation value $g_*(\beta, v)$ of the invariant circle. The enlargement in the bottom panel of Figure 6.8 shows that the curve SN of points g_* moves to the left and approaches $g = 1$ as the intensity of choice β increases.[19]

The main economic consequence from this analysis is that, if traders' sensitivity to differences in fitness is high (i.e., the intensity of choice β is high) then the interaction between weakly extrapolating trend followers (i.e., for trend parameters g close to 1) and fundamentalists leads to coexistence of attractors and agents may coordinate on a stable limit cycle around the locally stable fundamental steady state.[20]

Figure 6.9 shows typical examples of attractors in the $p_t - p_{t+1}$ plane, for three different g-values with all other parameters fixed. Since $g < 2R$ *these attractors coexist with a locally stable fundamental steady state.* For $g = 1.6$ an attracting quasi-periodic circle occurs, whereas for $g = 1.7$ a stable limit cycle of period 16 occurs. For $g = 2$, after a complicated sequence of bifurcations, the invariant circle has turned into a strange attractor. The numerical simulations in Figure 6.9 thus suggest that in our 2-type ABS, a strange attractor with chaotic dynamical behavior may coexist with a locally stable fundamental steady state. In Figure 6.9c, the unstable invariant circle created at the Chenciner bifurcation can be seen as the inner boundary between the strange attractor and the locally stable fundamental steady state.

Figure 6.10 illustrates what happens after the supercritical Hopf bifurcation in the model. An important difference between the two figures is that the parameter v, that is, the factor with which fundamentalists expect prices to move toward the fundamental value, has been decreased from $v = 0.6$ in Figure 6.9 to $v = 0.3$ in Figure 6.10. Numerical simulations suggest that for $g = 2$ the fundamental steady state is globally stable, whereas for $g = 2.09$ an invariant attracting circle, with quasi-periodic (or periodic with high period) dynamics, has appeared. For $g = 2.4$, the invariant circle has developed into a strange attractor. Notice that the strange attractor in Figure 6.10c seems to contain the (unstable) fundamental steady state, suggesting that price fluctuations get close to the fundamental steady state occasionally. The corresponding chaotic time series suggests

[19] See Gaunersdorfer et al. (2005) for a plot in the 3-D parameter space $\{(g, v, \beta)\}$
[20] Hommes et al. (2005b) have carried out laboratory forecasting experiments using a similar asset pricing framework. In these experiments both possibilities, with human subjects either learning to coordinate on the fundamental price or learning to coordinate on an oscillatory pattern, have been observed; see Chapter 8 for a detailed discussion of these experiments.

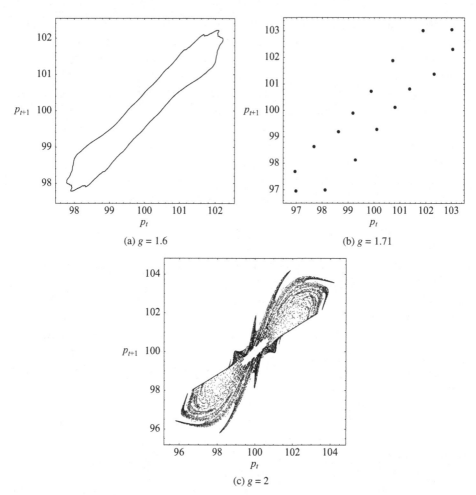

(a) $g = 1.6$

(b) $g = 1.71$

(c) $g = 2$

Figure 6.9. Projections of a quasi-periodic (a), a periodic (b) and a chaotic attractor (c) on the p_t–p_{t+1} plane. Not drawn is the locally stable fundamental steady state at $p^* = 100$. Parameters are $\beta = 4$, $v = 0.6$, $R = 1.01$, $\alpha = 10$, and $g = 1.60$ (a), $g = 1.71$ (b), and $g = 2.00$ (c). These parameter values lie in the region where two attractors coexist. The fixed point undergoes a subcritical Hopf bifurcation at $g = 2.02$. In (c) the unstable invariant circle can be seen as the inner boundary of the strange attractor.

intermittent chaos, characterized by phases of growing prices and phases of close to the fundamental price fluctuations.

There is a strikingly simple economic intuition why intermittent chaos may in fact be expected when chartists are strong trend extrapolators (i.e., the trend parameter g is large) and fundamentalists are strongly stabilizing (i.e., the parameter v is close to zero). In the presence of strong trend extrapolators the fundamental steady state is locally unstable, because trend followers strongly extrapolate small deviations from the fundamental steady state leading to oscillatory, diverging prices. When prices diverge

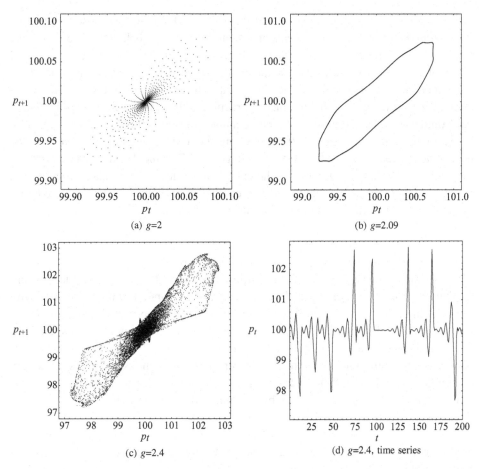

Figure 6.10. Projection of the attractors on the p_t–p_{t+1} plane. Parameters are $\beta = 4$, $v = 0.3$, $R = 1.01$, $\alpha = 10$ and $g = 2$ (a), $g = 2.09$ (b) and $g = 2.4$ (c). The fundamental steady state is attracting in (a): points spiraling towards it are shown. It undergoes a supercritical Hopf bifurcation at $g = 2.02$, has a quasi-periodic attractor for $g = 2.09$ and a strange attractor for $g = 2.4$, with corresponding time series in the plot (d) showing intermittent chaos.

and move away far above or below the fundamental value, technical traders conditioning their charts upon market fundamentals will abandon their rule and the upward or downward price trend will stop and most technical analysts will start following the fundamental rule. When fundamentalists are strongly stabilizing, prices will then quickly move into a small neighborhood of the fundamental steady state. Due to the strong trend extrapolators, the fundamental steady state is locally unstable and prices start oscillating again and the story then repeats. This mechanism suggests that the evolutionary interaction causes the fundamental steady state to have a saddle point structure with a locally destabilizing force due to strong trend extrapolation and a globally stabilizing force due to strong stabilization by fundamentalists.

This economic intuition suggests that this 2-type ABS is in fact close to having a *homoclinic orbit* and its associated complicated dynamical behavior. The economic intuition also suggests reasons why the dynamics might be chaotic. A set of initial states of the system close to the fundamental will be *stretched out* during the phase when technical traders dominate and extrapolate a trend. At the point where the fundamentalists start to become the dominating fraction in the market, the set will be *folded back* onto itself. The action of the fundamentalists transports this folded set back close to the fundamental. It is precisely this stretching and folding which lies at the root of the occurrence of chaos in dynamical systems in general. Technical trading causes stretching, whereas the conditioning of technical trading rules upon fundamentals causes folding, and the interaction between these competing strategies in the adaptive belief system forms a natural environment for intermittent chaos .

6.6.3 An endogenous mechanism for volatility clustering

Many financial time series exhibit volatility clustering, that is, an irregular switching between "quiet phases," with low market volatility, and "turbulent" phases, with high volatility. In the ABS volatility clustering arises endogenously due to the interaction between fundamentalists and technical analysts, and the switching between these strategies driven by adaptive, evolutionary learning. In the 2-type example with fundamentalists versus conditional trend followers, two endogenous mechanisms explain clustered volatility: intermittent chaos and coexistence of attractors.

Intermittent chaos is characterized by irregular switching between phases where fundamentalists dominate the market and price fluctuations are close to the fundamental steady state, and phases where trend followers dominate the market and prices follow temporary bubbles, ending by sudden market crashes (see, e.g., the time series in Figure 6.10d).

In the case of coexisting attractors, small noise may force the ABS to switch irregularly between the different basins of attraction. Figure 6.11 shows a noisy time series of the 2-type ABS in the case of a locally stable fundamental steady state coexisting with a strange attractor. In this stochastic simulation, a noise term ϵ_t (normally distributed, with standard deviation $\sigma = 0.5$) has been included in the equilibrium pricing equation (6.43), which is equivalent to adding a small fraction of noise traders, who trade randomly, to the market clearing equation (6.4). Due to the presence of noise traders, the market switches irregularly between a low-volatility phase, dominated by fundamentalists with prices close to the fundamental value, and a high-volatility phase, dominated by trend followers with prices exhibiting temporary bubbles. These temporary bubbles are triggered by noise traders and reinforced by trend followers.

There is a simple *economic intuition* why in the 2-type ABS both intermittent chaos and coexistence of a locally stable fundamental steady state and a stable limit cycle occur, depending upon the strength of trend extrapolation (as measured by the trend parameter g) and the strength of fundamental stabilization (as measured by the factor v with which fundamentalists expect prices to move toward the fundamental value).

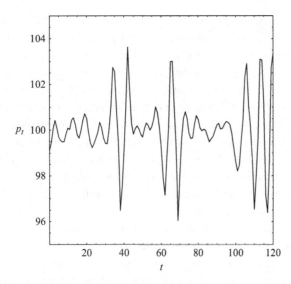

Figure 6.11. Stochastic simulation of prices for the model with fundamentalists and conditional chartists together with a small fraction of noise traders. Parameters $v = 0.6$ and $g = 2$ are such that a stable fundamental steady state and a strange attractor coexist (see Figure 6.9c). Due to the noise traders, price fluctuations switch irregularly between a low-volatility phase, with prices close to the fundamental value, and a high-volatility phase, with prices exhibiting temporary bubbles. These temporary bubbles are triggered by noise trader and reinforced by trend followers.

In the presence of strongly extrapolating chartists, small price deviations from the fundamental will be reinforced by trend extrapolation. The fundamental steady state will therefore be locally unstable and prices move away from their fundamental value. When the price deviation from the fundamental becomes too large, however, chartists will abandon their rules since they condition their charts on market fundamentals. Most technical traders will thus start following a fundamental rule and, when fundamentalists are strongly stabilizing, prices will quickly move back close to the fundamental value, and the story repeats. The evolutionary system with interactions between strongly extrapolating chartists and strongly stabilizing fundamentalists has homoclinic orbits, leading to a strange attractor with intermittent chaos and irregular price fluctuations switching between phases of low and high volatility, as illustrated in Figure 6.10.

When the chartists are only weak trend extrapolators, the fundamental steady state is locally stable. The trend extrapolators may be strong enough, however, to reinforce a price trend far away from the fundamental steady state. This upward trend, say, cannot continue forever, since chartists condition their rule upon market fundamentals and at some point will switch to become fundamentalists. Prices will then return in the direction of the fundamental value, and a downward trend will start. If fundamentalists are only weakly stabilizing, prices will only move slowly downward and will not get close enough to the (locally stable) fundamental steady state. Trend followers will extrapolate the downward trend, until the point when prices move too far away from their fundamental value and the downward trend will be reversed into an upward trend, and the story repeats. This mechanism leads to a market in which a locally stable fundamental steady state coexists with a stable limit cycle or strange attractor. When the intensity of choice to switch strategies is high, coordination on a stable limit cycle around a locally stable fundamental steady state may arise even when trend followers are only weakly extrapolating (i.e., for g-values close to 1). When traders are highly sensitive to differences in fitness, the evolutionary interaction between weak trend extrapolators and weakly stabilizing fundamentalists may thus lead to a stable limit cycle (or a more complicated attractor) around a (locally) stable fundamental steady state. In the presence of noise, the market then switches irregularly between phases of low volatility and phases of high volatility.

The model studied here is admittedly simple and should only be viewed as a stylized, analytically tractable behavioral model. Volatility clustering arises, at least in a qualitative sense. We have proposed intermittency and coexistence of attractors (e.g., arising from a Chenciner bifurcation) as an *endogenous explanation* of clustered volatility. Both intermittency and coexistence of attractors are "generic" phenomena, and similar phenomena are therefore likely to occur in more complicated, nonlinear dynamical models.

6.7 Many trader types

In the stylized heterogeneous agent models discussed in this book so far, the number of trader types is small, typically two, three or four types. In agent-based simulation models it is easy to build in many different agent types. Analytical tractability, however, often comes at the cost of restricting attention to just a few different types. What happens in evolutionary ABS when the number of different types becomes large? In this section, we discuss results of Brock, Hommes and Wagener (2005), who developed a theoretical framework to study evolutionary markets with *many* different trader types. They introduce the notion of *large type limit (LTL)*, a simple, low-dimensional system approximating an evolutionary market with many different trader types. The notion of LTL was developed within a general market clearing setting, but here we focus on its application to the asset pricing model.[21]

Recall from (6.16) that in the asset market with H different trader types, the equilibrium price (in deviations x_t from the fundamental benchmark) is given by

$$x_t = \frac{1}{1+r} \sum_{h=1}^{H} n_{ht} f_{ht}. \tag{6.54}$$

---

[21] Anufriev et al. (2012) contains a recent application of LTL to macroeconomics, in particular to a frictionless DSGE macro-model and study the stabilizing effect of monetary policy interest rate rules under hetergeneous expectations.

Using the *multinomial logit* probabilities (6.18) for the fractions n_{ht} we get

$$x_t = \frac{1}{1+r} \frac{\sum_{h=1}^{H} e^{\beta U_{h,t-1}} f_{ht}}{\sum_{h=1}^{H} e^{\beta U_{h,t-1}}}. \tag{6.55}$$

The equilibrium equation (6.55) determines the evolution of the *system with H trader types* – this defines the *evolution map* $\varphi_H(\mathbf{x}, \lambda, \vartheta)$:

$$\varphi_H(\mathbf{x}, \lambda, \vartheta) = \frac{1}{1+r} \frac{\sum_{h=1}^{H} e^{\beta U(\mathbf{x}, \lambda, \vartheta_h)} f(\mathbf{x}, \lambda, \vartheta_h)}{\sum_{h=1}^{H} e^{\beta U(\mathbf{x}, \lambda, \vartheta_h)}}, \tag{6.56}$$

where $\mathbf{x} = (x_{t-1}, x_{t-2}, \cdots)$ is a vector of past deviations from the fundamental, λ is a structural parameter vector (including, e.g., the risk free interest rate r, the risk aversion parameter a, the intensity of choice β, etc.) and the *belief variable* ϑ_h is now a multidimensional *stochastic* variable which characterizes the belief of type h. At the beginning of the market, a large number H of beliefs is sampled from a general distribution of beliefs. For example, all forecasting rules may be drawn from a linear class of rules with L lags,

$$f_t(\vartheta_0) = \vartheta_{00} + \vartheta_{01} x_{t-1} + \vartheta_{02} x_{t-2} + \cdots + \vartheta_{0L} x_{t-L}, \tag{6.57}$$

with ϑ_{0h}, $h = 0, \cdots, L$, drawn from a multivariate normal distribution.

The evolution map φ_H in (6.56) determines the dynamical system corresponding to an *asset market with H different belief types*. When the number of trader types H is large, this dynamical system contains a large number of stochastic variables $\vartheta = (\vartheta_1, ..., \vartheta_H)$, where the ϑ_h are IID, with *distribution function* F_μ. At the beginning of the market a large number, H belief types, are drawn from this distribution, and these H types then compete against each other. The distribution function of the stochastic belief variable ϑ_h depends on a multidimensional parameter μ, called the *belief parameter*. This setup allows one to vary the population out of which the individual beliefs are sampled at the beginning of the market. For example, in the case of linear forecasting rules with L lags as in (6.57), the belief parameter vector μ includes the means and standard deviations of all coefficients ϑ_{0h}.

Observe now that both the denominator and the numerator of the evolution map φ_H in (6.56) may be divided by the number of trader types H and thus may be seen as sample averages. The evolution map ψ of the large type limit (LTL) is then simply obtained by *replacing sample averages in the evolution map φ_H by population means*:

$$\psi(\mathbf{x}, \lambda, \mu) = \frac{1}{1+r} \frac{E_\mu \left[e^{\beta U(\mathbf{x}, \lambda, \vartheta_0)} f(\mathbf{x}, \lambda, \vartheta_0) \right]}{E_\mu \left[e^{\beta U(\mathbf{x}, \lambda, \vartheta_0)} \right]} = \frac{1}{1+r} \frac{\int e^{\beta U(\mathbf{x}, \lambda, \vartheta_0)} f(\mathbf{x}, \lambda, \vartheta_0) dv_\mu}{\int e^{\beta U(\mathbf{x}, \lambda, \vartheta_0)} dv_\mu}. \tag{6.58}$$

Here ϑ_0 is a stochastic variable, distributed in the same way as the ϑ_h, with density v_μ. The *structural* parameter vector λ of the evolution map φ_H and of the LTL evolution map ψ coincide. However, while the evolution map φ_H in (6.56) of the heterogeneous agent system contains H randomly drawn multidimensional stochastic variables ϑ_h, the LTL evolution map ψ in (6.58) only contains the *belief parameter* vector μ describing the joint probability distribution. Taking a large type limit thus leads to a huge reduction from a large number H randomly drawn belief parameters to a relatively small number of stochastic belief parameters that determine the belief distribution. In the example of the linear forecasting rules with L lags in (6.57), the number of parameters is reduced from H (which could be thousands or millions) to $2(L+1)$ belief parameters representing the means and standard deviations of all coefficients for all lags L.

The main result in Brock, Hommes and Wagener (2005) is the *LTL-theorem*, stating that, as the number H of trader types tends to infinity, the H-type evolution map φ converges almost surely to the LTL-map ψ. This implies that the LTL dynamical system generated by the LTL-map ψ in (6.58) is a good approximation of the dynamical behavior in a heterogeneous asset market with H types in (6.55) when the number of belief types H is large. In particular, all *generic* and *persistent* dynamic properties will be preserved with high probability. For example, if the LTL-map exhibits a bifurcation route to chaos for one of the structural parameters, then, if the number of trader types H is large, the H-type system also exhibits such a bifurcation route to chaos with high probability. A rational route to randomness for the LTL system therefore implies that a rational route to randomness is likely to occur in the H-type system when the number of types H is large.

LTL systems can be computed using moment generating functions. For example, in the case of linear forecasting rules (6.57) with three lags ($L = 3$), the corresponding LTL becomes a 5-D nonlinear system given by

$$(1+r)x_t = \mu_0 + \mu_1 x_{t-1} + \mu_2 x_{t-2} + \mu_3 x_{t-3} \tag{6.59}$$
$$+ \eta(x_{t-1} - Rx_{t-2} + a\sigma^2 z^s)(\sigma_0^2 + \sigma_1^2 x_{t-1} x_{t-3}$$
$$+ \sigma_2^2 x_{t-2} x_{t-4} + \sigma_3^2 x_{t-3} x_{t-5}),$$

where $\eta = \beta/(a\sigma^2)$, and μ_h and σ_h^2, $0 \le h \le 3$ are the means and variances of the coefficients ϑ_{0h}.

The simplest special case of (6.59) that still leads to interesting dynamics is obtained when all $\vartheta_{0h} = 0$, $1 \le h \le d$, that is, when the forecasting function (6.57) is purely biased: $f_t(\vartheta_0) = \vartheta_{00}$. The LTL then simplifies to the linear system

$$Rx_t = \mu_0 + \eta\sigma_0^2 \left(x_{t-1} - Rx_{t-2} + a\sigma^2 z^s\right). \tag{6.60}$$

This simplest case already provides important economic intuition about the (in)stability of the (fundamental) steady state in an evolutionary system with many trader types. When there is no intrinsic mean bias, that is when the mean of the biases ϑ_{00} equals 0 (i.e., $\mu_0 = 0$), and the risk premium is zero ($z^s = 0$), the steady state of the LTL (6.60) coincides with the fundamental: $x^* = 0$. When the mean bias and risk premium are both positive (negative) the steady state deviation x^* will be positive (negative) so that the steady state will be above (below) the fundamental. The natural bifurcation parameter tuning the (in)stability of the system is $\eta\sigma_0^2 = \beta\sigma_0^2/a\sigma^2$. We see that instability occurs

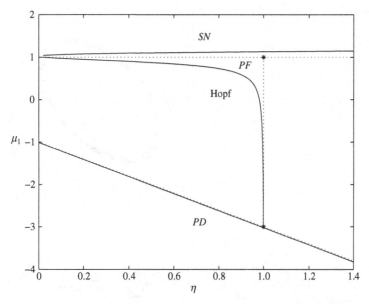

Figure 6.12. Bifurcation diagrams in the (η, μ_1) parameter plane for the large type limit (LTL) (6.59), where μ_1 represents the mean of the first order stochastic trend variable ϑ_{01} in the forecasting rule (6.57). For $\mu_0 = a\sigma^2 = 0$, with μ_0 the mean of the constant ϑ_{00} in the forecasting rule (6.57), the LTL is symmetric and thus non-generic (dotted curves); when $\mu_0 \neq 0$ the LTL is non-symmetric and generic. The diagrams show Hopf, period-doubling (PD), pitchfork (PF) and saddle-node (SN) bifurcation curves in the (η, μ_1) parameter plane, with other parameters fixed at $R = 1.01$, $z^s = 0$, $\mu_2 = \mu_3 = 0$, $\sigma_0 = \sigma_1 = \sigma_2 = 1$ and $\sigma_3 = 0$. Between the PD and Hopf curves (and the PF curve when $\mu_0 = 0$) there is a unique, stable steady state. This steady state becomes unstable when crossing the Hopf or the PD curve. Above the PF curve or the SN curve the system has three steady states. The PF curve is non-generic and only arises in the symmetric case with mean bias $\mu_0 = 0$. When the symmetry is broken by perturbing the mean bias to $\mu_0 = -0.1$, the PF curve "breaks" into generic Hopf and SN curves.

if and only if η increases beyond the bifurcation point $\eta_c = 1/\sigma_0^2$. Hence this simple case already suggests forces that may destabilize the evolutionary system: an increase in choice intensity β for evolutionary selection, a decrease in risk aversion a, a decrease in conditional variance of excess returns σ^2, or an increase in the diversity of purely biased beliefs σ_0^2. All of these forces can push η beyond η_c, thereby triggering instability of the (fundamental) steady state.

Figure 6.12 shows a two-dimensional bifurcation diagram in the (η, μ_1) parameter plane for the 5-D LTL (6.59). Here μ_1 represents the mean of the first-order stochastic trend variable ϑ_{01} in the forecasting rule (6.57). Recall that μ_0 is the mean of the constant term ϑ_{00} in the forecasting rule (6.57); it models the "mean bias" of the trader types. When $\mu_0 = 0$ and $a\sigma^2 z_s = 0$ (expressing that the risk premium is zero), the LTL is symmetric with respect to the fundamental steady state.

In the symmetric case (dotted lines in Figure 6.12), for parameter values in the region enclosed by the Hopf, period-doubling (PD) and pitchfork (PF) bifurcation curves, the

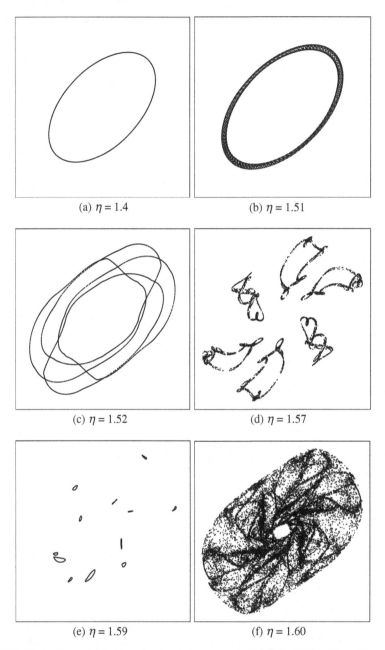

(a) $\eta = 1.4$

(b) $\eta = 1.51$

(c) $\eta = 1.52$

(d) $\eta = 1.57$

(e) $\eta = 1.59$

(f) $\eta = 1.60$

Figure 6.13. Projections of attractors in the phase space for the 5-D LTL (6.59), with parameters $R = 1.01$, $z^s = 0$, $\mu_0 = 0$, $\mu_1 = 0$, $\mu_2 = \mu_3 = 0$, $\sigma_0 = \sigma_1 = \sigma_2 = \sigma_3 = 1$: (a) immediately after the Hopf bifurcation (quasi-)periodic dynamics on a stable invariant circle occurs; (b–c) after the Hopf bifurcation (quasi-)periodic dynamics on a stable invariant torus occurs; (d–f) breaking up of the invariant torus into a strange attractor.

fundamental steady state is unique and stable. As the parameters cross the PF curve, two additional non-fundamental steady states are created, one above and one below the fundamental. Another route to instability occurs when crossing the Hopf curve, where the fundamental steady state becomes unstable and a (stable) invariant circle with periodic or quasi-periodic dynamics is created. The pitchfork bifurcation curve is *non-generic*, and only occurs in the symmetric case. When the symmetry is broken by a non-zero mean bias $\mu_0 \neq 0$, as illustrated in Figure 6.12 (bold curves) for $\mu_0 = -0.1$, the PF curve disappears, and "breaks" into two generic codimension 1 bifurcation curves, a Hopf and a saddle-node (SN) bifurcation curve. When crossing the SN curve from below, two additional steady states are created, one stable and one unstable. Notice that, as illustrated in Figure 6.12, when the perturbation is small (in the figure $\mu_0 = -0.1$), the SN and the Hopf curves are close to the PF and the Hopf curves (dotted lines) in the symmetric case. In this sense the bifurcation diagram depends continuously on the parameters, and it is useful to consider the symmetric LTL as an "organizing" center to study bifurcation phenomena in the generic, non-symmetric LTL.

Figure 6.13 illustrates the dynamical behavior of the LTL after the (fundamental) steady state loses stability through a Hopf bifurcation as η increases. After the Hopf bifurcation periodic and quasi-periodic dynamics on a stable invariant circle occur, and for increasing values of η a bifurcation route to strange attractors occurs. Figure 6.13 thus presents numerical evidence of the occurrence of a *rational route to randomness*, that is, a bifurcation route to strange attractors when the intensity of choice to switch forecasting strategies increases or when traders become less risk averse (i.e., the coefficient of risk aversion a decreases). If such rational routes to randomness occur for the LTL in (6.59), the LTL convergence theorem implies that in evolutionary systems with many trader types using linear forecasting rules with three lags rational routes to randomness occur with high probability. In a many trader types evolutionary world, fundamentalists will in general *not* drive out all other types and asset prices need not converge to their fundamental value but exhibit complicated dynamical behavior and excess volatility.

7 Empirical validation

In the previous chapters we have seen a number of stylized complexity models with heterogeneous expectations and heterogeneous trading strategies. What is the empirical relevance of heterogeneous expectations complexity models? In the last two chapters we discuss the empirical validation of heterogeneous expectations. In this chapter we discuss the empirical validity of the asset pricing model with heterogeneous beliefs compared to financial time series data, while the final chapter discusses the empirical relevance, both at the micro and at the macro level, of cobweb and asset pricing heuristic switching models in laboratory experiments with human subjects.

There is already a large literature on heterogeneous agent models (HAMs) replicating important stylized facts of financial time series on short time scales (say daily or higher frequency), such as fat tails and long memory in the returns distribution and clustered volatility. In fact, an important motivation to develop behavioral heterogeneous agent models has been the dissatisfaction with standard rational representative agent models to match stylized facts of financial time series. Many examples of heterogeneous agent models replicating stylized facts of financial markets have appeared in the literature, e.g., Brock and LeBaron (1996), Arthur et al. (1997b), Brock and Hommes (1997b), Youssefmir and Huberman (1997), LeBaron et al. (1999), Lux and Marchesi (1999, 2000), Farmer and Joshi (2002), Kirman and Teyssière (2002), Hommes (2002), Iori (2002), Cont and Bouchaud (2000) and Gaunersdorfer and Hommes (2007). The recent survey by Lux (2009) contains an extensive and stimulating survey of behavioral interacting agent models mimicking the stylized facts of asset returns with many more references; see also DeGrauwe and Grimaldi (2006) for an extensive discussion and applications in exchange rate modeling. In the stylized models discussed in this book, we have seen examples of simple heterogeneous agent models mimicking temporary bubbles and crashes and we have also discussed an endogenous mechanism for clustered volatility (either through intermittent chaos or through a co-existing stable steady state with a limit cycle or a more complicated attractor; see Subsection 6.6.3). In this chapter our focus will be whether observed bubbles and crashes in real markets can be explained by heterogeneous expectations models.

There is growing empirical evidence that heterogeneous expectations switching models explain observed fluctuations in various financial time series. Shiller (1984) already presented a HAM with rational "smart money" traders versus ordinary investors and estimated the fraction of smart money investors using stock market data over the period 1926–1983; Shiller found considerable fluctuations in the fractions over a range between 0 and 50%. Baak (1999) and Chavas (2000) estimated HAMs on hog and beef market data, and found evidence for the heterogeneity of expectations, with naive, rational and quasi-rational agents in the market. Winker and Gilli (2001) and Gilli and Winker (2003) estimated the model of Kirman (1991, 1993) with fundamentalists and chartists, using the daily DM–US$ exchange rates 1991–2000. Their estimated parameter values correspond to a bimodal distribution of agents indicating investor heterogeneity. Westerhoff and Reitz (2003) also estimated a HAM with fundamentalists and chartists to exchange rates and showed considerable fluctuations of the market impact of fundamentalists. Alfarano et al. (2005) estimated an agent-based herding model where agents switch between fundamentalist and chartist strategies using gold prices and stock market data. Branch (2004, 2007) estimates a simple switching model with heterogeneous expectations (with naive, adaptive expectations and a VAR forecasting rule) on exchange rate survey data and finds considerable time variation of heterogeneous expectations. More recently, switching models with heterogeneous expectations have been estimated on stock prices (Amilon, 2008, de Jong et al., 2009), stock option prices (Frijns et al., 2010), exchange rates (de Jong et al., 2010; Jongen et al., 2012), oil prices (ter Ellen and Zwinkels, 2010) and US inflation (Cornea et al., 2012).

In this chapter, we discuss the estimation of a simple 2-type asset pricing model with heterogeneous beliefs on yearly S&P 500 data, 1871–2003, in Boswijk et al. (2007). The model is very similar to the model discussed in Section 6.5. As we will see, this kind of switching model can, for example, explain the dot-com bubble in the late 1990s and the subsequent market crash in early 2000.

7.1 The model in price-to-cash flows

In all previous examples of the asset pricing model with heterogeneous beliefs, for simplicity, the stochastic dividend process of the risky asset has been assumed to be stationary and IID, so that the fundamental price is constant. To estimate the model, a more realistic dividend process with a time-varying fundamental price is needed. In particular, using yearly data of more than a century, the dividend process is growing over time and thus nonstationary. Before estimating the model, Boswijk et al. (2007) therefore reformulated the asset pricing model with heterogeneous beliefs in terms of price-to-cash flows. Recall from (6.5) that, under the assumption of zero net supply of the risky asset, the equilibrium pricing equation is

$$p_t = \frac{1}{1+r} \sum_{h=1}^{H} n_{h,t} E_{h,t}(p_{t+1} + y_{t+1}), \qquad (7.1)$$

or equivalently

$$r = \sum_{h=1}^{H} n_{h,t} \frac{E_{h,t}[p_{t+1} + y_{t+1} - p_t]}{p_t}. \tag{7.2}$$

In equilibrium the average required rate of return for investors to hold the risky asset equals the discount rate r. In the estimation of the model the discount rate r has been set equal to the sum of the (risk free) interest rate and the required risk premium on stocks. A simple, nonstationary process that fits cash flow data (dividends or earnings) well is a stochastic process with a constant growth rate. More precisely, assume that $\log y_t$ is a Gaussian random walk with drift, that is,

$$\log y_{t+1} = \mu + \log y_t + \upsilon_{t+1}, \qquad \upsilon_{t+1} \sim \text{i.i.d. } N(0, \sigma_\upsilon^2), \tag{7.3}$$

which implies

$$\frac{y_{t+1}}{y_t} = e^{\mu + \upsilon_{t+1}} = e^{\mu + \frac{1}{2}\sigma_\upsilon^2} e^{\upsilon_{t+1} - \frac{1}{2}\sigma_\upsilon^2} = (1+g)\varepsilon_{t+1}, \tag{7.4}$$

where $g = e^{\mu + \frac{1}{2}\sigma_\upsilon^2} - 1$ and $\varepsilon_{t+1} = e^{\upsilon_{t+1} + \frac{1}{2}\sigma_\upsilon^2}$, so that $E_t(\varepsilon_{t+1}) = 1$. As before, we assume that all types have correct beliefs on the cash flow, that is,

$$E_{h,t}[y_{t+1}] = E_t[y_{t+1}] = (1+g)y_t E_t[\varepsilon_{t+1}] = (1+g)y_t. \tag{7.5}$$

Since the cash flow is an *exogenously* given stochastic process it seems natural to assume that agents have learned the correct beliefs on next period's cash flow y_{t+1}. In particular, boundedly rational agents can learn about the constant growth rate, for example, by running a simple regression of $\log(y_t/y_{t-1})$ on a constant. In contrast, prices are determined *endogenously* and are affected by *expectations* about next period's price. In a heterogeneous world, agreement about future prices therefore seems more unlikely than agreement about future cash flows. Therefore we assume homogeneous beliefs about future cash flow, but heterogeneous beliefs about future prices.[1] The pricing equation (7.1) can be reformulated in terms of price-to-cash flow (PY) ratio, $\delta_t = p_t/y_t$, as

$$\delta_t = \frac{1}{R^*}\left\{1 + \sum_{h=1}^{H} n_{h,t} E_{h,t}[\delta_{t+1}]\right\}, \qquad R^* = \frac{1+r}{1+g}. \tag{7.6}$$

In the special case, when all agents have *rational expectations* the equilibrium pricing equation (7.1) simplifies to $p_t = (1/(1+r))E_t(p_{t+1} + y_{t+1})$. In the case of a constant discount rate r and a constant growth rate g for dividends, according to the static Gordon

---

[1] Barberis et al. (1998) consider a model where agents have psychological biases in forming expectations about future cash flows. In particular, agents may overreact to good news about economic fundamentals because they believe that cash flows have moved into another regime with higher growth. Their model is able to explain continuation and reversal of stock returns.

growth model (Gordon, 1962), the rational expectations fundamental price, p_t^*, of the risky asset is given by

$$p_t^* = \frac{1+g}{r-g} y_t, \qquad r > g. \tag{7.7}$$

Equivalently, in terms of price-to-cash flow ratios the fundamental is

$$\delta_t^* = \frac{p_t^*}{y_t} = \frac{1+g}{r-g} \equiv m. \tag{7.8}$$

We will refer to p_t^* as the *fundamental price* and to δ_t^* as the fundamental PY ratio. When all agents are rational the pricing equation (7.6) in terms of the PY ratio, $\delta_t = p_t/y_t$, becomes

$$\delta_t = \frac{1}{R^*} \{1 + E_t[\delta_{t+1}]\}. \tag{7.9}$$

In terms of the *deviation from the fundamental ratio*, $x_t = \delta_t - \delta_t^* = \delta_t - m$, this simplifies to

$$x_t = \frac{1}{R^*} E_t[x_{t+1}]. \tag{7.10}$$

Under heterogeneity in expectations, the pricing equation (7.6) is expressed in terms of x_t as

$$x_t = \frac{1}{R^*} \sum_{h=1}^{H} n_{h,t} E_{h,t}[x_{t+1}]. \tag{7.11}$$

Hence, the reformulation of the asset pricing model with heterogeneous beliefs in terms of price-to-cash flow leads to essentially the same pricing equation as in (6.16).

7.1.1 Heterogeneous beliefs
The expectation of type h about next period PY ratio is given by

$$E_{h,t}[\delta_{t+1}] = E_t[\delta_{t+1}^*] + f_h(x_{t-1}, ..., x_{t-L}) = m + f_h(x_{t-1}, ..., x_{t-L}), \tag{7.12}$$

where δ_t^* represents the fundamental PY ratio, $E_t(\delta_{t+1}^*) = m$ is the rational expectation of the PY ratio available to all agents, x_t is the *deviation* of the PY ratio from its fundamental value and $f_h(\cdot)$ represents the expected deviation of the PY ratio from the fundamental value by type h. The information available to investors at time t includes present and past cash flows and past prices. In terms of deviations from the fundamental PY ratio, x_t, we get

$$E_{h,t}[x_{t+1}] = f_h(x_{t-1}, ..., x_{t-L}). \tag{7.13}$$

Note again that the rational expectations, fundamental benchmark is nested in the heterogeneous agent model as a special case when $f_h \equiv 0$ for all types h. We can express (7.11) as

$$R^*x_t = \sum_{h=1}^{H} n_{h,t} f_h(x_{t-1}, ..., x_{t-L}).$$ (7.14)

From this equilibrium equation it is clear that the adjustment toward the fundamental PY ratio will be slow if a majority of investors has persistent beliefs about it.

Agents are boundedly rational and switch between different forecasting strategies according to recently realized profits. We denote by $\pi_{h,t-1}$ the realized profits of type h at the end of period $t - 1$, given by (cf. (6.19) and (6.20))

$$\pi_{h,t-1} = R_{t-1} z_{h,t-2} = R_{t-1} \frac{E_{h,t-2}[R_{t-1}]}{a V_{t-2}[R_{t-1}]},$$ (7.15)

where $R_{t-1} = p_{t-1} + y_{t-1} - (1+r)p_{t-2}$ is the realized excess return at time $t - 1$ and $z_{h,t-2}$ is the demand of the risky asset by belief type h, as given in (6.3), formed in period $t - 2$. As before, we assume that the beliefs about the conditional variance of excess returns are homogeneous and equal to fundamentalists beliefs about conditional variance, that is,

$$V_{h,t-2}[R_{t-1}] = V_{t-2}[P_{t-1}^* + y_{t-1} - (1+r)P_{t-2}^*] = y_{t-2}^2 \eta^2,$$ (7.16)

where $\eta^2 = (1+m)^2(1+g)^2 V_{t-2}[\epsilon_{t-1}]$, with ϵ_t IID noise driving the cash flow. The fitness measure can be rewritten in terms of the deviation $x_t = \delta_t - m$ of the PY ratio from its fundamental value, with $m = (1+g)/(r-g)$ as

$$\pi_{h,t-1} = \frac{(1+g)^2}{a\eta^2} (x_{t-1} - R^*x_{t-2}) (E_{h,t-2}[x_{t-1}] - R^*x_{t-2}).$$ (7.17)

This fitness measure has a simple, intuitive explanation in terms of forecasting performance for next period's deviation from the fundamental. A positive demand $z_{h,t-2}$ may be seen as a bet that x_{t-1} would go up more than was expected on average from R^*x_{t-2} (note that R^* is the growth rate of rational bubble solutions). The realized fitness $\pi_{h,t-1}$ of strategy h is the realized profit from that bet and it will be positive if both the realized deviation $x_{t-1} > R^*x_{t-2}$ and the forecast of the deviation $E_{h,t-2}[x_{t-1}] > R^*x_{t-2}$. More generally, if both the realized absolute deviation $|x_{t-1}|$ and the absolute predicted deviation $|E_{h,t-2}[x_{t-1}]|$ to the fundamental value are larger than R^* times the absolute deviation $|x_{t-2}|$, then strategy h generates positive realized fitness. In contrast, a strategy that wrongly predicts whether the asset price mean-reverts back toward the fundamental value or moves away from the fundamental generates a negative realized fitness.

At the beginning of period t investors compare the realized relative performances of the different strategies and withdraw capital from those that performed poorly and move it to better strategies. The fractions $n_{h,t}$ evolve according to a discrete choice model with multinomial logit probabilities, that is (cf. (6.18)),

$$n_{h,t} = \frac{\exp[\beta\pi_{h,t-1}]}{\sum_{k=1}^{H}\exp[\beta\pi_{k,t-1}]} = \frac{1}{1+\sum_{k\neq h}\exp[-\beta\Delta\pi_{t-1}^{h,k}]}, \qquad (7.18)$$

where $\beta > 0$ is the *intensity of choice* as before, and $\Delta\pi_{t-1}^{h,k} = \pi_{h,t-1} - \pi_{k,t-1}$ denotes the difference in realized profits of belief type h compared to type k.

7.2   Estimation of a simple 2-type example

Consider the simplest case of two types, both predicting next period's deviation by extrapolating past realizations in a linear fashion, that is[2]

$$E_{h,t}[x_{t+1}] = f_h(x_{t-1}) = \varphi_h x_{t-1}. \qquad (7.19)$$

The dynamic asset pricing model with two types can be written as

$$R^* x_t = n_t\varphi_1 x_{t-1} + (1-n_t)\varphi_2 x_{t-1} + \epsilon_t, \qquad (7.20)$$

where φ_1 and φ_2 denote the coefficients of the two belief types, n_t represents the fraction of investors that belong to the first type of traders and ϵ_t represents a disturbance term. The value of the parameter φ_h can be interpreted as follows. If it is positive and smaller than 1, investors expect the stock price to mean-revert toward the fundamental value. Agents of this type represent *fundamentalists*, because they expect the asset price to move back toward its fundamental value in the long run. The closer φ_h is to 1 the more persistent are the expected deviations. If the beliefs parameter φ_h is larger than 1, it implies that investors believe the deviation of the stock prices to grow over time at a constant speed. We will refer to this type of agents as *trend followers*. Note in particular that when one group of investors believes in a strong trend, i.e., $\varphi_h > R^*$, this may cause asset prices to deviate further from their fundamental value. In the case with two types with linear beliefs (7.19), the fraction of type 1 investors is

$$n_t = \frac{1}{1+\exp\{-\beta^*[(\varphi_1-\varphi_2)x_{t-3}(x_{t-1}-R^*x_{t-2})]\}}, \qquad (7.21)$$

where $\beta^* = \beta(1+g)^2/(a\eta^2)$.

Boswijk et al. (2007) estimated the 2-type model (7.20) and (7.21) using an updated version of the data set in Shiller (1989), consisting of annual observations of the S& P 500 index from 1871 to 2003. Here we present the estimation results with earnings as cash flows, but using dividends as cash flows gives similar results. The valuation ratios are then the price-to-earnings (PE) ratios.[3]

---

[2] In the estimation of the model higher-order lags turned out to be insignificant, see Manzan (2003). Therefore we focus on the simplest case with only one lag in the function $f_h(\cdot)$, with φ_h the parameter characterizing the strategy of type h.

[3] Since earnings data are noisy, to determine the fundamental valuation the practice of Campbell and Shiller (2005) to smooth earnings by a 10 years moving average has been followed.

Recall that according to the static Gordon growth model the fundamental price is given by

$$p_t^* = m y_t, \qquad m = \frac{1+g}{r-g}. \tag{7.22}$$

The fundamental value of the asset is a multiple m of its cash flow where m depends on the discount rate r and the cash flow growth rate g. The multiple m can also be interpreted as the PD and PE ratios implied by the PVM model. Figure 7.1 shows the (log) of yearly S&P 500 data together with the fundamental benchmark as well as their PE ratios. The figure shows a clear long-term co-movement of the stock price and the fundamental value. However, the PE ratio takes persistent swings away from the constant value predicted by the PVM model. This suggests that the fundamental value does not account completely for the dynamics of stock prices, as was suggested in the early debate on mean-reversion by Summers (1986). A survey of the on going debate is given in Campbell and Shiller (2005). Here we use the simple constant-growth Gordon model for the fundamental price and estimate the 2-type model on deviations from this benchmark.[4]

Recall that $R^* = (1+r)/(1+g)$, where g is the constant growth rate of the cash flow and r is the discount rate equal to the risk free interest rate plus a risk premium. In order to obtain R^*, an estimate of the risk premium – the difference between the expected return on the market portfolio of common stocks and the risk free interest rate – is used, as in Fama and French (2002). The risk premium satisfies

$$RP = g + y/p - i, \tag{7.23}$$

where g is the growth rate of dividends, y/p denotes the average dividend yield y_t/p_{t-1} and i is the risk free interest rate. For annual data from 1871 to 2003 of the S&P 500 the estimates are $RP = 6.56\%$, $i = 2.57\%$, so that $r = 9.13\%$ and $R^* = 1.074$. The corresponding average price-earnings ratio is 13.4, as illustrated in Figure 7.1.

Using yearly data of the S&P 500 index from 1871 to 2003, Boswijk et al. (2007) estimate the parameters $(\varphi_1', \varphi_2', \beta^*)$ in 7.20) and (7.21) using nonlinear least squares (NLLS). The estimation results are as follows:

$$R^* x_t = n_t \{0.80 \ x_{t-1}\} + (1 - n_t)\{1.097 x_{t-1}\} + \widehat{\epsilon}_t, \tag{7.24}$$
$$\underset{(0.074)}{\phantom{R^* x_t = n_t \{}} \qquad \underset{(0.052)}{\phantom{+ (1 - n_t)\{1.097 x_{t-1}\}}}$$

$$n_t = \{1 + \exp[-7.54 \ (-0.29 x_{t-3})(x_{t-1} - R^* x_{t-2})]\}^{-1}.$$
$$\underset{(4.93)}{\phantom{n_t = \{1 + \exp[-}}$$

$R^2 = 0.77$, $AIC = 2.23$, $AIC_{AR(1)} = 2.29$, $\varphi_{AR(1)} = 0.983$, $Q_{LB}(4) = 0.94$, $F^{boot}(p\text{-value}) = 10.15$ (0.011)

---

[4] The same approach can be used for more general, time-varying fundamental processes. Manzan (2003) shows that a dynamic Gordon model for the fundamental price, where the discount rate r and/or the growth rate g are time varying does not explain the large fluctuations in price-to-cash flow ratios, and in fact yields a fundamental price pattern close to that for the static Gordon model. Boswijk et al. (2007) also estimate a version of the model allowing for time variation in the growth rate of the cash flow, and obtain similar results.

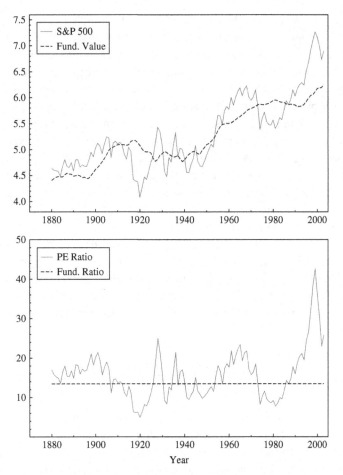

Figure 7.1. Yearly S&P 500, 1871–2003 and benchmark fundamental $p_t^* = m y_t$, with $m = (1 + g)/(1 + r)$. The top panel shows logs of S&P 500 and the fundamental p_t^*, while the bottom panel shows the PE ratio of the S&P 500 around the constant fundamental benchmark.

The belief coefficients are strongly significant and different from each other. On the other hand, the intensity of choice β^* is not significantly different from zero. This is a common result in nonlinear switching-type regression models, where the parameter β^* in the transition function is difficult to estimate and has a large standard deviation, because relatively large changes in β^* cause only small variation of the fraction n_t. Teräsvirta (1994) argues that this should not be worrying as long as there is significant heterogeneity in the estimated regimes.[5] The nonlinear switching model achieves a lower value for the AIC selection criterion compared to a linear AR(1) model. This suggests that the model is capturing nonlinearity in the data. This is also confirmed by

---

[5] See also the references cited at the beginning of this chapter, where endogenous switching models have been estimated on various financial times series and in most cases a significant intensity of choice parameter has been obtained.

the bootstrap F-test for linearity, which strongly rejects the null hypothesis of linearity in favor of the heterogeneous expectations model. The residuals of the regression do not show significant evidence of autocorrelation at the 5% significance level.

The estimated coefficient of the first regime is 0.80, corresponding to a half-life of about three years. The first regime can be characterized as *fundamentalist* beliefs, expecting the asset price to move back toward its fundamental value. In contrast, the second regime has an estimated coefficient close to 1.1, implying that in this regime agents are *trend followers*, believing the deviation of the stock price to grow over time at a constant speed larger than $R^* \approx 1.074$. At times when the fraction of investors using this belief is equal or close to 1 we have explosive behavior in the PE ratio. The sentiment of investors switches between a stable fundamentalists regime and a trend-following regime. In normal periods agents consider the deviation as a temporary phenomenon and expect it to revert back to fundamentals quickly. In other periods, a rapid increase of stock prices not paralleled by improvements in the fundamentals causes losses for fundamentalists and profits for trend followers. Evolutionary pressure will then cause more fundamentalists to become trend followers, thus reinforcing the trend in prices.

Figure 7.2 shows the time series of the fraction of fundamentalists and the *average market sentiment*, defined as

$$\varphi_t = \frac{n_t \varphi_1 + (1 - n_t)\varphi_2}{R^*}. \tag{7.25}$$

It is clear that the fraction of fundamentalists varies considerably over time with periods in which it is close to 0.5 and other periods in which it is close to either of the extremes 0 or 1. The series of the average market sentiment shows that there is significant time variation between periods of strong mean-reversion when the market is dominated by fundamentalists and other periods in which φ_t is close to or exceeds 1 and the market is dominated by trend followers. These plots also offer an explanation of the events of the late 1990s: for six consecutive years the trend-following strategy outperformed the fundamentalists strategy and a majority of agents switched to the trend-following strategy, driving the average market sentiment beyond 1, thus reinforcing the strong price trend. However, at the turn of the market in 2000 the fraction of fundamentalists increased again, approaching 1 thus contributing to the reversal toward the fundamental value in subsequent years.

The estimation results show that there are two different belief strategies: one in which agents expect continuation of returns and the other in which they expect reversal. We also find that there are some years in which one type of expectations dominates the market. It is clear that the expectation of continuation of positive returns dominated the market in the late 1990s, with the average market sentiment coefficient φ_t in (7.25) larger than 1 in the late 1990s. Despite the awareness of the mispricing, in this period investors were aggressively extrapolating the continuation of the extraordinary performances realized in the past years. Our model endogenizes the switching of agents among beliefs.

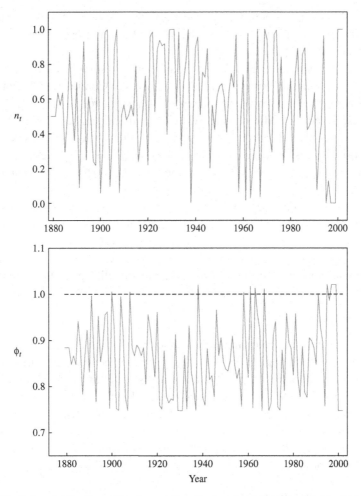

Figure 7.2. Estimated fraction of fundamentalists (top) and average extrapolation factor φ_t (bottom) in (7.25), for switching model with fundamentalists versus trend followers.

The evolutionary mechanism that relates predictor choice to their past performance is supported by the data.

These results are in line with previous empirical evidence that performance-based reinforcement learning plays an important role in investment decisions in real markets. For example, Ippolito (1989), Chevalier and Ellison (1997), Sirri and Tufano (1998), Rockinger (1996) and Karceski (2002) showed for mutual funds data that money flows into past good performers, while flowing out of past poor performers, and that performance persists on a short term basis. Pension funds are less extreme in picking good performance but are tougher on bad performers (Del Guerico and Tkac, 2002). Recently, Benartzi and Thaler (2007) have shown that heuristics and biases play a significant role in retirement savings decisions. For example, using data from Vanguard they showed that the equity allocation of new participants rose from 58% in 1992 to 74% in 2000, following a strong rise in stock prices in the late 1990s, but dropped back to 54% in 2002, following a strong fall in stock prices.

Survey data show similar results. Based on answers to a survey, Shiller (2000) constructed indices of "Bubble Expectations" and of "Investor Confidence." In both cases, he finds that the time variation in the indices is well explained by the lagged change in stock prices. Based on a different survey, Fisher and Statman (2002) find that in the late 1990s individual investors had expectations of continuation of recent stock returns while institutional investors were expecting reversals. This is an interesting approach to identify heterogeneity of beliefs based on the type of investors rather than the type of beliefs.

In the view of our model, the bubble in the 1990s was triggered by good news about economic fundamentals (a new internet technology), and strongly reinforced by trend extrapolating behavior. The bubble slowed down and reversed due to bad news about economic fundamentals (excessive growth cannot last forever and is not supported by earnings), and the crash was accelerated by switching of beliefs back to fundamentals.

7.3   Empirical implications

In this section we discuss some empirical implications of the estimation of our nonlinear evolutionary switching model with heterogeneous beliefs. We start with some simulations of the estimated model. Next, we investigate the response to a positive shock to fundamentals when the asset is overvalued. Finally, we address the question concerning the probability that a bubble may resume by comparing the evolution of the valuation ratios in a switching model to a linear representative agent model. These simulation experiments show the importance of considering *nonlinear* effects in the dynamics of stock prices.

7.3.1   Bubble and crash dynamics

Figure 7.3 shows a time series simulation of the estimated 2-type model (7.24) with fundamentalists versus trend followers with normally distributed shocks (with the same standard deviation as for the estimated residuals). This simulation is characterized by temporary bubbles and crashes of the PE ratio, with a peak over 40 toward the end of the simulation, consistent with the S&P 500 data (cf. Figure 7.1). Comparing the time series of the PE ratio to the time series of the fraction of fundamentalists, it is clear that during bubbles the market is dominated by trend-following behavior with an average extrapolation coefficient exceeding 1.

Straightforward computation shows that for the estimated parameter values the fundamental steady state is locally stable.[6] A typical stochastic simulation of the 2-type

---

[6] The model is similar to the 2-type example, fundamentalists versus trend followers, in Subsection 6.5.1. At the fundamental steady state, since both types predict the steady state and there are no costs for fundamentalists, the fractions of the two types are equal to 0.5. The fundamental steady state is locally stable, because the average extrapolation coefficient at the steady state, $\varphi = (\varphi_1 + \varphi_2)/(2R^*) \approx 0.88 < 1$.

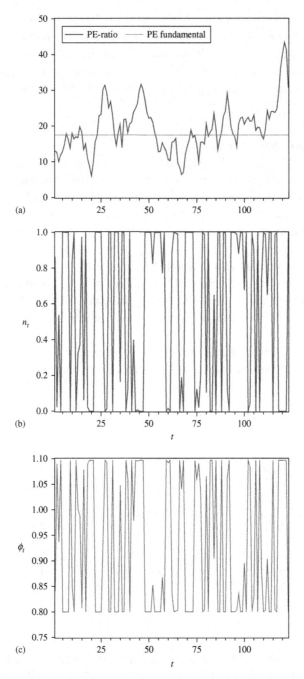

Figure 7.3. Simulated time series of the PE ratio (a), the fraction of fundamentalists (b) and the average extrapolation coefficient (7.25) (c), for estimated 2-type model with fundamentalists versus trend followers with normally distributed shocks with mean 0 and $\sigma = 2.975$. Parameters are $g_1 = 0.80$, $g_2 = 1.097$ and $\beta = 7.54$.

model (7.24) is characterized by fluctuations around the fundamental benchmark with irregular temporary bubbles consistent with the data. These simulations thus show that temporary bubbles are triggered by shocks to economic fundamentals, reinforced by trend-following extrapolation, and occasionally strongly amplified causing extremely high spikes, similar to what has been observed in the S&P 500 data in the end of the 1990s.

7.3.2   *Response to a fundamental shock*
The estimated model can be used to investigate the response of the market valuation to good news. Assume that at the beginning of period t the cash flow increases due to a permanent increase in the growth rate. This implies that the asset has a higher fundamental valuation ratio, but what is the effect on the market valuation? We address this question both for the linear model and the nonlinear 2-type switching model. The linear model may be interpreted as a model with a representative agent believing in an average mean-reversion toward the fundamental. Assume that at $t-1$ the fundamental valuation ratio was 15 and the good news at time t drives it to 17. Assume also that the equilibrium price at $t-1$ was 16. Figure 7.4 shows the valuation ratio dynamics in response to the good news for both the linear representative agent and the heterogeneous agent model.

The figure shows the average price path over 2000 simulations of the estimated model. There is a clear difference between the linear and the nonlinear models. In the

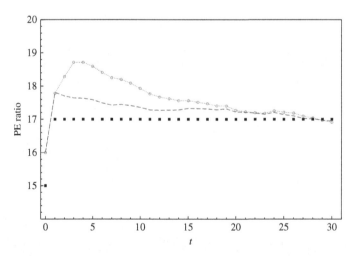

Figure 7.4. Average response (over 2000 simulations) to a shock to the fundamental for linear representative agent model (dotted) and nonlinear 2-type switching model (bold). At period 0 there is a permanent shock to the fundamental price from 15 to 17. The simulation uses the estimated parameter values for the PD ratio, with a representative agent average belief parameter $\varphi = 0.968$ and heterogeneous agent parameters $\varphi_1 = 0.762$ and $\varphi_2 = 1.135$ (see Boswijk et al., 2007). The nonlinear heterogeneous agent model exhibits overreaction, leading to short-run continuation of positive returns due to trend-following behavior, and long term mean-reversion.

linear case, the positive shock to the fundamental value leads to an immediate increase of the price followed by a mean-reversion thereafter. In contrast, for the nonlinear heterogeneous agent switching model, the pattern that emerges is consistent with *over-reaction* and short run continuation of positive returns followed by long term reversal toward the fundamental price. After good news, the agents incorporate the news into their expectations and they also expect that part of the previous period overvaluation will persist. One group – the trend followers – overreacts and expects a further increase of the price, while the other group – the fundamentalists – expects the price to diminish over time. The equilibrium price at time *t* overshoots and almost reaches 18. In the following two periods trend followers continue to buy the stock and drive the price (and valuation ratio) even higher, thus reinforcing the good news. Finally, the reversal starts and drives the ratio back to its long run fundamental value. Initially, the aggressive investors interpret the positive news as a confirmation that the stock overvaluation was justified by forthcoming news. However, the lack of further good news convinces most investors to switch to the mean-reverting expectations and the stock price is driven back toward the fundamental.

In summary, in a linear representative agent world after a positive shock to fundamentals prices mean-revert back to their fundamental value. In contrast, in a heterogeneous world after good news about economic fundamentals, trend followers amplify an increase in asset prices and cause prices to overreact to good news. Only after a few periods, the lack of additional good news gradually causes prices to mean-revert toward their fundamental value.

7.3.3   *Will the bubble resume?*

As a forecasting exercise, Boswijk et al. (2007) simulated the evolution of the valuation ratios using the estimated heterogeneous agent model to predict the evolution of the ratio conditional on the value realized at the end of their sample 2003. Innovations were obtained by reshuffling the estimated residuals. Instead of focusing attention only on the mean or the median of the distribution, the quantiles were considered corresponding to 10, 30, 50, 70% and 90% probability over 2000 replications of the estimated model in (7.24) for the PE ratio. Figure 7.5 shows the 1 to 5 periods ahead quantiles of the predictive distribution for the estimated nonlinear switching model as well as the linear representative agent model.

The linear model (right plot) predicts that the valuation ratio reverts back toward the mean at all quantiles considered. In contrast, the nonlinear switching model predicts that there is a significant probability that the ratio may increase again as a result of the activation of the trend-following regime. The 70% and 90% quantiles clearly show that the PE ratio may increase again to levels close to 35. Stated differently, the heterogeneous agent model predicts that with probability over 30% the PE ratio may increase to more than 30. Note however that the median predicts that the ratio should decrease as implied by the linear mean-reverting model. Another implication of the switching model is that if the first (mean-reverting) regime dominates the beliefs of investors, it will enforce a much faster adjustment than predicted by the linear model. This is clear

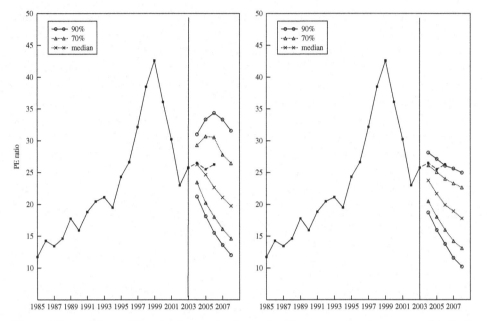

Figure 7.5. Prediction of PE ratios 5 years ahead, based on linear representative agent model (right) and nonlinear 2-type switching model (left). The estimated belief parameters are $\varphi = 0.983$ for the representative agent and $\varphi_1 = 0.80$ and $\varphi_2 = 1.097$ for the 2-type switching model. The quantiles corresponding to 10%, 30%, 50%, 70% and 90% probability over 2000 replications are shown.

from the bottom quantiles of the distributions. These simulations show that predictions from a linear, representative agent model versus a nonlinear, heterogeneous agent model are quite different. In particular, extreme events with large deviations from the benchmark fundamental valuation, either upward or downward, are much more likely in a nonlinear world.

8 Laboratory experiments

In Chapter 6 we have seen many examples of the simple asset pricing model with heterogeneous beliefs exhibiting complex dynamics characterized by temporary bubbles and crashes, triggered by exogenous news about economic fundamentals and strongly amplified by self-fulfilling expectations and trend-following trading strategies. While the previous chapter focused on the empirical relevance of the heterogeneous expectations switching model by comparing it to real financial time series, the current chapter confronts the heterogeneous expectations switching model with laboratory experimental data, both at the individual micro and at the aggregate macro level. Laboratory experiments with human subjects are well suited to discipline the class of behavioral modes or individual heuristics that boundedly rational subjects may use in economic decision making. This chapter discusses a number of "learning-to-forecast experiments" in the cobweb and asset pricing framework, where human subjects must forecast the price of an asset or a commodity, whose realized market price is an aggregation of individual expectations. These experiments may be seen as a testing of the heterogeneous expectations hypothesis in the lab. This chapter is based on the survey of laboratory experiments in Hommes (2011), with some recent updates.

In real markets, it is hard to obtain detailed information about individual expectations. One way to collect data on individual expectations is by survey data analysis; see, e.g., Pesaran and Weale (2006) for a stimulating overview. Survey data analysis can focus exclusively on the expectations-generating process, avoiding the dilemma of testing joint hypotheses. There is already quite some evidence on forecasting heterogeneity in survey data. Frankel and Froot (1987, 1990a and b), Allen and Taylor (1990) and Taylor and Allen (1992), for example, found that financial experts use different forecasting strategies to predict exchange rates. They tend to use trend extrapolating rules at short horizons (up to 3 months) and mean-reverting fundamentalists rules at longer horizons (6 months to 1 year). Moreover, the weight given to different forecasting techniques changes over time. Shiller (1987, 2000) and Vissing-Jorgensen (2003) present evidence of heterogeneity and time variation in the sentiment of investors in stock market data. For example, Shiller (2000) finds evidence that investor's sentiment changes over time, with both institutions and individual investors becoming more optimistic in response to recent significant increases of the stock market in the late 1990s. Mankiw et al. (2003), Capistran and Timmermann (2009) and Pfajfar and Santoro (2010) find evidence for heterogeneity and time variation in inflation expectations. Branch (2004, 2007) estimates a simple switching model with heterogeneous expectations, along the lines of Brock and Hommes (1997a) (see Chapters 5 and 6), and provides empirical evidence that models which allow the degree of heterogeneity to change over time provide a better fit on exchange rate survey data.

Laboratory experiments with human subjects provide an alternative, complementary method to study the interactions of individual expectations and the resulting aggregate outcomes. An advantage is that the experimenter has full control over the underlying economic fundamentals. It is remarkable that, despite a huge theoretical literature on expectations formation and learning with boundedly rational agents, relatively few laboratory experiments with human subjects have been performed to study how individuals form expectations and learn from experience, and how the market aggregates individual forecasts.

In this chapter, we discuss a number of laboratory experiments with human subjects that can be used to empirically validate the expectations hypothesis and, in particular to see whether heterogeneous expectations switching models are consistent with experimental data. Lucas (1986) already stressed the importance of laboratory experiments in studying expectations and stability under adaptive learning:

> Recent theoretical work is making it increasingly clear that the multiplicity of equilibria ... can arise in a wide variety of situations involving sequential trading, in competitive as well as finite-agent games. All but a few of these equilibria are, I believe, behaviorally uninteresting: They do not describe behavior that collections of adaptively behaving people would ever hit on. I think an appropriate stability theory can be useful in weeding out these uninteresting equilibria ... But to be useful, stability theory must be more than simply a fancy way of saying that one does not want to think about certain equilibria. I prefer to view it as an experimentally testable hypothesis, as a special instance of the adaptive laws that we believe govern all human behavior. (Lucas, 1986, pp. S424–425).

Learning-to-forecast experiments (LtFEs) provide a controlled environment to study individual expectations, their interactions and feedbacks and the resulting aggregate outcomes, and investigate questions such as:

- How do *individuals* form expectations and how do they *learn* from mistakes and *adapt* their behavior?
- How do individual forecasting rules *interact* at the *micro* level and which *aggregate outcome* do they co-create at the *macro* level?
- Will *coordination of expectations* occur, even when there is limited information, or will *heterogeneity* persist?
- What is the *aggregate effect* of coordination of individual expectations?

- When does *learning* enforce convergence to REE and when do non-REE "learning equilibria" arise?

The chapter is organized as follows. Section 8.1 discusses some general background of LtFEs and some related literature. Section 8.2 describes an experiment in the cobweb framework, while Section 8.3 focuses on asset pricing experiments. In Section 8.4 a heterogeneous forecasting heuristics switching model, where agents switch between different forecasting rules based upon their recent performance, is fitted to the asset pricing experiments. In Section 8.5 the same switching model is fitted to experimental data in different market settings, cobweb as well as asset pricing, where the *only* difference comes from the type of expectations feedback, positive for the asset pricing versus negative for the cobweb. Section 8.6 contains some final remarks on markets as complex systems.

8.1   Learning-to-forecast experiments (LtFEs)

Laboratory experiments with human subjects, with full control over the market environment and economic fundamentals, form an ideal environment to study how interactions of individual decisions shape aggregate market behavior. See Duffy (2008a,b) for stimulating discussions and up to date surveys of "experimental macroeconomics." Here, we focus on so-called *learning-to-forecast experiments* (LtFEs), where subjects' *only* task is to forecast the price of an asset or a commodity repeatedly, say for 50–60 periods, with the realized market price in each period determined by (average) individual expectations. In LtFEs subjects' forecasting decisions are separated from market-trading decisions. The subjects in the experiments do not participate themselves directly in other market activities, such as trading or producing, but are forecasters (say advisors to large producers or financial investors) whose earnings increase when forecasting errors decrease. At the beginning of each period, individual forecasts are collected, which feed directly into (unknown) demand and/or supply functions and computerized trading yields a market price, derived from equilibrium between aggregate demand and supply, that becomes available to the subjects at the end of the period. Demand and supply curves are derived from maximization of expected utility, profit or wealth and thus market-trading decisions are consistent with rational optimizing behavior.

The LtFEs were motivated directly by the bounded rationality literature, as a way to empirically validate different theories of expectations and learning. Sargent (1993), for example, emphasizes two different requirements of rational expectations. The first requirement imposes that individuals maximize an objective function (utility, profit, wealth, etc.) subject to perceived constraints, while the second requirement imposes mutual consistency between perceptions and realizations. Marimon and Sunder (1994) were the first to set up experiments testing individual rationality and mutual consistency either jointly or separately and used different experimental designs to distinguish between "learning-to-optimize" versus "learning-to-forecast" experiments (Marimon and Sunder, 1994, p. 134). The LtFEs focus exclusively on the role of expectations, using computerized optimal individual demand and supply schedules once these individual forecasts have been made.[1]

In LtFEs, subjects typically only have *qualitative* information about the market. They know that the price p_t is an aggregation of individual forecasts, derived from equilibrium between demand and supply, and they are able to infer the type of expectations feedback, *positive* or *negative*. Positive (negative) feedback means that an increase of (average) individual forecasts leads to a higher (lower) market equilibrium price. Positive feedback is important in speculative asset markets, where higher market expectations lead to an increase of speculative demand and therefore to an increase of the realized asset price. Negative feedback may be dominant in supply driven commodity markets, where an increase in expected prices leads to higher production and thus to a lower realized market price. Subjects in the LtFEs know past prices and their own past forecasts and earnings, typically in table as well as in graphic form, as illustrated in Figure 8.1. Subjects, however, do *not* know the forecasts of other participants, the exact market equilibrium equation, the exact demand and supply schedules and the exact number of other demanders and/or suppliers in the market. The type of information in the experiment is thus very similar to models of bounded rationality and adaptive learning, where agents try to learn a perceived law of motion, based upon time series

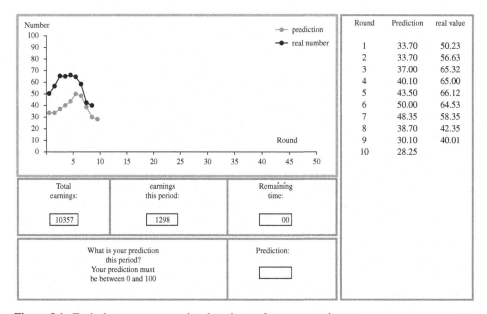

Figure 8.1. Typical computer screen in a learning-to-forecast experiment

[1] Other recent LtFEs in the literature include Adam (2007), Pfajfar and Zakelj (2011) and Assenza et al. (2011); see also Bao et al. (2011) for a recent experiments comparing learning-to-forecast versus learning-to-optimize treatments.

observations without knowing the underlying actual law of motion of the market. The type of information in the experiment is also similar to what agents (do not) know in real complex markets.

A learning-to-forecast experiment may be seen as a test bed for the expectations hypothesis in a benchmark model, assuming that all other assumptions such as rational utility and/or profit maximizing behavior are satisfied. A learning-to-forecast experiment thus provides *clean data* on *individual expectations* as well as *aggregate price behavior*. We will discuss learning-to-forecast experiments based on two benchmark models: the cobweb model (as in Chapter 5) and a standard asset pricing model (as in Chapter 6). The underlying laws of motion are of the form

$$p_t = F(p_{1,t}^e, \cdots, p_{H,t}^e) \qquad \text{cobweb}, \qquad (8.1)$$

$$p_t = F(p_{1,t+1}^e, \cdots, p_{H,t+1}^e) \qquad \text{asset pricing}. \qquad (8.2)$$

In the cobweb LtFE experiments in Hommes et al. (2007), the realized market price p_t in (8.1) is a (nonlinear) function of all individual one-period-ahead forecasts $p_{h,t}^e$. In the asset pricing LtFE in Hommes et al. (2005b, 2008) the realized market price p_t in (8.2) is a (nonlinear) function of all two-period-ahead individual forecasts $p_{h,t+1}^e$ of next period's price p_{t+1}. There is another important difference between the cobweb and the asset pricing LtFEs: negative versus positive expectations feedback. The asset pricing experiments exhibit positive feedback, that is, the realized market price increases when individual price forecasts increase, an important characteristic of speculative asset markets; mathematically it means that the map F in (8.2) is an increasing function of individual forecasts. The classical cobweb framework, describing a supply driven commodity market with a production lag, exhibits negative feedback, that is, a higher expected price leads to increased production and thus a lower realized market price; the map F in (8.1) underlying the cobweb experiments is decreasing in individual forecasts. In Section 8.5 we will compare aggregate behavior in positive versus negative feedback systems. Despite the fact that the *only* difference will be the sign (positive versus negative) of the coefficient in a linear price-expectations feedback rule, the aggregate price behaviors and individual expectations turn out to be very different.

8.2 Cobweb experiments

The LtFEs in Hommes et al. (2007) use the classical cobweb framework, exactly the same framework employed in the seminal paper of Muth (1961) introducing rational expectations.[2] The cobweb LtFEs may be seen as a direct test of the REH in the cobweb model, assuming that all other modeling assumptions, such as, producers' profit maximization and consumers' utility maximization, are satisfied. The participants were asked to predict next period's price of a commodity under limited information on the

---

[2] See Carlson (1967), Holt and Villamil (1986), Wellford (1989) and Hommes et al. (2000) for earlier cobweb experiments.

structural characteristics of the market. Participants were only informed about the basic principles of the cobweb-type market. They were advisors to producers, whose only job is to accurately forecast the price of the good for 50 subsequent periods. Pay-offs were defined as a quadratic function of squared forecasting errors, truncated at 0^3:

$$E = \text{Max}\{1300 - 260(p^e_{i,t} - p_t)^2, 0\}. \tag{8.3}$$

Participants were informed that the price would be determined by market clearing and that it would be within the range $[0, 10]$. Furthermore, they knew that there was (negative) feedback from individual price forecasts to realized market price in the sense that if their forecast would increase, the supply would increase and consequently the market clearing price would decrease. Subjects, however, did not know how large these feedback effects would be, as they had no knowledge of underlying market equilibrium equations. Subjects thus had *qualitative* information about the market, but no quantitative details.

The realized price p_t in the experiments was determined by the (unknown) market equilibrium between demand and supply:

$$D(p_t) = \sum_{i=1}^{K} S(p^e_{i,t}), \tag{8.4}$$

with $p^e_{i,t}$ the price forecast of participant i at time t. In each market there were 6 subsects, i.e., $K = 6$. Notice that the model underlying the experiment is exactly the same as the cobweb model with heterogeneous expectations in Chapter 5. Demand was exogenously given by a simple linear schedule:

$$D(p_t) = a - dp_t + \eta_t, \tag{8.5}$$

with η_t a small stochastic shock drawn from a normal distribution representing small random demand fluctuations. Supply $S_\lambda(p^e_{i,t})$ was determined by the nonlinear schedule

$$S_\lambda(p^e_{i,t}) = \tanh(\lambda(p^e_{i,t} - 6)) + 1. \tag{8.6}$$

This increasing, nonlinear supply schedule can be derived from producer's expected profit maximization with a convex cost function. Subjects in the experiment thus do not participate themselves in production decisions, but supply is computed as if each individual producer maximizes expected profit, given his/her individual price forecast. The parameter λ tunes the nonlinearity of the supply curve and the stability of the underlying cobweb model. The resulting equilibrium price is obtained as:

$$p_t = D^{-1}\left(\sum_{i=1}^{K} S_\lambda(p^e_{i,t})\right) = \frac{a - \sum_{i=1}^{K} S_\lambda(p^e_{i,t})}{d} + \epsilon_t, \tag{8.7}$$

where $\epsilon_t = \eta_t/d$. Given the parameters a, d and λ the aggregate realized price p_t depends on individual price expectations as well as the realization of the (small) stochastic

---

[3] 1300 points corresponded to 0.5 euro, so that maximum earnings per session were 25 euro's.

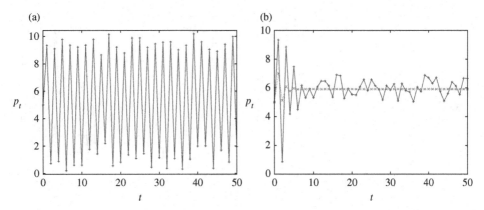

Figure 8.2. Cobweb price dynamics in the strongly unstable treatment ($\lambda = 2$) in two benchmark simulations: (a) convergence to a (noisy) 2-cycle under naive expectations; (b) convergence to (noisy) RE equilibrium price under learning by sample average.

shocks. While the parameters of the demand function and the realizations of the noise component remained unchanged across all treatments at $a = 13.8$, $d = 1.5$ and $\epsilon_t = \frac{n_t}{d} \sim N(0, 0.5)$, the slope parameter of the supply function was varied. Here we consider two treatments. A stable treatment had $\lambda = 0.22$, for which under naive expectations the price converges quickly to the rational expectations equilibrium. In another strongly unstable treatment, with $\lambda = 2$, under naive expectations the RE price is unstable and prices converge to a 2-cycle, as illustrated in Figure 8.2a. Along the 2-cycle producers are "irrational" in the sense that they make "systematic forecasting errors", predicting a high (low) price when realized market price will be low (high).

Under rational expectations, all individuals would predict the unique price p^*, at which demand and supply intersect. Given that all individuals have rational expectations, realized prices will be given by

$$p_t = p^* + \epsilon_t, \tag{8.8}$$

that is, small random fluctuations around the RE steady state. Given the limited market information one cannot expect that all individuals have rational expectations at the outset, but one can hope that in such a simple, stationary environment individuals would *learn to have rational expectations*. For example, if price expectations are given by the *sample average* of past prices, convergence to the RE price is enforced, as illustrated in Figure 8.2b. The LtFE has in fact been designed to test whether individuals are able to learn from their systematic mistakes under naive expectations and coordinate on a learning algorithm, such as learning by average, enforcing convergence to the RE steady state.

Figure 8.3 shows time series of the individual forecasts (top panels) as well as the realized market prices together with the average price forecast (bottom panels) for two typical experimental groups, one stable treatment (left panels) and one strongly unstable treatment (right panels). An immediate observation is that in the stable treatment, after

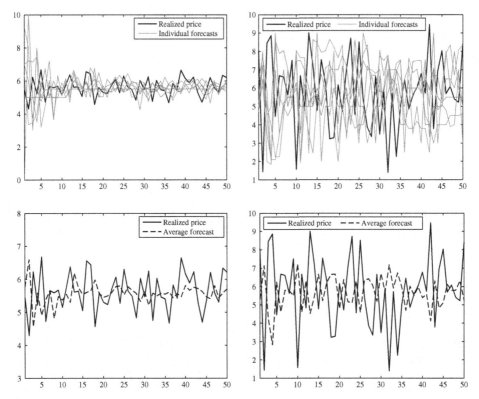

Figure 8.3. Two typical cobweb learning-to-forecast-experiments. In the stable treatment (left panels) coordination on RE occurs; in the strongly unstable treatment (right panels) heterogeneity persists causing excess price volatility. Top panels: individual forecasts and realized prices; bottom panels; average forecast and realized prices.

a short learning phase of about 10 periods, the price volatility is low and individual forecasts as well as average forecasts are very close to the RE benchmark, with price fluctuations almost entirely driven by the small random shocks in the experiments. This is an example where in an unknown market environment with limited information individuals are able to learn and coordinate on a rational expectations equilibrium. Aggregate price behavior and individual forecasts are very different, however, in the strongly unstable treatment. Realized prices exhibit large fluctuations, while individual forecasts are very volatile, even toward the end of the experiment. Hence, in the classical cobweb framework used in Muth (1961) to introduce rational expectations, our LtFEs show that *only* in the stable cobweb case, the interaction of individual forecasting rules enforces convergence to the RE benchmark. In the unstable treatment, *heterogeneity in forecasting is persistent and leads to an aggregate effect upon prices characterized by excess volatility.*

The behavior in Figure 8.3 is typical for all cobweb experiments. Hommes et al. (2007) summarize the *stylized facts* of the cobweb LtFE experiments as follows: (1) the sample mean of realized prices is close to the RE benchmark p^* in all treatments; (2) the sample variance of realized prices depends on the treatment: it is close to the RE benchmark in the stable treatment, but significantly higher in the unstable treatments; (3) realized market prices are irregular and do not exhibit significant linear autocorrelations.

These stylized facts across different treatments appear hard to explain by standard learning mechanisms offered by the theoretical literature. For example, naive expectations is inconsistent with the experiments, because in the unstable treatment it predicts too much regularity (convergence to a 2-cycle) in aggregate price behavior. Average price expectations, which is just the simplest form of *adaptive learning* obtained when regressing prices on a constant, is also inconsistent with the experiments, because for both treatments it predicts convergence to the RE benchmark (see Figure 8.2b). None of the homogeneous expectations rules or learning algorithms discussed in Chapter 4 is consistent with these experimental findings across both the stable and the strongly unstable treatment. Therefore, *heterogeneity* in forecasting rules must play a role to explain the stylized facts of the cobweb experiments across different treatments. Apparently, there is some form of individual learning, since agents do *not* coordinate on a simple stable 2-cycle with systematic mistakes. In the experiments, the interaction of agents' individual forecasting and learning rules washes out all linear predictability in aggregate price behavior. In the stable treatment, this interaction leads to coordination on the "correct" RE benchmark steady state, but in the unstable treatment heterogeneity persists and prices are excessively volatile.

Hommes and Lux (2013) present a model of heterogeneous individual learning via genetic algorithms (GAs) explaining all three stylized facts in the cobweb LtFEs. Genetic algorithms require a functional specification of the forecasting rule, whose fitness-maximizing parameter values are searched for via the evolutionary algorithm. They use a simple first-order autoregressive rule:

$$p^e_{i,t+1} = \alpha_i + \beta_i(p_t - \alpha_i). \tag{8.9}$$

Such a first-order autoregressive AR(1) rule seems a natural forecasting scheme as agents could implement it using the sample average as their estimate of α_i and the first-order sample autocorrelation as the estimate of β_i.[4] Moreover, the AR(1) forecasting rule (8.9) has a simple *behavioral* interpretation, with α_i representing an anchor or observed average price level around which the market price fluctuates, and β_i representing the observed persistence or antipersistence of price fluctuations.[5]

The interaction of individual GA learning rules simultaneously reproduces all stylized facts in aggregate price behavior observed in the experiments across the different treatments. Figure 8.4 shows typical price time series under GA learning as well as

---

[4] See Hommes and Sorger (1998) and Chapter 4, Section 4.7, where the parameters of an AR(1) rule are updated according to sample autocorrelation (SAC) learning. See also Chapter 5, Section 5.4 for a heterogeneous expectations cobweb model with SAC learning versus naive expectations.

[5] In similar cobweb LtFE experiments Heemeijer et al. (2009) estimated individual forecasting rules, and many individuals actually used forecasting rules of the simple AR(1) form (8.9).

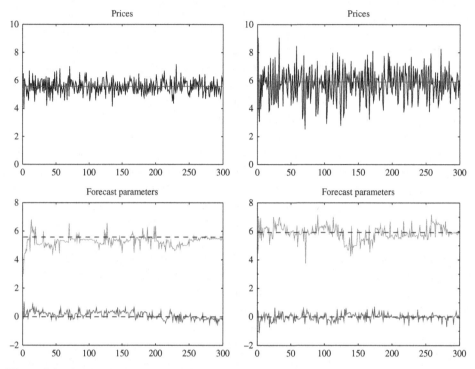

Figure 8.4. Simulated prices and learning parameters under GA learning of six AR(1) forecasting rules (8.9) in the same cobweb model as in the experiment.

time series of the two parameters in the AR(1) forecasting rule for the stable treatment (left panel) and the strongly unstable treatment (right panel). In the stable treatment the parameters converge to a neighborhood of the RE benchmark, consistent with the observed coordination of individual forecasts in the experiments, while in the strongly unstable treatment parameters continue to fluctuate and prices keep moving away from the RE benchmark, consistent with the persistent heterogeneity of expectations and excess volatility in the strongly unstable treatment of the experiments (cf. Figure 8.3).

8.3   Asset pricing experiments

In this section, we discuss the asset pricing learning-to-forecast experiments (LtFEs) in Hommes et al. (2005b). There are two assets, a risk free asset paying a fixed rate of return r and a risky asset, with price p_t, paying an uncertain stochastic dividend y_t. The asset market is populated by 6 large pension funds and a small fraction of fundamentalist robot traders. Six subjects are forecast advisors to each of the pension funds. Subjects' only task is to forecast the price p_{t+1} of the risky asset for 50 periods and, based on this forecast, the pension fund then decides how much to invest in the risky asset according to a mean-variance demand function (the same as in the asset pricing model of Chapter 6, Eq. 6.3). The fundamentalist trader always predict the *fundamental price* p^f and trades based upon this prediction.

The realized asset price in the experiment is determined by market clearing, as in the standard asset pricing model with heterogeneous beliefs in Chapter 6 (cf. Eq. 6.5):

$$p_t = \frac{1}{1+r}\left((1-n_t)\bar{p}^e_{t+1} + n_t\, p^f + \bar{y} + \varepsilon_t\right), \tag{8.10}$$

where $p^f = \bar{y}/r$ is the fundamental price, $\bar{p}^e_{t+1} = (\sum_{h=1}^6 p^e_{h,t+1})/6$ is the average two-period-ahead price forecast over six individuals and ε_t are small shocks, e.g., representing small random fluctuations in asset demand. Subjects do *not* know the underlying law of motion (8.10), but they do know the mean-dividend $\bar{y}$ and the interest rate r, so they can in principle use these to compute the fundamental price and use it in their forecast. The fraction n_t in (8.10) is the share of computerized fundamental robot traders, given by

$$n_t = 1 - \exp\left(-\frac{1}{200}|p_{t-1} - p^f|\right). \tag{8.11}$$

The fraction of robot traders increases as the price moves further away from the fundamental benchmark. The fundamental trader thus acts as a "far from equilibrium" stabilizing force in the market, mimicking the feature that more traders in the market expect the price to return in the direction of the fundamental when the deviation becomes large.[6] Subjects' earnings depend on forecasting performance and are given by a quadratic scoring rule

$$e_{i,t} = \begin{cases} 1 - \left(\dfrac{p_t - p^e_{i,t}}{7}\right)^2 & \text{if} \quad |p_t - p^e_{i,t}| < 7, \\ 0 & \text{otherwise}, \end{cases} \tag{8.12}$$

so that forecasting errors exceeding 7 would result in no reward at a given period. At the end of the session the accumulated earnings of every participant were converted to euros (1 point computed as in (8.12) corresponded to 50 cents).

8.3.1 Benchmark simulations

Figure 8.5 shows simulations of realized prices, which would occur if all subjects would coordinate on the corresponding homogeneous benchmark expectations rule. When all individuals use the rational, fundamental forecasting rule, $p^e_{i,t+1} = \bar{y}/r = p^f$, for all i and t, the realized price $p_t = p^f + \varepsilon_t/(1+r)$ randomly fluctuates around the fundamental level $p^f = 60$ with small amplitude, due to the small shocks. In the experiment, one cannot expect rational behavior at the outset, but aggregate prices

---

[6] In the experiment n_t never exceeds 0.25, while the weights of the other traders are equal to $(1-n_t)/6$. Hommes et al. (2008) investigate price behavior in asset pricing LtFEs *without* robot traders. Bottazzi et al. (2011) ran an asset pricing LtFE where subjects had to forecast price returns and price volatility.

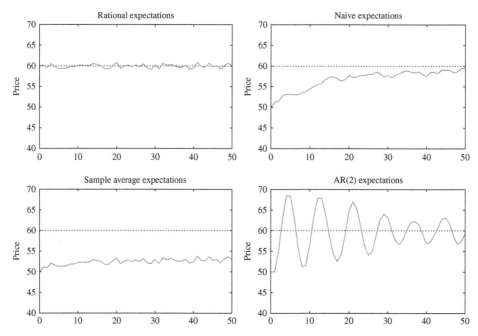

Figure 8.5. Simulation benchmarks: top panels RE (left) and naive expectations (right); bottom panels: learning by sample average (left) and AR(2) trend-following rule $p_{t+1}^e = (60 + p_{t-1})/2 + (p_{t-1} - p_{t-2})$.

might converge to their fundamental value through individual learning. Under naive expectations the price slowly converges (monotonically) toward its fundamental value (top right panel). The same is true under learning by average, the simplest form of adaptive learning obtained when regressing the price on a constant, but the convergence under average price expectations is extremely slow (bottom left panel). Finally, if all subjects would use the simple AR(2) rule

$$p_{t+1}^e = \frac{60 + p_{t-1}}{2} + (p_{t-1} - p_{t-2}), \qquad (8.13)$$

price oscillations as illustrated in the bottom right panel of Figure 8.5 arise. This is an example of an *anchoring and adjustment* rule, which play an important role in psychology (Tversky ad Kahneman, 1974), because it extrapolates the last price change from a reference point or *anchor* $(p^f + p_{t-1})/2$ describing the "long run" price level.[7]

---

[7] At this stage one could argue that the anchor of this rule, defined as the average between the last observed price and the fundamental price, was unknown in the experiment, since subjects were not provided explicitly with the fundamental price 60. It is remarkable, however, that for a number of subjects the estimated linear forecasting rule was surprisingly close to the anchor and adjustment rule (8.13). In Section 8.4 we will fit a heterogeneous expectations switching model to the experimental data and one of the (four) rules will be obtained by replacing the fundamental price 60 in (8.13) by the observable sample average of past prices.

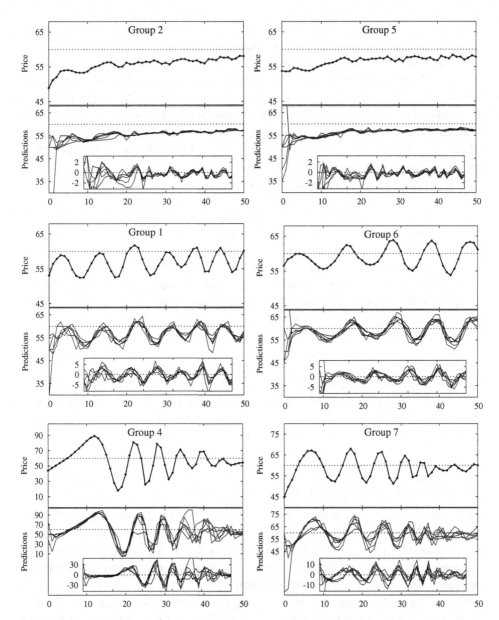

Figure 8.6. Asset pricing experiments in six different groups: realized market prices, six individual predictions (middle part of each panel) and individual errors (bottom part of each panel).

8.3.2 *Experimental results*

Figure 8.6 shows time series of prices, individual predictions and forecasting errors in six different markets of the experiment. A striking feature of aggregate price behavior is that three different qualitative patterns emerge. The prices in groups 2 and 5 converge slowly and almost monotonically to the fundamental price level. In groups 1 and 6 persistent oscillations are observed during the entire experiment. In groups 4 and 7 prices are also fluctuating but their amplitude is decreasing.[8]

A second striking result in the experiments concerns individual predictions. In all groups participants were able to *coordinate* their forecasting activity. The forecasts, as shown in the lower parts of the panels in Figure 8.6, are dispersed in the first periods but then, within 3–5 periods, move close to each other in all groups. The coordination of individual forecasts has been achieved in the absence of any communication between subjects, except through the realized market price, and without any knowledge of past and present predictions of *other* participants.

To summarize, in the asset pricing LtFEs the following stylized facts are observed:

1. Participants were unable to learn the rational, fundamental price; only in some cases individual predictions moved (slowly) in the direction of the fundamental price towards the end of the experiment.
2. Although the sessions were designed exactly the same, three different price patterns were observed: (i) slow, (almost) monotonic convergence, (ii) persistent price oscillations with almost constant amplitude, and (iii) large initial oscillations dampening slowly towards the end of the experiment.
3. Already after a short transient phase, participants were able to coordinate and submit similar forecasts in every period.

One would like to have a model explaining all these stylized facts simultaneously. To our best knowledge, there is no homogeneous expectations model fitting all these experiments. The fact that qualitatively different aggregate outcomes can arise suggests that *path dependence* and *heterogeneous expectations* must play a key role.

8.4   Fitting a heterogeneous expectations model

In this section, we discuss a heuristics switching model, which has been fitted to the asset pricing LtFEs by Anufriev and Hommes (2012a,b). The heuristics switching model is an extension of the heterogeneous expectations model (Brock and Hommes, 1997a), where agents tend to switch toward forecasting strategies that have performed better in the recent past, as discussed in Chapters 5 and 6.

Agents can choose from a number of simple *forecasting heuristics*. To discipline the wilderness of bounded rationality, the set of forecasting heuristics needs to be carefully chosen. The forecasting heuristics chosen here are similar to those obtained from estimations of linear models on individual forecasting data in the LtFEs. To discipline the wilderness of bounded rationality *evolutionary selection* or *performance based reinforcement learning* takes place, that is, agents evaluate the *performances* of

---

[8] Price dynamics in group 3 (not shown) is more difficult to classify. Similar to group 1 it started with moderate oscillations, then stabilized at a level below the fundamental, suddenly falling in period $t = 40$, probably due to a typing error of one of the participants.

all heuristics, and tend to switch to more successful rules. Hence, the impact of each of the rules is evolving over time.

To keep the model as simple as possible, Anufriev and Hommes (2012a,b) restricted attention to only four forecasting heuristics:

$$\text{ADA} \quad p_{1,t+1}^e = 0.65\, p_{t-1} + 0.35\, p_{1,t}^e, \tag{8.14}$$

$$\text{WTR} \quad p_{2,t+1}^e = p_{t-1} + 0.4\,(p_{t-1} - p_{t-2}), \tag{8.15}$$

$$\text{STR} \quad p_{3,t+1}^e = p_{t-1} + 1.3\,(p_{t-1} - p_{t-2}), \tag{8.16}$$

$$\text{LAA} \quad p_{4,t+1}^e = \frac{p_{t-1}^{av} + p_{t-1}}{2} + (p_{t-1} - p_{t-2}), \tag{8.17}$$

were $p_{t-1}^{av} = \sum_{j=0}^{t-1} p_j$ is the sample average of past prices. The first *adaptive expectations* (ADA) rule predicts that the price is a weighted average of the last observed price p_{t-1} and the last price forecast p_t^e. This ADA rule was obtained as the estimated linear rule of a number of subjects in the converging groups 2 and 5. The second and the third rules are both *trend-following rules*, with a weak trend (WTR) parameter 0.4 and a strong trend (STR) parameter 1.3 respectively. These rules were obtained as the estimated linear rules for quite a number of subjects in the oscillatory markets 1, 4, 6 and 7, with 0.4 and 1.3 obtained as the smallest and largest trend extrapolating coefficients. Finally, the fourth rule is an anchor and adjustment rule, obtained from the linear AR(2) rule (8.13), discussed in Subsection 8.3.1, by replacing the (unknown) fundamental price p^f by a proxy given by the (observable) sample average of past prices p_{t-1}^{av}. The weight coefficient of the ADA rule and the trend parameters of trend-following rules have been fixed and it appears that the simulations below are robust with respect to small changes of these parameters. The LAA rule exhibits a simple form of *adaptive learning*, since the anchor of the rule is the average of the last observed price and the sample average of all observed prices.

Subjects switch between the different forecasting rules based upon quadratic forecasting errors, consistent with the earnings incentives in the experiments. The fitness or performance measure of forecasting heuristic i is given by

$$U_{i,t-1} = -\left(p_{t-1} - p_{i,t-1}^e\right)^2 + \eta\, U_{i,t-2}, \tag{8.18}$$

where the parameter $\eta \in [0,1]$ measures, the strength of the agents' *memory*. Switching is described by a discrete choice model with *asynchronous updating* (see Chapter 5, Eq. 5.10)

$$n_{i,t} = \delta\, n_{i,t-1} + (1-\delta)\, \frac{\exp(\beta\, U_{i,t-1})}{\sum_{i=1}^{4} \exp(\beta\, U_{i,t-1})}. \tag{8.19}$$

In the special case $\delta = 0$, (8.19) reduces to *the discrete choice model* with synchronous updating. The more general case, $0 \le \delta \le 1$, gives some persistence or inertia in the impact of rule h, reflecting the fact (consistent with the experimental data) that not all the participants update their rule in every period or at the same time. Hence, δ may be interpreted as the average per period fraction of individuals who stick to their previous strategy. In the extreme case $\delta = 1$, the initial impacts of the rules never change; if $0 < \delta \leq 1$, in each period a fraction $1 - \delta$ of participants update their rule according to the discrete choice model. The parameter $\beta \geq 0$ represents the intensity of choice measuring how sensitive individuals are to differences in strategy performance. The higher the intensity of choice β, the faster individuals will switch to more successful rules. In the extreme case $\beta = 0$, the impacts in (8.19) move to an equal distribution independent of their past performance. At the other extreme $\beta = \infty$, *all* agents who update their heuristic (i.e., a fraction $1 - \delta$) switch to the most successful predictor.

In all simulations below, the parameters are fixed at the benchmark values $\beta = 0.4, \eta = 0.7, \delta = 0.9$[9] and the initial fractions of the four strategies are equal, i.e., $n_{ht} = 0.25$. The simulations thus only differ in their initial prices, which have been chosen exactly the same as in the first two periods in the corresponding experimental group.

Figure 8.7 compares the experimental data with the *one-step ahead predictions* made by the heuristics switching model, for one converging group (group 5), one oscillating group (group 6) and one dampened oscillating group (group 7); the other groups yield very similar results. Figure 8.7 suggests that the switching model with four heuristics fits the experimental data quite nicely. The one-step ahead predictions of the nonlinear switching model in Figure 8.7 use past *experimental price data* to determine the forecasts and the fractions of the strategies at each period t, i.e., the model simulation uses exactly the same information that was available to participants in the experiments. An immediate observation by comparing these simulations is that the one-period-ahead forecasts can easily follow the different patterns in aggregate price behavior, slow monotonic convergence, sustained oscillations as well as dampened oscillations.

The right panels in Figure 8.7 show the corresponding fractions of the four strategies for each group. In different groups different heuristics are dominating the market, after starting off from a uniform distribution. In the monotonically converging group, the impact of the different rules stays more or less equal, although the impact of adaptive expectations gradually increases and slightly dominates the other rules in the last 25 periods. In the oscillatory group the LAA rule dominates the market from the start and its impact increases to about 90% toward the end of the experiment. Finally, for the group with the dampened oscillations, one-step-ahead forecast produces a rich evolutionary selection dynamics (bottom right panel), with three different phases where the STR, the LAA and the ADA heuristics subsequently dominate. The STR dominates during the initial phase of a strong trend in prices, but starts declining after it misses the first turning point of the trend. The LAA does a better job in predicting the trend reversal, because of its more slowly time-varying anchor and its impact starts increasing. The LAA takes the lead in the second phase of the experiment, with oscillating prices, and its share increases to almost 90% after 35 periods. But the oscillations slowly dampen

---

[9] These values were obtained in Anufriev and Hommes (2012a) after some trial and error simulations. The simulation results, however, are fairly robust with respect to small changes in the parameter values.

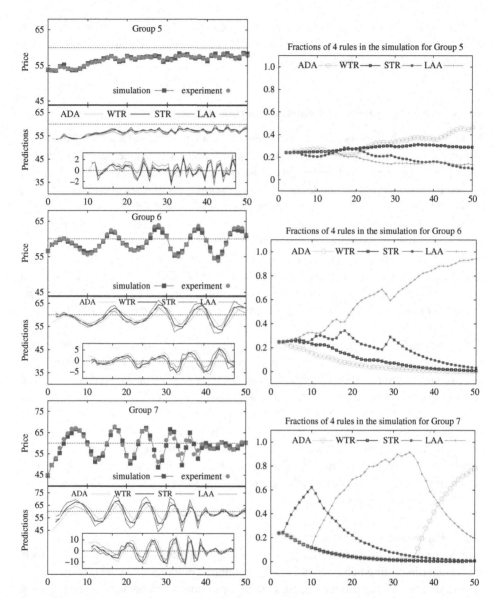

Figure 8.7. Left panels: prices for asset pricing laboratory experiments in different groups with corresponding one-step ahead predictions of the heuristics switching model. Lower parts of left panels show predictions and forecasting errors (inner frames) of four heuristics. Right panels: evolution of impacts of four forecasting heuristics during the one-step-ahead predictions of the model: adaptive expectations (ADA), weak trend followers (WTR), strong trend followers (STR) and anchoring adjustment heuristic (LAA).

and therefore, after period 35, the impact of adaptive expectations, which has been the worst performing rule until that point, starts increasing and adaptive expectations dominates the group in the last 9 periods.

8.5   Positive versus negative feedback experiments

Aggregate price behaviors in the cobweb and the asset pricing LtFEs are very different. In the cobweb framework the price fluctuates around its fundamental value, with a sample average of realized prices very close to the RE price. In contrast, in the asset pricing experiments persistent deviations from the fundamental price with long-lasting periods of under- or over-valuation are observed. An important difference between the cobweb and asset pricing experiments is the type of expectations feedback: the asset pricing (cobweb) framework exhibits positive (negative) feedback, that is, the realized price depends positively (negatively) on the average price forecast. In the case of positive (negative) feedback, an increase of an individual forecast causes the realized market price (slightly) to go up (down). A natural question then is *whether the type of expectations feedback, positive or negative, explains the observed differences in aggregate price behavior.*

In most markets both types of feedback may play a role. Positive feedback, however, seems particularly relevant in speculative asset markets. If many agents expect the price of an asset to rise they will start buying the asset, aggregate demand will increase and so, by the law of supply and demand, will the asset price. High price expectations thus become self-confirming and lead to high realized asset prices. In markets where the role of speculative demand is less important, e.g., in markets for non-storable commodities, negative feedback may play a more prominent role. Consider, e.g., a supply-driven commodity market. If many producers expect future prices to be high they will increase production which, according to the law of supply and demand, will lead to a low realized market price.

8.5.1   *Experiments with small shocks*

Heemeijer et al. (2009) investigate how the expectations feedback structure affects individual forecasting behavior and aggregate market outcomes by considering market environments that *only* differ in the sign of the expectations feedback, but are equivalent along all other dimensions. In this section we discuss these experiments and apply the heterogeneous expectations model of Section 8.4 to see whether it can explain individual learning as well as the different aggregate outcomes.[10]

---

[10] The distinction between positive and negative expectations feedback is related to the concepts of strategic complements versus strategic substitutes (Haltiwanger and Waldman, 1985). In their experiments, Fehr and Tyran (2001, 2005, 2008) study the impact of different strategic environments (strategic complementarity versus strategic substitutability) on individual rationality and aggregate outcomes. Sutan and Willinger (2009) investigate a new variant of beauty contest games (BCG) in which players' actions are strategic substitutes versus strategic complements and find that chosen numbers are closer to rational play in the case of strategic substitutes.

The (unknown) price generating rules in the *negative* and *positive* feedback systems were respectively:

$$p_t = 60 - \frac{20}{21}\left[\left(\sum_{h=1}^{6}\frac{1}{6}p_{ht}^e\right) - 60\right] + \epsilon_t, \qquad \text{negative feedback} \qquad (8.20)$$

$$p_t = 60 + \frac{20}{21}\left[\left(\sum_{h=1}^{6}\frac{1}{6}p_{ht}^e\right) - 60\right] + \epsilon_t, \qquad \text{positive feedback} \qquad (8.21)$$

where ϵ_t is a small random shock to the pricing rule. First we will consider positive and negative feedback systems with small IID shocks ϵ_t, $\epsilon_t \sim N(0, 0.25)$, and in Subsection 8.5.2 with large permanent shocks.

A common feature of the positive and negative feedback systems (8.20) and (8.21) is that both have the same RE equilibrium steady state $p^* = 60$. The *only* difference between (8.20) and (8.21) is therefore the sign of the slope of the linear map, $20/21 \approx +0.95$ resp. $-20/21 \approx -0.95$.[11]

Figure 8.8 shows realized market prices as well as individual predictions in two typical groups. A striking feature is that aggregate price behavior is very different in the positive versus negative feedback cases. In the negative feedback case, the price relatively quickly settles down to the RE steady state price 60, while in the positive feedback case, the market price oscillates slowly around its fundamental value. Individual forecasting behavior is also different for the different feedback treatments: in the case

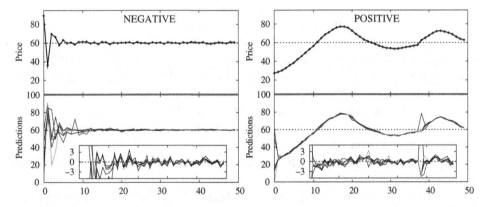

Figure 8.8. Negative (left panel) vs. positive (right panel) feedback experiments with small IID shocks; prices (top panels), individual predictions (bottom panels) and forecast errors (small panels). In the negative expectations feedback market the realized price quickly converges to the RE benchmark 60. In the positive feedback market individuals coordinate on the "wrong" price forecast and as a result the realized market price persistently deviates from the RE benchmark 60.

---

[11] In both treatments, the absolute value of the slopes is 0.95, implying in both cases that the feedback system is stable under naive expectations. Recall from (8.10) in Section 8.3 that the asset pricing experiments had almost the same coefficient $1/(1+r) = 1/1.05 \approx 0.952$, while the stable treatment ($\lambda = 0.22$) of the cobweb experiments in Section 8.2 had a slope coefficient of -0.87 at the steady state.

of positive feedback, coordination of individual forecasts occurs extremely quickly, within 2–3 periods. The coordination, however, is on a "wrong" non-fundamental price. In contrast, in the negative feedback case coordination of individual forecasts is slower and takes about 10 periods. More persistence in heterogeneity of individual forecasts, however, ensures that, after 10 periods, individual predictions as well as the realized market price are very close to the RE benchmark of 60.

As already noted in Muth's classical paper on rational expectations, a key issue for their aggregate effect is whether the deviations of individual expectations from the rational forecast are *correlated* or not. To quote Muth (1961, p. 321, emphasis added):

> Allowing for cross-sectional differences in expectations is a simple matter, because their aggregate effect is negligible as long as the deviation from the rational forecast for an individual firm is *not strongly correlated with those of the others*. Modifications are necessary only if the correlation of the errors is large and depends systematically on other explanatory variables.

Our learning-to-forecast experiments show that for the cobweb model considered by Muth, because of the negative expectations feedback, heterogeneity of individual forecasts around the rational forecast 60 persists in the first 10 periods, correlated individual deviations from the rational, fundamental forecast do not arise and the realized market price converges quickly to the RE benchmark. In contrast, our learning-to-forecast experiments show that in an environment with positive expectations feedback individual deviations from the rational fundamental forecast may be strongly correlated. For example, in Figure 8.8 (right panel) within 2–3 periods, individual forecasts are strongly coordinated substantially below the rational fundamental forecast. In positive expectations feedback markets, at the aggregate level the market price may therefore persistently deviate from the rational fundamental price.

Can the heterogeneous expectations model of Section 8.4 explain these different outcomes in individual and aggregate behavior? Figure 8.9 shows realized market prices together with the simulated prices (top panels) and the corresponding evolution of the fractions of the four strategies (bottom panels) of the heuristics switching model with the same benchmark parameters as before, i.e., $\beta = 0.4, \eta = 0.7, \delta = 0.9$. The model matches aggregate price behavior in both the negative and positive feedback treatments. Furthermore, the time series of the fractions of the different forecasting heuristics (Figure 8.9, bottom panels) provide an intuitive explanation of how individual learning leads to different aggregate price behavior. In the negative feedback treatment, the adaptive expectations strategy performs best and within 20 periods it captures more than 90% of the market, thus enforcing convergence toward the fundamental equilibrium price. In contrast, in the positive feedback treatment the impact of the strong trend-following rule (STR) quickly increases and it captures more than 75% of the market after 15 periods. Thereafter, the impact of the STR rule gradually declines, while the fraction of weak trend followers (WTR) gradually increases due to the fact that the STR rule makes (somewhat) larger mistakes (especially at the turning points) than the WTR rule.

The difference in aggregate behavior is thus explained by the fact that *trend-following rules are successful in a positive feedback environment* reinforcing price oscillations

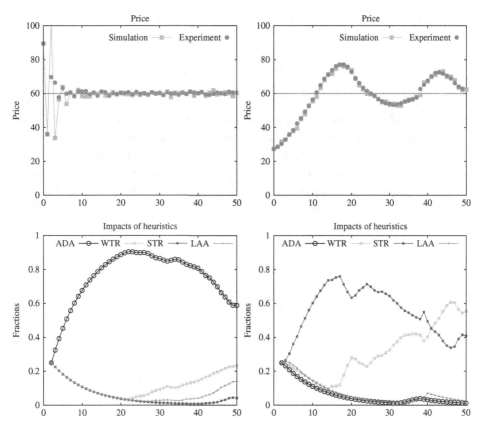

Figure 8.9. Negative feedback (left panels) and positive feedback (right panels) markets with small shocks. Realized and simulated prices (top panels) and corresponding evolution of fractions of 4 strategies in heuristics switching model (bottom panels). In the negative feedback market the adaptive expectations (ADA) rule dominates and enforces quick convergence to the RE fundamental price 60. In the positive expectations feedback market, the strong (STR) and the weak (WTR) trend-following rules perform well and reinforce price oscillations, leading to persistent deviations from the RE fundamental price.

and persistent deviations from the fundamental equilibrium benchmark price, while the trend-following rules are driven out by adaptive expectations in the case of negative feedback. Self-confirming coordination on trend-following rules in a positive expectations feedback environment has an aggregate effect, with realized market prices deviating significantly and persistently from the RE benchmark.

8.5.2 Experiments with large shocks

Finally, we discuss some recent experiments by Bao et al. (2012), who ran similar LtFEs with large unanticipated permanent shocks ϵ_t to the price generating mechanisms (8.20) and (8.21). These shocks have been chosen such that, both in the negative and positive feedback treatments, the fundamental equilibrium price p_t^* changes over time according to

$$p_t^* = 56, \qquad 0 \le t \le 21,$$
$$p_t^* = 41, \qquad 22 \le t \le 43, \qquad\qquad (8.22)$$
$$p_t^* = 62, \qquad 44 \le t \le 65.$$

The purpose of these experiments was to investigate how the type of expectations feedback may affect the speed of learning of a new steady state equilibrium price, after a relatively large shock to the economy. Figure 8.10 shows realized market prices together with the simulated market prices (top panels), together with the evolution of the fractions of the four strategies of the heuristics switching model (bottom panels) for a typical group of the negative feedback (left panels) and the positive feedback

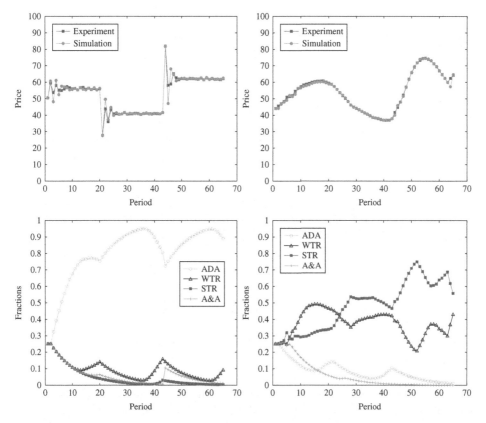

Figure 8.10. Negative feedback (left panels) and positive feedback (right panels) markets with large permanent shocks to the equilibrium steady state level. Realized and simulated prices (top panels) and evolution of fractions of the 4 strategies in heuristics switching model (bottom panels). In the negative feedback market, after each large shock the market quickly settles down to the new RE price, with the adaptive expectations rule dominating. In the positive feedback market, prices do not converge to RE, but persistently oscillate due to the relatively good performance of the weak and the strong trend-following strategies.

treatment (right panels). The heuristics switching model is exactly the same as before, with the same benchmark parameters, i.e., $\beta = 0.4, \eta = 0.7, \delta = 0.9$. As before, there is a striking difference between positive and negative feedback markets. In the negative feedback market, after each large shock the price quickly (within 5 periods) settles down to the new RE steady state, while in the positive feedback market the price slowly oscillates with persistent deviations from the RE benchmark. The heuristics switching model matches both patterns quite nicely and provides an intuitive, *behavioral explanation* why these different aggregate patterns occur. In the negative feedback market, trend-following strategies perform poorly and the adaptive expectations strategy quickly dominates the market (more than 50% within 10 periods) enforcing quick convergence to the RE benchmark after each large shock. In contrast, in the positive feedback treatment, trend-following strategies perform well, the weak trend-following rule dominates in the first 20 periods, while the strong trend-following rule starts dominating after the first large shock in period 22. The survival of trend-following strategies in the positive feedback markets causes persistent deviations from the RE steady states, overreaction and persistent price fluctuations.

Figure 8.11 reveals some other striking features of aggregate price behavior and individual forecasts. The left panel shows the time variation of the median distance to the RE benchmark price over all (eight) groups in both treatments. For the negative feedback treatment, after each large shock the distance spikes but converges quickly back (within 5–6 periods) to 0, while for the positive feedback treatment after each shock the distance to the RE benchmark shows a similar spike but does not converge to 0 and only decreases slowly. The right panel shows how the *degree of heterogeneity*, that is, the median standard deviation of individual forecasts, changes over time. For the positive feedback treatment after each large shock heterogeneity decreases very

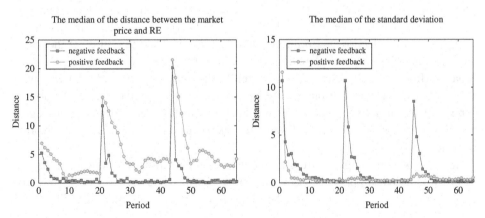

Figure 8.11. Positive/negative feedback markets with large shocks. These plots illustrate price discovery (left panel) and coordination of individual expectations (right panel). The left panel shows the median absolute distance to RE fundamental price, while the right panel shows the median standard deviation of individual predictions.

quickly and converges to (almost) 0 within 3–4 periods, while in the negative feedback treatment heterogeneity is more persistent for about 10 periods after each large shock. One may summarize these results in saying that in the positive feedback treatment individuals quickly coordinate on a common prediction, but that coordination on the "wrong" non-fundamental price occurs. On the other hand, in the negative feedback treatment coordination is slower, heterogeneity is more persistent but price convergence is quick. Stated differently, positive feedback markets are characterized by quick coordination and slow price discovery, while negative feedback markets are characterized by slow coordination, more persistent heterogeneity and quick price discovery. Our simple heterogeneous expectations switching model provides a simple and intuitive explanation of individual forecasting as well as aggregate price behavior in both positive and negative feedback markets.[12]

8.6   Final remarks and future outlook

Learning-to-forecast experiments (LtFEs) can be used to test different theories of expectations and learning. In laboratory experiments, different types of aggregate behavior have been observed in different market settings. To our best knowledge, *no homogeneous expectations model* fits the experimental data across different market settings. Quick convergence to the RE benchmark *only* occurs in stable (i.e., stable under naive expectations) cobweb markets with negative expectations feedback, as in Muth's (1961) seminal rational expectations paper. In all other market settings persistent deviations from the RE fundamental benchmark seem to be the rule rather than the exception.

The laboratory experiments suggest that *heterogeneity* is a crucial aspect of a theory of expectations for at least two reasons. First, a *heterogeneous expectations model* can explain the *path dependence* and the different aggregate outcomes in the same market environment, as observed for example in the asset pricing LtFEs. Second, a single model of heterogeneous expectations can explain different aggregate outcomes across different market settings. Indeed a simple heuristics switching model based on evolutionary selection and reinforcement learning provides an intuitive theory of individual learning and an explanation of the different observed types of aggregate price behavior. In positive feedback markets a trend-following strategy does relatively well and reinforces price oscillations and persistent deviations from the RE benchmark. In contrast, when negative expectations feedback dominates, trend-following strategies perform poorly and are driven out by adaptive expectations which enforces stable price behavior.

An important challenge to a research program in behavioral economics and finance based on bounded rationality is to come up with a plausible and general theory of heterogeneous expectations. The fact that the same simple heuristics switching model (with

---

[12] These findings are, e.g., in line with Schunk (2009, 2011) who uses laboratory panel data from an intertemporal choice task and shows that (i) a small set of both rational and rule of thumb types explains almost all observed decisions, (ii) there is evidence of type stability, i.e., individuals stick to a strategy for a while, and (iii) the type distribution is affected by the decision environment.

fixed parameters) fits experimental data in different economic environments suggests that a general heterogeneous expectations hypothesis may explain individual expectations and the aggregate behavior their interaction co-creates across different market settings. More research in this area is called for to test the robustness of these findings and its broader empirical relevance.

The recent macroeconomic literature stresses the importance of managing expectations in the formulation of monetary policy (Woodford, 2003, p. 15). The way in which individual expectations shape aggregate macroeconomic variables is crucial for the transmission and effectiveness of monetary policy. For policy it makes a big difference whether these expectations are rational or whether they are boundedly rational and heterogeneous. The question how to manage expectations when forecasting rules are heterogeneous has only recently moved to the forefront of macroeconomic research; for example, DeGrauwe (2010a,b,c) stresses the importance of taking boundedly rational heterogeneous expectations into account for macro economic policy. Anufriev et al. (2012) introduce a simple frictionless DSGE model with heterogeneous expectations to study the effect of monetary policy interest rate rules upon macroeconomic stability.

Pfajfar and Zakelj (2011) and Assenza et al. (2011) have recently conducted learning-to-forecast experiments in a standard New Keynesian macroeconomic framework and found evidence for heterogeneity of individual expectations. Assenza et al. (2011) use the same heuristics switching model as in Section 8.4 to explain coordination of individual expectations and aggregate macro behavior for two different variables, inflation and the output gap, observed in the laboratory experiments. Interestingly, the heuristics switching model explains coordination on different forecasting rules for the two variables within the same economy, with a weak trend-following rule dominating inflation forecasting and adaptive expectations dominating output forecasting. The simple heterogeneous expectations switching model thus also fits individual learning as well as aggregate outcomes in the standard New Keynesian macroeconomic setting.

For financial market regulation the expectations hypothesis – rational expectations versus heterogeneous bounded rationality– also makes a big difference. A recent example of completely different policy implications has been given in Brock et al. (2009), who study the effect of financial innovation in the asset pricing model with heterogeneous beliefs of Chapter 6. In standard financial economics the conventional wisdom is that financial innovation is beneficial, because it would stabilize market prices and improve welfare. But this is only true under the assumption that all agents are perfectly rational. Brock, et al. (2009) show that in the asset pricing model with heterogeneous, boundedy rational beliefs the introduction of additional futures markets in the form of Arrow securities may *destabilize* markets, and thus increase price volatility, and at the same time may decrease average welfare. This stylized model explains how the introduction of complex financial instruments in real markets with boundedly rational investors may have contributed to market instability and excess volatility in the 2008–2012 financial-economic crisis.

Policy makers become increasingly aware that the economy is a complex system. Complexity models with boundedly rational heterogeneous expectations provide important tools in understanding complex phenomena and sudden, unpredictable transitions in the global economy. Economists must recognize complexity research as a serious alternative to the standard rational paradigm, which may particularly be relevant and useful at extreme times. It is about time the economics profession turned its attention to a more realistic complexity approach to assist in developing more effective tools for economic policy in managing the current financial-economic crisis and preventing or limiting the damage of future crises.

Bibliography

Adam, K. (2007), Experimental evidence on the persistence of output and inflation. *The Economic Journal* 117 (520), 603–636.

Akerlof, G.A. and Shiller, R.J. (2009), *Animal Spirits: How Human Psychology Drives the Economy, and Why It Matters for Global Capitalism*. Princeton University Press, Princeton, NY.

Alfarano, S., Lux, T. and Wagner, F. (2005), Estimation of agent-based models: the case of an asymmetric herding model. *Computational Economics* 26, 19–49.

Allen, H. and Taylor, M.P. (1990), Charts, noise and fundamentals in the London foreign exchange market. *Economic Journal* 100 (400), Conference Papers, 49–59.

Amilon, H. (2008), Estimation of an adaptive stock market model with heterogeneous agents. *Journal of Empirical Finance* 15, 342–362.

Anderson, P.W, Arrow, K.J. and Pines, D. (eds.) (1988), *The Economy as an Evolving Complex System*. Addison-Wesley, Reading, MA.

Anderson, S., de Palma, A. and Thisse, J. (1993), Discrete choice theory of product differentiation. MIT Press, Cambridge, MA.

Anufriev, M. and Hommes, C.H. (2012a), Evolution of market heuristics, *Knowledge Engineering Review, The Knowledge Engineering Review* 27, 255–271.

Anufriev, M. and Hommes, C.H. (2012b), Evolutionary selection of individual expectations and aggregate outcomes in asset pricing experiments. *American Economic Journal: Microeconomics* 2012, 4 (4).

Anufriev, M., Assenza, T., Hommes, C.H. and Massaro, D. (2012), Interest rate rules and macroeconomic stability under heterogeneous expectations. *Macroeconomic Dynamics*, in press.

Aoki, M. (2002), *Modeling Aggregate Behavior and Fluctuations in Economics. Stochastic Views of Interacting Agents*. Cambridge University Press, Cambridge.

Arifovic, J. (1994), Genetic algorithm learning and the cobweb model. *Journal of Economic Dynamics and Control* 18, 3–28.

Arthur, W.B. (1994), Increasing returns and path dependence in the economy. University of Michigan Press, Ann Arbor, MI.

Arthur, W.B. (1995) Complexity in economic and financial markets. *Complexity* 1, 20–25.

Arthur, W.B. (2006), Out-of-equilibrium economics and agent-based modeling. In Tesfatsion, L. and Judd, K.L. (eds.), *Handbook of Computational Economics, Volume 2: Agent-Based Computational Economics*, chapter 23. North-Holland, Amsterdam, pp. 1551–1564.

Arthur, W.B., Durlauf, S.N and Lane, D.A. (eds.) (1997a), *The Economy as an Evolving Complex System II*. Addison-Wesley, Reading, MA.

Arthur, W.B., Holland, J.H., LeBaron, B., Palmer, R. and Tayler, P. (1997b), Asset pricing under endogenous expectations in an artificial stock market. In Arthur, W., Lane, D. and Durlauf, S.

(eds.), *The Economy as an Evolving Complex System II*. Addison-Wesley, Reading, MA, pp. 15–44.

Artstein, Z. (1983) Irregular cobweb dynamics. *Economics Letters* 11, 15–17.

Assenza, T., Heemeijer, P., Hommes, C.H. and Massaro, D. (2011), Individual expectations and aggregate macro behavior. *CeNDEF Working Paper*. University of Amsterdam, July 2011.

Baak, S.J. (1999), Tests for bounded rationality with a linear dynamic model distorted by heterogeneous expectations. *Journal of Economic Dynamics and Control* 23, 1517–1543.

Bao, T., Duffy, J. and Hommes, C.H. (2011), Learning, forecasting and optimizing: an experimental study. *CeNDEF Working Paper*. University of Amsterdam, October 2011.

Bao, T., Hommes, C.H., Sonnemans, J. and Tuinstra, J. (2012), Individual expectation, limited rationality and aggregate outcome. *Journal of Economic Dynamics and Control*, 36, 1101–1120.

Barberis, N. and Thaler, R. (2003), A survey of behavioral finance. In Constantinidis, G.M. Harris, M. and Stulza, R. (eds.) *Handbook of the Economics of Finance*. Elsevier, Amsterdam, pp. 1051–1121.

Barberis, N., Shleifer, A. and Vishny, R. (1998). A model of investor sentiment. *Journal of Financial Economics* 49, 307–343.

Benartzi, S. and Thaler, R.H. (2007), Heuristics and biases in retirement savings behavior. *Journal of Economic Perspectives* 21, 81–104.

Benhabib, J. and Day, R.H. (1982), A characterization of erratic dynamics in the overlapping generations model. *Journal of Economic Dynamics and Control* 4, 37–55.

Blume, L. and Easley, D. (1992), Evolution and market behavior. *Journal of Economic Theory*, 58, 9–40.

Blume, L. and Easley, D. (2006), If you're so smart, why aren't you rich? Belief selection in complete and incomplete markets. *Econometrica* 74, 929–966.

Bollerslev, T., Engle, R. and Nelson, D. (1994), Arch models. In Engle, R. and McFadden, D. (eds.), *Handbook of Econometrics*, Volume IV. North Holland, Amsterdam, pp. 2961–3038.

Boswijk, H.P., Hommes, C.H. and Manzan, S. (2007), Behavioral heterogeneity in stock prices. *Journal of Economic Dynamics and Control* 31, 1938–1970.

Bottazzi, G., Devetag, G. and Pancotto, F. (2011). Does volatility matter? Expectations of price return and variability in an asset pricing experiment, *Journal of Economic Behavior and Organization* 77, 124–146.

Bouchaud, J.-P. (2009), Economics needs a scientific revolution. *Nature* 457, 147.

Bouchaud, J.-P., Farmer, J.D. and Lillo, F. (2009), How markets slowly digest changes in supply and demand. In Hens, T. and Schenk-Hoppé, K.R. (eds.), *Handbook of Financial Markets: Dynamics and Evolution*. Elsevier, Amsterdam, pp. 57–160.

Branch, W.A. (2004), The theory of rationally heterogeneous expectations: evidence from survey data on inflation expectations. *Economic Journal* 114, 592–621.

Branch, W.A. (2006), Restricted perceptions equilibria and learning in macroeconomics. In Colander, D. (ed.), *Post Walrasian Macroeconomics: Beyond the Dynamic Stochastic General Equilibrium Model*. Cambridge University Press, New York, pp. 135–160.

Branch, W.A. (2007), Sticky information and model uncertainty in survey data on inflation expectations. *Journal of Economic Dynamics and Control* 31, 245–276.

Branch, W.A. and Evans, G.W. (2006), Intrinsic heterogeneity in expectation formation. *Journal of Economic Theory* 127, 264–295.

Branch, W.A. and McGough, B. (2005), Consistent expectations and misspecification in stochastic non-linear economies. *Journal of Economic Dynamics and Control* 29, 659–676.

Bray, M.M. and Savin, N.E. (1986), Rational expectations equilibria, learning, and model specification. *Econometrica* 54, 1129–1160.

Brock, W.A. (1993) Pathways to randomness in the economy: emergent nonlinearity and chaos in economics and finance. *Estudios Económicos* 8, 3–55.

Brock, W.A. (1997), Asset price behavior in complex environments. In Arthur, W.B., Durlauf, S.N., and Lane, D.A. (eds.), *The Economy as an Evolving Complex System II*. Addison-Wesley, Reading, MA, 385–423.

Brock, W.A. and Hommes, C.H. (1995), Rational routes to randomness. *SSRI Working Paper 9506*. Department of Economics, University of Wisconsin.

Brock, W.A. and Hommes, C.H. (1997a), A rational route to randomness. *Econometrica* 65, 1059–1095.

Brock, W.A. and Hommes, C.H. (1997b), Models of complexity in economics and finance. In Hey, C. et al. (eds.), *System Dynamics in Economic and Financial Models*, Chapter 1, Wiley, New York, pp. 3–41.

Brock, W.A. and Hommes, C.H. (1998), Heterogeneous beliefs and routes to chaos in a simple asset pricing model. *Journal of Economic Dynamics and Control* 22, 1235–1274.

Brock, W.A. and Hommes, C.H. (1999), Rational animal spirits. In Herings, P.J.J., Laan, van der G. and Talman, A.J.J. (eds.), *The Theory of Markets*. North-Holland, Amsterdam, pp. 109–137.

Brock, W.A. and LeBaron, B. (1996), A structural model for stock return volatility and trading volume. *Review of Economics and Statistics* 78, 94–110.

Brock, W.A. and Sayers, C.L. (1988), Is the business cycle characterized by deterministic chaos? *Journal of Monetary Economics* 22, 71–90.

Brock, W.A., Hsieh, D. and LeBaron, B. (1991), *Nonlinear Dynamics, Chaos and Instability: Statistical Theory and Economic Evidence*. MIT Press, Cambridge, London.

Brock, W.A., Lakonishok, J. and LeBaron, B. (1992), Simple technical trading rules and the stochastic properties of stock returns. *Journal of Finance* 47, 1731–1764.

Brock, W.A., Dechert, W.D., Scheinkman, J.A. and LeBaron, B. (1996), A test for independence based on the correlation dimension. *Econometric Reviews* 15, 197–235.

Brock, W.A., Hommes, C.H. and Wagener, F.O.O. (2005), Evolutionary dynamics in markets with many trader types. *Journal of Mathematical Economics*, 41, 7–42.

Brock, W.A., Hommes, C.H. and Wagener, F.O.O. (2009), More hedging instruments may destabilize markets. *Journal of Economic Dynamics and Control* 33, 1912–1928.

Bullard, J. (1994), Learning equilibria. *Journal of Economic Theory* 64, 468–485.

Bullard, J., Evans, G.W. and Honkapohja, S. (2008), Monetary policy, judgment and near-rational exuberance. *American Economic Review* 98, 1163–1177.

Bullard, J., Evans, G.W. and Honkapohja, S. (2010), A model of near-rational exuberance. *Macroeconomic Dynamics* 14, 166–188.

Camerer, C.F. (2003), *Behavioral Game Theory*. Princeton University Press, Princeton, NJ.

Campbell, J.Y. and Shiller, R.J. (2005), Valuation ratios and the long-run stock market outlook: an update. In Thaler, R.H. (ed.), *Advances in Behavioral Finance*, volume 2. Princeton University Press, Princeton, NJ, pp. 173–201.

Campbell, J.Y., Lo, A.W. and MacKinlay, A.C. (1997), *The Econometrics of Financial Markets*. Princeton University Press, Princeton, NJ.

Capistrán, C. and Timmermann, A. (2009), Disagreement and biases in inflation expectations. *Journal of Money, Credit and Banking* 41, 365–396.

Carlson, J. (1967), The stability of an experimental market with a supply response lag. *Southern Economic Journal* 33, 305–321.

Chavas, J.P. (1996) *On the economic rationality of market participants: the case of expectations in the U.S. pork market*. Department of Economics, University of Wisconsin.

Chavas, J.P. (2000) On information and market dynamics: the case of the U.S. beef market. *Journal of Economic Dynamics and Control* 24, 833–853.

Chevalier, J. and Ellison, G. (1997), Risk taking by mutual funds as a response to incentives. *Journal of Political Economy* 105, 1167–1200.

Cheysson, Ê. (1887), *La statistique géometrique méthode pour la solution des problèmes commerciaux et industrièles*. Legenie Civil, Paris.

Chiarella, C. (1988) The cobweb model. Its instability and the onset of chaos. *Economic Modelling* 5, 377–384.

Chiarella, C. (1992), The dynamics of speculative behaviour. *Annals of Operations Research* 37, 101–123.

Chiarella, C. and He, X. (2001), Asset price and wealth dynamics under heterogeneous expectations, *Quantitative Finance* 1, 509–526.

Chiarella, C. and He, X. (2002), Heterogeneous beliefs, risk and learning in a simple asset pricing model. *Computational Economics* 19, 95–132.

Chiarella, C. and He, X. (2003), Heterogeneous beliefs, risk and learning in a simple asset pricing model with a market maker. *Macroeconomic Dynamics* 7, 503–536.

Chiarella, C., Dieci, R. and Gardini, L. (2002), Speculative behaviour and complex asset price dynamics: a global analysis. *Journal of Economic Behavior and Organization* 49, 173–197.

Chiarella, C., Dieci, R. and Gardini, L. (2006), Asset price and wealth dynamics in a financial market with heterogeneous agents. *Journal of Economic Dynamics and Control*, 30, 1755–1786.

Chiarella, C., Dieci, R. and He, X. (2009), Heterogeneity, market mechanisms, and asset price dynamics. In Hens, T. and Schenk-Hoppé, K. R. (eds.), *Handbook of Financial Markets: Dynamics and Evolution*. Elsevier, Amsterdam, pp. 277–344.

Clarida, R.G., Gali, J. and Gertler, M. (1999), The science of monetary policy: a New Keynesian perspective. *Journal of Economic Literature* 37, 1661–1707.

Clark, C.W. (1985), *Bioeconomic Modelling and Fisheries Management*. Wiley-Interscience, New York.

Clark, C.W. (1990), *Mathematical Bioeconomics: The Optimal Management of Renewable Resources*, 2nd ed. Wiley-Interscience, New York.

Colander, D., Goldberg, M., Haas, A., Juselius, K., Kirman, A. Lux, T. and Sloth, B. (2009), The financial crisis and the systemic failure of economics profession, *Critical Review: A Journal of Politics and Society* 21, 249–267.

Collet, P. and Eckman, J.-P. (1980), *Iterated Maps on the Interval as Dynamical Systems*. Birkhäuser, Basel.

Conlisk, J. (1980), Costly optimizers versus cheap imitators. *Journal of Economic Behavior and Organization* 1, 275–293.

Conlisk, J. (1996), Why bounded rationality? *Journal of Economic Literature* 34, 669–700.

Cont, R. (2001), Empirical properties of asset returns: stylized facts and statistical issues. *Quantitative Finance* 1, 223–236.

Cont, R. and Bouchaud, J.-P. (2000), Herd behavior and aggregate fluctuations in financial markets. *Macroeconomic Dynamics* 4, 170–196.

Cornea, A., Hommes, C.H. and Massaro, D. (2012), Behavioral heterogeneity in U.S. inflation dynamics. *CeNDEF Working Paper*. University of Amsterdam.

Cutler, D.M., Poterba, J.M. and Summers, L.H. (1989), What moves stock prices? *Journal of Portfolio Management* 15, 4–12.

Dacorogna, M.M., Müller, U.A., Jost, C., Pictet, O.V., Olsen, R.B. and Ward, J.R. (1995), Heterogeneous real-time trading strategies in the foreign exchange market. *European Journal of Finance* 1, 383–403.

Day, R.H. (1994), *Complex Economic Dynamics Vol. I. An Introduction to Dynamical Systems and Market Mechanisms*. MIT Press, Cambridge, MA.

Day, R.H. and Hanson, K.A. (1991), Cobweb chaos. In Kaul, T.K. and Sengupta, J.K. (eds.), *Economic Models, Estimation and Social Systems, Essays in Honor of Karl A. Fox*. North-Holland, Amsterdam.

Day, R.H. and Huang, W. (1990), Bulls, bears and market sheep. *Journal of Economic Behavior and Organization* 14, 299–329.

DeGrauwe, P. (2010a), Top-down versus bottom-up macroeconomics. *CESifo Economic Studies* 56(4), 465–497.

DeGrauwe, P. (2010b), *Behavioral macroeconomics*. Manuscript, University of Leuven, September 2010.

DeGrauwe, P. (2010c), Animal spirits and monetary policy, *Economic Theory* 47, 423–457.

DeGrauwe, P. and Grimaldi, M. (2006), *The Exchange Rate in a Behavioral Finance Framework*. Princeton University Press, Princeton, NJ.

DeGrauwe, P. and Markiewicz, A. (2012), Learning to forecast the exchange rate: two competing approaches. *Journal of International Money and Finance* 2012, in press.

DeGrauwe, P., Dewachter, H. and Embrechts, M. (1993) *Exchange Rate Theory. Chaotic Models of Foreign Exchange Markets*. Blackwell, Oxford.

Del Guerico, D. and Tkac, P.A. (2002), The determinants of the flow of funds of managed portfolios: mutual funds versus pension funds. *Journal of Financial and Quantitative Analysis* 37, 523–557.

Delli Gatti, D., Gallegati, M. and Kirman, A. (eds.) (2000), Interaction and market structure. Essays on heterogeneity in economics. *Lecture Notes in Economics and Mathematical Systems 484*. Springer Verlag, Berlin.

Delli-Gatti, D., Gaffeo, E., Gallegati, M., Giulioni, G. and Pallestrini, A. (2008), *Emergent Macroeconomics. An Agent-based Approach to Business Fluctuations*. Springer Verlag, Milan.

DeLong, J.B., Shleifer, A., Summers, L.H. and Waldmann, R.J. (1990a), Noise trader risk in financial markets. *Journal of Political Economy* 98, 703–738.

DeLong, J.B., Shleifer, A., Summers, L.H. and Waldmann, R.J. (1990b), Positive feedback investment strategies and destabilizing rational speculation. *Journal of Finance* 45, 379–395.

Devaney, R.L. (2003), *An Introduction to Chaotic Dynamical Systems*, 2nd edn. Westview Press.

Dieci, R. and Westerhoff, F. (2010), Heterogeneous speculators, endogenous fluctuations and interacting markets: a model of stock prices and exchange rates. *Journal of Economic Dynamics and Control* 34, 743–764.

Diks, C.G.H. and Weide, R. van der (2005), Herding, a-synchronous updating and heterogeneity in memory in a CBS. *Journal of Economic Dynamics and Control* 29, 741–763.

Diks, C.G.H., Hommes, C.H., Panchenko, V. and Weide, R. van der (2008), E&F Chaos: a user friendly software package for nonlinear economic dynamics. *Computational Economics*, 32, 221–244.

Droste, E., Hommes, C.H. and Tuinstra, J. (2002), Endogenous fluctuations under evolutionary pressure in Cournot competition. *Games and Economic Behavior* 40, 232–269.

Dudek, M.K. (2010), A consistent route to randomness. *Journal of Economic Theory* 145, 354–381.

Duffy, J. (2006), Agent-based models and human-subject experiments. In Tesfatsion, L. and Judd, K.L. (eds.), *Handbook of Computational Economics*, volume 2. North Holland, Amsterdam, 949–1011.

Duffy, J. (2008a), Experimental macroeconomics. In Durlauf, S. and Blume, L. (eds.), *The New Palgrave Dictionary of Economics*, 2nd ed. Palgrave Macmillan, New York.

Duffy, J. (2008b), Macroeconomics: a survey of laboratory research. In Kagel, J. and Roth, A.E. (eds.), *Handbook of Experimental Economics*, volume 2, Working Paper 334. University of Pittsburgh.

Ellen, ter, S. and Zwinkels, R.C.J. (2010), Oil price dynamics: a behavioral, finance approach with heterogeneous agents. *Energy Economics* 32(6), 1427–1434.

Erev, I. and Roth, A.E. (1998), Prediction how people play games: reinforcement learning in games with unique strategy equilibrium. *American Economic Review* 88, 848–881.

Evans, G.W. and Honkapohja, S. (2001), *Learning and Expectations in Macroeconomics*. Princeton University Press, Princeton, NJ.

Evans, G.W. and Ramey, G. (1992), Expectation calculation and macroeconomic dynamics. *American Economic Review* 82, 207–224.

Ezekiel, M. (1938) The cobweb theorem. *Quarterly Journal of Economics* 52, 255–280.

Falconer, K. (1990), *Fractal Geometry. Mathematical Foundations and Applications*. Wiley, Chichester.

Fama, E.F. (1965), The behavior of stock market prices. *Journal of Business* 38, 34–105.

Fama, E.F. (1970), Efficient capital markets: a review of theory and empirical work. *Journal of Finance* 25, 383–423.

Fama, E.F. and French, K.R. (2002), The equity premium. *Journal of Finance* 57, 637–659.

Farmer, J.D. (2002), Market force, ecology, and evolution. *Industrial and Corporate Change* 11, 895–953.

Farmer, J.D. and Foley, D. (2009), The economy needs agent-based modelling. *Nature* 460, 685–686.

Farmer, J.D. and Geanakoplos, J. (2009), The virtures and vices of equilibrium and the future of financial economics. *Complexity* 14, 11–38.

Farmer, J.D. and Joshi, S. (2002), The price dynamics of common trading strategies. *Journal of Economic Behavior and Organization* 49, 149–171.

Fehr, E. and Tyran, J.-R. (2001), Does money illusion matter? *American Economic Review* 91, 1239–1262.

Fehr, E. and Tyran, J.-R. (2005), Individual irrationality and aggregate outcomes. *Journal of Economic Perspectives* 19, 43–66.

Fehr, E. and Tyran, J.-R. (2008), Limited rationality and strategic interaction: the impact of the strategic environment on nominal inertia. *Econometrica* 76, 353–394.

Finkenstädt, B. and Kuhbier, P. (1992), Chaotic dynamics in agricultural markets. *Annals of Operations Research* 37, 73–96.

Fisher, K.L. and Statman, M. (2002), Blowing bubbles. *Journal of Psychology and Financial Markets* 3, 53–65.

Franke, R. and Westerhoff, F. (2011), Estimation of a structural stochastic volatility model of asset pricing. *Computational Economics*, 38, 53–83.

Frankel, J.A. and Froot, K.A. (1986), Understanding the US dollar in the eighties: The expectations of chartists and fundamentalists. *Economic Record*, special issue, pp. 24–38. (Also published as NBER working paper No. 0957, December 1987.)

Frankel, J.A. and Froot, K.A. (1987), Using survey data to test standard propositions regarding exchange rate expectations. *American Economic Review* 77, 133–153.

Frankel, J.A. and Froot, K.A. (1990a) Chartists, fundamentalists and the demand for dollars. In Courakis, A.S. and Taylor, M.P. (eds.), *Private Behaviour and Government Policy in Interdependent Economies*. Oxford University Press, New York, pp. 73–126. (Also published as NBER Working Paper No. r1655, October 1991.)

Frankel, J.A. and Froot, K.A. (1990b), The rationality of the foreign exchange rate. Chartists, fundamentalists and trading in the foreign exchange market. *American Economic Review* 80(2), AEA Papers and Proceedings, 181–185.

Friedman, M. (1953), The case of flexible exchange rates. In M. Friedman (ed.) *Essays in Positive Economics*. University of Chicago Press, Chicago, IL.

Frijns, B., Lehnert, B and Zwinkels, R. (2010), Behavioral heterogeneity in option prices. *Journal of Economic Dynamics and Control* 34, 2273–2287.

Froot, K.A. and Frankel, J.A. (1989), Forward discount bias: is it an exchange rate premium? *Quarterly Journal of Economics* 104, 139–161.

Gallegati, M. and Kirman, A. (eds.) (1999), *Beyond the Representative Agent*. Edward Elgar, Northampton.

Gaunersdorfer, A. (2000), Endogenous fluctuations in a simple asset pricing model with heterogeneous beliefs. *Journal of Economic Dynamics and Control* 24, 799–831.

Gaunersdorfer, A. (2001), Adaptive belief systems and the volatility of asset prices. *Central European Journal of Operations Research* 9, 5–30.

Gaunersdorfer, A. and Hommes, C.H. (2007), A nonlinear structural model for volatility clustering. In Teyssière, G. and Kirman, A.P. (eds.), *Long Memory in Economics*. Springer Verlag, Berlin, pp. 265–288.

Gaunersdorfer, A., Hommes, C.H. and Wagener, F.O.O. (2005), Nonlocal onset of instability in an asset pricing model with heterogeneous agents. In Dumortier, F., Broer, H., Mawhin, J., Vanderbauwhede, A. and Lunel, S.V. (eds.), *EQUADIFF 2003: Proceedings of the International Conference on Differential Equations*. Hasselt, Belgium, July 22–26, 2003. World Scientific, Hackensack, NJ, pp. 613–618.

Gaunersdorfer, A., Hommes, C.H. and Wagener, F.O.J. (2008), Bifurcation routes to volatility clustering under evolutionary learning. *Journal of Economic Behavior and Organization* 67, 27–47.

Gigerenzer, G. and Selten, R. (eds.) (2001), *Bounded Rationality. The Adaptive Toolbox*. MIT Press, Cambridge, MA.

Gigerenzer, G., Todd, P.M. and the ABC Research Group (1999), *Simple Heuristics That Make Us Smart*. Oxford University Press, Oxford.

Gilli, M. and Winker, P. (2003), A global optimization heuristic for estimating agent based models. *Computational Statistics and Data Analysis* 42, 299–312.

Gleick, J. (1987), *Chaos. Making a New Science*. Viking, Harrisonburg, VA.

Goeree, J.K. and Hommes, C.H. (2000), Heterogeneous beliefs and the non-linear cobweb model. *Journal of Economic Dynamics and Control* 24, 761–798.

Goldbaum, D. (2005), Market efficiency and learning in an endogenously unstable environment. *Journal of Economic Dynamics and Control* 29, 953–978.

Goodwin, R.M. (1947), Dynamical couplic with especial reference to markets having production lags. *Econometrica* 15, 181–204.

Gordon, M. (1962), *The Investment Financing and Valuation of the Corporation*. Irwin, Homewood, IL.

Grandmont, J.-M. (1985), On endogenous competitive business cycles. *Econometrica* 53, 995–1045.

Grandmont, J.-M. (1998), Expectation formation and stability in large socio-economic systems. *Econometrica* 66, 741–781.

Grassberger, P. and Procaccia, I. (1983), Characterization of strange attractors. *Physical Review Letters* 50, 346–349.

Guckenheimer, J. and Holmes, P. (1983), *Nonlinear Oscillations, Dynamical Systems and Bifurcations of Vector Fields*. Springer Verlag, New York.

Haltiwanger, J. and Waldman, M. (1985), Rational expectations and the limits of rationality: an analysis of heterogeneity. *American Economic Review*, 75(3), 326–340.

Heemeijer, P., Hommes, C.H., Sonnemans, J. and Tuinstra, J. (2009), Price stability and volatility in markets with positive and negative expectations feedback, *Journal of Economic Dynamics and Control*, 33, 1052–1072.

Hénon, M. (1976), A two-dimensional mapping with a strange attractor. *Communications in Mathematical Physics* 50, 69–77.

Hens, T. and Schenk-Hoppé, K.R. (eds.) (2009), *Handbook of Financial Markets: Dynamics and Evolution*. Elsevier, Amsterdam.

Hicks, J.R. (1950), *A contribution to the theory of the trade cycle*. Clarendon Press, Oxford.

Holmes, J.M. and Manning, R. (1988), Memory and market stability. The case of the cobweb. *Economics Letters* 28, 1–7.

Holt, C.A. and Villamil, A.P. (1986), A laboratory experiment with a single person cobweb. *Atlantic Economic Journal* 14, 51–54.

Hommes, C.H. (1991a), Adaptive learning and roads to chaos. The case of the cobweb. *Economics Letters* 36, 127–132.

Hommes, C.H. (1991b), Chaotic dynamics in economic models. Some simple case studies. *Groningen Theses in Economics, Management & Organization*. Wolters-Noordhoff, Groningen.

Hommes, C.H. (1994), Dynamics of the cobweb model with adaptive expectations and nonlinear supply and demand. *Journal of Economic Behaviour and Organization* 24, 315–335.

Hommes, C.H. (1995), A reconsideration of Hicks' nonlinear trade cylce model. *Structural Change and Economic Dynamics* 6, 435–459.

Hommes, C.H. (1998), On the consistency of backward-looking expectations. The case of the cobweb. *Journal of Economic Behaviour and Organization* 33, 333–362.

Hommes, C.H. (2000), Cobweb dynamics under bounded rationality. In Dockner, E.J. et al. (eds.), *Optimization, Dynamics and Economic Analysis – Essays in Honor of Gustav Feichtinger*. Springer Verlag Berlin, pp. 134–150.

Hommes, C.H. (2001), Financial markets as nonlinear adaptive evolutionary systems. *Quantitative Finance* 1, 149–167.

Hommes, C.H. (2002), Modeling the stylized facts in finance through simple nonlinear adaptive systems. *Proceedings of the National Academy of Sciences* 99, 7221–7228.

Hommes, C.H. (2005), Heterogeneous agents models: two simple examples. In Lines, M. (ed.), Nonlinear Dynamical Systems in Economics. CISM Courses and Lectures No. 476. Springer, Berlin, pp. 131–164.

Hommes, C.H. (2006), Heterogeneous agent models in economics and finance. In Tesfatsion, L. and Judd, K.L. (eds), *Handbook of Computational Economics, Volume 2: Agent-Based Computational Economics*, chapter 23. North-Holland, Amsterdam, pp. 1109–1186.

Hommes, C.H. (2009), Bounded rationality and learning in complex markets. In Rosser, J.B. (ed.), *Handbook of Research on Complexity*, Edward Elgar, Cheltenham, pp. 87–123.

Hommes, C.H. (2011), The heterogeneous expectations hypothesis: Some evidence from the lab, *Journal of Economic Dynamics and Control* 35, 1–24.

Hommes, C.H. and Lux, T. (2013), Individual expectations and aggregate behavior in learning to forecast experiments, *Macroeconomic Dynamics*, in press.

Hommes, C.H. and Manzan, S. (2006), Comments on "Testing for nonlinear structure and chaos in economic time series". *Journal of Macroeconomics* 28, 169–174.

Hommes, C.H., and Rosser, J. Barkley Jr., (2001) Consistent expectations equilibria and complex dynamics in renewable resource markets, *Macroeconomic Dynamics* 5, 180–203.

Hommes, C.H. and Sorger, G. (1998), Consistent expectations equilibria. *Macroeconomic Dynamics* 2, 287–321.

Hommes, C.H. and Wagener, F.O.O. (2009), Complex evolutionary systems in behavioral finance. In Hens, T. and Schenk-Hoppé, K.R. (eds.), *Handbook of Financial Markets: Dynamics and Evolution*. Elsevier, Amsterdam, pp. 217–276.

Hommes, C.H. and Zhu, M. (2012), Behavioral learning equilibria. *CeNDEF Working Paper*. University of Amsterdam.

Hommes, C.H., Sonnemans, J. and van de Velden, H. (2000), Expectation formation in an experimental cobweb economy, In: D. Delli Gatti, M. Gallegati and A. Kirman (eds.). Interaction and Market Structure: Essays on Heterogeneity in Economics, *Lecture Notes in Economics and Mathematical Systems*, volume 484, Berlin: Springer-Verlag, pp. 253–266.

Hommes, C.H., Sorger, G., Wagener, F., (2013), Consistency of linear forecasts in a nonlinear stochastic economy, In: Bischi, G.I., Chiarella, C. and Sushko, I. (Eds.), *Global Analysis of Dynamic Models in Economics and Finance*, Springer-Verlag, Berlin, pp. 229–287.

Hommes, C.H., Huang, H. and Wang, D. (2005a), A robust rational route to randomness in a simple asset pricing model. *Journal of Economic Dynamics and Control* 29, 1043–1072.

Hommes, C.H., Sonnemans, J., Tuinstra, J., and van de Velden, H., (2005b) Coordination of expectations in asset pricing experiments, *Review of Financial Studies* 18, 955–980.

Hommes, C., Sonnemans, J., Tuinstra, J. and Velden, H. van de, (2007), Learning in cobweb experiments, *Macroeconomic Dynamics* 11 (S1), 8–33.

Hommes, C.H., Sonnemans, J., Tuinstra, J. and Velden, H. van de, (2008), Expectations and bubbles in asset pricing experiments, *Journal of Economic Behavior & Organization* 67, 116–133.

Hommes, C.H., Kiseleva, T., Kuznetsov, Y. and Verbic, M. (2012), Is more memory in evolutionary selection (de)stabilizing?, *Macroeconomic Dynamics*, 16, 335–357.

Hong, H. and Stein, J. (1999), A unified theory of underreaction, momentum trading and overreaction in asset markets. *Journal of Finance* 55, 265–295.

Ingrao, B. and Israel, G., (1990), *The Invisible Hand. Economic Equilibrium in the History of Science*, Cambridge, MA,: MIT Press.

Iori, G. (2002), A microsimulation of traders activity in the stock market: the role of heterogeneity, agents' interactions and trade frictions. *Journal of Economic Behavior and Organization* 49, 269–285.

Ippolito, R.A. (1989), Efficiency with costly information: a study of mutual fund performance, 1965–1984. *Quarterly Journal of Economics* 104, 1–23.

Ito, K. (1990), Foreign exchange rate expectations. *American Economic Review* 80, 434–449.

Jacobson, M.V. (1981), Absolutely continuous invariant measures for one-parameter families of one-dimensional maps. *Communications in Mathematical Physics* 81, 39–88.

Jensen, R.V. and Urban, R. (1984), Chaotic price behaviour in a nonlinear cobweb model. *Economics Letters* 15, 235–240.

de Jong, E., Verschoor, W.F.C. and Zwinkels, R.C.J. (2009), Behavioural heterogeneity and shift-contagion: evidence from the Asian crisis. *Journal of Economic Dynamics and Control* 33, 1929–1944.

de Jong, E., Verschoor, W.F.C. and Zwinkels, R.C.J. (2010), Heterogeneity of agents and exchange rate dynamics: evidence from the EMS. *Journal of International Money and Finance* 29, 1652–1669.

Jongen, R., Wolf, C.C.P., Zwinkels, R.C.J. and Verschoor, W.F.C. (2012), Explaining dispersion in the foreign exchange market: a heterogeneous agent approach, *Journal of Economic Dynamics and Control*, 36, 719–735.

Kahneman, D. (2003), Maps of bounded rationality: Psychology for behavioral economics. *American Economic Review* 93, 1449–1475.

Kahneman, D. and Tversky, A. (1973), On the psychology of prediction. *Psychological Review* 80, 237–251.

Kaldor, N. (1934), A classificatory note on the determinateness of equilibrium. *Review of Economic Studies* 1, 122–136.

Kantz, H. and Schreiber, T. (1997), *Nonlinear Time Series Analysis*. Cambridge University Press, Cambridge.

Karceski, J. (2002), Returns-chasing behavior, mutual funds, and beta's death. *Journal of Financial and Quantitative Analysis* 37, 559–594.

Keynes, J.M. (1936), *The General Theory of Unemployment, Interest and Money*. Harcourt, Brace and World, New York.

Kindleberger, C.P. (1996), *Manias, Panics, and Crashes. A History of Financial Crises* 3rd edn. Wiley, New York.

Kirman, A. (1991), Epidemics of opinion and speculative bubbles in financial markets. In M. Taylor (ed.), *Money and Financial Markets*, Macmillan, New York.

Kirman, A. (1992), Whom or what does the representative individual represent? *Journal of Economic Perspectives* 6, 117–136.

Kirman, A. (1993), Ants, rationality and recruitment. *Quarterly Journal of Economics* 108, 137–156.

Kirman, A. (1999), Aggregate activity and economic organisation. *Revue Européene des Sciences Sociales* XXXVII(113), 189–230.

Kirman, A. (2010), *Complex Economics: Individual and Collective Rationality*. Routledge, Oxford.

Kirman, A. and Teyssière, G. (2002), Microeconomic models for long memory in the volatility of financial time series. *Studies in Nonlinear Dynamics and Econometrics* 5(4), 281–302.

Kurz, M. (ed.) (1997), *Endogenous Economic Fluctuations*. Springer Verlag, New York.

Kuznetsov, Y. (1995), *Elements of Applied Bifurcation Theory*. Springer Verlag, New York.

Kydland, F.E. and Prescott, E.C. (1982), Time to build and aggregate fluctuations. *Econometrica* 50, 1345–70.

Lansing, K.J. (2009), Time-varing U.S. inflation dynamics and the new Keynesian Phillips curve. *Review of Economic Dynamics* 12, 304–326.

Lansing, K.J. (2010), Rational and near-rational bubbles without drift. *Economic Journal* 120, 1149–1174.

Lasselle, L., Svizzero, S. and Tisdell, C. (2005), Stability and cycles in a cobweb model with heterogeneous expectations. *Macroeconomic Dynamics* 9, 630–650.

LeBaron, B. (2000), Agent based computational finance: suggested readings and early research. *Journal of Economic Dynamics and Control* 24, 679–702.

LeBaron, B. (2002), Short-memory traders and their impact on group learning in financial markets. *Proceedings of the National Academy of Sciences (USA)* 99(Suppl. 3), 7201–7206.

LeBaron, B. (2006), Agent-based computational finance. In Tesfatsion, L., Judd, K.L. (eds.), *Handbook of Computational Economics, Volume 2: Agent-Based Computational Economics*, chapter 24. North-Holland, Amsterdam, pp. 1187–1233.

LeBaron, B., Arthur, W.B. and Palmer, R. (1999), Time series properties of an artificial stock market. *Journal of Economic Dynamics and Control* 23, 1487–1516.

Leontief, W.W. (1934), Verzögerte Angebotsanpassung und partielles Gleichgewicht. *Zeitschrift für Nationalökonomie*, V(5), 670–676.

Levy, M., Levy, H. and Solomon, S. (1994), A microscopic model of the stock market. *Economics Letters* 45, 103–111.

Li, T.Y. and Yorke, J.A. (1975), Period three implies chaos. *American Mathematical Monthly* 82, 985–992.

Lichtenberg, A.J. and Ujihara, A. (1989), Application of nonlinear mapping theory to commodity price fluctuations. *Journal of Economic Dynamics and Control* 13, 225–246.

Lines, M. and Westerhoff, F. (2010), Inflation expetations and macroeconomic dynamics: the case of rational versus extrapolative expectations. *Journal of Economic Dynamics and Control* 34, 246–257.

Lorentz, E.N. (1963), Deterministic nonperiodic flow. *Journal of the Atmospheric Sciences* 20, 130–141.

Lorenz, H.W. (1993), *Nonlinear Dynamical Economics and Chaotic Motion*, 2nd, revised and enlarged ed. Springer-Verlag, Berlin.

Lucas, R.E. (1972a), Econometric testing of the natural rate hypothesis. In Eckstein, O. (ed.), *The Econometrics of Price Determination*. Conference, Board of Governors of the Federal Reserve System and Social Science Research Council, Washington DC, pp. 50–59.

Lucas, R.E. (1972b), Expectations and the neutrality of money. *Journal of Economic Theory* 4, 103–124.

Lucas, R.E. (1986), Adaptive behavior and economic theory, *Journal of Business* 59(4), S401–S426.

Lux, T. (1995), Herd behavior, bubbles and crashes. *The Economic Journal* 105, 881–896.

Lux, T. (1997), Time variation of second moments from a noise trader/infection model. *Journal of Economic Dynamics and Control* 22, 1–38.

Lux, T. (1998), The socio-economic dynamics of speculative markets: interacting agents, chaos, and the fat tails of return distribution. *Journal of Economic Behavior and Organization* 33, 143–165.

Lux, T. (2009), Stochastic behavioral asset pricing models and the stylized facts. In Hens, T. and Schenk-Hoppé, K.R. (eds.), *Handbook of Financial Markets: Dynamics and Evolution*. Elsevier, Amsterdam.

Lux, T. and Marchesi, M. (1999), Scaling and criticality in a stochastic multi-agent model of a financial market. *Nature* 397(February) 498–500.

Lux, T. and Marchesi, M. (2000) Volatility clustering in financial markets: a micro-simulation of interacting agents. *International Journal of Theoretical and Applied Finance* 3, 675–702.

Mankiw, N., Reis, R. and Wolfers, J. (2003), Disagreement about inflation expectations, *NBER Macroecomics Annual 2003*, volume 18, 209–248.

Mandelbrot, B.B. (1982), *The Fractal Geometry of Nature*. Freeman, San Francisco, CA.

Manski, C. and McFadden, D. (1981), *Structural Analysis of Discrete Data with Econometric Applications*. MIT Press, Cambridge, MA.

Mantegna, R.N. and Stanley, H.E. (2000), *An Introduction to Econophysics. Correlations and Complexity in Finance*. Cambridge University Press, Cambridge.

Manzan, S. (2003), Essays in nonlinear economic dynamics. PhD thesis, *Tinbergen Institute Research Series 317*. Thela Publishers, Amsterdam.

Marimon, R. and S. Sunder (1994), Expectations and learning under alternative monetary regimes: an experimental approach. *Economic Theory* 4, 131–162.

May, R.M. (1976), Simple mathematical models with very complicated dynamics. *Nature* 261, 459–467.

Medio, A. (1992), *Chaotic Dynamics. Theory and Applications to Economics*. Cambdridge University Press, Cambridge.

Medio, A. and Lines, M. (2001), *Non-linear Dynamics. A Primer*. Cambridge University Press, Cambridge.

de Melo, W. and van Strien, S. (1993), *One-dimensional Dynamics*. Springer Verlag, Berlin.

Menkhoff, L. and Taylor, M.P. (2007), The obstinate passion of foreign exchange professionals: technical analysis. *Journal of Economic Literature* 45, 936–972.

Merton, R.C. (1980), On estimating the expected return on the market. An exploratory investigation. *Journal of Financial Economics* 8, 323–361.

Muth, J.F. (1961), Rational expectations and the theory of price movements. *Econometrica* 29, 315–335.

Nerlove, M. (1958), Adaptive expectations and cobweb phenomena. *Quarterly Journal of Economics* 72, 227–240.

Nicholson, W. (1995), *Microeconomic Theory. Basic Principles and Extensions*, 6th edn. Dryden Press, Fort Worth, TX.

Palis, J. and Takens, F. (1993), *Hyperbolicity and Sensitive Chaotic Dynamics at Homoclinic Bifurcations*. Cambridge University Press, Cambridge.

Pashigian, B.P. (1987), Cobweb theorem. In Eatwell, J., Milgate, M. and Newman, P. (eds.), *The New Palgrave. A Dictionary of Economics*, volume 1, MacMillan, Basingstoke.

Pesaran, H.M. and Weale, M. (2006), Survey expectations. In Elliott, G., Granger, C.W.J. and Timmermann, A. (eds), *Handbook of Economic Forecasting*. Amsterdam, North-Holland, pp. 715–776.

Pfajfar, D. and Santoro, E. (2010), Heterogeneity, learning and information stickiness in inflation expectations. *Journal of Economic Behavior and Organization* 75, 426–444.

Pfajfar, D. and Zakelj, B. (2011), Inflation expectations and monetary policy design: evidence from the laboratory. *CentER Discussion Paper*. Tilburg University, July 2011.

Plott, C.R. and Sunder, S. (1982), Efficiency of experimental security markets with insider information: an application of rational expectations models. *Journal of Political Economy* 90, 663–698.

Poincaré, H. (1890), Sur le problème des trois corps et les equations de la dynamique (Mémoire couronné du prise de S.M. le roi Oscar II de Suède). *Acta Mathamatica* 13, 1–270.

Ricci, U. (1930), Die "synthetisch Ökonomie" von Henry Ludwell Moore, *Zeitschrift für Nationalökonomie* I(5), 649–668.

Rockinger, M. (1996), Determinants of capital flows to mutual funds. Working paper, HEC School of Management, Paris.

Rosser, J.B., Jr. (2000), *From Catastrophe to Chaos: A General Theory of Economic Discontinuities*, 2nd ed. Kluwer Academic Publishers, Boston.

Rosser, J.B., Jr. (2004), *Complexity in Economics: The International Library of Critical Writings in Economics 174*, (3 volumes). Edward Elgar, Aldergate.

Rosser, J.B., Jr. (2009), *Handbook of Economic Complexity*. Edward Elgar, Cheltenham.

Ruelle, D. and Takens, F. (1971), On the nature of turbulence. *Communications in Mathematical Physics* 20, 167–192.

Sakai, H. and Tokumaru, H. (1980), Autocorrelations of a certain chaos, *IEEE Transactions on Acoustics, Speech and Signal Processing* 28, 588–590.

Sargent, T.J. (1993), *Bounded Rationality in Macroeconomics*. Clarendon Press, Oxford.

Sargent, T.J. (1999), *The Conquest of American Inflation*. Princeton University Press, Princeton, NJ.

Sargent, T.J. (2008), Evolution and intelligent design. *American Economic Review* 98, 5–37.

Scheinkman, J.A. and LeBaron, B. (1989), Nonlinear dynamics and stock returns. *Journal of Business* 62, 311–337.

Schönhofer, M. (1999), Chaotic learning equilibria. *Journal of Economic Theory* 89, 1–20.

Schultz, H., (1930), Der Sinn der Statistischen Nachfragekurven. In Altschul, E. (ed.), *Veröffentlichungen der Frankfurter Gesellschaft für Konjunkturforschung 10*.

Schunk, D. (2009), Behavioral heterogeneity in dynamic search situations: theory and experimental evidence. *Journal of Economic Dynamics and Control* 33, 1719–1738.

Schunk, D. (2011), Heterogeneous agnets in intertemporal choice: theory and experimental evidence. Working paper, University of Zürich, 2011.

Shefrin (2000), Beyond greed and fear. Understanding behavioral finance and the psychology of investing. Harvard Business School Press, Boston, MA.

Shiller, R.J. (1981), Do stock prices move too much to be justified by subsequent changes in dividends? *American Economic Review* 71, 421–436.

Shiller, R.J. (1984), Stock prices and social dynamics. *Brookings Papers in Economic Activity* 2, 457–510.

Shiller, R.J. (1987), Investor behavior in the October 1987 stock market crash: survey evidence. *NBER working paper* No. 2446, November 1987 (Published in Shiller, R.J., *Market Volatility*, MIT Press, Cambridge, MA 1989, chapter 23.)

Shiller, R.J. (1989), *Market Volatility*. MIT Press, Cambridge, MA.

Shiller, R.J. (2000), Measuring bubble expectations and investor confidence. *Journal of Psychology and Financial Markets* 1, 49–60.

Simon, H.A. (1955), A behavioral model of rational choice. *Quarterly Journal of Economics* 69, 99–118.

Simon, H.A. (1957), *Models of Man*. Wiley, New York.

Simon, H.A. (1984), On the behavioral and rational foundations of economic dynamics. *Journal of Economic Behavior and Organization* 5, 35–55.

Sims, C.A. (1980), Macroeconomics and reality. *Econometrica* 48, 1–48.

Sirri, E.R. and Tufano, P. (1998), Costly search and mutual fund flows. *Journal of Finance* 53, 1589–1621.

Smale, S. (1963), Diffeomorhphisms with many periodic points. In Cairns, S.S. (ed.), *Differential and combinatorial topology*. Princeton University Press, Princeton, NJ, pp. 63–80.

Smith, V.L., (1962), A experimental study of competitive market behavior. *Joural of Political Economy* 70, 111–137.

Smith, V.L., Suchanek, G.L. and Williams, A.W. (1988), Bubbles, crashes and endogenous expectations in experimental spot asset markets. *Econometrica*, 56, 1119–1151.

Sögner, L. and Mitlöhner, H. (2002), Consistent expectations equilibria and learning in a stock market. *Journal of Economic Dynamics and Control* 26, 171–185.

Sonnemans, J., Hommes, C.H., Tuinstra, J. and van de Velden, H. (2004), The instability of a heterogeneous cobweb economy: a strategy experiment in expectation formation. *Journal of Economic Behavior and Organization* 54, 453–481.

Sorger, G. (1998), Imperfect foresight and chaos: an example of a self-fulfilling mistake. *Journal of Economic Behavior and Organization* 33, 363–383.

Summers, L.H. (1986), Does the stock market rationally reflect fundamental values?, *Journal of Finance* 41, 591–601.

Sunder, S. (1995) Experimental asset markets: a survey. In Kagel, J.H. and Roth, A.E. (eds.), *Handbook of Experimental Economics*. Princeton University Press, Princeton, NJ, pp. 445–500.

Sutan, A. and Willinger, M. (2009), Guessing with negative feedback: an experiment. *Journal of Economic Dynamics and Control* 33, 1123–1133.

Takens, F. (1981), Detecting strange attractors in turbulence: In Rand, D.A. and Young, L.S. (eds.), *Dynamical Systems and Turbulence*. Lecture Notes in Mathematics 898. Springer Verlag, Berlin, pp. 366–381.

Taylor, M.P. and Allen, H. (1992), The use of technical analysis in the foreign exchange market. *Journal of International Money and Finance* 11, 304–314.

Tesfatsion, L., (2006), Agent-based computational economics: a constructive approach to economic theory. In Tesfatsion, L. and Judd, K.L. (eds), *Handbook of Computational Economics Volume 2: Agent-Based Computational Economics*. North-Holland, Amsterdam, pp. 831–880.

Tesfatsion, L. and Judd, K.L. (eds), 2006, *Handbook of Computational Economics, Volume 2: Agent-Based Computational Economics*. North-Holland, Amsterdam.

Teräsvirta, T. (1994), Specification, estimation, and evaluation of smooth transition autoregressive models. *Journal of the American Statistical Association* 89, 208–218.

Thaler, R., (1994) *Quasi Rational Economics*. Russel Sage Foundation.

Tinbergen, J. (1930), Bestimmung und Deutung von Angebotskurven. Ein Beispiel, *Zeitschrift für Nationalökonomie*, (5), 669–679.

Tong, H., (1990), *Non-linear Time Series. A Dynamical System Approach*. Clarendon Press, Oxford.

Tuinstra, J. (2003), Beliefs equilibria in an overlapping generations model, *Journal of Economic Behavior and Organization* 50, 145–164.

Tuinstra, J., and Wagener, F.O.O. (2007), On learning equilibria. *Economic Theory 30*, 493–513.

Tversky, A. and Kahneman, D. (1974), Judgment under uncertainty: heuristics and biases. *Science* 185, 1124–1131.

Vilder, de, R. (1996), Complicated endogenous business cycles under gross substitutability. *Journal of Economic Theory 71*, 416–442.

Vissing-Jorgensen, A. (2003), Perspective on behavioral finance: does 'irrationality' disappear with wealth? Evidence from expectations and actions. In: Gertler, M. and Rogoff, K. (eds.), *NBER Macroeconomics Annual*. MIT Press, Cambridge, MA.

Waugh, F.V. (1964), Cobweb models, *Journal of Farm Economics* 46, 732–750.

Wellford, C.P. (1989), A laboratory analysis of price dynamics and expectations in the cobweb model. *Discussion Paper No. 89–15*. Department of Economics, University of Arizona

Westerhoff, F.H. (2004), Multi-asset market dynamics. *Macroeconomic Dynamics* 8, 596–616.

Westerhoff, F.H. and Dieci, R. (2006), The effectiveness of Keynes–Tobin transaction taxes when heterogeneous agents can trade in different markets: a behavioral finance approach. *Journal of Economic Dynamics and Control* 30, 293–322.

Westerhoff, F.H. and Reitz, S. (2003), Nonlinearities and cyclical behavior: the role of chartists and fundamentalists. *Studies in Nonlinear Dynamics and Econometrics* 7(4), article 3.

Williams, A.W. (1987) The formation of price forecasts in experimental markets. *Journal of Money, Credit and Banking*, 19, 1–18.

Winker, P. and Gilli, M. (2001), Indirect estimation of the parameters of agent based models of financial markets. *FAME Research Paper* No. 38. University of Geneva, November 2001.

Woodford, M. (2003), *Interest and Prices: Foundations of a Theory of Monetary Policy*, Princeton University Press, Princeton, NJ.

Youssefmir, M. and Huberman, B.A. (1997), Clustered volatility in multi agent dynamics. *Journal of Economic Behavior and Organization* 32, 101–118.

Zeeman, E.C. (1974), The unstable behavior of stock exchange. *Journal of Mathematical Economics* 1, 39–49.

Index

Printed in the United States
By Bookmasters